Too Good To Be True
Alcan's Kemano Completion Project

Bev Christensen

Talonbooks   Vancouver   1995

Published with the assistance of the Canada Council.

Talonbooks
201 - 1019 East Cordova Street
Vancouver, British Columbia
Canada V6A 1M8

Typeset in Bembo and Optima and printed and bound in Canada by Hignell
Printing Ltd.

First Printing: April, 1995

Canadian Cataloguing in Publication Data

Christensen, Bev.
        Too good to be true

        Includes bibliographical references.
        ISBN 0-88922-354-8

    1. Kemano Completion Project (B.C.)—History. 2. Alcan Aluminum Limited.
3. Aluminum   industry   and   trade—British   Columbia—Kemano   River
Watershed—History.. 4. Hydroelectric power plants—British Columbia—
Kemano River Watershed—History.. 5. British Columbia, Northern—Social
conditions. 6. Aluminum industry and trade—Environmental aspects—British
Columbia—Kemano River Watershed. 7. Hydroelectric power plants—
Environmental aspects—British Columbia—Kemano River Watershed. I. Title.
TD195.A37C57 1995   338.2'74926'097111   C95-910107-1

Contents

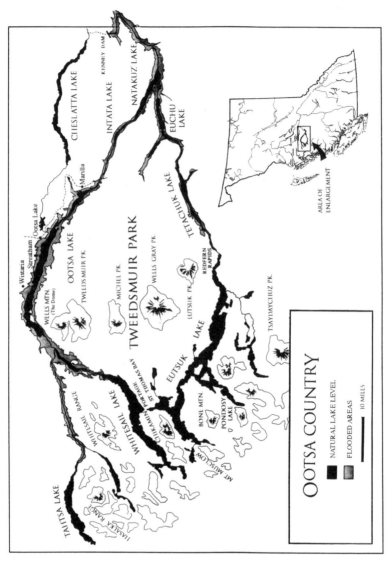

Ootsa country: Map drawn by and reproduced courtesy of Brian Giesbrecht.

Preface

On January 23, 1995, British Columbia's NDP Premier, Mike Harcourt, announced he was cancelling the Kemano Completion Project, a $1.3 billion Nechako River water diversion project the Aluminum Company of Canada had started to add on to its vast existing hydroelectric empire which it had been operating in the central-interior of the province since the 1950s. His announcement engendered a collective sigh of relief from the residents of the Nechako River Valley, most of whom had opposed the project for years, and brought a rash of smiles to the faces of other residents of the province, primarily those earning their livelihood in the province's vibrant and extensive fishing communities, who had become convinced that diverting more water from this river would cause irreparable damage to the Fraser River into which the waters of the Nechako flow.

There can be no doubt that the province-wide sense of relief and vindication expressed in the hours and days following Premier Harcourt's surprise announcement was entirely premature. It would be foolish indeed for anyone to believe that such a simple political statement had finally ended the long fight over who has the right to control the water flows in the Nechako River: Alcan; the Province of British Columbia; or the Government of Canada. Anyone harbouring such a naïve belief has a lot to learn from the residents of the Nechako River Valley who have discovered—all too well—in their long struggle to prevent more water from being diverted out of this river, that you cannot always trust governments to act on, much less carry out, their promises.

This book has been written because Harcourt's announcement of January 23, 1995, marks not the end of a long-standing debate, but the beginning of a steep escalation in that debate. It is intended to provide readers with information they will need to understand both the history of the dispute, and the far-ranging issues the future outcome of this debate will raise. Not the least of these issues is the question of who will have to pay Alcan how much, if any, compensation for the province's decision (if indeed it prevails) to cancel what Harcourt has described as a "flawed project."

This controversy has been simmering away in the resource-rich central-interior of British Columbia for more than fifteen years. During that period many acrimonious claims have surfaced: charges by scientists that the project has been allowed to proceed on the basis of flawed scientific evidence; and allegations that the decision to allow the Kemano Completion Project (the KCP) to proceed was a political decision, reached during a suspicious closed-door workshop. If Alcan either carries out its threat to ask the court to force the province to live up to the terms of its agreements with the company, dating primarily from 1950 and 1987, or proceeds through the courts to obtain compensation for the violation of those agreements, it will be important to understand that the opponents of this project have already tried the avenue of the courts in their effort to force the federal government to withdraw the Cabinet order exempting Alcan's KCP from its own legislation requiring it to be subjected to a full environmental review. This exemption was ruled unconstitutional by the Rules Committee of the House of Commons, and the project's opponents rejoiced when the federal court set aside the 1987 agreement and ruled there must be an environmental review. Jubilation turned to despair when that decision was overturned by an appeal court and opponents of the project were denied the right to appeal this second decision to the Supreme Court of Canada. These lengthy and ultimately unsuccessful court battles have left the two groups who led the fight—the Rivers Defense Coalition and the Carrier Sekani Tribal Council—exhausted and, in the Coalition's case, deeply in debt. Both groups, however, remain determined to carry on.

The KCP fight has been one that, over the years, has developed many unique features, not the least of which is that it has united First Nations and non-native residents of the Nechako River Valley for the first time in their history, enabling them to present a united front of opposition to a project they are convinced will severely curtail future development in their environment, and destroy forever their way of life in a vast region of their province.

When Harcourt first announced the controversial project had been cancelled, it was primarily these residents who looked at each other with amazement and congratulated themselves on finally succeeding in their long, uphill, David-and-Goliath battle to ensure their once mighty river would retain enough water to avoid becoming a stagnant, weed-choked stream. Other BC residents celebrated with them. They included sport and commercial fishers, unionists, church leaders, naturalists, trappers, First Nations and wildlife activists who had joined the fight to stop the project when they learned about the dangers the KCP posed to the annual salmon runs migrating through BC's largest river, the Fraser.

Within days of the announcement, Alcan had again threatened to sue the Province. That threat caused other BC residents to begin to worry publicly about who would pay the enormous legal and expropriation costs that will result from the Province's unilateral decision to cancel Alcan's half-finished project. Harcourt attempted to soothe these fears by charging that Alcan had already received $900 million in deferred tax credits from the federal government. That statement quickly proved to be incorrect. But even $900 million may not be enough to characterize accurately the total cost to BC and Canadian taxpayers of all the benefits bestowed on the company by both the federal and the provincial governments during the forty years it has been generating electricity and smelting aluminum in BC. Add to these past inducements and tax benefits the enormous costs that BC and Canadian taxpayers would have to bear in the future should Alcan's project be completed, the public costs of the project become so high they cannot be justified. Those who argue it is reasonable to incur these public costs in order to ensure that this multinational company continues to make a profit from its BC operations and create jobs, need to take another look. While this project does create short-term construction jobs, it will generate few long-term jobs once the project is built, and less than no benefits to the people living in the river valley from which the water is to be diverted.

Harcourt also alleged in his announcement that federal politicians were responsible for the flawed political and scientific decision-making process that led to the signing of the agreement in 1987, which cleared the way for the KCP to proceed. But the federal government, and particularly the federal minister responsible for fisheries and oceans, moved quickly to distance themselves from any financial responsibility for the Province's unilateral decision to cancel the project. This inter-governmental posturing and straight-arming is directly linked to the background to the coming battle over who is responsible for having approved this flawed project. Is it the federal government, which allowed the KCP to proceed despite warnings from its own scientists that the millions of fish inhabiting the river would not survive in the lower, warmer water flows? Or is it a succession of provincial governments, one of which introduced and approved legislation giving Alcan complete control over a piece of the province more than twice the size of Prince Edward Island, another of which was a full participant in the federal-provincial decision-making process allowing Alcan to remove even more water from the river?

This book explains the complex fifty-year history of Alcan's activities in BC, during which successive federal and provincial governments cleared a path and provided public enticements to enable Alcan to take corporate advantage of one of the cheapest power generating sites in the world. But this is more than a history book. It is also, in part, the story of the once naïve, but always determined and resourceful residents of the Nechako River Valley who dug in their heels and stood up to one of Canada's largest multinational companies. These are not wild-eyed environmentalists. They are earthy, friendly, honest people who live close to their communities and the wilderness that surrounds them. When they began to realize that Alcan, and their federal and provincial governments, might have been deceiving them about their long-term plan for the river, they fought long and hard to reverse the corporate and political agenda to allow even more water to be diverted into Alcan's reservoir. During the course of writing this book I came to admire and respect these people and, wherever possible, have used their own eloquent words at the bottom of these pages in an effort to help readers understand the sincerity of their convictions.*

When Alcan began the first phase of its developments in the interior of BC during the 1950s, their industrial activities were hailed as the biggest project to break through the Rockies since the coming of the transcontinental railways. Originally, the project was intended to provide cheap electrical power to smelt aluminum at the company's facilities in Kitimat. At that time, aluminum was emerging as the miracle metal of the twentieth century, which could be used to manufacture anything from aircraft parts to beer cans. But between the 1950s and the 1980s, increasing amounts of the cheap hydroelectric power the company was able to generate at Kemano were being sold by the privately-held company to the power grid of BC Hydro, the Crown Corporation controlling the distribution and sale of electrical power not only to consumers within the province, but also, and increasingly, to consumers in Alberta and the United States of America. And, when valley residents learned late in 1979 that Alcan planned to reduce the flows in the upper reaches of the Nechako River to a trickle in its effort to generate even more hydroelectric power, not necessarily for use to smelt more aluminum in Kitimat at all, they began to object. The company countered with a smoothly crafted publicity campaign that ignited fierce debates in the communities along the river initially pitting neighbour against neighbour.

One of the things that remained hidden from view during all these years of deception and intrigue surrounding the project was the destruction of the self-sufficient lifestyle of the isolated First Nations community living around Cheslatta Lake in the area which was flooded in the 1950s by Alcan's huge reservoir. To make way for the project, they were displaced to a windy plateau outside their traditional territory, where diseases like tuberculosis and alcoholism have taken their toll. They too went to court seeking compensation for the forgeries and breaches of trust that led to their displacement from their traditional territories. Their claims were finally addressed by a multi-million-dollar out-of-court settlement with the federal government in March, 1993.

Toward the end of puzzling out the complex and hidden details of this story, it came as a complete surprise to me that, as important and valid as the concerns of those people directly affected by the project are, there are other, larger issues at play in this debate which will affect not only all Canadians, but every citizen of every country that becomes a co-signatory of international trade agreements like the FTA, the NAFTA, and the GATT—affecting most immediately, of course, the citizens of the United States of America and Mexico. These trade agreements are leading Canadians into a trading maze in which there is a very clear indication that the Canadian Provinces and the Canadian Government itself will be forced to surrender their ability to control the natural resources, including water and power, within their boundaries.

In the end, this book is a case study of how the power of ordinary citizens, democratically vested in their governments, was voluntarily abrogated by those governments to the interests of a multinational company. The lessons learned by the residents of one British Columbia valley should serve as a warning to all citizens in an increasingly continentalized North America.

* The majority of my quotations of these speakers are taken from the Transcripts of the BC Utilities Commission Hearings (BCUCH), unless otherwise indicated. They are cited by the volume and page number: e.g., *BCUCH* 1.64.

359 Billion Beer Glasses

That was the image of giant mega-projects which were full of romantic images of taming nature's resources or showing man's undaunted spirit over the unchecked forces of nature. All one needs is the vision, the tools, the cash and courage to spend it for the benefit of man.[1]

The most westerly part of the 218-mile-long freshwater boating adventure known as the Great Circle Water Route once began 368 miles north of Vancouver, 20 miles east and one-half-mile above the Pacific Ocean.

It was the longest inland boating route in BC.

There, high in the mountains, lay 19-mile-long Tahtsa Lake, which was described in a 1931 government bulletin as "glacier-fed, cold and emerald green with magnificent scenery, especially at the western end, where craggy Mount Tahtsa rises above a glacier and snow-fields."[2] One of the first Europeans to see this beautiful wilderness lake was railway surveyor, Charles Horetzky, who walked into the area in 1874 searching for a route for a transcontinental railway. He described the atmosphere in the steep-sided mountain pass leading into Tahtsa Lake as follows: "A terrible silence, broken only now and again by the dreadful crash of some falling avalanche, reigned over this scene of desolation."[3] But, when his party of three white men and four Indians walked through a gap in the mountains and saw beneath them the waters of Tahtsa Lake shining like a jewel in the wilderness, he described the lake as having a "brilliant light blue colour," and as the first excitement to greet his eyes for many weeks.[4]

From the point where the blue waters of the western end of Tahtsa Lake lapped against the Coast Range, it was only 20 miles to where the tides of the Pacific Ocean moved up and down the beaches of Kemano Bay on Gardner Canal. Horetzky's discovery was subsequently shared by only the most ambitious and adventurous of BC's early canoeists who arduously made their way in to the lake. To reach it, they were required to pole, pull or paddle their boats more than 45 miles up the Tahtsa River from the western end of Ootsa Lake.

Adventurous tourists paddling over the Great Circle Water Route during the 1930s and '40s usually began their journey further east near the middle of Ootsa Lake, south of Burns Lake. In 1931 that community was a thriving pioneer settlement containing "11 post offices, 11 schools, five general stores, three hotels, a hospital and good roads connecting them."[5]

Early visitors to Ootsa Lake were Lord and Lady Tweedsmuir who, in August, 1937, used the lake as a starting point for their tour to see for themselves the 5,400-square-mile park that had been named in Lord Tweedsmuir's honour the previous year. Their hosts included many of the first white settlers who had walked into Ootsa Lake near the beginning of the twentieth century from tide water at Bella Coola, 100 miles to the south on Bentinck Arm. The trail they used was one on which generations of First Nations people had moved back and forth between central British Columbia's inland areas and the coast at Bella Coola.

From the eastern end of Ootsa Lake the Bella Coola trail ran south through One Eye Creek Valley to Chelaslie River, then over a rolling 3,500-foot high jackpine plateau to join the main Bella Coola Trail from Ulkatcho, six miles to the south. This route has now been designated as a national heritage trail known as the

---

"In the 1940s this northern half of the Park had been advertised by the Ministry of Parks...as being a park of great and extensive beauty. Tweedsmuir Park became renowned not only for its superb fresh water fishing, but because of the attraction of the Great Circle Tour, a chain of lakes with connecting rivers...." *Will Koop of Project North (Vancouver), an associate group of the ecumenical church organization, The Aboriginal Rights Coalition. BCUCH 6.961.*

Nuxalk-Carrier Grease Trail (Alexander Mackenzie Voyageur Route, in honour of the local First Nations people who, in 1793, guided Alexander Mackenzie and his men from the Fraser River to Bella Coola. When Mackenzie and his men arrived at the Pacific Ocean near Bella Coola they became the first non-Natives to travel overland across North America. Many of these Ootsa Lake pioneers walked and rode horses over that long, rough trail seeking cheap but productive farm land. At Ootsa Lake they found what they were looking for. A pamphlet describes what government officials saw in 1931 when they entered the valley in which the lake is located:

> The great fertility of [the] soil is indicated by [the] remarkable growth of wild grasses, peavine, vetch, cow parsnip, and fireweed etcetera which attain heights of five to six feet and in places grow so dense that it is hard to force a way through.[6]

Most of the pioneers settled on the north side of Ootsa Lake where the spring sun would warm the soil early, coaxing forth some welcome green pasture for their horses and cattle. The mountainous country to the south of the lake was populated only by prospectors and trappers, and by the Cheslatta First Nations people who had lived in peaceful isolation there for generations.

From Ootsa Lake these pioneers could pole and paddle their boats far up the Tahtsa River to Tahtsa Lake, deep in the Coast Range, to catch large amounts of fish. Cyril Shelford, the son of pioneer Jack Shelford, who arrived in the area in 1911, describes how he and his brother took a boat up there every year to catch "a ton of kokanee" to feed the foxes they were raising on their ranch at Ootsa Lake. Kokanee are a land-locked salmon which, although small, have an oil-rich, deep-red flesh which makes them delicious eating for humans and also, apparently, for foxes.

After reaching the western end of Ootsa Lake, the early adventurers paddling over the Great Circle Water Route continued their travels by making their way up a short river leading into Whitesail Lake. In 1931 it was described as 2,750 feet above sea level, mountain-ringed, crescent-shaped and subject to violent winds from the mountain passes to the west.

At that time, boaters paddled to a southern bay on Whitesail Lake where they hauled their boats over a mile-long portage. Since the 1930s the portage had been equipped with railway tracks to ease the job of transporting heavy boats into 50-mile-long Eutsuk Lake, the largest lake in the chain, which was described this way in the 1931 bulletin: "To [the] south [the] scenery is splendid, the glaciers on Mount Haven stretching almost to lake level. The mountains hug the shore for half the length, Atna Bay lying completely within them."[7]

A short river containing some challenging white-water rapids around which most paddlers portaged, connected Eutsuk Lake with 18-mile-long Tetachuck Lake. The land to the north and south of this lake rose to a rolling plateau dotted by many timbered ridges, with mosquito-infested swamps in the lower areas. To the north, the plateau was broken by a hill spur from the west which had an average height of 4,000 feet. Beyond that was an almost level, heavily timbered plateau.

Boaters left Tetachuck Lake by paddling and portaging down four-mile-long Tetachuck River, which descended 150 feet over a succession of waterfalls, the highest of which was 25 feet. This river carried the paddlers into 12-mile long Euchu Lake, which in addition to being fed by the Tetachuck River, also received water from the Chelaslie River to the west and the Entiako River to the south. A short outflow river with one small riffle to challenge canoeists linked Euchu Lake to the western arm of Natalkuz Lake. It is believed Euchu and Natalkuz Lakes were once one lake, until the western end of what now forms Euchu Lake was cut off by a dam of alluvial material deposited by the Entiako River. The Natalkuz-Euchu-Eutsuk Lakes system was the second prong of the two-pronged lake system known as the Great Circle Water Route. The first prong was formed by the Ootsa-Tahtsa-Whitesail Lakes system. The waters of the two prongs of the circular lake system mingled when they both drained into Natalkuz Lake.

Prior to 1950, the merged water of these two chains of lakes flowed out of Natalkuz Lake into the east-flowing Nechako River which merges with the Fraser River near Prince George. In 1931 the outlet to the river was described as "a fine stream, 140 feet wide" and "swift, but smooth-flowing." This is a deceptive description, because downstream the river became a raging torrent when its entire width was compressed into a canyon 50 feet wide. The 1931 bulletin uses these words to describe the torrent of water that once raged through the Nechako River canyon:

> The Grand Canyon is 7 miles long, in the lower 3 miles is a box canyon cut sheer 300 feet deep. Above the water is not continuously bad, but the gorge is deep, and shorter box canyons and bad chutes frequent, especially at [the] head of the canyon. Down the lower 3 miles is a wild cascade with a 60 foot drop, below which water races down a narrow cleft, in places not over 50 feet wide and very deep. A rise of 3 feet in the broad river above would pile water 30 feet higher in this chasm. At one right-handed bend a cave has been cut 100 feet long, 60 feet deep, the water surging below in boiling eddies under the overhanging cliff.

Astute readers will have noticed that, while this 1931 description is written in the present tense, my description of the Great Circle Water Route has used the past tense throughout. The reason for this difference? This unique system of wilderness lakes and rivers over which tourists travelled during the 1930s and '40s was changed forever in the 1950s when Alcan began constructing the Kenney Dam across the Nechako River upstream from the river's Grand Canyon.

The dam impounded the water draining from an area more than twice the size of Prince Edward Island,[8] turning what had once been the Great Circle Water Route of interconnected lakes and rivers into what is now one long, two-pronged lake. The reservoir covers 358 square miles and is twice the size of the original lakes.[9]

The hydroelectric potential of this complex lake system, which was already naturally impounded at its western border by the Coast Range, was first recognized by two people during the 1920s: northern surveyor Frank Swannell and engineer Frederick Knewstubb, who later became BC's chief hydraulic engineer. During the 1930s, Knewstubb developed a plan for a project to produce hydroelectric power by damming portions of the east-flowing circular water route which foreshadowed the more ambitious plans Alcan developed during the 1940s. When Alcan put these plans into action and began constructing the dam south of Vanderhoof during the 1950s, the reservoir and the

15

power facilities at Kemano were described as the largest engineering project undertaken in Canada during the first half of the twentieth century.

One of the first challenges faced by the engineers designing the dam was finding a way to drain the riverbed. The Nechako River Canyon was too deep and narrow for the construction of a coffer dam to divert water away from the dam site. Instead, a tunnel was built to carry the water 1,539 feet in a sweeping arc into the bank of the river, emptying it back into the riverbed well below the dam site. That project was completed in two months during the summer of 1951.[10]

When the riverbed at the dam site had dried out, workers began stripping the canyon walls and the riverbed down to solid bedrock. A thick concrete slab was placed at the base of the canyon as an anchor for the dam and, on May 20, 1952, a thousand workers began blasting and scooping more than four million cubic yards of rock, sand and clay out of the surrounding terrain and dumping it into the Grand Canyon of the Nechako River over the concrete foundation.[11] The dam's impervious core was created from 514,671 cubic yards of the blue clay which is abundant throughout the Nechako River Valley.[12] The rock was obtained from the deposit of basalt found a half-mile from the dam site and suitable gravel was found along the river.

"Mr. Knewstubb, after whom the reservoir is named,...all he could see, because he was a hydrologist working for the province of British Columbia, all he could see was hydro-electric power.... Today we must also see the Nechako as a beautiful river and be, like the botanist, able to determine all the other qualities of a river and how it functions to supply and yet, at the same time, live off its surroundings." *Vanderhoof pioneer Dr. Al Mooney, BCUCH 3.379-80.*

"The challenge of financing the cost of the Aluminum Company of Canada, Ltd.'s activities in Canada—estimated at $200 million—matched the engineering challenge of the project. Combined with other expansion projects such as the $40 million being spent in Jamaica to develop the bauxite which would be reduced to pure aluminum at Kitimat, the parent company, Aluminum Limited, had to raise a total of $390 million. At that time it was described as 'one of the largest private financing ventures in recent years'." *L.L. Wise, "Setting Up Shop," Engineering News-Record 1952.*

Portal of the tunnel built to divert the Nechako River away from the site where they built the dam. BC Archives & Records Service, Province of BC photo no. d-05740.

A fleet of 30 to 40, ten- to seventeen-cubic-yard capacity trucks worked around the clock to transport this material along the four-lane divided highway connecting the quarry with the dam site one mile away. The central control tower used to allocate where each truck went for its next load was instrumental in achieving an average turnaround time of 12 minutes from dam site to quarry. One load of rocks—some of which weighed as much as 20 tons—were dumped into the canyon every 45 seconds.[13] In preparation for being placed on the dam, sand and gravel from nearby pits were screened and stockpiled in small mountains containing 208,777 cubic yards of sand measuring from zero to three-quarters of an inch, 164,680 cubic yards of gravel measuring three-quarters of an inch to three inches, and 136,697 cubic yards of gravel measuring three inches to ten inches.

View of the Grand Canyon of the Nechako River before Alcan built the Kenney Dam there, stopping the flow. Photo courtesy of the Jean Giesbrecht Collection.

That was not all.

Millions of yards of dirt and rocks had to be removed to prepare the dam site, clear the overburden from the quarries and build the roads required to construct the dam, including a 60-mile road south from Vanderhoof to the dam site over which men, equipment and half a million tons of supplies were hauled. It was said that if the loaded trucks required to transport these mountains of material from the quarries and dump them into the canyon were lined up bumper to bumper, they would form a line-up stretching from Vancouver almost to Halifax.[14]

Fortunes were made by the contractors hired to transport the more than 4.2 million gallons of petroleum products used during the construction of the dam and the owners of the airplanes that flew approximately three-quarters of a million miles hauling workers and supplies to and from the site.[15]

The dam was completed in six months. It was the largest sloping, rock-filled, clay-core dam in the world. The base of the dam lies over the concrete pad and along 1,170 feet of the bottom of the canyon. From there the dam rises in a series of terraces to 317 feet above the canyon floor. The top of the dam is 1,500 feet long and 40 feet wide. When the reservoir is filled the water laps against the boulders 25 feet below the top of the dam.[16] When it was completed the builders boasted it was so solid its life would be measured in geological, not historical time.[17]

The diversion tunnel around the dam was closed on October 8, 1952, and the water began rising behind the Kenney Dam. The reservoir contains 35 million acre feet of water[18] and covers the 358 square miles which once contained the Great Circle Water Route.[19] That's enough water to cover Vancouver Island to a depth of four feet. A more colourful explanation of the amount of water the reservoir holds is that it is enough to fill 359 billion eight-ounce beer glasses.[20] When the dam was completed, Harry Jomini, Alcan's resident engineer on the dam project, proudly declared, "This formerly wasted water is now, thanks to the Kenney dam, available for useful services."[21]

What he didn't say was, as the water rose behind the dam, it drowned all the prime timber growing around the perimeter of the reservoir. At the time it was thought this timber was uneconomi-

The Kenney Dam with the reservoir in the background. Photo courtesy of the *Prince George Citizen*.

cal to log, because there were no roads into the area. Forty years later, the driftwood created by that drowned forest is piled along the shore of the reservoir, and the tops of the dead trees, turned silvery-grey with age, still poke through its surface as silent reminders of the waste that occurred there.

The rising water in the reservoir also had a major impact on Tweedsmuir Park, the wilderness park established in 1936 to protect and preserve the natural features of a 5,400-square-mile area including the 218-mile Great Circle Water Route. When it was established, the park was roughly triangular. But Alcan's Kemano I Project resulted in seven of the park's lakes—Tahtsa, Sinclair, Whitesail, Tetachuk, Eutsku, Euchu and Chelaslie—becoming part of the large reservoir. The park boundaries were radically altered after the project was completed. The original triangular shape was truncated in the northeast and a southern leg was added which included the Rainbow Range, the Atnarko Valley and other areas south of the Dean River. In recognition of high wilderness values, Eutsuk Nature Conservancy (260,000 hectares) was established in northern Tweedsmuir in 1967 and the Rainbow Nature Conservancy (50,000 hectares) was established in the southern portion of the park in 1970.

In March, 1986, Tweedsmuir was one of the parks investigated by the Wilderness Advisory Committee,[22] appointed by the Socred provincial govenment's Environment Minister Austin Pelton. The committee used these words to describe the degrading impact Alcan's Kemano I Project had had on the northern portion of Tweedsmuir Park, rendering it unsuitable for permanent park status and more suitable for logging:

> Because this area's scenic values have suffered from the condition of Ootsa Reservoir (which is choked by drowned forest) the Parks Division considers it to have low park value. The Ministry of Forests indicates that its forest values are significant. The Ministry of Environment is concerned about caribou habitat.[23]

No mention was made of the recreation opportunities that had already been lost by the flooding that occurred there in the 1950s.

Although the Parks Division wanted to protect Tweedsmuir Park by upgrading it to Class A status, the committee did not concur. Instead it recommended that only areas of high recreational and conservation value should remain in the park, and areas of low park value and those with potentially severe management problems be deleted from the park or redesignated as recreation areas.[24] The Parks Division also considered the park value of the central area of Tweedsmuir, between the southern boundary of the Eutsuk Nature Conservancy and the Dean River, to be low. The problems here were the number of trees killed by mountain pine beetles and forest fires which had left large accumulations of dry timber which could result in a forest fire over a large area. The value of the forests remaining in the area were still considered low because of the long hauls required to get the timber to existing mills.

The environment ministry spoke out in defence of the significant wildlife population in the remote park, especially the relatively intact wilderness system in which predators such as

---

"[T]here are aspects of the original Kemano project that we would all do differently today. For example, it would be unacceptable today to flood standing timber. Back then, nobody wanted the timber and no one, including us, wanted to go to the expense of clearing such a huge site for the sake of tidiness." *Alcan's BC vice-president, Bill Rich, BCUCH 11.1630.*

21

wolves hunted prey such as moose, in a naturally controlled cycle in which, if the moose population rose, the wolf population would increase accordingly.

In its final report the committee recommended:

(1) The study of the Eutsuk caribou herd now under way be continued until the Wildlife Branch has adequate information to identify the areas that need to be protected to ensure the survival of the caribou herd living both within and outside the park;

(2) No lands identified by the Parks Division as having low park value along Ootsa and Whitesail Lakes should be deleted from Tweedsmuir Park until a management agreement has been reached among the Wildlife Branch, the Parks Division and the Ministry of Forests to cover the Eutsuk caribou herd and its range;

(3) Following the agreement referred to in (2) lands identified as having low park value along Ootsa and Whitesail Lakes not needed for protecting the caribou herd could be deleted from Tweedsmuir Park and added to the Provincial Forest. Of particular interest was the land around Lindquist Lake where the Deer Horn Mine is located;

(4) If the committee's recommendation regarding a wilderness designation is accepted, the central belt of the Park on the Nechako Plateau identified by the Parks Division as having low park values should be designated a Wilderness Conservancy, along with key areas of caribou winter range on its boundary to the east and north. If the recommendation is not accepted, the area should remain within the park, but be designated a recreation area with management directed toward wildlife.

The creation of the Kenney Dam was not the only industrial activity Alcan undertook in the remote area occupied by Tweedsmuir Park during the 1950s. The company's ambitious plan to harness the waters of the Upper Nechako River was made up of five different engineering projects: the Kenney Dam and storage reservoir; the 10-mile-long tunnel underneath Mount DuBose; the cavernous underground powerhouse carved out of the rock one-third of a mile inside Mount DuBose's western slope; and the 50-mile-long power-line built over the gale-torn Kildala Pass to carry electricity to what was then the largest aluminum smelter in the world, being built at Kitimat.

About 150 miles away from where the convoy of trucks was

Alcan's existing powerhouse at Kemano which is located inside a cavernous room blasted out of the interior of Mount DuBose. It was located there during the Korean War scare, to protect it from atomic bombs. No one thought about what would happen if the dam were to be bombed. Photo courtesy of the *Prince George Citizen*.

Mount DuBose with Kemano at its base. The giant "seven" on the mountain marks the spot where the penstocks emerge from the mountain and carry the water drawn out of Tahtsa Lake into the turbines inside the mountain. Photo courtesy of the *Prince George Citizen*.

working day and night to place a giant rock and clay plug in the Nechako River Canyon, another small army of workers was drilling, blasting and excavating 1.8 million cubic yards of underground rock out of the centre of Mount DuBose. They were building the system of sloping tunnels required to carry the water from the reservoir into the underground powerhouse being blasted from the inside of the base of the mountain. When it was completed, the length of this mammoth rock cathedral to hydroelectric power was 700 feet—longer than two football fields placed end-to-end—its roof an 80-foot-wide parabolic arch standing 120 feet above the top of the pits in which the eight turbines were to be installed.[25]

The crews began boring the main tunnel into Mount DuBose at the western end of Tahtsa Lake on October 22, 1951 and, on November 4, 1951, another crew started boring into the seaward side of the mountain. The 10-mile-long, horseshoe-shaped tunnel is 25 feet in diameter, and leads from the Western end of Tahtsa Lake through Mount DuBose. Inside the mountain it separates into two penstocks leading to four 54-inch spherical valves.[26] When the project was completed, 77,634 feet or 14.7 miles of tunnels had been drilled and blasted from the interior of the mountain.[27]

To create these mammoth works inside a mountain, a total of 529 miles of drill holes and 70 miles of blast holes were punched into the mountain to receive the more than 1,396 tons of dynamite required to open up these underground works. More than 260,990 cubic feet of a liquid mixture of cement were forced into cracks and sprayed on the walls of the tunnel, and 237,534 cubic yards of concrete were used to waterproof and reinforce the tunnels and the powerhouse.[28]

Mobilizing the men and equipment to construct this portion of the project proved to be a monumental task. There were neither roads nor railways close to the construction site and deep snows covered the mile-high mountain pass separating the worksites at the tunnel-building project's eastern and western ends. To bring workers and supplies to the construction site at Tahtsa Lake, in 1951 a road was built 105 miles from the Canadian National

Railway lines at Burns Lake to the east end of the lake. A barge was used to transport equipment, supplies and workers 18 miles along the lake to the site of the Tahtsa Lake camp built to accommodate 520 single employees and 44 families. At the western end of the project another road was built from the muskeg flats at the mouth of the Kemano River 12 miles to the construction camp at the base of the mountain.

A 25-ton tramway was constructed up the side of the mountain to carry supplies and workers to the site where the main tunnel emerged from the mountain and the metal penstocks were being installed to carry the water to the powerhouse. Another seven-mile road was built up the steep valley beside the fast-flowing creek named after Charles Horetzky, to a point near where the rocky crags of the Coast Range hold back the water of Tahtsa Lake. There they located Horetzky Camp, in which 500 single workers and nine families lived in Quonset huts. Their job was to drill the adit, or access tunnel, into the centre of the main tunnel.

The main camp near the powerhouse grew into a small community, with accommodation for 2,450 single employees and 44 families, and included a school, commissary, theatre, recreation building, a plant to reconstitute powdered milk, bakery, laundry, guest houses, a bank and a post office. Eight hundred workers could be fed at one time in the mess hall. At peak workforce, they were fed in three shifts.

"Recruiters also scoured Canada to find workers experienced in the type of underground work being carried out deep inside Mount DuBose. Many of these workers came from Ontario and 60 key supervisors were American citizens. The project also provided employment for the flood of post-war immigrants arriving in Canada many of whom were journeymen electricians, plumbers and carpenters." L.L. Wise, "Setting Up Shop."

"All hiring for the Kemano I project was done through Vancouver. In 1951, when workers were being assembled for the project, people were being hired at the rate of 100 per day. The turnover rate was high during the first year's operation but, by 1952, the hiring rate had dropped to 200 per week. By that time it was estimated there were 4,500 people employed on the construction of the hydroelectric facilities alone. That was 13 per cent of estimated 35,000 construction workers in B.C." L.L. Wise, "Setting Up Shop."

Horetsky Creek winds its way down the steep-sided mountain valley leading up from Kemano toward the site where the adit was drilled into Mount DuBose. Photo courtesy of the *Prince George Citizen*.

Other camps built at the western end of the construction site included: a camp at tidewater to house the 60 workers employed in building the docks; a camp for privately-owned trailers,

The village of Kemano, owned by Alcan, by the Kemano River. Photo courtesy of the *Prince George Citizen*.

approximately 40 small, prefabricated plywood houses, a school, commissary and recreation centre built two miles from the main camp which, at the peak of the construction period, provided housing for an additional 250 people; two tent camps perched high on the western slopes of Mount DuBose to provide accommodation for 120 employees working on the penstocks and 310 employees working on the main tunnel. Before the onset of winter the tents were replaced with small, winterized frame buildings with aluminum roofs.

The final obstacle faced by the engineers was designing a low-risk-of-failure, high-voltage, flexible and efficient powerline to transmit the power generated in the underground powerhouse at Kemano to the smelter being built at Kitimat. Any interruption of the power flowing over the line could damage the aluminum reduction cells inside the plant. Two routes were considered: a 78-mile route down the Kemano River and along the coast to Kitimat, or a 51-mile transmission line over the 5,300-foot-high Kildala Pass.

The shorter route was found to be cheaper despite the difficulties presented by its construction. During a helicopter reconnaissance of the area in September, 1949, the engineers saw for the first time the problems they would face building transmission towers through the narrow valleys and over the steep ridges and alpine passes on this route. Further investigation disclosed the terrain over which the transmission line was to be built was subject to avalanches, heavy ice accumulations, gale-force winds and flash floods during which the swift-flowing mountain streams and rivers carved new channels from the surrounding mountains.

Temperatures in Kildala Pass drop to -24°F during the winter. Turbulent weather conditions are created when warm, moist air masses coming off the Pacific Ocean are raised into the freezing temperatures high in the Coast Range where the new powerline was to be strung. The result is gale-force winds reaching maximums of 100 miles per hour, whipping the area's heavy winter snowfalls into 50-foot snowdrifts. Coupled with the severe climatic conditions prevailing throughout the route, engineers also had to cope with the rugged topography over which the lines had to be built and the unusually heavy electrical loads which had to be carried over the long spans strung over the mountainous terrain.

The engineers' efforts were hampered by the lack of accurate information about weather conditions in the pass. Apart from the members of the Kitimaat and Haisla Indian Bands, few people lived

Camp 11 at the high point of the Kildala Pass, between Kemano and Kitimat. Powerlines carry the electricity from the powerhouse at Kemano to the smelter at Kitimat. There are two transmission lines: one with conventional steel towers, the other with aluminum towers after a design used in Europe. Both lines had problems because of severe weather conditions and either one or both were relocated to less slide-prone areas and modified later. The camp was about 6,000 feet above sea level. Photos on pages 32-33 and 34, courtesy of Earl Warner.

in the area. No one knew how much ice and rime would build up on the powerlines during the winter. Nor did they know how the shifting ice and snow and the steep mountain slopes would affect the towers on which the lines were strung. In 1949, a lonely weather observation station was established on the west side of the mountain at the mouth of the Kildala River, where West Coast guide Herb Skuce recorded snowfalls of up to 20 feet and the amount of snow drifting and icing that would occur on the transmission lines on this route.

The following year, weather observation stations were established 3,000 feet up the Kildala Valley and near the mountain's 5,300-foot high summit. Twenty-foot spans of extra-large aluminum conductors equipped with recording instruments were erected near these sites and shelters were built for the six-man crews, whose job it was to record the weather conditions and the amount of ice and rime forming on the lines. Conditions were so severe at the summit of the pass that steel cables were passed over the small shelters and bolted into the rocky summit to keep the shelters from being pushed down the mountain by the force of the creeping snowpack. The only break in the monotony of the job of the observation crews was the arrival of the helicopters bearing supplies and someone to relieve them when they were taken down to the construction camps at Kemano. Adverse weather conditions were so lengthy in the pass that weeks would go by before it was safe for a helicopter to fly in the pass and land on the small landing pad. The observations of these crews helped to create the design criteria on which the engineers proceeded.

Later, these crews observed the performance of the experimental hollow-legged aluminum towers designed to carry the power over the pass.

At first the 80-foot-high legs of these experimental towers wobbled wildly, leading an early observer stationed on the mountain to describe their action during high winds to be like five-legged monsters trying to walk off the mountains. Engineers were able to stop this action with the aid of a system of shock absorbers.[29]

Despite their lack of long-term knowledge about the weather conditions, Alcan's engineers set to work designing the towers and large conductors required for the project. Alcan vice-president McNeeley DuBose visited high-altitude transmission lines erected in similar winter conditions in Switzerland and Norway, and high-head, underground power stations in Switzerland and Sweden, to learn more about the difficulties they had experienced. His concern and caution about the construction of the powerline were justified. The design of a failure-proof power transmission line was critically important to the successful operation of the smelter. DuBose knew even a brief power outage could cause serious damage to the aluminum reduction pots being built at Kitimat. His solution was to install two lines through the worst parts of the pass, one utilizing conventional steel towers and the second the experimental five-legged aluminum towers.

The smelting pots at Kitimat are actually huge electrolytic cells containing a seething molten mass of black-crusted, bright red liquid cryolite and aluminum oxide or alumina, which resembles the molten lava that pours from an erupting volcano. They are an awesome example of humanity's ability to harness vast amounts of electricity and turn it to its own use.

The electrical energy surging through the fiery cryolite-alumina mixture separates the alumina into oxygen which collects on the carbon anodes immersed in the electrolyte, and molten aluminum which settles to the bottom of the carbon-lined cell, which acts as the cathode. More powdered alumina can be added to the molten cryolite as long as the carbon is active and there is enough electrical current surging between the anode and the cathode for the smelting process to continue. A power outage can be disastrous to the process because, as it cools, the molten mass quickly solidifies, forming a lump of metallic salts so hard it must be broken up by jack hammers. Restarting the potline is a slow, costly process and, in some cases, the damaged pots cannot be restarted and must be replaced. That high-risk factor was critically important in the design for the transmission lines carrying the electrical power from Kemano over Kildala Pass to the smelter.

On entering the smelter, one's first impression is of how few people can actually be seen working in the smoky, cavernous room. The workers stay in ventilated areas, protected from overexposure to the contaminants—carbon monoxide, sulphur dioxide, hydrogen flouride and small particles of cryolite and aluminum flouride—which are by-products of the smelting process. Workers emerge from these ventilated areas only when there is something

Kitimat smelter, 1955. BC Archives & Records Service, Province of BC photo no. na-15619.

to be done. One of their tasks is breaking up the black crust which forms on top of the red-hot electrolyte to prevent flare-ups or eruptions of pent-up gases. When I visited the smelter this was done by poking pitch-covered pine poles into the crusty electrolyte, causing the gases and the poles to erupt dramatically into flames.

So much energy is sizzling around each of the 900 pots at Alcan's Kitimat smelter that the air is magnetized for yards around the pots. The energy field inside the smelter is so strong it can render watches inoperative and expose the film inside a camera if kept in the pot room too long. As a result, visitors entering the cavernous buildings in which the pots are located are advised to remove all electronic devices and watches and leave their cameras behind. Those who have pace-makers inserted in their chests are advised not to enter the buildings housing the potlines.

The air outside the smelter is so polluted that high emissions of flourides are blamed for a 19% to 28% reduction in the growth of trees on the 17,400 surrounding acres, and the death of the trees formerly growing on 80 acres north of the smelter.[30] Evidence of elevated flouride levels are found in the waters of nearby Douglas Channel, where waste from the smelter is dumped and polycyclic aromatic hydrocarbons on surface sediments and sediment cores taken from Kitimat Arm are attributed to the burning of carbon paste in the potlines.[31]

By 1994 Alcan had been on BC's worst polluter's list for seven years.

Alcan's original plans for the Kemano project called for it to be developed in four stages over 18 years, during which increasing amounts of water would be diverted into the powerhouse at Kemano as more generators were brought into action. The first stage would have seen a small dam built at the outlet of Tahtsa Lake so that its water would be diverted into the tunnel. Next they would tap the waters of the Upper Skeena by diverting the water of the Nanika-Kidprice system into the Tahtsa Lake reservoir through a second three-mile tunnel drilled through the mountain ridge separating the two river systems. The Kenney Dam in the Nechako River Canyon would have been built during the third stage, when a second tunnel would be drilled through Mount DuBose to deliver water to the underground powerhouse. During the fourth stage the number of generators in the powerhouse would be expanded from 10 to 16.[32]

World events intervened and, with the outbreak of the Korean War in June of 1950, and the resultant increase in the demand and price for aluminum, the plans for the project were accelerated. With the exception of the Nanika-Kidprice diversion, most of the first three stages of the original construction proposal were completed in 42 months, and by July, 1958, seven generators were already humming in the underground powerhouse. An eighth generator was added in 1967, raising the plant's maximum generating capacity to 900 million watts,[33] and raising the generating capacity it could guarantee to deliver steadily to the smelter to 750 million watts.[34] What became known as the Kemano I Project delivered enough power to supply the average electrical requirements of a city containing 75,000 BC homes.[35] Assuming an average of three people live in each home, that is enough power to meet the annual electricity needs of 225,000 BC residents.[36]

The Sound of a River Dying

I understand why the B.C. government invited Alcan to this region of the province in the early fifties. They wanted to open up this area to develop-ment. They wanted to make money. They wanted flood control for the peo-ple down south. In the fifties we were not aware of the environment, nor were we learned enough to understand that environment and economy can-not be separated. When you destroy one you destroy the other. Nor were they thinking of the people who inhabited this region. After all, they were only a bunch of natives and backwoods people. They were expendable for the benefit of the rest of the province and for profit.[1]

When Alcan began building its industrial colossus in the rugged hinterland of BC in 1950, a Canadian news magazine described the project as the biggest thing that had happened to BC since the first transcontinental railway punched a right-of-way through the Rockies in 1885.[2] Despite that type of national promotion, few people in BC understood the magnitude of what was happening in the sparsely-populated Nechako River Valley during the 1940s and '50s. Some blame their ignorance on the remoteness of the area in which the project was being built and on the absence of such sophisticated electronic communications systems as exist today. Others believed then, and continue to believe today, that it was acceptable to turn over control of the province's apparently limit-less resources to large industrial firms which, it was assumed, would provide the stable industrial base they believed was essential to solve BC's chronic economic and unemployment problems. There are also those who continue to argue that Alcan's Kemano I

Project was beneficial to the Nechako River because it reduced the flooding that frequently occurred along the river, especially at Prince George, near its mouth. However, reports prepared for Alcan show the operation of the Nechako Reservoir provided only moderate flood relief in the 30 years following its construction.[3] And environmentally concerned citizens point out there are less expensive, less damaging methods for reducing flooding than inundating 358 square miles of land.

My own ignorance of what was happening to the Nechako River is only one example of how residents of the area failed to recognize the problems that would be created when, in 1952, all the water flowing into the river from an area more than two times the size of Prince Edward Island (or four and a half times the size of Rhode Island) was diverted into Alcan's reservoir.[4]

Although I lived in the area during the time the project was being built, and both my brothers and many of my friends had worked on the project, I didn't see the damage it has caused until more than 30 years after the dam was completed. In 1979, I was visiting Alcan's Nechako Reservoir with friends and family for a weekend of cross-country skiing and snowmobiling in the area. On the second morning of our stay, I crept out of my bed to go for an early morning ski. Overnight the temperature had plunged to well below zero and, as I moved across the snow covering nearby Knewstubb Lake, the shrunken lake ice sporadically cracked beneath my skis, sending a dull booming thud echoing and re-echoing off the low surrounding hills. The only other sound interrupting the silence of my solitary ski trip was the chorus of wild howls sent up by a pack of wolves prowling through a valley somewhere in the distance.

I have never returned to that place in winter. But I hope, when age and infirmity may lock me into a more sedentary lifestyle, I will still have the imaginative power to evoke the essence of that ski trip across the lake: the feel of my muscles driving my skis over the thin layer of hard-packed snow covering the windswept ice, the wolves' howls, the sting of the intense cold on my face, the sight of my breath emerging from my mouth and the feel of it as it froze on my eyelashes, hair and parka. Overriding everything was an intense feeling of internal calm and oneness with the universe.

Etched in my memory, too, is the time later that day when I joined my friends and family on a spine-jolting overland snow-mobile trip to the spot where ice-shrouded Cheslatta Falls plunged into a clear pool. The sound of our vehicles roaring along the trail startled a flock of swans overwintering on the pool. They rose sedately into the clear, blue winter sky where they circled, watching as we struggled through the waist-deep snow to peer into the torpid depths of the pool where fat, semi-dormant fish lolled. Before we left, we stamped out a sitting area in the snow where we ate our lunch, accompanied by the cries of the birds flying overhead and the muffled sound of the nearby waterfall. It was a magic moment.

That brief winter recreational trip in the wilderness south of Vanderhoof had some disturbing lessons to teach me the following summer, when I learned I had not been skiing on a lake at all. Instead, the snow-covered ice I had skied across covered part of Alcan's huge reservoir; and Cheslatta Falls, where the swans had circled over us as we ate lunch, was part of the release system carrying "surplus" water back into the Nechako River from behind Alcan's Kenney Dam.

My mistake was understandable. Many maps don't clearly identify this chain of flooded lakes as a reservoir. Instead, the area is shown as part of Tweedsmuir Park and many of the once-pristine wilderness lakes retain their original names: Tetachuk, Ootsa, Whitesail, Tahtsa, Natalkuz and Eutsuk. Nearby Chelaslie Lake, which was once connected to Natalkuz Lake by a short river, was also flooded, raising its water level until it is now shown on maps as Chelaslie Arm on the northern shore of Natalkuz Lake. When the water level rose in the reservoir, it also raised the water level of the rivers connecting the lakes, transforming them into long, narrow channels which are now identified on maps as Tahtsa Narrows and Intata Reach.

During a summertime visit to the "lake" in 1980, my friends took me across the reservoir in their power-boat to a bay where a surreal landscape had been created by the silvery-grey tops of drowned trees poking above the surface of Tetachuk Lake. These were some of the trees left standing when the water built up 40 years ago behind the Kenney Dam. As we proceeded cautiously

View of the huge canyon torn out of the surrounding hillsides by torrents of water released through Skins Lake Spillway. Photo taken from the top of the Spillway. Photo courtesy of the Cheslatta First Nations.

through the tangle of trees and drifting deadheads, my friends pointed out an occupied osprey's nest near the top of one of the dead trees which stood about five feet above the surface of the water. The female osprey and her mate were circling overhead screaming warnings down to us.

The level of the reservoir is not constant: Depending on the rainfall, and on the amount of water being sucked into the tunnel drilled through Mount DuBose, or the amount being released back into the Nechako River, it can rise and fall more than ten feet. So when we returned to that same dead forest a month later, heavy rains had raised the level of the reservoir and the osprey nest was covered with water. As we stared down through six inches of water at the three eggs in the nest, the parents again circled above us, their cries now sounding more like laments than threats.

Looking at a map later I realized where once there was wilderness, there is now a reservoir stretching 135 miles from the Kenney Dam to the natural western boundary formed by the Coast Range. In 1949 it was predicted that the reservoir would provide a deepwater recreational site providing access to natural resources in Tweedsmuir Park which, until then, had not been easily accessible.[5] Today, the driftwood ringing the shores of the reservoir and the dangers posed by half-submerged snags and floating debris make access to areas of the park difficult for all but the most experienced boaters and canoeists.

During that summertime trip to the lake I stood for the first time on the 1,500-foot-long Kenney Dam. It is a stunning sight. When it was erected in the early 1950s, it was proudly proclaimed to be the largest sloping, rock-filled, clay-core dam in the world. After it was completed and the reservoir it created filled with water, the level of Tahtsa Lake, 136 miles west of the dam, rose by 18 feet, to where the water is drawn off into the 10-mile-long tunnel drilled through Mount DuBose to feed Alcan's hydro-electric generators at Kemano. Looking toward the reservoir today, you see the water lapping against the rip-rap protecting the face of the dam. The downstream face of the dam falls 320 feet—the height of a 32-storey building—into what was once the Grand Canyon of the Nechako River.

Alcan's reservoir flooded more than 38 square miles of Crown land, 14 square miles of private land and numerous native reservations and graveyards that the federal government held in trust for the Cheslatta Indian Band. When the Kenney Dam was finished in 1952, Alcan invited members of the Nadleh Whet'en band who

Tetachuk Crossing, circa 1910-20, which now lies under the reservoir. Photo by pioneer surveyor Frank Swannell.

live near the dam site to witness what they were told would be "a big blast" that would close off the diversion tunnel. Among those attending was elder Matthew Ketlo, who was then 29 years old. The trapping territory he had acquired from his father, Achille, was located below the dam. He says he watched in amazement as "they blew the whole mountain on the west side right into the river. It's a pitiful sight now. The dam looks nice but it ruined the whole country," he says today.

After the river was closed off by the blast, it took four years for the reservoir to fill up behind the dam. During that time, no water flowed in the riverbed between the dam and the Nautley River 50 miles downstream, except for that coming from a few small streams. When the water stopped flowing, fish were trapped and died in the deeper pools of remaining water, and the animals who used that portion of the river moved away. Dr. A.W. "Al" Mooney describes the scene and the Nechako Valley residents' reaction to the closing off of their river:

"I have seen the destruction from the air. Each swollen lake is encircled by a ring of broken trees and rotting vegetation several hundred yards deep, a labyrinth of deadfalls drowned in the rising waters. No energy crisis in the world is worth this obscenity." *Pierre Berton, Drifting Home.*

The people of Vanderhoof are reported as being overjoyed when the by-pass tunnel was closed to start filling the reservoir. This is not true. There was sorrow. I was there. I had never thought of a river as a living thing. When that gate crashed down and the river struck the gates there was a crying sound which permeated the whole area. Unnerving—the sound of a river dying. Mr. Elmer Kerr put out his next issue of the Nechako Chronicle edged in black. The front page said "Death of a River."[6]

Matthew Ketlo remembers a time during the "Dirty Thirties" when he accompanied his father on trips to the Nautley River to spear the big spring salmon found there. "Our parents would get me and my friend to pack those salmon home on a stick between our shoulders and their tails would be dragging on the ground," he said. Only the occasional big spring finds its way up the Nechako and into the Nautley River these days. During a meeting at Stoney Creek with Alcan and Department of Indian Affairs executives, Celina John (the elder adviser to the Carrier Sekani Tribal Council) used a characteristically colourful Carrier anecdote to describe what happened to the upper reaches of the Nechako River: "When I was young that river was so powerful a strong horse couldn't swim across it. Now my little kitty can walk across it without getting her feet wet," she said.

Below the spot where water now re-enters the river at Cheslatta Falls, the water level rises and falls many times throughout each summer and autumn when the company adjusts the releases of water from the reservoir through the Skins Lake Spillway. Matthew Ketlo tells a story about how "one smart beaver" coped with the fluctuating water levels by building one lodge near the low water mark and a high-water lodge above it where the family lived when

---

"The dam is terraced, like a huge Inca temple, and standing on it, straining to hear a trickle of water in the river-bed below, you have to wonder what God you should worship here." *Mark Hume, The Run of the River: Portraits of Eleven British Columbia Rivers, 42.*

"The licence gave the Aluminum Company of Canada a carte blanche permit to harness the Upper Nechako River, with no consideration whatever to the salmon or any environmental effects." *Murray Rankin and Arvay Finlay, Alcan's Kemano Project: Options and Recommendations, 17.*

Two views of the Nechako River from the same spot, showing the full summer flow and fall's reduced flow. If Alcan is allowed to proceed, the summer flows will be less than the fall flows shown here. Photo courtesy of Pam Sholty.

the water was higher. "It was a two-storey beaver condo," he says.

Ketlo's life has been profoundly affected by Alcan's Kemano I Project. "First Alcan took the water. Then the BC Forest Service took all the trees off my trapline so about 10 years ago we had to sell it for practically nothing," he said.

Jack Shelford was a pioneer at Ootsa Lake. In 1911 he moved into the lake area from Hazelton with his brother Arthur, to establish the original Shelford Ranches. Jack's son, Cyril, has travelled on foot and by boat through the area now covered by the dam. He describes it as being a hunter's and fisherman's paradise, teeming with waterfowl, game and fish. "We had a river boat. But in the early years we had no motor so every year we poled and paddled our way to Tahtsa Lake to catch kokanee," he said. Portions of the Shelford family's land now lie under 140 feet of water. He said that before the Kenney Dam was built, Tetachuck Lake south of Ootsa Lake was very shallow and warm during the summer. Now the lake is much deeper and too cold for swimming.

In 1951, when construction crews moved into the remote area south of Vanderhoof to begin building a dam on the upper Nechako River, the environmental price tags were not visible on Alcan's plans for a huge industrial development in the region. Indeed, a public opinion poll conducted during May, 1949, revealed 93.9% of the BC residents surveyed supported Alcan's plans for a hydroelectric development in the Nechako River Valley.[7] The poll results reflected the commonly held belief of that time: Industrial development held the promise of a brighter, more prosperous future. Few of the people polled in the survey understood the long-term repercussions the project would have on the environment, or realized that the company had been given the right to remove all the water from the upper Nechako River.

The project was being built in a sparsely populated area far from the prying eyes of reporters and at a time when most BC residents thought the province's forest and water supplies were limitless. Few could envision a time when concerns about the health of the Nechako River or that of the fish swimming in it would cause environmentally-concerned residents to begin to question the

---

"When the water dropped, fisheries officers were able to walk the upper Nechako and for the first time get a firm assessment of the river's fisheries value. They found 4000 chinook spawning redds." *Hume, 46.*

company's right to remove even more water from the river, or to add up the environmental and economic costs of the project.

The agreement paving the way for what became known as Kemano I was signed by representatives of the BC government and Alcan on December 29, 1950. It was greeted with enthusiastic endorsement from business and political leaders from throughout the province. Regional representatives were assured the project would provide the economic stability that had, until then, eluded the population living in the area from Prince Rupert to Prince George. An editorial in the July 28, 1949, edition of the *Burns Lake Review* described the difficulties Nechako Valley residents had understanding the immensity of the project: "It is possibly just a little hard to realize the impact of a new $500,000,000 industry for British Columbia and right in our own part of the country" exclaimed the editor.

The people living in the area to be flooded by the dam were understandably less enthusiastic about the prospect of watching their homes disappear under the water. Their objections were brushed aside by Alcan's BC vice-president McNeely DuBose and BC's Water Comptroller Major R.C. Farrow after they held a half-day hearing at Wistaria near Ootsa Lake on October 24, 1949. There are two versions of that meeting.

In the report he forwarded to Alcan president R.E. Powell, DuBose says:

> [A]bout 100 people, men, women, and children were present. The hearing convened at 10:35 a.m. and was finished at 1:30 p.m. At first it appeared that there might be some flaring up on the part of local people who did not want their present way of life to be disrupted, but everything turned out smoothly and after the hearing the assembled gathering, including our representatives and those of

---

"[W]hat worries me on these low flows, like when the river goes down to 500 [cubic feet per second] what will the beaver do in the winter time that had built their house for a much higher flow because it freezes the mouth [of the beaver lodge].... [T]hen all of a sudden somebody decides to put the river up to 2,000, 3,000 [cubic feet per second] with the ice still on the river, they had did it, and them beaver are drowned out because they live in there and the ground is frozen and they can't get out." *Trapper Burt Irvine, BCUCH 3.330.*

the Government, were given sandwiches and coffee and every evidence of hospitality by the local people.[8]

But the pioneer residents of the area have different memories of that meeting.

After DuBose explained what the company was planning, Jack Shelford was appointed as spokesman for the residents. They had identified six concerns about the project:

- They did not want to be flooded out.
- They would like to stop the whole thing but they believed it was too big for them to stop.
- They believed they should have an agreement on compensation before a water licence was granted.
- They were concerned about what the basis of compensation would be and felt it should provide enough money to enable them to re-establish themselves elsewhere.
- Compensation should also be paid for "the general upset to their lives" as well as for the actual damage.
- The lives of those not flooded out would also be changed because their community would be destroyed and they should receive compensation also.[9]

DuBose said he agreed with Shelford "100 per cent."

Burns Lake resident William MacNeil told the hearing he believed that if the area were left untouched, mining and mineral claims there would eventually result in the development of industry in the area planned to be flooded by the reservoir.[10] At that point, DuBose reminded the residents that, although the company was conducting studies of possible dam sites on the Nechako River, the site of the dam had not yet been chosen, and the company might have to "revert to the original plan prepared by government engineers."[11] That plan called for the construction of dams at Eutsuk, Whitesail and Tahtsa Lakes to be connected by a series of tunnels or canals. If none of these plans proved to be eco-

---

"It would be contrary to general practice and manifestly unfair to expect the applicant to continue spending large sums of money in investigating the possibilities of a project for its practical use without any assurance that it would be granted licences or on what terms." *Major Farrow, BC's Water Comptroller in 1950, BCUCH 4.438.*

nomically viable, the company would take another look at its original plan to build a dam on the Chilko River near Williams Lake, Dubose said. The residents of Ootsa Lake were reassured it would be "a long period of years"[12] before the engineering studies for the project would be completed, the site of the dam selected and the dam built, so they would have plenty of time to re-establish themselves elsewhere.[13] In fact, construction crews began building the Kenney Dam on the Nechako River the following year.

Jack Shelford describes the meeting as "lively" with plenty of shouting. He says the residents left the meeting feeling "sad," "as if they'd lost their best friend," wondering what they could do to prevent the project and how much money they would be paid for their land.[14]

The hearing at Wistaria was adjourned and reconvened in Victoria one week later, on October 31. During this meeting, Major Farrow clarified the way in which compensation to Ootsa Lake residents would be determined. He informed the settlers that according to BC's Water Act, if they could not agree on a price, the matter would be settled by binding arbitration.[15] Arbitrated settlements were something the settlers feared because land values were low and unlikely to provide them with enough money to resettle elsewhere in the province, where land prices were higher. When the first offers were as low as $3,000 for a house and a half-section of land, they became alarmed.

More formal opposition to Alcan's proposal to divert water from the upper Nechako was heard during the Victoria meeting, when representatives of the federal Department of Fisheries and the fishing industry warned Farrow there was not enough information available to evaluate the consequences of the project on BC's salmon-fishing industry.[16] They recommended that any licence issued to Alcan include conditions providing for ongoing research to determine the extent of the project's effects on the fisheries. The federal government and the International Pacific Salmon Fisheries Commission recommended that provision be made for releasing flows of water through the dam to cool the upper reaches of the river when it contained migrating salmon. That recommendation was not acted upon until 1987, when an agreement was reached enabling Alcan to remove all but 12% of the pre-dam water flows from the Nechako.

A preliminary report prepared by fisheries biologist Dr. Peter Larkin for the BC Game Department in 1949 stated that the project threatened the health of the freshwater fish in the lakes and would pose a major threat to the spawning grounds on which future generations of freshwater fish would be born. Ironically, in 1993 Dr. Larkin was one of the people appointed by the Province of BC to the commission to investigate how the incremental damages caused to the Nechako River Valley could be lessened. In his report he also accurately predicted what would happen should the area not be logged before it was flooded:

> The flooding of the margins of the lakes will undoubtedly result in the presence of innumerable snags and large amounts of debris in the near shore area which would impair fishing conditions and recreational sites and make navigation near the shore dangerous. This effect on the "fishability" might mean that although fish were as abundant as they had been or possibly more abundant, they would not represent the potential sport fishery of any consequence.[17]

Larkin recommended that one or two years be spent studying both the project's potential effect on the local sports fishery, and the possibility that if clearing all the future flood area around the lakes were not economically feasible, consideration should be given to removing the timber in areas where recreational developments would be most desirable.

A submission presented to the 1949 hearing by the Canadian Department of Fisheries recognized the need for power and fish to develop together in BC. The report states that developing the

---

"[O]n one occasion we had difficulty getting into shore when the wind came up and a storm blew in. There was a lot of standing timber along the shoreline and there appeared to be only one place we could get into shore and, when we got in there, there was about 60 or 70 feet of drift wood that was between us and the shore. So we stayed there for about 45 minutes and then had to go back out into the lake because we obviously couldn't stay there any longer." *Prince George resident, Arlene Galisky, describing the dangers posed by the drowned forest surrounding the Nechako Reservoir, BCUCH 6.1063.*

hydroelectric power potential of the Chilko River would irreparably damage the river's salmon fishery, and less damage would be done by Alcan's proposed dam on the Nechako River. This report also contains early estimates of the reduction of water flows which would result from the building of the dam: Diverting the upper reaches of the Nechako would remove 95% of the water flow from below the proposed dam to Fort Fraser; 80% of the water flowing in the river from Fort Fraser to the confluence of the Stuart and Nechako Rivers; and 55% below the confluence of the Stuart and Nechako Rivers to Prince George.[18] The report concludes that these reduced flows would present "transportation difficulties" to the sockeye and spring salmon and steelhead trout migrating through the river to their spawning grounds.[19] This early report also states:

> The matter before this board covers the use of the water resources in British Columbia which are available for power on the one hand, and for fisheries on the other. The provincial government has authority over the former aspect of water development and the federal government, through the Department of Fisheries, has authority over the latter aspect.

A handwritten comment on this particular page of the record of the hearings, on file at the BC Archives in Victoria, asks "Do they have jurisdiction over the water at all?" The answer to that question threatened to become a legal issue 30 years later when Alcan attempted to initiate the second half of its agreement with the province.

In 1951, not all federal fisheries representatives agreed with the concerns being expressed about the effects of Alcan's proposed project on the fish using the river. Among them was federal fisheries representative Dr. A.L. Pritchard, who said the salmon using the Nechako would be safe because the dam was being built above the rapids and falls of the river's Grand Canyon, which already made that portion of the river inaccessible to fish.[20] The belief that migrating salmon would not be affected adversely by the dam persisted in some government circles up until the hearings held during the 1990s to determine the potential damage of the KCP.

In the 1940s, the sockeye salmon run up the Stuart River—the

Nechako's main tributary that flows into it below the falls—was considered to be less important than the Chilko River run.

Concerns for the well-being and survival of the wildlife living in the future flood area were raised in a report prepared by Dr. Ian McTaggart Cowan in 1949 for the BC Game Commission. He began his report by complaining he had been given insufficient time to prepare an adequate report (he had only been notified of the hearings on August 10, 1949) and that "it is obviously impossible, under these circumstances, to anything but outline the possible consequences in a general way."[21] He did conclude that waterfowl, big game and fur-bearing animals living in the area would be affected by the proposed flooding.

The habitat of large numbers of Canada geese and ducks who "nest in the islands and other sequestered places and congregate later on the delta of the Tahtsa River,"[22] would be flooded by the reservoir. Of more concern was the flock of approximately 100 trumpeter swans (representing one-eighth of Canada's population of this rare species) which spent the winters feeding in the rapids of the Tetachuck River. McTaggart Cowan stated that "[e]xperience has shown, if the area is flooded, they are unlikely to move elsewhere."[23]

The area to be flooded around the perimeter of the reservoir was also the winter feeding ground of the large population of moose, he pointed out. These animals spent the summer grazing in the higher altitudes and moved down near the lakes in the fall. If this winter range were to be lost, the animals would be forced to spend the winters at higher levels where there is less protection from the icy wind and food is scarcer. A total of 102 traplines were registered, wholly or in part, in the area to be covered by the reservoir. In most instances, the most productive portion of these traplines was near the lakes and streams. "Substantial changes in the water level will flood out the animal populations of the lower levels and remove many acres of productive fur land permanently from production," McTaggart Cowan said in his report.[24] He predicted that the damage to beaver colonies in the area from which many of the trappers received a large portion of their annual income would be particularly severe. To lessen the damage to wildlife, he recommended that the project be delayed for a year to enable the Game Commission to undertake a more detailed study of the area, and that any water licenses granted should include provisions to protect the wildlife. The BC Forest Service also recommended the project be delayed until "all areas to be flooded should be properly cleared in accordance with the specifications drawn up by the Forest Service."[25]

Asked if the project's postponement, recommended so that the fisheries and wildlife experts would have more time to evaluate the proposal, would make it difficult for the company to proceed, DuBose replied:

> I would say this, that if the people who would profit by having it postponed would agree to go on a bond to return the money that we would spend on engineering during the next two years providing the permission of the license was not then granted, why that would take away most of the objections, of course.[26]

Local residents, however, voiced their own objections and alarm. Pioneer Ootsa Lake resident Alice Harrison says she and her husband Alfred were "very shaken" when they learned what was going to happen. "We thought we would be there forever. In the end we didn't starve to death but it was pretty upsetting."[27]

In a letter to the editor which appeared in the *Burns Lake Review* on November 3, 1949, Ootsa Lake resident B.R. "Buster" Harrison wrote:

> The most of us in the Ootsa Lake district are here by choice, some of us have been here for forty years, had we wanted to leave we would have done so long ago.
>
> It appears now if the Alcan takes this project some of us will have to go if we want to or not.
>
> We have tried to find out from the Alcan just what they will do for us in the way of compensation for taking our property, businesses and upsetting our way of life. So far all we have had is a promise that we will be looked after. How we are going to be looked after seems very vague in the minds of the Company officials as well as the water comptroller. The water comptroller did tell us that should anyone refuse to sell to the Company said Company could expropriate property or businesses and it would be placed in

the hands of an arbitration board as to value. If this is so then my conception of a Democracy and the free enterprise system is all wrong, I thought that in Canada one was allowed to own property in ones own right. This seems to be true as long as some company don't want what you have. In fact the water comptroller seemed to be more interested in giving the Alcan what they want than he was in protecting the interests of the people who are paying his salary.

The most of us do not feel that we can stop this project from going through, although it will ruin one of the most beautiful chain of lakes and rivers on the Continent as well as the duck and goose shooting and quite a per cent of the winter feed for moose, the fishing also will be ruined. However we feel that no license should be granted to any Company until said Company has first taken care of the people whose lives and property are to be affected.

I think that most everyone will agree that the people here should have the right to protect their homes and business to the best of their ability, and the only way we can do this is to prevent the grant-ing of this license, for once the license is granted they can start on their dam, and could only be forced to pay damages to properties flooded, and one is not in a very good bargaining position when the water is up around the neck.

We know that the Government is very anxious to sell this pro-ject to the Alcan and therefore will give us little help in getting a good settlement from the Company once the license is granted, this is why we have objected to the granting of this license. We would like to stop the project if we could, if we can't stop it we want to make the best deal we can, which will be little enough at the best.

Mr DuBose, Vice-President of Alcan, told us that they did not know if they were going to take this project or not. If this is true, then why grant the license at this time. Our Government will pro-tect them in not letting anyone else have a license as long as they are interested.

The Government could guarantee the license if and when they decide to take the project and as soon as they own the properties to be affected.

By 1951 the Ootsa Lake residents were becoming impatient with their lack of success in getting the provincial government to protect them. They decided to try to force the government to act by sending a delegation, led by Jack Shelford, to Victoria to meet

View of the water rising over farmers' fields beside Ootsa Lake after Alcan built the Kenney Dam and began diverting the Nechako River. Photo courtesy of the Jean Giesbrecht Collection.

with Premier Johnson.[28] The other members of the delegation were Buster Harrison, Mrs. Arthur (Polly) Pelletier, G.R. Anderson and Mrs. Myles Shelford. Jack Shelford says they tried to include the members of the Cheslatta Band living on Ootsa Lake in their negotiations with Alcan. "But the Department of Indian Affairs told us to mind our own business. They were wards of the federal government and it was a federal matter," he said during a 1993 interview at his summer home on Francois Lake.

Once in Victoria, the six-member delegation was unsuccessful in convincing either Johnson or the Leader of the Opposition, Harold Winch, to help them. Their visit was reported in the *Victoria Daily Colonist*, which described Alcan's "high-pressure tactics" in attempting to force the settlers to agree to relinquish their lands for "small and niggardly prices."[29] "We'll stay there until the furniture is floating around our ears, unless everyone gets a fair settlement," the paper quotes Ootsa Lake guide-outfitter and lakeshore property owner Buster Harrison as saying. In the *Daily Colonist* article, the Ootsa Lake residents charged the provincial government with threatening to use the expropriation process improperly to protect "an enterprise which is not a public utility

54

but which has invaded our district and will flood us out for profit to itself and its shareholders."

But the government's failure to protect them and Alcan's reluctance to pay them a fair price for their land were not the only issues concerning the Ootsa Lake delegation. They pointed out that it was unfair to consider only the value of the land when establishing prices for their property, as many of them combined several ways of making a living—farming in the summer, guiding hunters in the fall and working in sawmills or trapping in the winter. Guides and trappers, they noted, paid for the right to operate in a set area within the territory to be flooded by Alcan's reservoir. Harrison, who had been guiding in the area for 30 years, owned 430 acres on which he'd constructed two homes, two cabins and nine other buildings, including a boat house, and had hacked 50 miles of horse trails out of the forest. More than 150 acres of his land would be flooded by the dam, including some of his best guiding areas, he said. For this he was being offered $19,000 which he claimed was not enough to re-establish himself elsewhere.

The delegation also told the *Daily Colonist* reporter about "Postmaster R. Nelson and Mrs. Nelson, an old couple in their 70s" who owned 160 acres beside Ootsa Lake of which 55 acres would be flooded, and for which they were being offered $3,000. "Mr. Nelson is crippled and he and his wife depend on neighbourhood help for chores and fuel," they told the reporter. The delegation charged that the flooding would necessitate the departure of more than 65 of the 77 families living along Ootsa Lake, and would thus destroy the community on which the Nelsons and other residents depended.

> They will lose their community, social life, neighbours, churches, post offices, telephone service, stores, delivery services, local markets for farm produce and chances for local employment.
> There will not be enough children left to justify schools and weekly movies will no longer be shown, the lake water will be polluted, the early range where the timothy grasses grows along the present lake shore will be flooded.

When the first Alcan project was complete, 12 of the families who formerly had been neighbours ended up living scattered along a 25-mile-long stretch of the lakefront.

Alcan decided to negotiate individually with the landowners. The result was that the 90 landowners received a total of $2.3 million or an average of $25,500 each. It was one of the few items in Alcan's original estimates of the cost of the project that came in below budget.[30]

Despite the opposition, the project moved ahead quickly. None of the inland fisheries studies were done and none of the forests along the lake cleared before they were drowned by the rising water.

The timber drowned by the flooding is particularly galling to Shelford:

> Before the dam was built my brother and I wanted to get the timber out of a place called Andrew's Bay but they wouldn't give it to us because it was part of Tweedsmuir Park. There were huge trees in there and when I pointed out to Ed Kenney [then Minister of Lands and Forests and the man after whom the Kenney Dam is named] it was going to be flooded, he still refused to let us cut them.

A 1992 report prepared for the BC government said 32,000 hectares of forest were flooded by the reservoir,[31] resulting in more than 8.7 million cubic metres of timber lying beneath the water of the reservoir. According to the BC government's 1993 stumpage manual, 26.85 cubic metres of lumber are required to construct a 1,400- to 1,500-square foot home. That means enough timber was flooded by the Nechako Reservoir in the early 1950s to construct 324,000 wood-frame homes of that size. Or, to look at that

---

"The...party policy, as stated by Harold Winch, leader of the opposition in 1951, [was] that the government should have developed the power for the aluminium company's use since power is one thing which should be controlled by the people. He accused the government of giving the company an empire and allowing the Alcan Company to reduce the resources of the province without proper compensation. Why should the province hand away this heritage, he asked." *Jill Kopy, president of the East Francois Lake Community Association, BCUCH 2.138.*

"As was common practice in those days, Alcan did not clear timber before flooding the reservoir.... The area was largely inaccessible. There was no market for the timber, and it would have been extremely costly to log." *Rankin and Finlay, 13.*

drowned timber in another way: It was removed from the forest resource base of the Nechako Valley region, thereby eliminating the jobs that would have been created by harvesting that wood. Three pioneer communities—Ootsa, Streatham and Wistaria—were flooded by the reservoir. Only Ootsa and Wistaria were relocated. Steatham disappeared off BC maps.

"I never thought I was too much of a sentimental person but the first time I went back to the lake my heart went down into my stomach," Alice Harrison says today. Underneath the water lies the land she and her husband cleared by hand, and the fields of alfalfa her husband had planted, and her big flower and vegetable garden. Many of the displaced families moved away from Ootsa, then came back to settle in the area. Alice and Alfred Harrison now live on the shore of Tchesinkut Lake south of Burns Lake.

In 1952 Jack Shelford ran as a Socred candidate and was elected to the provincial legislature, representing the Omineca riding, which includes Ootsa Lake. He was a popular MLA but, after being elected he, too, fell in with the popular view of the day which held that the Kemano I Project was good for BC's economy. He held the seat until 1972 and was elected again in 1978 and 1979. He now lives in Victoria during the winter but spends the summers at his comfortable log home on the shore of Francois Lake, north of Ootsa Lake.

Knocking on the Floodgates of Opportunity

The Alcan agreement grew out of greed and ignorance. Mr. Reid, the Minister of Fisheries, was from New Westminster and was only known for playing the bagpipes on the steps of the Parliament Buildings in Ottawa. The Provincial Minister for Lands, Forest and Water Resources was Mr. Kenny [sic] from Terrace, B.C. The Alcan development was to be located in his backyard. His daughter (a competent and pleasant nurse) was the manager of the short stay hospital at Kenny Dam during construction. Kenny was to have his name given to the dam.[1]

How did Canada become a prime producer of aluminum, the twentieth-century metal?

It wasn't because this nation is home to rich ore deposits, for although aluminum-bearing ore is the most abundant mineral in the earth's crust, Canada lacks commercial deposits of bauxite—a reddish-brown ore formed when aluminum-rich rocks are exposed to oxygen under tropical conditions—the ore from which aluminum is smelted.[2] After bauxite is mined, it is washed and treated to produce a chalky white powder called alumina—the product fed into Alcan's reduction furnaces, or "pots," in Kitimat. There are many natural phenomena and resources for which Canada is known world-wide: a bauxite-yielding tropical climate is not one of them.

It was not, then, the fruits of its climate but rather Canada's rugged geography, particularly its mountains and large river systems, that made it so attractive to the aluminum industry. The ability of Canada's seemingly infinite water resources to sustain the industry's enormous appetite for electricity has led to its becoming the world's second largest producer of refined aluminum.

The first step toward making the twentieth century the Age of Aluminum followed the discovery of the electrolytic process for smelting the metal in 1886 by two men: Charles Hall of the United States and Paul-Louis Tossaint Herault of France. Prior to the development of this process, aluminum was rarer than gold and so costly to produce it was used only for making jewellery.[3] The first aluminum smelter using the electrolytic aluminum smelting process was built by Hall in Pittsburgh. It had one main drawback: Steam was used to produce electric power, and at $5 a pound, the metal was still too expensive to attract buyers' interest. The price of electricity was cheaper in the outskirts of Pittsburgh, so in 1891 Hall borrowed $1 million and constructed a bigger smelter in a suburb of the city known as New Kensington. This was the first in a series of moves the aluminum industry would make in search of the cheapest possible source of electricity. Eventually the search led the industry into Quebec, then into the wilderness of central British Columbia.

Hall's New Kensington smelter could produce cheaper aluminum but, even at one dollar a pound, the metal still wasn't attracting many buyers. So the fledgling company went into the business of manufacturing aluminum cooking pots. This venture initially encountered a marketing problem when storekeepers refused to purchase the thick-walled, light-weight aluminum pots because they thought their customers still preferred the heavy iron pots their ancestors had used for generations. So the company sent persistent armies of unemployed college and university students out on the road as door-to-door salesmen, intent on introducing these new-fangled aluminum pots directly to North America's homemakers.

One of these door-to-door salesmen was Ray Edwin "Rip" Powell, who was so certain aluminum was *the* twentieth-century metal, he stuck with the industry, rising through the ranks until he became the president of the Aluminum Company of Canada. Late in his career he was instrumental in Alcan's move into British Columbia.

The company now commonly referred to as Alcan came into being in 1928 as a holding company set up to acquire and expand the Canadian holdings of its US parent company, the Aluminum Company of America (Alcoa).[4] At that time Alcan's principle holdings were the aluminum smelting plants established by Alcoa at Shawinigan, Quebec in 1901, and at Arvida, Quebec in 1926. Alcan also had a controlling interest in the first hydroelectric plant constructed on the Saguenay River in Quebec, several smaller smelters in Europe and bauxite and mining operations in Guyana, South America and Europe.

Alcoa's decision to establish Alcan by permitting only those investors who already held shares in the parent company to purchase shares in the new Canadian-based company resulted in a long anti-trust court battle in the United States which began in 1937. Named as defendants were Alcoa, 25 of its subsidiaries and affiliated companies including Alcan, and 37 of its directors, officers and shareholders.[5] The parent company was also charged with seeking to monopolize the US aluminum market. The action ended in June, 1950 when, in a step intended to ensure the aluminum industry remained competitive, investors holding shares in both Alcoa and Alcan were ordered to dispose of their interests in one of the companies.[6] This move established Alcan as an independent, Canadian company which, to this day, competes with Alcoa for markets, but co-operates with Alcoa and other major aluminum producers to control production as a means of maintaining higher prices. This co-operative relationship worked until the 1990s, when prices started falling: The former Soviet Union had begun to dismantle and, instead of trading only among themselves, a clutch of formerly Communist, newly independent countries began placing large blocks of their lower-priced aluminum for sale on international metal markets.

Despite the on-going legal entanglements in its early years, Alcan began preparing for a vast expansion of its operations in Quebec. The first site they looked at was Shipshaw where, in 1928, the company announced plans to build what was at the time the world's largest power development. Then came the Great Depression, which hit the rapidly expanding Canadian aluminum industry hard as demand for aluminum was cut in half.[7] The first section of the Shipshaw project, which could produce 260,000 horsepower, was completed. But the second, larger phase was postponed. When demand for aluminum fell further, the Shipshaw project was shut down completely after it was determined that 30,000 tons of lower-cost aluminum being produced annually at Arvida were enough to meet the demand for the metal.

What seemed like an economic disaster for the aluminum industry soon turned into an advantage when the inevitability of World War Two became apparent and countries from around the world, including Germany, Japan and Russia, began placing orders for immediate delivery of Canadian aluminum. Between 1937 and 1939 Alcan doubled its aluminum production at Arvida and Shipshaw. This was just the beginning. After war was declared, a frantic race began to build the military aircraft vital to winning the battles being fought in the air over Britain. When the US entered the war in 1941, it too purchased large quantities of the metal from Alcan's Quebec operations. Most of the aluminum produced in the province during World War Two was used to build Allied airplanes. It has been said the air forces of Germany and Japan were first defeated on the aluminum pot lines of Quebec.[8]

To achieve that rapid increase in production the second section of the Shipshaw development was completed in 18 months. It was a spectacular wartime engineering achievement involving the stationing of a huge police force outside the construction site to guard against sabotage.[9] New smelters were also built at Beauharnois near Montreal, at Shawinigan Falls and LaTuque, Quebec, and another hydroelectric plant was built on the St. Maurice River in that province.

Alcan's rapid expansion of production to meet wartime demand was not entirely public-spirited. It was completed with considerable help from Canadian tax-payers. In 1940, C.D. Howe, Canada's powerful minister of munitions and supply in Mackenzie King's Liberal government, devised a plan to assist Alcan in developing its smelting operations in Canada by accelerating the time over which companies were allowed to depreciate the cost of new industrial plants from the previous rate of 10 to 50 years, to four years.

Major James "M.J." Coldwell,[10] the leader of the Co-operative Commonwealth Federation (the CCF: predecessor of the New Democratic Party), claimed this government move to assist Alcan was "the greatest financial grab ever pulled off in the history of

Canada."[11] Those concerned about the future of the Nechako River today charge that this plan amounted to a $179.5 million interest-free loan to Alcan from Canadian tax-payers.[12]

Coldwell also charged that Alcan was involved in an aluminum cartel which was profiting from the war by inflating the price it charged for aluminum it sold to Allied Forces. Three countries contributing to the Allied war effort—Britain, the United States and Australia—had loaned Alcan more than $108 million to help them build the new aluminum plants in Quebec.

Aluminum was considered such an essential product to the wartime effort that, although power was rationed in Quebec, the electricity-guzzling smelting pots operated at full bore throughout the war. In three years alone, hydroelectric output in Quebec tripled, the annual production of aluminum ingots in Alcan's smelters increased from 45,000 tonnes to 500,000 tonnes a year and the company was supplying more than one-third of the Allied Force's need for aluminum.[13] The positive impact of World War Two on Alcan's corporate success can be found in the company's financial statistics which record that the company's annual sales rose 492% in six years—from $49 million in 1937 to $290 million in 1943—and dropped to $259 million in 1944.[14]

When the war ended, Alcan's sales of aluminum rose from $200 million in 1949 to $9 billion in 1989,[15] as Alcan shifted its marketing attention toward promoting consumer products. By 1992 Alcan was producing 1.8 million tonnes annually[16] and the company had begun moving away from being a producer of aluminum ingots toward the production of aluminum alloys and the manufacture of automobile parts, doors, windows and siding, electrical wiring, cooking foil and utensils, and pop and beer cans.[17]

Most of Alcan's aluminum fabrication is done in the United States through the company's US-based sales subsidiary, the Alcan

---

"As early as 1943, Alcan vice-president McNeely DuBose met Premier John Hart, head of the Liberal/Conservative coalition that governed B.C. Pressured by the CCF opposition to bring in more war industry, Premier Hart was aggressively advocating a plan for industrial development." *Rankin and Finlay, 14.*

Aluminum Corporation (Alcancorp). By 1974, the US was importing approximately 75% of its aluminum ingots from Alcan.[18] The report of a 1977 Royal Commission on Corporate Concentration in Canada states:

> As a result of Alcan's investment into fabrication in the U.S., there is a very high degree of corporate interdependence and integration between Alcan Canada and Alcancorp. This explains why Alcan actively encourages the creation of a North American free trade arrangement, at least in primary aluminium.[19]

One of the keys to Alcan's international success has been its ownership of sources of cheap electrical power to feed its smelters in Quebec and BC. In 1973 it was estimated it cost Alcan one cent for the electricity required to produce one pound of aluminum, compared to four cents for US aluminum producers and six to eight cents for European and Japanese aluminum producers.[20] Alcan's ability to take advantage of the low cost of producing hydroelectric power in Canada and its American fabricating plants' ability to provide consumer products for the large US market meant it was well-positioned to become a world leader in the production of aluminum.

Other Canadian provinces, particularly BC which has more than its share of good hydroelectric sites, had watched with envy as the aluminum industry blossomed in Quebec. Finally, on November 3, 1941, BC's Liberal Premier Duff Pattullo telephoned Alcan executive R.E. Powell—the former aluminum pot salesman—in Montreal to see if the company would be interested in locating a planned new hydroelectric development in the province. According to Powell, Pattullo indicated the provincial government was willing "to do almost anything to get the company to establish itself there."[21] Pattullo was aware BC's mountainous terrain held many potential sites for installing the hydroelectric generating facilities needed to produce the large amounts of low-cost electricity required to smelt aluminum.

On January 26, 1943, Alcan vice-president McNeeley DuBose wrote BC's comptroller of water rights, Ernest Davis, seeking permission to investigate the Chilko-Taseko River system west of Williams Lake as a possible source of a one-million-horsepower hydroelectric development.[22] Alcan was also considering sites in the southern United States, Newfoundland and British Guyana.[23]

The company's request was timely. The provincial government had been looking for potential dam sites along the Fraser River since 1929. Three possible sites for hydroelectric developments had been identified: the Fraser River itself and two of its main tributaries, the Chilcotin and Nechako Rivers.[24]

But Alcan had ideas of its own about the best site for a hydroelectric development in BC. During May, 1943, DuBose travelled to Victoria to meet with Liberal-Conservative Coalition Premier John Hart, who had replaced Pattullo in December, 1941, to discuss the company's proposal to construct a dam on the Chilko-Taseko river system west of Williams Lake. After the meeting, he reported to Alcan's Canadian president, who was now R.E. Powell, that he had informed Hart the province would not be considered for the site of the company's proposed smelter unless it agreed to co-operate fully.[25]

Hart stepped down as party leader in December, 1947 and was replaced that same month by another Liberal-Conservative coalition premier, "Boss" Johnson, an ardent advocate of rapid industrial growth in BC. In 1947, Johnson again approached Alcan to reconsider plans to establish an aluminum industry there, and the company conducted preliminary engineering surveys on a number of potential sites during 1948. In 1949 it was decided the most interesting site was the Tahtsa-Kemano project which included a dam on the Nechako River high enough to impound all the lakes draining eastward into the river.[26]

By this time, the Cold War was being waged against the Communist Bloc and was used as the excuse by C.D. Howe[27] to convince the federal Liberal government to introduce, once more, accelerated depreciation as a means of expanding Canada's industrial war effort. Between 1951 and 1954 more than $515 million

---

"After the war the government of British Columbia came back to Alcan and asked it once more to look to the west. The offer was water from the Eutsuk-Tahtsa Basin of the Nechako River in exchange for investment that would develop a new source of energy and create a new industry in a remote corner of B.C...." *Alcan's BC vice-president Bill Rich, BCUCH 11.1603.*

of new Canadian industrial assets were eligible for what had earlier been identified as "interest-free loans" by Canadian tax-payers to industrialists. Again, Alcan took advantage of this program to help finance its industrial developments in central BC.

Most central BC residents remained unaware of what was being planned for the region. One of the first hints of what was looming came during a speech Johnson made in Prince George on April 26, 1949 when he talked about the industrial opportunities opening up in the province including "plans to install a hydro plant which, for sheer size, dwarfs into insignificance any local scheme." The "local schemes" he was referring to were the calls being heard in Victoria, from residents of Quesnel and Prince George, for the provincial government to build a dam on the north fork of the Quesnel River that would generate cheap hydroelectric power for the region. Originally, they had proposed the power plant be built in a canyon on the West Road River, now known as the Blackwater River. That plan was rejected because its hydroelectric potential was less than that of the site on the more rapidly flowing Quesnel River.[28]

Ironically, while the provincial government was acting quickly to clear the way for Alcan to divert the water from the upper Nechako River for its own industrial purposes, it acted upon neither of the proposals for providing cheap industrial power to central interior BC communities.

Alcan's engineers were obviously impressed with the potential hydroelectric generating sites they found within BC's high mountain ranges, the sites abutting the Coast Range being particularly attractive. The mountains would provide a natural barrier for water captured by raising the level of the numerous finger-shaped lakes located on the province's 2,000- to 4,000-foot-high interior plateau.

The western side of the Coast Range is marked by deep fjords that were gouged out of the mountains during the Ice Age when several thousand feet of ice ground away the softer soils. Many of these steep-sided fjords reach hundreds of miles inland from the ocean. The Alcan-dominated communities of Kitimat and Kemano are located on Gardner Canal, at the head of one of these deep inland channels. Just 20 miles away from Kemano and 2,800 feet above it—or 16 times the height of Niagara Falls[29]—lies Tahtsa Lake which, before the Kenney Dam was built, drained 700 miles east and south into the Pacific Ocean through the Nechako and Fraser Rivers. Engineers had known about the power potential of the area for years but were deterred by the magnitude of the problems they would encounter in harnessing it and the knowledge that even the smallest development there would be gigantic by prevailing standards. In other words, the engineering challenges were as huge and unknown as the potential benefits.

Whether they chose the Chilko-Teseko or the Tahtsa-Kemano project, Alcan's engineers knew what they had to do: Impound the water flowing eastward from mountains along BC's western boundary, drain it off through tunnels drilled through the mountains and feed it into turbines located at tidewater on Bute or Jervis Inlet (if the Chilko-Taseko river were dammed) or the Gardner Canal or Douglas Channel (were the Nechako River to be chosen).

R.E. Powell, now Alcan's Canadian president, travelled to BC in May, 1948, to tour Bute Inlet, which would have been the site of its developments if the company had chosen to dam up a more southerly river system. While he was there, he asked Premier Johnson whether BC residents would approve of the company's proposal to invest $250 to $300 million to construct a one-million-horsepower hydroelectric plant in the province. Johnson is reported to have assured Powell repeatedly that he would do everything required to persuade Alcan to choose BC as the site of its new smelter.[30]

Two months later, Lands and Forests Minister Ed Kenney gave Alcan's officials assurance BC would lay down the welcome mat for the project. In a letter dated June 16, 1948, he said BC was officially inviting the company to build a hydroelectric generating plant and smelter in BC, "[i]n view of the desire of the Government of British Columbia to promote the establishment of industry within our province, having in mind particularly the development of large blocks of water power somewhat remote from major centres...."[31] To demonstrate the province's seriousness and to encourage the company to investigate the possibilities for industrial development in BC, Kenney said the province had placed reserves on the watersheds and associated Crown lands along the Chilko-Taseko, Eutsuk-Kimsquit and the Tahtsa-Kemano Rivers. No reserve was placed on the Nechako River, but the Eutsuk-Kimsquit and the Tahtsa-Kemano River systems were part of the company's final proposal to the province.

Kenney went further.

He also promised Alcan that if it decided to proceed with the project in BC, the provincial government would issue all required water licences at the minimum rates provided for in BC's Water Act and Regulations and amend any laws standing in the way of the project.[32]

Liberal MPs' concerns for the future of the salmon industry killed plans for Alcan's proposed developments of the more southerly Chilko-Taseko-Southgate system. On June 25, 1948, Liberal Senator Tom Reid of New Westminister questioned the power-minded BC government's support for Alcan's proposal to dam the Chilko-Tasiko-Southgate river system, which he said produced 66% of the Fraser River's lucrative sockeye salmon run. Reid was also a member of the International Pacific Salmon Fisheries Commission (IPSFC) which had been assigned the task of protecting the salmon interests of Canada and the United States.[33]

IPSFC was instrumental in building the first fishway at Hell's Gate in the Fraser Canyon, where the river's flow had been blocked in the late 1930s by a rockfall during blasting on a nearby railway right-of-way. The fishways built at Hell's Gate to enable migrating salmon to swim past the rockfall had been a major factor in rebuilding the Fraser River's sockeye salmon runs. One of the most successful restocking efforts had been in the Chilko-Tasiko-Southgate river system. Although the salmon runs past Hell's Gate were restored, no one knows how many of the individual runs returning to a specific creek or lake were unable to survive the blockage of the river. It is now known each individual salmon

---

"Newspaper and magazine articles at the time reveal that fishing interests were bitterly opposed to a possible hydro development on the Chilko River, but less opposed to development on the Nechako." *Rankin and Finlay, 16.*

stock represents a different gene pool which, once lost, weakens the capacity of the river's salmon run to survive.

Protection of migrating salmon is a federal responsibility, so Reid urged the federal minister of fisheries, R.W. Mayhew (MP for Victoria), to investigate the project and take whatever steps were necessary to protect the fish using the Chilko-Tasiko-Southgate river system by ensuring that Alcan's project was built on a BC river that did not produce salmon.[34]

With assurances of the province's support, Alcan ignored Reid's warnings and hired a San Francisco-based engineering firm, International Engineering Company Inc.,[35] to begin assessing the three hydroelectric sites reserved by the government in July, 1948.

The budget for the first year's work was $100,000. It would be spent investigating the feasibility of a project involving Chilko and Taseko Lakes and the Southgate River.[36] After the best site was selected from among the 24 potential sites identified, it was estimated it would take a budget of a further $1 million and two years to complete the engineering studies for the huge project.

In January, 1949, DuBose evaluated the engineers' preliminary investigations of the 24 potential sites and reported to Powell that it was too early to make a final conclusion. He believed, however, that further investigation would show the cost of the power developed by the Tahtsa-Kemano project would be 65% less than that developed by the Chilko project.[37] He also estimated one million horsepower could be developed at Kemano in the first stage for almost the same cost per h.p. as developing the project to its full potential of 1.66 million h.p.[38] Alcan's engineers were instructed to conduct further investigations of the Tahtsa-Kemano project, partly because of its potential to produce lower-cost power, and partly because of the opposition to the Chilko-Taseko project by people representing international fishing interests. The final cost of the northern project would depend on whether or not engineers encountered difficulties locating a foundation for the dam in the Nechako River, or if the company would be faced with the job of clearing timber from the edges of the reservoir, which DuBose described as "very poorly timbered according to B.C. standards."[39]

Senator Reid's objections to including any salmon-producing rivers in any power project developed in the province were expanded in a lengthy letter which appeared in the December 15, 1949 edition of the *Burns Lake Review*:

It is not generally known or recognized that what the aluminium interests are principally after is B.C.'s water power which if granted them either in Nechako area or in the Chilko, the two districts for which applications have been made, will enable them in that event to control British Columbia's greatest heritages.

Two applications have been made by this large and powerful corporation to the Water Rights Branch at Victoria. One of these applications is for the water rights of the Nechako lake and river system comprising some 400 square miles, from which it is reliably estimated 1,850,000 gross horsepower could be developed. The other application placed by this powerful corporation to the Water Rights Branch at Victoria is for the Chilko lake system and from this area it is reliably estimated that about 850,000 to 1,000,000 gross horsepower could be developed. The International Pacific Salmon Fisheries Commission of which I am a member, have taken strong objection to the granting of water rights for hydro electric development on the Chilko on account of the fact that any dam built at the outlet of the Chilko River from Chilko Lake would completely destroy one of the greatest runs of sockeye salmon to the Fraser River system. As a matter of information it should be pointed out that the sockeye spawn in the three mile area on the Chilko river at the point where the Chilko river leaves the lake. The young fry that hatch later, enter the lake and make their home there for from ten to eighteen months in the lake before proceeding downstream for the open sea.

Reid feared any dams on the River would cause "the young fingerlings to perish by the millions."

Later in the letter he writes:

What I fear is that the Provincial Government might hand over to the powerful aluminium interests any one of these water sheds in which event the company might obtain all the water rights thereby enabling them to completely control for all time all the future industrial development requiring hydro electric power in the interior of British Columbia. The point should not be overlooked that the company does not require all the power that can be developed either in Nechako or Chilko for the manufacture of aluminium. They particularly want to be able to sell and ship the surplus power developed south of the U.S. line to the Northwest pool in the United States. I doubt if this powerful corporation would want to simply develop an aluminium plant were it not for the fact that there is a ready market in the United States for the surplus power and to the Northwest electrical pool.

As I say, the citizens of British Columbia have a right to know what the powerful corporation is going to get and before these rights are given away by Premier Johnson and his government. I want to warn the people of British Columbia that the aluminium corporation is out at the moment not particularly in the interests of developing industries in British Columbia or in the interests of the development of an aluminium plant,—they are principally concerned with the obtaining by any manner of means the entire hydro potentialities of British Columbia. And they are spending lots of money in an effort to do so. One has only to read the story of the all powerful holds this great cartel or corporation has on the manufacture of aluminium throughout the world to realize how financially powerful these interests are and naturally they have lots of friends. Again one has only to read the history of how this world wide corporation obtained the large blocks of hydro power at Shipshaw and Arvida as well as in dozens of other places, to realize how easily the people of British Columbia could have it put over them by the propaganda of industrial development of British Columbia. Once this powerful corporation obtains these water rights they will then hold the development of British Columbia in their own hands and when it is realized that they control the making of aluminium throughout almost every country in the world today, the question could very well be asked what is the real purpose behind this entire scheme.

In an article of this kind one cannot go as fully into all phases of the matter as one would like to, my chief purpose at this time however, is to draw attention of our people to the potential dangers of allowing such an all powerful and ruthless corporation to obtain a heritage belonging to all the people and without the Provincial Government first making public the details of any proposed lease or grants.

Personally I am not against the developing of hydro electric power, in fact I am all in favour of every possible encouragement being given to industry to locate in our province. There are however certain watersheds in British Columbia which could be developed without the developing of the same destroying an important industry like the salmon fishing industry. To my mind these should be explored and developed first. To simply hand over however, the water rights of large areas like Nechako without provision being made to see that in the first instance, surplus power will not be exported to the United States to the detriment of Canadian or B.C. industries, and secondly we should see to it that provision is also made to prevent the Aluminium Company or any other company from denying power to some other industrial concern that may wish to locate. Finally we should see to it that any rates charged in the future should not be prohibitive as they could be should all the hydro power of either the Nechako or the Chilko be handed over to such an all-powerful corporation as the Aluminium Company of Canada who are not by any manner or means a Canadian concern.

Reid's words proved to be uncannily prophetic.

They are also in sharp contrast to the sentiments expressed by Powell in a letter he sent from Alcan's Montreal office to DuBose on February 14, 1949:

There is a lot of thoughtless and repetitious talk about natural resources—at least, such is my humble opinion. I hold the view that it is in general interest for enterprising and energetic persons—who might under certain circumstances be called "suckers"—to develop such resources as land, forests, mines and flowing rivers so that all of the people may have food, shelter and other requirements of modern life, even though some of them don't want to work. But the development and operation of natural resources certainly do provide work.

Getting down to cases, what have certain rivers in northern British Columbia ever done for the people? I'd say that they have done little or nothing so far—and that they probably won't do much without a terrific amount of work by someone—and, unless that someone is willing to "work like a dog", there won't be any enjoyment to share. I'd think that the people of British Columbia would leap at an opportunity to acquire money and people who, without the assurance of any reward, will proceed with developments, which, even if successful, will do a lot for the people as distinct from the Government.

And while distinction between the people and the Government may have little or nothing to do with natural resources, I call to your attention the fact that representatives of governments are often so concerned about their own succession that they forget the interests of the people, the majority of whom must have employment provided for them, unless we are to go back to the good (?) old days when each Indian with a bow and arrow was self-sufficient.

No doubt there are those who envy persons prominent in business, but I venture to say that many such persons have found that they labour principally for others—not because they want to but because they get caught in a machine from which they can't easily escape. I don't pretend that they are unselfish or high-minded. I merely say that they are "suckers."[40]

Prominent federal Liberal politician James "Jimmy" Sinclair, whose daughter Margaret would marry the future Prime Minister Pierre Trudeau, was the federal member representing the riding in which Alcan first proposed to build the Chilko River and Bute Inlet project. Because he had campaigned to obtain the fishways at Hell's Gate he, too, objected to the threat the proposed Chilko-Tasiko development posed to the Fraser River sockeye salmon runs. The government and Alcan then identified the Eutsuk-Tahtsa Lake system as the second choice for locating a dam.

Coalition MLA Henry Robson Bowman, who represented Prince George until 1949, and his successor, Socred MLA Llewellyn Leslie King, did not object, nor did most of their constituents. They saw the construction of the multi-million-dollar project both as an opportunity to end, finally, the area's dependence on the boom-and-bust cycles of the lumber market, and as a means of opening the region to further industrial development.

Alcan's plans to locate a huge industrial complex in central and northern BC was a major issue during the provincial election held June 15, 1949. The company and the government interpreted the results of the election, in which voters gave the Johnson-led coalition 61% of their votes, as a sign of public support for its plans. The CCF, who opposed the project, received 35% of the votes.

Of particular interest to Alcan was the Grand Canyon of the Nechako River. In the 1930s, hydraulic engineer Frederick Knewstubb had proposed portions of the Great Circle Water Route be dammed, to develop the Nechako's hydroelectric power potential. In 1949, the BC government took the first concrete step toward carrying out Knewstubb's vision. On March 24 of that year,

Johnson's government approved Bill 66, the Industrial Development Act, giving the provincial Cabinet sweeping powers that enabled it to clear the way for Alcan to proceed with the construction of an aluminum smelter somewhere in BC.[41] It is now thought the province chose to facilitate Alcan's project—by approving the Industrial Development Act—in order to avoid any meaningful public hearings. Although there were half-day hearings related to the project held in 1949 at Wistaria near Ootsa Lake and in Victoria, their format was such that the government and the company reported only to interested parties, and any public input that was voiced was ignored. Lands and Forests Minister Kenney dismissed concerns about the future safety of the fish in the rivers, saying:

> Insofar as the objections of the fisheries interests are concerned, it is felt the value to the economy of the Province outweighs a possible loss to the fisheries and that this water power could be developed at a comparatively small expense to the fishing industry.[42]

In 1950 the Cabinet used its new powers, acquired under the Industrial Development Act, to issue a conditional water licence to Alcan, giving the company the water rights to all the flows of the upper Nechako River above the Kenney Dam and to the Nanika River downstream of Nanika Falls at the outlet of Kidprice Lake.[43] The protection granted to Alcan—in the 1950 agreement and the associated water licence and flooding permits—was unprecedented in Canada. It has been described as giving Alcan a form of sovereignty association,[44] inasmuch as it prevents anyone else from using the Crown land and the mineral and forestry resources within the defined watersheds. The agreements also exempted the company from paying a significant portion of provincial and local government taxes and attempted to prevent any future public examination of its water rights agreement. In later years the agree-

---

"The cost of Kemano 1 today would be $5 billion." *BCUCH 11.1632.*

"[T]he root of Alcan's entitlements can be traced to the Industrial Development Act and to the 1950 agreement." *Rankin and Finlay, 26.*

ment was described by a provincial water rights official as "an aberration on our books, more wide-ranging than anything we've ever issued, even back then."[45] According to Howard DeBeck, Comptroller of Water Rights, the licence was issued "back in the postwar years when the government thought it had to hand over sweeping powers as the price it had to pay for development."[46]

And the company was also given:

- The right to divert all the flow of the Nechako River above the dam to be constructed in a canyon 100 miles southwest of Prince George into a 137-mile-long reservoir;
- The right to divert into the reservoir all the water flowing in the Nanika River below Nanika Falls near the outlet of Kidprice Lake. The Nanika River flows into the Skeena River which empties into the Pacific Ocean at Prince Rupert, north of Kitimat;
- Timber rights on all the land flooded by the 358-acre reservoir that would be created from what had been a series of five wilderness lakes. There was neither requirement that the forests be cleared from the land flooded by the reservoir,[47] nor requisition that stumpage fees be paid for any trees cut;
- Mineral rights on all Crown lands flooded;
- The right to buy approximately 14,000 acres of land, in what is now known as Kitimat, for appoximately $1.60 an acre for use as the site of a smelter and a city—the eventual population of which was optimistically predicted to be 50,000 people.[48] (By 1986 the population of Kitimat was 11,196.);[49]
- A perpetual water licence, to be granted December 31, 1999, cov-

---

"[I]t seems that the legislative intent is clear. Alcan was to be given all the legal assurances necessary to permit it to undertake the massive development [in 1950].... [T]here can be no doubt that the legislative intent of the Industrial Development Act was to provide Alcan with the basis for making billions of dollars worth of expenditures. The 1949 act has never been repealed." *Rankin and Finlay, 32, 33.*

"Winch generally favoured the development but objected to the sale and the perpetual agreement. An Amendment was introduced to limit Cabinet's authority in the bill to selling or leasing land only; water, in all the forms listed in the bill, could not be sold or leased. Rather, the Cabinet was given the authority to license the storage or use of 'unrecorded water' for a rental considered advisable." *Rankin and Finlay, 16.*

ering all facilities installed on the Nechako River above the dam and above another proposed dam that would be built on the Nanika-Kidprice River by that date;

• Favourable water-rental rates based on the price of aluminum at Kitimat. Thus, by 1992, the company was paying less than 10% of the rate paid for water by other hydroelectric producers;[50]

• Municipal status for Alcan's dams, other hydroelectric developments and the Village of Kemano, with the result that the required lands were ceded directly to Alcan who, of course, is exempted from paying provincial or regional taxes on any of these properties.

The Industrial Development Act included provisions for the protection of fish.[51] But the conditional water licence the province issued to Alcan effective August 3, 1949, contained no indication of the amount of flows the province considered necessary to protect the fish using the river.

After the agreement was signed, Alcan president W.E. Powell said the BC government had refused his original offer to have the government develop the power and sell it to the company. He predicted the day would come when politicians would try to take over the company's hydroelectric developments in BC, and had insisted on including a preamble to the agreement which would create difficulties for any government that would attempt such a move.[52]

The plans for the Nechako River dam were made public during January, 1951. It was the largest such project ever undertaken in Canada.

In March, 1951, CCF MLA Harold Winch criticized the Alcan

"[T]he truth is that both the federal and provincial governments achieved substantial concessions from Alcan in the 1987 Settlement Agreement.... [T]he proposal Alcan contemplated in the 1970's was to divert virtually all of the remaining water from the Eutsuk-Tahtssa drainage basins of the Nechako and all of the water to which we're entitled in the Nanika River watershed to the limit of our rights under the conditional water licence. This would have provided for an increase in firm hydroelectric energy production of about 550 megawatts. The proposal put forward by Alcan in 1983 scaled the project back to one that would have generated about 350 megawatts, and the project we're talking about today, as a result of the 1987 agreement, will generate 285 megawatts." *BCUCH 11.1666.*

agreement as being "too open handed." He believed water to be a natural resource belonging to the people and, therefore, should not be given to a company. Instead, he said, the BC government should have agreed to Alcan's original request that the province develop the power and sell it to the company for the smelter Alcan would construct at Kitimat. He also criticized the government for giving the company an "empire" and enabling it to exploit BC's resources without proper compensation being paid to the province.[53]

Concerns about the safety of the salmon were expressed during the meeting of the Prince George Board of Trade held March 24, 1951. Arthur Seeger, a representative of the Pacific Coast Salmon Canneries Operating Committee and a former employee of the Dominion Fisheries Department, warned the meeting the province should take steps to avoid any threat to the rich Stuart sockeye salmon run when selecting a site for the development.[54]

That advice was ignored.

Beginning in 1949, the DFO continually expressed concerns about the diversion of water from the Nechako and its effect on the fish.[54] The province and the company also ignored these concerns and, upon its issue in August, 1949, Alcan's water licence included no provisions requiring the company to release more water into the river to make it safe for both migrating salmon and the fish living in the river all year round, including sturgeon, rainbow trout, dolly varden and mountain whitefish.

Thirty years later that omission would return to haunt Alcan and the federal and provincial governments.

Coffins in the Lake

I've been asked by many people why are the people of Cheslatta standing outside in 20 below, beating drums? Why are they not [in] here? There's the opportunity. And I ask the commission to please consider the historical circumstances and how deep a hurt like that goes. The tradition, the language, the culture, the very essence of a group of people was destroyed on April 21st of 1952.[1]

The Nechako River Valley has a long and vivid history. For more than 10,000 years it has been the home of the aboriginal people now known as the Carrier First Nations. As is often the case in Canada, the river's present name is an Anglicized version of the local native name for it: "Nechako" is based on the Carrier name "Incha-Khoh," which means "Big River."

The rich harvest of furs to be found in the area first drew the aggressive Scottish, English and other European explorers from the Montreal-based North West Company into the Nechako River Valley. In 1793, the first European contact occurred in the valley: That year Alexander Mackenzie journeyed up the Peace and Parsnip Rivers, then down a portion of the Fraser River past the mouth of the Nechako and overland to Bella Coola, searching for a route to the Pacific Ocean and hence to the lucrative fur markets in the Far East.

One of the oldest unsolved mysteries of the early exploration of BC is why Mackenzie did not record passing the mouth of the Nechako River in his journal, in which he made detailed notations on many smaller streams. Three entries in his journal on the day he passed the mouth of the river, June 19, 1793, gave rise to theory that Mackenzie failed to see the mouth of the Nechako because it was either obliterated by fog or smoke from a forest fire.[2] Another theory holds that at that point in its history, the Nechako River entered a tributary of the Fraser River, which then flowed on the other side of a prominent hill standing near the centre of the present-day city of Prince George. Evidence of this old river channel was apparent until, as the city developed, the old riverbed, which had by then been reduced to a mosquito-infested slough, was filled in for use as commercial and recreational property. In any case, the course of BC history might have been changed had Mackenzie or his men seen the mouth of this large river and chosen to make their way to the Pacific Ocean using the Nechako and Skeena River systems, instead of the arduous overland route they took along First Nations' trails to Bella Coola.

Simon Fraser did not repeat Mackenzie's oversight when, in 1803, he followed his own route down the Fraser River. On July 11, 1806 he described the river in his journal:

> At sunset we got to the [Nechako] River. This River is not mentioned by Sir A.M.K [Sir Alexander Mackenzie], which surprizes [sic] me not a little, it being full in sight and a fine large River and in the state we saw it equal in size to the Athabasca and forms what Mr. McDougall in his journal of last spring calls the great Fort.[3]

Earlier in his journal Fraser explained Mackenzie's failure to record his sighting of the Pack River which flows into McLeod Lake, noting that "he used to indulge himself sometimes with a little sleep...."[4] He also criticized Mackenzie's navigational skills, saying "he pretends to have been very exact but was qualified to make observations and [were I] inclined to find fault with him, I could prove that he seldom or ever paid the attention he pretends to have

---

"The Nechako River is a heritage river, although, not officially designated as such.... Prior to white contact, the Nechako served the many needs of the indigenous people for countless generations. The thousands of food cache pits which lie in the banks of the river attest to the importance of the river in the lives of the past inhabitants of this valley." *Doug Goodwin, BCUCH 3.349.*

done, and that many of his remarks were not made by himself but communicated by his men."[5]

Fraser and his voyageurs used paddles, poles and towlines to make their way up the Nechako and Stuart Rivers into Stuart Lake. When the rivers were too deep or there was no safe footpath on the river banks along which they could walk while pulling their two birchbark canoes, they stayed in the canoes, pulling themselves along by grabbing the overhanging tree branches. Fraser's goal was to build a fur-trading empire for the North West Company centred at Fort St. James, which became BC's first fur-trading post in 1806. He named the area New Caledonia because the clear lakes surrounded by evergreen-clad mountains reminded him of his mother's descriptions of her Scottish birthplace.

Later in the summer of 1806, Fraser and his voyageurs paddled back down the Stuart River and poled their canoes up the Nechako and Nautley Rivers into Fraser Lake where they established Fort Fraser. Here Fraser established what is thought to be the first farm in BC where vegetables, especially root crops, were grown for use in his expanding chain of forts during the winter.

Fraser spent the winter of 1806-1807 at Fort Fraser with a native, or "country," wife. The following year he travelled down the Nechako River to its junction with the Fraser River where, in 1807, he established his fourth fort in New Caledonia,[6] naming it Fort George in honour of King George III. On May 22, 1808, Fort George was the launching site for Fraser's epic journey down the tumultuous river—the river he thought to be the Columbia, and which now bears his name—to the Pacific Ocean near New Westminster.

Fort St. James was established as BC's first administrative centre, a position it held until 1857, when the administration of the growing colony was moved to New Westminister so officials could provide stronger control over the people who were moving into the area from the United States on their quest for gold on the sandbars of the Fraser River. During the time Fort St. James was the fur-trading capital of New Caledonia, the Stuart and Nechako Rivers were the routes used by the annual brigades of huge birchbark canoes carrying the winter's fur catch eastward to Montreal via Fort Chipewyan and, later, south to Fort Alexandria on the Fraser

River and on to Fort Langley.[7]

Other historical figures who used the river during BC's early fur-trading history included the province's first Governor General, Sir James Douglas, Daniel Harman, Peter Ogden, John Stuart and David Douglas, the Scottish botanist who identified and named the Douglas Fir. Fur-traders, free traders and those employed by the North West Company and later the Hudson's Bay Company, followed Mackenzie and Fraser.

Since the days of these early fur-traders, central BC has drawn waves of settlers seeking to benefit from the region's rich natural resources. The discovery of gold in Barkerville brought the next group of settlers seeking land and wealth to central BC. In 1862 a large group of Overlanders arrived in Fort George at the mouth of the Nechako River. They had separated from the rest of the party at Tête Jaune Cache and undertaken an ill-conceived journey—fatal for some—down the Fraser River on a jerry-built flotilla of rafts and canoes on what they mistakenly thought was an easier route to the gold fields at Barkerville. Four men died while making their way down the turbulent river to Fort George.

They were followed in 1868 by prospectors on their way to the minor gold rush along the Parsnip and Finlay Rivers, northeast of Prince George and, in 1872, by gold seekers on their way to the Cassiar Mountains where a major gold discovery had been made. The discovery of large gold nuggets in Bonanza Creek on the Klondike River in 1896 led to yet another rush of people travelling through the area on their way north. Among this group were Chilcotin ranchers who, in May 1898, set out to drive herds of beef cattle 1,500 miles through the wilderness to the Klondike, where they hoped to make their fortune selling beef to the miners swarming into the area.[8]

In the first part of the twentieth century another wave of settlers began arriving in the vicinity of the Nechako River Valley, seeking riches in the cheap land and jobs provided by the building of the Grand Trunk Pacific Railway that passed through Prince George and along the Nechako and Skeena River Valleys to a Pacific Ocean port at Prince Rupert. Many of these railway followers used clumsy rafts and canoes made from hollowed-out cottonwood trees to make their way down the Fraser from Tête

Jaune Cache to its confluence with the Nechako, where a steel bridge would be built to carry the railcars over the river. Others made their way northward into the area on foot or on horseback over the Blackwater Trail from Quesnel. The more affluent among them arrived aboard one of the many small paddlewheelers then plying the Fraser and Nechako Rivers north of Soda Creek.

But the key players for the concerns of this book were those men who were part of the fourth large contingent of non-natives who moved into the area in pursuit of the money to be made from its natural resources—briefcase-toting businessmen who flew in by plane during and after the Second World War. Their goal was to gain control of the riches they knew could be extracted from the area's network of lakes and rivers and the thick carpet of evergreen trees covering the region.

Among this fourth invasion of settlers were some who had been extended official invitations: representatives of Alcan. Successive governments in Ottawa and Victoria had wooed the company into the province to develop the hydroelectric potential of northwestern BC and build an aluminum smelter at Kitimat.

The Cheslatta T'en—the First Nations people who lived in the area that would eventually be flooded by Alcan's Nechako Reservoir—were not intimately aware of the comings and goings of these successive waves of settlers and businessmen situating themselves along the more easterly portion of the Nechako River. They continued to live off the land, as they had done for centuries, in their isolated territory surrounding the Cheslatta and Murray Lakes on the western edge of the Fraser River system.

The reports and diaries prepared by early missionaries reveal that the Cheslatta T'en had developed a peaceful lifestyle, drawing their sustenance from the supply of readily accessible food: freshwater fish—trout, char, kokanee and whitefish; wild game like bear and moose; and berries and herbs. They had also developed farms on which they raised hay for their horses and cattle and grew gardens to supplement the food they gathered from the wilderness. Their extensive trapline systems stretched from Tahtsa Lake to Uncha Lake and south into the Chilcotin country of the Ulkatcho people. Their traditional territory was criss-crossed by systems of wagon roads and trails over which they travelled to trade with

Indians living at Ulkatcho, Bella Coola, Moricetown and Stuart Lake.[9]

For centuries they and the neighbouring Carrier tribes had depended on the extensive chains of lakes and rivers draining into the Nechako River as a source of food and as a transportation route. In his account of his travels through the region, *Sixteen Years in Indian Country*, Daniel Harmon recorded this view of the Carrier People:

> The natives of New Caledonia, we denominate Carriers; but they call themselves Ta-cullies, which signifies people who go upon water. This name originated from the fact that they generally go from one village to another, in canoes....
>
> ...
>
> The men, however, make canoes which are clumsily wrought of the aspin [sic] tree, as well as of the bark of the spruce fir. The former, will carry from half a ton to a ton and an half burthen, while the latter, will carry from one to four grown persons. The women make excellent nets of the iner [sic] bark of the willow tree, and of nettles, which answer better for taking small fish, than any which we can obtain from Canada, made of twine or thread."[10]

They used these nets to harvest the freshwater fish and the sockeye and chinook salmon which swam past their villages on their migration to their spawning grounds upstream.

By 1916 the federal government had established 16 separate Indian Reservations in the vicinity of Cheslatta and Murray Lakes. Here the Cheslatta people lived in relatively self-sufficient isolation and, until 1952, they had little contact with representatives of the non-native government. "These people, the Cheslatta People, were at the time gainfully employed. They ran farms. They trapped for a living. They hunted. They were a stable, productive and employed society. Any suggestion that may be made—and I have heard some suggestions like this—that the situation was otherwise

---

"In the 1940s they were regarded as just a bunch of backward Indians who didn't even require fair and human treatment, but heed my warning well, for today they are educated. They have some funding, they are demanding fair treatment, and they are hell-bent to right the wrongs done to them in the past." *Pam Sholty, BCUCH 4.558.*

prior to 1952, is categorically untrue," Prince George lawyer Richard Byl said in 1993.[11]

Without their knowledge, during the later part of the 1940s, the BC government and Alcan were about to begin a massive engineering project on a scale never before seen in Canada—a project that would leave deep emotional, physical and financial scars on their lives.

The first hint the Cheslatta people had that their peaceful, self-sufficient lifestyle was ending came on April 3, 1952 when a federal Indian Agent arrived in one of their villages. He had come to tell them they must leave their village immediately because in two days the water would begin rising behind a temporary dam built by Alcan across the outlet of Murray Lake. "My people were shocked to hear that," says the present-day Cheslatta Chief Marvin Charlie.

The forced evacuation of the Cheslatta people from their traditional territory was a direct result of a decision made by the federal DFO, who failed to insist that Alcan design the Kenney Dam so that water was permitted to be released through the dam to protect the salmon migrating, spawning and living in the Nechako River below the dam. Alarmed by the potential damage that would be caused to the millions of salmon migrating through the Nechako—should Alcan close off all flows into the upper reaches of the river for years while their reservoir filled—government representatives ordered Alcan to build a dam on Murray Lake instead, so that water in it and Cheslatta Lake could be spilled into the Nechako, to cool it when the fish were in the river. The plan was to return some water to the river from the Cheslatta-Murray Lake system, down the Murray River and over Cheslatta Falls below the dam on the Nechako. When the reservoir was filled—a process that took four years to complete—water was to be released from the reservoir into the Cheslatta-Murray Lake system through the Skins Lake Spillway.

At this critical time in their history, the Cheslatta T'en had not yet selected a chief to replace their hereditary chief who had died the previous year. This circumstance afforded the Indian Agent the opportunity to use the powers of the Indian Act to appoint a chief and two councillors to act on behalf of the Cheslatta T'en during the negotiations. He then ordered them to tell the Cheslatta T'en to meet with him again at Bel-ga-tse No. 5 Reserve on April 16, 1952, to sign the surrender documents required by the DIA.

It is important, here, to note some significant dates: The decision to build the temporary dam was made in February or March of 1952; the Cheslatta people were first advised that some of their traditional territory would be flooded on April 3, 1952; and the water licence required to build the temporary dam was not issued until July 26, 1952, four months after the dam was completed.

All the Cheslatta T'en, except those away on their traplines, gathered at Bel-ga-tse Reserve on April 16 to learn more about what was going to happen to them and their land. The day came and went but the DIA representatives failed to show up. The Cheslatta T'en became worried because it was growing dark, the lake continued to rise and some buildings were already flooded.[12] By the time the Alcan helicopter bearing the DIA representatives arrived in the village three days later, the residents were short of food, and of hay for their horses.

The first meeting with the Cheslatta people came 30 months after BC's Water Rights Comptroller, R.C. Farrow, and Alcan's BC vice-president, McNeeley DuBose, met with the non-native residents of Ootsa Lake to begin negotiating to buy the land that would be flooded by the reservoir.[13] While the Cheslatta people were instructed that they must sign the documents surrendering their land and leave immediately, the negotiations with the non-native Ootsa Lake residents continued until 1953, when they were required to leave their homesteads. In the end, the Cheslatta people received one-fifth of the price non-native Ootsa Lake residents

---

"The federal government, in fact, did arrive at Reserve Number 5 on April the 19th of 1952 by a helicopter supplied by Alcan along with a high Alcan official by the name of Mr. Clark. Meetings went on for a couple of days and they were not, from reading the records of all parties involved...the meetings were very tense and the Cheslatta people did not want to leave.... I want the Commission to take note of the fact that Alcan did not—or its predecessor—obtain a Water License from the B.C. Water Controller [sic] until approximately three months later, some time in July of 1952. And all that I read into that, as a lawyer, is that at the time that the Murray Lake Dam was built its existence was illegal." *Richard Byl, BCUCH 5.682, 683.*

received for their property.[14] "I think they just forgot about the Cheslatta people when they started building the temporary dam to protect the fish," says Mike Robertson, a non-Indian resident of Grassy Plains who has worked as a researcher for the Cheslatta band for many years.

Until the day Alcan's helicopter arrived in their village, the Cheslatta T'en had had little contact with non-native officialdom. The only band member who could understand and speak English well enough to act as an interpreter was 29-year-old Abel Peters. He had learned to speak English while serving with the Canadian Armed Forces in France during the Second World War. "When they started the meeting the first thing they [the Department of Indian Affairs] told us was we were not supposed to take notes," Peters said in 1991.[15]

The official surrender documents were presented for the people to sign. Peters outlined the Cheslatta T'en's counterdemands to the government and Alcan officials. In return for surrendering their land they wanted new land and buildings to be purchased before they moved, a monthly pension paid to each band member for life, additional compensation for their traplines and new roads built to the reserves they were not surrendering.[16]

The DIA said their demands were unreasonable, and explained that if they surrendered the land, they would receive fair compensation. If they refused to surrender the land, they would still have to move, but they would receive no compensation. The Cheslatta People refused to sign the documents saying the money they were being offered was not enough to replace the land and buildings that would be destroyed by the flooding.

At that point, the Alcan and government representatives left to spend the night at Alcan's construction site near the Kenney Dam. During a meeting held that night to discuss the situation, Alcan pointed out they had more time to negotiate because the water was not going to rise as quickly as they had originally thought.[17] But the DIA representatives did not want to wait. They feared if the Indians had more time to think about what was happening, they would become more difficult to deal with. Instead of negotiating with the band, they wanted to begin negotiating with each band member separately.

Abel Peters, the World War II veteran who negotiated with Alcan and DFO in the 1950s because he could speak English. Photo by Tim Pelling.

That was the strategy in place when the officials returned to Belga-tse to resume their work the next day. Again, the officials painted a picture of the urgent need for the Cheslatta T'en to leave their homes before they were flooded out by the rising water. Lawyer Richard Byl, in his 1994 submission to hearings into Alcan's KCP, stated:

There was much confusion amongst the Band members as to what was being discussed and decided, and issues of critical importance to the Band in making an informed decision were not even discussed. The meeting dragged on for hours and particular individuals were subjected to verbal and threatening abuse by the officials.[18]

Peters continued to negotiate as best he could for his people, and the Cheslatta T'en continued to refuse to sign the surrender document. They were advised that if they didn't leave, the RCMP would be sent in to remove them. They were told they could take only what they would need on the trail: food, blankets, tents, cooking utensils. The demoralized and confused Cheslatta T'en left behind their homes, barns, farming tools and trapping equipment. To this day the elders of the band who were alive when the fateful meeting was held in 1952 deny that they signed the documents surrendering the land to the DIA so they could sell it to Alcan.

DIA records, however, show the Cheslatta T'en unanimously approved the surrender of 2,600 acres of their reserves on Cheslatta and Murray Lakes for $129,000, "provided that this amount is sufficient to re-establish our Band elsewhere to our satisfaction on a comparable basis."[19]

The total cost of moving and re-establishing the people was to be borne by the Aluminum Company of Canada. Many of the signatures on the documents consist only of an "X," witnessed by one of the officials present as being the mark of that person.

The band members claim they were neither advised that they could refuse to surrender their traditional lands, nor that they had the right to be advised by a lawyer. The Cheslatta T'en were unaware the Indian Act sets out the procedures to be used when a band is being asked to surrender its lands—or that those people who were demanding that they immediately relinquish their lands were violating those guidelines and procedures.

As soon as the Cheslatta people were gone, the Catholic church they'd built, their homes, barns and outbuildings were bulldozed into piles and burned, to prevent the people from returning to the site. Before they abandoned their villages, the people hid some of their personal possessions including tools and traps that were too heavy for them to carry with them when they walked overland to Grassy Plains. When they returned to claim their possessions, everything had disappeared.

Abel Peters had a wagon and a team of horses, so he was paid $150 to help the people move their belongings. But the $50 most

View of the Cheslatta settlement at Reserve No. 2 before all the buildings were bulldozed and burned and the village flooded in 1952. Photo courtesy of the Jean Giesbrecht Collection.

of the Cheslatta people received was all the money they had to purchase food, clothing and other essentials until May, 1953. Worse yet, the money was paid by cheques which were of little use in a country where there were no banks.

The memories of that day still haunt Peters. "At that time I was younger and I was careless about the idea. I could have done better because I didn't think about the future of the people. I thought mostly about myself," he said in 1991.[20]

Marvin Charlie, the soft-spoken, present-day chief of the Cheslatta Band, was only eight years old when the fateful 1952 meeting took place. But he says he can remember everything about the move from their isolated villages around the lakes to a windy plateau above Francois Lake called Bickle Flats. In April, overnight temperatures drop below freezing in that part of BC. But during the day the lake ice became soft and slushy, making it unsafe to walk on. The trails along the lake were muddy and the snow still lay in deep drifts on the higher ground. These were the conditions the people faced when they left their villages and walked or rode wagons and horses more than 30 miles from Cheslatta Lake to the nearest settlement at Grassy Plains. It took them three days to get

88

The Roman Catholic Church built in 1915 on Cheslatta Reserve No. 2 which was bulldozed and burned before the village was flooded in 1952. Photo courtesy of the Cheslatta First Nations.

there. "It was a nightmare for the people when they were asked to move immediately. The snow was pretty deep and some of them took wagons and some of the boys took saddle horses to break the trail so the travelling was very slow," Chief Charlie says.

One of the major concerns of the Cheslatta T'en was what would happen to the bodies of their ancestors buried in hundreds of graves around the lake. They claim they were assured no grave-yards would be flooded or damaged by the rising waters.

After the Cheslatta T'en left the village, the federal Indian Commissioner took charge of the two cemeteries containing approximately 100 graves that were to be flooded. Only the two most recent graves and some of the headstones were moved.[21] The spirit houses and grave markers were removed from the remaining graves and burned. The ashes were placed under a stone cairn built above the high water mark.[22] An aluminum marker placed on the site reads: "This monument was erected in 1952 to the memory of

"The Aboriginal people were not involved in the initial negotiations with Alcan. Instead, they were forced to deal with the effects of Kemano I after the fact." *Rankin and Finlay, 17.*

Cheslatta Chief Marvin Charlie with Skins Lake Spillway in the background. Photo by Tim Pelling.

the Indian men, women and children of the Cheslatta Band, laid to rest in the cemetery on Reservation Four, now under water. MAY THEY REST IN PEACE."

At the time the more than 100 band members abandoned their villages, many of the men were out in the surrounding wilderness attending their traplines. When they returned to their villages, they were shocked to find them empty—their homes in smouldering ruins and no sign whatsoever of what had happened to the people.

"Brian Peters used to live at reserve number five. When he and George Louis returned to that reserve in June they found the houses burned, destroyed and flooded, so they walked to reserve number seven where George Louis lived and they found the same thing, everything burned and destroyed and the land wetted," says Chief Charlie. The two men then walked to reserve number nine, which was also abandoned and destroyed, so they walked on to Grassy Plains where they finally found some of the Cheslatta T'en and learned what had happened while they were absent.

The worst was yet to come.

After the Cheslatta people reached Grassy Plains they camped under large trees, in abandoned sawmills and in tents for most of the next year while they waited for the DIA to find them new land on which to settle. They became ill, confused and depressed. Some died. Others, including their present Chief, Marvin Charlie, contracted tuberculosis and spent years recovering in a sanatorium.

"The position and the lot of the Cheslatta People in this period of time can only be described as absolutely terrible and I am sorry to say that it will stand out as a blight and as a shame on the conscience of this province and this country for a long time," says lawyer Richard Byl.[23]

Peters says the overland trek and living outdoors was particularly hard on the elders. "Many of them died off because they were camping out all summer waiting to get money so we could buy new land," he said.

"The DIA kicked them off and forgot them," says Mike Robertson. "For almost 40 years they have been struggling to get back on their feet and it has taken its toll."

The agreement signed by the Cheslatta people during the 1952 meeting in the village stated that Alcan would replace their property to their satisfaction. Alcan says it paid the DIA $129,000 for the 10 Cheslatta reserves, totalling 1,820.6 acres, flooded by the reservoir.[24] Half of the money was for land and buildings and the remainder was relocation compensation. The band has never received an account of how the money was used.

Six months after the Cheslatta T'en evacuated their villages, the DIA finally began to relocate them on farm lands at 11 different locations near Grassy Plains. Today you have to drive more than 150 miles to visit all the families. The forced migration and the long distances they now live from each other has destroyed their close-knit communities and the self-sufficient lifestyle which had enabled them to live in their isolated villages for centuries.

The indignities inflicted on the Cheslatta People did not end when they were forced out of their homes and off their lands. When some of the people tried to move back to their traditional territory, the federal Indian Agent, identified only as Mr. Demere[25] advised them that they were trespassing. "As this is now their [Alcan's] property, they've also requested that you be told to get off their land. We are asking you to remove any personal effects as soon as possible and to arrange your trapline in the area with the game warden in such manner that you would not cause the Alcan any

Cheslatta elder George Louis who, as a young man, returned from a trapping trip to Cheslatta Lake to find his village destroyed. Photo courtesy of the Cheslatta First Nations.

inconvenience or trouble," he said in a letter written to Chief Peters.

Cheslatta Lake was not flooded by Alcan's reservoir. Originally it was flooded by the temporary dam built across the outlet from Murray Lake. Before the Kenney Dam was completed, a spillway was built 47 miles west of the dam on the north shore of Ootsa Lake. When the reservoir was filled, the water had risen 140 feet behind Skins Lake saddle dam, and the spillway built into that smaller dam became the only means for returning water into the dry Nechako riverbed below. Since 1980 the flows through the spillway have been regulated by an injunction and, later, by the terms of the 1987 Settlement Agreement. Larger amounts of surface water are released during the summer to cool the temperatures of the water in the Nechako River, for the benefit of migrating salmon on their way to their spawning grounds in the river and its tributaries.

This inefficient and artificial way of cooling the waters downstream in the Nechako did not go unnoticed. It was of concern even when the project was being planned. During 1951 and 1952, the International Pacific Salmon Fisheries Commission had been unsuccessful in its efforts to have Alcan rebuild the temporary diversion tunnel—built around the Kenney Dam site while the dam was being constructed—to turn it into a permanent cold-water release facility.

Before the building of the dam and the spillway connecting the newly filled reservoir with the Murray-Cheslatta Lake system, the Cheslatta River was a small creek with an average flow of 100 cubic feet per second. Its size changed drastically with the dam. One of the worst floods on the Cheslatta River occurred in 1957, when the gates of the Skins Lake Spillway appear to have malfunctioned, resulting in torrents of water being sent down the 20- to 30-mile-long Cheslatta River,[26] and thus raising the level of Cheslatta Lake more than 12 feet. The tremendous gush of water ripped away the river banks and tore a canyon hundreds of feet wide and 75 to 100 feet deep from the low hills surrounding the once-peaceful little river. Had it occurred in a more populated area, the 1957 flood would have been a catastrophe.

But that was not the only time there were large water releases through the Skins Lake Spillway. Over the years, all the soil torn from the 25-mile-long canyon created below the spillway has been

---

"We have heard stories of forged documents and forced evacuations. If these stories are true, there is nothing I can say in defence of such treatment. All I can say is that the people representing Alcan at the time dealt with the Department of Indian Affairs as they had been instructed to do by the federal government of the day." Alcan's BC vice-president, Bill Rich, BCUCH 11.1676.

Researcher Mike Robertson on the shore of the Cheslatta River. Note the erosion caused by surges of water released through Skins Lake Spillway. Photo by Tim Pelling.

deposited in Cheslatta and Murray Lakes, or carried further downstream and deposited in what is now known as the Cheslatta Fan—the huge, delta-like deposit of debris which has built up in the Nechako riverbed at the base of Cheslatta Falls.

The sudden floods also washed away the banks protecting the Cheslatta graveyard at Bel-ga-tse Reserve Number 9. The Cheslatta T'en have a deeply-felt respect for their ancestors, and were profoundly offended when some of their remains were washed into the lake. "That is the part I will never forget," Chief Charlie says today. "When we found out the graves had been washed down the river and we found the grave houses and coffins floating around on the lakes, the people began walking the riverbanks looking for their loved ones' graves they had lost."

Although the flooding and the damage to the graveyard was ignored by the rest of the province, it did not go unnoticed by Indian Agent Demere. In July, 1957, he wrote the following letter to his supervisor, R. Neil:

Approximately seventeen graves were completely washed away by the high water in the river. This high water is caused by the opening of the floodgates at Skins Dam. The water level is reported by the gauge reader, Mr. Jim Clark, at Cheslatta to be in excess of 12 feet, the expected level. The Aluminium Company of Canada is aware of this, and they ordered the gate shut in order to inspect the damage, saw that it was irreparable, and reordered the gates open. There is absolutely no vestige of the cemetery left to the eye. I've taken pictures of the area, if they are required. The Cheslatta Indians are not aware that this has happened as yet. I am informed that they will raise proper hell when they find out, and that is the reason for me taking the liberty of writing to you personally on this subject.[27]

The band's tragic history came into the spotlight in 1990 when Chief Marvin Charlie travelled to Prince George to announce that his people had launched a $122-million court case charging the federal government with fraud, duress and breach of trust resulting from DIA's failure to protect them in 1952. In preparation for the court case, the band asked forensic expert Don Brown, a retired RCMP superintendent, to examine the signatures on the surrender documents signed during the 1952 meeting. Ninety-two of the people had signed the documents with an X. Brown concluded that the 92 X-marks could not have been made by aboriginals because they don't make an X, they make a cross (+) "All those X's were beautifully done.... I have investigated other marks from Native people. They are usually trembly marks."[28]

In an out-of-court settlement announced in March 1993, Ottawa agreed to pay $6.95 million[29] to compensate the band for the government's failure to compensate them adequately for the loss of their land in 1952 and the reduction in the value of the remaining reserve lands caused by the flooding.[30] They also received $475,970 for a second claim in which they charged they had not received all of the $129,000 Alcan paid the DIA in 1952.[31]

"I am acutely aware of the perceived injustices and deep emotional scars left in the particular community from the original Kemano project. I think they are something that none of us, as Canadians, can be proud of." *John Watson, BC Regional Director, Department of Indian Affairs and Northern Development, BCUCH 85.16023.*

The more than $7.4 million has been placed in a trust fund and the interest is to be used to improve elders' housing and the economic and social needs of the Cheslatta People.

In 1989, Alcan agreed to return the reserve lands at Cheslatta Lake to the band once the KCP is completed. In 1991, the Cheslatta T'en returned to the lake to assess the damage caused by 39 years of rapid fluctuations in the level of the lake and to lay plans for rehabilitating the lake so they can return there to live. They found the shores of the lake eroded, the grassy areas on which they had lived now barren, rocky wastes with up to 200 metres of debris floating offshore and littering the beaches of the 25-mile lake. They have developed a plan to rehabilitate the lake and develop it into a wilderness tourist site where visitors will be able to experience the life they once lived there.

The loss of their self-sufficient lifestyle following the trek away from their land is cited by Chief Charlie, Abel Peters and Mike Robertson as the prime reason behind the high suicide and violent-death rate among band members. "The people have lost their way. The young people don't know what we had. That's why we're going back to the lake to live each summer," Charlie says.

No mention is made of the devastation inflicted upon the lives of the Cheslatta T'en in the 1,495 page, three-volume company-

---

"In one swift move, an entire Cheslatta cemetery at Chislatlate Reserve, containing the bodies of about 25 Cheslatta people, washed away. The body of Chief Louie, Cheslatta's most prominent chief, was among those which disappeared into the lake. Since then over 25 bodies have been washed into the lake by erosion of a cemetery at Scilchola Reserve, the former site of one of three main Cheslatta villages and cemeteries located on the lakeshore. The erosion has made Cheslatta Lake a watery grave for the remains of at least 50 Cheslatta people." *The Watershed, October, 1993.*

"Just a few lines to say that we have seen for ourselves the graveyard that used to be at Cheslatta Number 9 Reserve.... It is all gone and we do not know where the dead have gone. We went to Cheslatta June 4th at four o'clock. All the dead have floated away and gone ashore anywhere. We didn't find any.... Bill Clark of Cheslatta seen a coffin floating in the middle of the lake on May 1. We look there ourselves.... We looked for coffins on the lakeshore but the boat we used was too small so we gave up." *Letter written to Kim Morris by Robert Skin, 6 June 1957, BCUCH 5.699.*

published history—*Global Mission: The Story of Alcan*, written by Duncan Campbell—which thoroughly documents the company's dealings with the provincial and federal governments as well as its engineering feats. In volume three, Alcan's BC vice-president Bill Rich refers to the meetings he had held with the Cheslatta people:

> We have had useful discussions with native organizations—not about land claims, that's for governments—but about other activities which could be undertaken while the land claims are being settled.
>
> These discussions have been about economic benefits that can accrue to native people through participation in projects such as KCP [the Kemano Completion Project]. This has helped us better understand the desires and aspirations of the native people, and we continue to be optimistic that we can reach agreements with them that will benefit all.

I have attended many meetings of First Nations people, Alcan representatives and government officials, at which aboriginal leaders struggled, with limited success, to explain their spiritual association to the land. I know now that the First Nations people at these meetings are trying to communicate across a vast cultural chasm. On one side of the chasm sit government representatives aiming to enforce policies, regardless of whether or not they make sense to the Indians; beside them are the serious-minded industrialists whose thoughts are habitually preoccupied with the potential for generating profits for their shareholders. On the other side of the

---

"Salmon hold in the current like kites in the wind. Some of them have in their mouths the bones of the Cheslatta people, spilled from the coffins in the flood. I hear an osprey outside my dream, flying up the Nechako toward the dam. I realize it's right near here, just below Cheslatta Falls, that the federal government has set aside land for a hatchery. Just in case." *Hume, 59.*

"Mr Robertson and myself and some other people retained one of the foremost forensic experts in Canada, a gentleman by the name of Donald Brown, to review these particular documents and to look at signature specimens that Mr. Robertson had identified over the course of 10 years' research. And the conclusion of Mr. Donald Brown—and it has never been challenged to this day by anyone—was that the surrender documents were forged." *Richard Byl, BCUCH 5.684.*

chasm sit native leaders and elders accustomed to surviving a level of poverty, isolation and insecurity the government representatives and business leaders could not possibly comprehend. The only constant factor in their troubled lives has always been their land's ability to provide them with shelter, medicines and food.

I saw the puzzlement on the faces of Alcan executives and bureaucrats during a meeting at Stoney Creek, when native elders tried to explain how they saw all humans, creatures, plants, water and the air itself as part of a larger web of life, to explain their belief that if one part of the web is damaged, everything suffers.

Puzzled looks also appeared among the technical experts when Stoney Creek elder Sophie Thomas rose to tell them how she'd heard the mountains and valleys along the Nechako River moaning with the pain caused by the environmental damage Alcan had wrought on the area. The university-trained experts didn't understand that kind of talk: They were members of a committee (established by the 1987 Nechako Settlement Agreement) to oversee the safety of the salmon using the Nechako River as a migration route. They had come to a meeting in Vanderhoof, loaded down with their charts, graphs and brochures to explain how they, not Mother Nature, were going to protect the salmon from harm when Alcan took more water from the river.

It took Alcan executives and the Catholic Church more than 40 years to begin to understand the words of the Cheslatta people when they spoke about their fears for the souls of their dead ancestors whose graves have been washed away by the water gushing from behind the company's dam at Skins Lake Spillway. Their ancestors' bones are still lying in the mud at the bottom of the lake that bears their name, and the people continue to search for the bones which are still being washed up on the shores of the lakes and rivers through which the water flows on its way back into the Nechako.

On July 6, 1993, Cheslatta Chief Marvin Charlie finally got his

---

"[I]t's taken literally 40 years in the wilderness—and the analogy might be apt for the people—under the magnificent leadership of Marvin Charlie and his council to come back to the point where they are today." *Richard Byl, BCUCH 5.685.*

From left to right: Cheslatta Chief Marvin Charlie, Elijah Harper and Councillor Richard Peters of Cheslatta, at ceremonies consecrating Cheslatta Lake as a cemetery. Photo courtesy of Dana Wagg.

wish when his ancestors' souls were laid to rest during a ceremony conducted by Father Nicholas Forde and Bishop Fergus O'Grady of the Catholic Church. Under Canon Law, the remaining grave-yards and the lake itself were consecrated as sacred ground. In preparation for the ceremony the scrub that had covered the site was cleared away and white spirit houses were erected over the restored grave sites. "I have waited many years for this day," Chief Marvin Charlie said following the ceremony.

Since the waters of Cheslatta Lake are now sacred, and since that lake water flows into the Nechako River, there are those who question why the river shouldn't *also* be considered sacred. "Assuredly, from the point of view of the Cheslatta people it is. I want the commission to not ever lose sight of the fact that the bodies of the ancestors of the Cheslatta people are buried in the mud and the sludge at the bottom of Cheslatta Lake today," Richard Byl told the members of the BCUC during hearings held November 25, 1993, in Prince George.

Few non-native Canadians understand First Nations peoples' deeply held beliefs about Mother Nature, the circle of life, the

Bishop O'Grady assisted by Father Forde during the ceremony consecrating the new cemetery and Cheslatta Lake, into which Cheslatta graves were washed, as sacred gound. Photo courtesy of the *Prince George Citizen*.

importance of their ancestors and their belief that their spirits pervade their universe. A man who had lived and worked among northern First Nations people for many years once told me First Nation's peoples' spiritual association with the land was so close it made them part of it:

> When you see a white person sitting on the bank of a river gazing at the river they may be admiring the view and enjoying the experience. But, when a spiritual native person sits on a bank gazing at the same river, they become part of everything around them: the trees, the air, the water, the grass and the land on which they stand. That makes them feel truly a part of the web of life.

Whether they admit it or not, many non-native Canadians have a similar spiritual association with the wilderness. They know only that they enjoy going into the wilderness which lies beyond the boundaries of their civilized life. They camp, fish, hunt, hike, and rest there because it provides them with the succour and solace missing in their daily urban lives. Consciously or unconsciously, they need to know the wilderness will always be there—hence the blockades to protect coastal rainforests, campaigns to save what is left of our wild rivers and the growing concern about the future of the animals, fish and birds who live there.

I once watched as the owner of a small business, whose life was beset with banking and personal problems, walked to the edge of a dark, northern lake, then stood there and stared off at the blaze of yellow autumn leaves mirrored on the water's quiet surface. For the first time in weeks, I saw his face begin to relax. When the maniacal cry of a loon split the silence, he smiled and said, "I love that sound."

We Are All River Gods

To some a trip down a river means water fights and wet summer fun. To others it is merely a testing of personal mettle, but to nearly all it is something more. Something ineffable yet deeply satisfying, as we join with ancient currents and flow for a brief moment in time between timeless banks. Rivers are greater than their grandest canyons and biggest drops. Their habitats for plant and animal species depend on the steady flow of water for survival. Among the species is man. On the river we recognize the identity we share with the people who have come before us. On the river we see in the faces of today's inhabitants, our own faces.... On the river we see ourselves as motes in God's bloodstream venturing along the planet's arteries, observing and perhaps inevitably changing as we go. For a while the rivers...still flow strongly or powerfully to the sea. In varying degrees all are under siege, be it by diversion, projects for irrigation, dams for hydro-electric power, or unthinking pollution. Yet we musn't look elsewhere for villains or turn aside in despair. We are all river gods, and whether we act as creator or destroyer...is up to us.[1]

From below the site where the Kenney Dam was built in the Grand Canyon of the Nechako River more than 40 years ago, the diverted river now flows eastward through the wilderness of central British Columbia's interior plateau until its waters merge with those of the Fraser River at Prince George. The river meanders past beaver lodges and thick stands of spruce, trembling aspen, black cottonwood and birch. On the higher, drier ground are stands of lodgepole pine—so named by early settlers, who preferred to use them in constructing their log buildings because the

102

diameter of the logs varies little from butt to tip.

From the river, boaters can see areas on the surrounding hills where the larger evergreens have been burned off by forest fires or removed by loggers. With time, they have become overgrown with aspen and willow, which are a favourite food of moose and mule deer who use the river as their source of water. Underneath the larger trees and in open spots along the river can be found shrubs such as wild roses, which bear sweet-smelling pink flowers during June, and soopolallie whose white berries are whipped into a froth and used to make Indian ice cream. Also found there are kinnikinnik, whose thin dark-green leaves with furry undersides can be used to make tea, and many edible berries including blueberries, saskatoons, high-bush cranberries, raspberries and bunchberries. More rare finds are edible wild onions, lettuce and mint.

Below the now dry canyon, migrations of Canada's largest species of salmon, the mighty chinook, once arrived each September after swimming more than 550 miles—against the current—from the Pacific Ocean and up the Fraser and Nechako Rivers. The big fish used their tails to fan out a shallow depression on one of thousands of sloping berms or redds of gravel that once lined the river bottom. There they laid the eggs that held the promise of the return of another generation in four or five years. When they died, their bodies littered the banks of the river for miles, serving as food for birds and animals alike. The freshwater fish inhabiting the river included rainbow trout, dolly varden, squawfish, suckers and the mysterious, slow-moving prehistoric white sturgeon.

Downstream from the dam, Cheslatta Falls cascades into the river. A few miles below the falls, dramatically pinnacled white cliffs of volcanic tuff rise from the water's edge. Another glacial feature present along the Nechako River are eskers: long, sinuous

---

"The 14 years that I have been taking clients on the Nechako River it has always been the highlight of their trips to the Fort Fraser area, the solitude and scenic beauty are memorable. You can float on the Nechako and always spot wildlife, whether it's beavers, eagles, ducks, bears, moose or wolves." *Colonel Anderson, a guide-outfitter who has lived near the banks of the Nechako River for 26 years, BCUCH 2.210.*

pyramidal ridges of gravel formed by erosion as the water flowed underneath the ice that once lay hundreds of feet deep over the area.

Along the segment of the river below the dam lies the former home of cowboy author Rich Hobson, whose autobiographical books made the region famous during the 1940s and '50s. His first book, *Grass Beyond the Mountains*, describes the struggles and adventures of Hobson and his partner, Panhandle Smith, during the 1930s, as they carved out a huge cattle empire from the bush and wild meadows that dot the area. This book established the style for his later books, which became international best-sellers and attracted a generation of American, European and Canadian adventure-seekers into the area he had portrayed as one of the last frontiers in North America—where tough men could live as they chose.

From the canyon the river flows north for more than 55 miles before it is joined by the Nautley River. This short river drains the waters of Fraser Lake. Into Fraser Lake drain two rivers—the Stellaquo, which originates in beautiful Francois Lake, and the Endako. Each summer fly-fishers gather from around the world along the banks of the swift-flowing Stellaquo to test their skills against the tough-mouthed, wild rainbow trout feeding there.

Near the point where the Nautley River flows out of the eastern end of Fraser Lake live the Nadleh Whut'en Band, whose elders remember the days when the river turned red when migrating chinook and sockeye salmon moved through it each fall. Near this section of the river, people walking along the shore of the Nechako can find small fist-sized clay concretions lying on the shores. These bizarre, bulbous shapes—known locally as "river babies" or "schmoos"—are created by the water's action on lumps of hard clay. Agate and jasper can also be found along the shore and amber can be found in black lignite beds south of Fort Fraser.

"If you could spend a day being in an untouched and peaceful forest, feeling the presence of all the beings around you, maybe you would understand, feel the breeze move softly against your cheek, see the trees gently dancing, hear the sound of the squirrel, the warning of the crow." *Fort Fraser resident Maya Sullivan, BCUCH 2.226-27.*

Near its junction with the Nautley River, the Nechako bends eastward and begins flowing through rich deposits of silty soils. The flat fields lying along each side of the river from Fraser Lake to 15 miles east of Vanderhoof are actually the bottom of an ancient lake that formed there at the end of the last Ice Age. The people who cultivate these fields have depended on the river and its related aquafers to provide the water to irrigate their crops of cereal feed grains, oilseed crops and forage crops. A settler who walked through the Nechako River Valley in 1907 described this section as being 500- to 600-feet wide and "one of the prettiest streams we saw on our trip. It has a gravel bottom, the water is clear and the current quite swift. Trout, sturgeon and whitefish are very plentiful in all the lakes and rivers. During the months of August and September the Nechako abounds with salmon which make their way from the sea to their spawning grounds. They are taken by the thousands by the Indians who dry them for their winter supply of food."[2]

In 1944, a bird sanctuary was established on the Nechako River within blocks of Vanderhoof's main business section. By the 1960s, as many as 63,000 Canada geese used the sanctuary as they migrated along the Pacific flyway. The Canada goose is such a feature of the life of Vanderhoof it has become the symbol of the community: Goose placards are displayed on telephone poles leading into the town and on signposts throughout the community. Along with the Canada geese in the sanctuary are snow geese, Ross' geese, ducks, and the elegant trumpeter swans which are now coming back from the brink of extinction. Joining the geese and other

---

"How many million days has this river greeted the sun as season passes into season, year into year, into century, into millennium? She has changed her course, been dammed and diverted by great blocks of ice, flooded and raged, and flowed, as now, placidly, silently, greatly." *Vanderhoof resident Todd Blattner, BCUCH 3.355-56.*

"I'm here to speak for the Nechako River. If ever there was a mother load [sic] of fertility, it is this meandering, friendly, nurturing body of water. It winds through the Nechako plateau, far beyond the sea it feeds with fish and far above the eye of most of the population of British Columbia." *Vanderhoof resident Audrey L'Heureux, BCUCH 3.327.*

birds using the river have been generations of Vanderhoof residents who have gathered there during the summer for picnics, to swim, float on rafts and enjoy other forms of water recreation.

During the first half of this century, the waters of the upper Nechako were so deep that two sturdy little stern-wheelers, the *Enterprise* and the *Nechacco*, made their way up the river.[3] In 1871 the 85-foot *Enterprise* navigated its way up the Nechako and Stuart Rivers en route to the Omineca gold fields. The captain was J.H. Bonser who, before the railway bridge was completed across the Fraser River at Prince George, became a legend delivering supplies to communities along the Nechako River such as Finmoore, now a ghost-town but which once rang to the sound of tie hackers' broadaxes, and Milne's Landing, now known as Vanderhoof.

In the spring of 1910 Bonser successfully navigated the upper part of the Nechako River as far as Fraser Lake. There, with the help of persuasion provided by a bottle of rum, he agreed to carry a survey party another 40 miles upstream to an area now known as Cutoff Creek. Surveyor George Copley, recorded the following description of an incident which occurred during this pioneering journey, illustrating Bonser's daring exploits:

> ...while steaming along in fair water, the captain saw a deer stand-
> ing on a rock cliff, staring down at the boat. He simply let the wheel
> go, grabbed his rifle which he always kept in the wheel-house, shot
> the deer and then had the ship straightened out before it had time
> to become crossways in the stream. He then edged the steamer to
> the river bank, where we retrieved the deer and had fresh liver and
> venison steaks for supper.[4]

Generations of people were drawn into the valley by the jobs created by the construction of the Grand Trunk Pacific Railway. And the incoming settlers were content to stay in the valley, with its vast stretches of rich farm land on the benches lining each side of the river. The fertile agricultural land spreading to the horizon in the Nechako River Valley near Vanderhoof was described this way during the late 1940s:

> At first the Nechako Valley appears barren and monotonous, a waste
> of jack pine. At the village of Vanderhoof it changes suddenly into
> a spacious flat, heavy with grain and so wide that you can imagine
> you are on the Canadian prairies.[5]

Downstream from Vanderhoof the river is joined first by the Sinkut River and, further downstream, by its largest tributary, the 68-mile-long Stuart River, out of which flows the water from Stuart, Trembleur and Takla Lakes to the north. (The only river entering the Nechako below the Stuart River is the Chilako River which carries water from Finger and Tatuk Lakes to the south.) Many of the spawning sockeye that make their way up the Nechako River on their mysterious annual migration turn right and swim into these lakes in search of their spawning grounds.

Here can be seen a patch of the 350-year-old Douglas Fir trees named after the adventurous Scottish botanist, David Douglas, who paddled through the area in 1833. Douglas came into the area seeking a route through New Caledonia to Europe via Siberia. His dream of being able to travel from North America to Europe through Russia was picked up during the 1860s by a group of Russian, American and Canadian adventurers who attempted to string a telegraph line from Seattle to Siberia.[6] The heroic venture was abandoned when a telegraph cable connecting North America with Europe was laid across the bottom of the Atlantic Ocean. By that time the overland trail had already been cut, and wire had been strung through the Nechako Valley. Remnants of the line can still be found along its route and pictures have been taken of bull moose who died locked in a mortal head grip when, during their fall rutting battles, their antlers became entangled in the remnants of the telegraph wire left behind when this venture ended. This old telegraph trail was also used by the Chilcotin ranchers who sought to capitalize on the rich beef markets in the Klondike Gold Rush by driving herds of cattle along the route.[7]

Near the junction of the Nechako and Stuart Rivers is Sturgeon Point, so named, local residents say, because in the early part of this century Chinese entrepreneurs caught some of the large number of the ancient fish found there, kept them alive by tying them up by their tails in the water and offered them for sale to passing settlers and gold seekers.

A major archaeological site, the large prehistoric Carrier Indian village of Chinlac, is also located near the confluence of the Stuart and Nechako Rivers. The remains of 13 rectangular lodges more than 1,000 square feet in area, and in excess of 2,200 cache pits have been located on a 7.2-acre site between the two rivers. In 1952 a centre-pierced Sung Dynasty Chinese coin minted in 1125 AD was found on the site. The coin provided corroborating evidence to First Nations peoples' statements that, prior to the arrival of European traders, the Carrier had used their extensive trail systems to travel and trade with Coastal Indians, who had traded with fur-traders who also traded with the Chinese. Chinlac is believed to have been abandoned in about 1745, following a raid by Chilcotin people from the Blackwater area to the south.[8] Most of the Carrier people living at Chinlac were massacred during the raid to avenge the death of a Chilcotin chief. Those spared included only the chief, Khahdintel, and some residents, all of whom were away from the village at the time of the raid.

The gory details of this raid are recorded by Father Morice in his book, *The History of the Northern Interior of British Columbia:*

> The spectacle which met Khahdintel's eyes on his return to his village was indeed heart-rending. On the ground, lying bathed in pools of blood, were the bodies of his own two wives and nearly all his countrymen, while hanging on transversal poles resting on stout forked sticks planted in the ground, were the bodies of the children ripped open and spitted through the out-turned ribs in exactly the same way as salmon drying in the sun. Two such poles were loaded from end to end with that gruesome burden.[9]

The Chinlac chief and his people who escaped the massacre at Chinlac abandoned their village and settled among the Carrier First Nations people living nearby. Three years later the Chinlac chief led a party of Carrier into Chilcotin territory to wreak equally bloody revenge on his neighbours.[10]

Boaters travelling the river between Vanderhoof and Prince George will undoubtedly see some of the wildlife that abounds in this area—moose, mule deer, black bear, coyote and beaver. Rarer species include a small population of elk near the lower Stuart River, and grizzlies on the sidehills near the upper Nechako. Wolves, lynx, marten, fisher, weasel, foxes and red squirrels are also common in this area but shy away from human contact. Quick-eyed observers may also spot some of the semi-aquatic animals that use the river including otter, mink and muskrat.

When the salmon are in the river, bald eagles can been seen resting in the trees along the Nechako and Stuart Rivers after feeding on the carcasses of the spawned-out fish. Golden eagles, osprey, northern harriers, red-tailed hawks, even the occasional peregrine falcon and rough-legged hawk can also be seen along the river which borders on the Pacific Flyway, along which millions of birds migrate each year. The rare trumpeter swan overwinters in Fraser Lake, the Nautley River and on open waters along the Nechako and Stuart Rivers.

George Copley recorded this account of an incident that occurred during a trip through the Isle Pierre Rapids near Prince George in 1910, aboard the stern-wheeler *Nechacco*:

> Our first obstacle on the Nechako River was a rapid known as Isle de Pierre...too steep for the steamer to navigate, but to Captain Bonser only an instance in his river career. All hands off to drag a one inch steel cable up to the head of the rapids to be made fast to a sizeable spruce tree.... All went well until the steamer was about half way up the rapids, then without warning the spruce tree came out roots and all. The steamer slewed around crosswise...and down we went bumpity bump over the rocks.[11]

The BC government established a reaction ferry service near the rapids in 1922 to carry people living in the farming community on the north side to the highway connecting Prince George and Vanderhoof built on the other side of the river.

Below the Isle Pierre rapids the Nechako River deepens and flows more sedately in sweeping bends past the series of high, sandy cutbanks formed along its north shore as the river eroded down through the glacial deposits left by the retreat of the last Ice Age. In this section of the river are ancient fishing sites of the Lheitli-T'en First Nations people who now claim a traditional territory which includes Prince George's downtown business centre and extends as far east as the Rocky Mountains.

Near the mouth of the river is the Island Cache, where in the early part of this century railway contractors Foley, Welch and Stewart built docks and warehouses to receive the supplies carried up the Fraser River by stern-wheeler during the construction of the Grand Trunk Railway. The stern-wheeler's usefulness ended when the railway was completed. When the warehouses were abandoned they "held hundreds of cases of canned goods rusted and with labels missing, old stationery, correspondence files and even typewriters just left to be destroyed by the elements."[12] Nearby two of the old stern-wheelers, the *Operator* and the *Conveyor*, were beached and abandoned, and eventually vandalized and stripped of their lumber, plumbing fixtures and windows.[13]

The Nechako empties into the Fraser River a few hundred yards north of the steel railway bridge built by the Grand Trunk Pacific Railway in 1914. From there the muddier waters of the Fraser River and the clearer waters of the Nechako run parallel before they finally mingle into one stream more than ten miles below the bridge.

I know this section of the Nechako River well. It was here I joined generations of Prince George children who swam there on hot summer days during the 1930s and '40s. When the weather was good you could always find a bonfire burning and a gang of friends at one of the many swimming places along the river. The favourite swimming spots in those days were in the main stream of the Nechako River below the cutbanks—in the side channels around the islands near what is now known as Cottonwood Island Park—or downstream from the Grand Trunk Pacific Railway Bridge, where the Nechako River begins to merge with the Fraser River.

At that time, even the strongest swimmers entering the Nechako River's main current below the cutbanks would be swept off their feet before they took two steps into the fast-flowing water. Braver swimmers walked miles west along the Canadian National Railway tracks to a point where they could slip back into the cold waters of the Nechako. The current was so strong they could just lie back and allow themselves to be carried downstream for a mile or two before swimming ashore. Whenever their ears were under the water, they could hear the dull, rumbling thud made by the boulders being rolled along the river's bed by its powerful current. Swimming in the side channels presented different hazards. Although these swimming spots were away from the river's strong current, they were often used to boom up the logs before they were fed into the sawmills lining the banks. To reach the deeper water, swimmers had to walk across the log booms. One misstep, and they dropped below them, then had to force the logs apart—

or, if it was close enough, swim underwater to the boom's edge—and then climb back up on the boom.

During periods of high water the river's current was also strong at another popular swimming spot near the confluence of the Nechako and Fraser Rivers. Here the dock which was used to tie up floatplanes also served as a diving raft. Stronger swimmers swam along with the current until it swept around a small point where a backwater made it easy to get ashore. After the water level dropped later in the summer, swimmers used the steel bridge to walk across the river to the point where they could climb down onto one of the concrete piers. From there it was a simple matter of climbing down a ladder onto a small island known as Goat Island which separated the currents of the Nechako and Fraser Rivers. Here, when the water was lower, safe swimming places could be found in the protected pools that formed around the piers of the bridge. In places where a strong current of shallow water continued to run between the gravelbars, it was possible to sit down and let the current push you along a watery roller coaster over the slippery rocks.

Near its mouth, the Nechako River becomes broader and shallower as it flows around the numerous small rocky islands formed from the sediments carried down by the current. During the first half of this century ice jams frequently occurred in this area. If the jam became thick and strong enough to block the flow of water, it would flood out over the Canadian National Railway lines onto the eastern end of First Avenue in downtown Prince George.

When Alcan built the dam, wide, rocky shores appeared between the former shoreline and the main stream of the river, making it less attractive for swimming. It was at about this time Prince George's young people stopped swimming in the river, congregating instead at the new outdoor swimming pool built by the city. In this way they lost the intimate contact with the river enjoyed by the previous generations of swimmers.

Today you rarely see people swimming in the Nechako. The water is so low most of the safer side channels are either dry or stagnant sloughs and the city has built a pumping station where young people once swam near the wooden bridge. Near its confluence with the Fraser, the river is now so dry during the summer most of the bridge's concrete piers are surrounded by dry riverbed, and it

Isle Pierre reaction ferry showing how the river used to look. BC Archives & Records Service, Province of BC photo no. na-41328.

has become a favourite spot for four-wheelers to test their vehicles. On hot summer days when the most water is being released into the river from behind the dam, flotillas of Prince George and Vanderhoof residents can be seen floating along with the current in the river aboard tubs, rafts and almost anything else that floats.

The most obvious changes to the river occurred upstream where the full force of the water had once surged through its Grand Canyon in a thunderous torrent, making it impassable to both humans and salmon.

The Nechako River canyon is now silent.

Unlike most other hydroelectric projects in which water from the reservoir is passed through the generators at the dam, then returned to the river, no water flows through the Kenney Dam. The canyon has virtually dried up and no water enters the Nechako for a six-mile section between the dam and Cheslatta Falls.

Below Cheslatta Falls where water once surged past at a mean annual rate of 7,407 cubic feet per second, 5,935 cubic feet per second—or 80% of the water flowing into that section of the river— has already been diverted, leaving only 1,472 cubic feet per second still flowing down the Nechako River. If the long-term flows of

The wide cobble-stone banks now lining the Nechako River near Prince George (Isle Pierre). The water flow shown in this photo is higher than what it would be if the KCP were to proceed. Photo by Bev Christensen.

the KCP are implemented after the second tunnel is completed through Mount DuBose, and the new generators start spinning in the powerhouse inside the mountain, the water flows below the dam will be reduced to 866 cubic feet per second, or only 12% of the amount of water flowing in the river prior to the construction of the dam.

It is almost impossible to understand how much water is represented by water equivalent to the 6,541 cubic feet per second which would disappear from the river if the KCP were allowed to proceed. But, if you visualize a room 10-feet high by 10-feet wide by 10-feet long, that is 1,000 cubic feet of room or, if you could fill it with water, 1,000 cubic feet of water. So before the Kenney Dam was built there were was the equivalent of almost seven rooms that size filled with water rushing through the canyon every second. If the project were to proceed, there would be less than one room that size filled with water left flowing through the river every second. In other words, the equivalent of 6.5-1,000 cubic foot rooms filled with water would have disappeared from the river every second, 390 rooms that size every minute, 17,400 every hour and 417,600 every day would have been diverted into the reservoir. Instead of flowing eastward, as it has done for centuries, that water would then flow westward through Alcan's generators and down the Kemano River into the Pacific Ocean.

There is a sharp contrast between the pre-dam flows when water rampaged through the canyon and the present-day scene in the canyon which is described this way:

The dry river bed now only supports a small creek and deep rock

---

"I was eight years old when I moved with my family to Vanderhoof, and the Kenney Dam had just been built. The water of the Nechako River had been cut off.... The country was changing. I remember the Reinhard kids coming out for a visit and expressing amazement at the pitiful amount of water in the river. Having never known the natural Nechako, my sister and I didn't understand. It was a hot day and we ran splashing from one side of the river to the other, stopping occasionally to watch the fish that were trapped in pools, where previously deep water had run. We had never known the beautiful circle of lakes and their connecting rivers alive with fish. We didn't know what had been lost. Few people did. And in those days it was chalked up to the price or progress." *Naturalist June Wood, BCUCH 3.305.*

bound pools. Existing trail access into the canyon is steep and dangerous. The volcanic basalts and tuffs of the canyon surrounded by sheer rock walls have been sculptured by the incredible force of the huge volume and velocity of the water that once rampaged through the gorge. Towering pinnacles, caves, stone bridges and grottoes have been worn over thousands of years by the turbulent flows. There are convoluted areas of rock, sinkholes and water-filled potholes up to 3 metres deep, some with rounded rocks inside that have worn the holes with their ceaseless turning in a "mortar and pestle" effect. High overhanging cliffs and colossal boulders create an awe-inspiring effect. At the downstream end of the canyon where it widens into the Cheslatta outwash fan a large basin and former eddy of the original river known as the Devil's Punchbowl forms a steep-walled lake where a rock island marks the entrance to the mouth of the canyon. A 25 cm. wide vein of attractive jasper agate occurs in the canyon and lignite, a brownish-black coal in which the texture of the original wood is distinct, can also be found. Large gypsum crystals are found in the canyon wall near the mouth.[14]

Six miles below the dam, Cheslatta Falls drops 60 feet into the Nechako river bed. The force of the falling water has created a giant charge pool at the base of the falls.

The original waterfall was created by the water flowing down Murray Creek. But the volume of water cascading down into the river was increased 25 to 46 times its natural flows when Alcan

---

"I don't see how dollar signs can be put on our river. I live near the river. I have swam in the river, fished in the river, canoed on the river, tubed on the river, along with many other people, and I believed that I would continue to do so for quite some time in the future but now with [the] Kemano Completion Project my river seems to be in jeopardy." *Nechako Valley resident Carl Derksen, BCUCH 4.520.*

"When the water went down, all the hollows of the river bed trapped many fish in stagnant pools of water. We had a lot of fun swimming in these little lakes because they weren't very deep, and the water was just a bit cooler than bath water. As the days went on and the water got even warmer, we were appalled at what was happening to all the fish. Trapped in these stagnant, warm water pools they became so lethargic that one of my friends was actually able to catch one with his bare hands. It hardly moved and pieces of flesh were missing. No doubt all those fish perished." *Barbara Klassen, BCUCH 7.1146.*

began releasing water through the Skins Lake Spillway, 47 miles to the west.[15]

Tons of debris have been dumped into the river during periods when large amounts of water were being released through the spillway. A particularly damaging spill occured in 1961 when the river broke through an upstream barrier, creating a new channel, by-passing Cheslatta Falls. The silt and debris torn out of the hillsides along the Murray-Cheslatta system by these floods were all carried down the Nechako River where it settled over salmon spawning grounds affecting the river's fish-carrying capacity.

Downstream from Cheslatta Falls the Nadleh Whut'en Band has watched helplessly as the flows in the Nautley River changed in response to the changing water level in the Nechako River. As the water level dropped in the Nechako, the Nautley began flowing faster, cutting into the banks surrounding the river. Today, when the Nechako River is low, so is the Nautley, and water conditions have deteriorated to the point where migrating salmon have difficulty making their way into the Nautley and into Fraser Lake beyond. By 1993 there were so few fish in the river, the Nadleh Whut'en people were forced to buy their year's supply from the Gitksan people who fish in the still untouched Skeena River, hundreds of miles to the west.[16]

South of Fort Fraser, the once-mighty Nechako River is nearly stagnant and choked with weeds during the summer. The lower water levels and slower flows have allowed the weeds to encroach on the river's flow, hindering canoeing opportunities in the once-pristine river. Weeds are also encroaching on the waters of Fraser Lake. "I think you would have to see a bay infested with pond weed in mid-August to understand the seriousness of the situation. Acres of what should be clear water look like a soggy lawn, the weeds grow so thick and so close to the surface," reports one Fraser Lake property owner.[17]

Near Vanderhoof swimmers still congregate at the river for a cooling dip and floatplanes can still land on the river. But, by 1993, the summer flows in the river were so low the BC government was no longer issuing water licences to farmers wishing to withdraw water from the river to irrigate their fields.

When Alcan began reducing the water flows in the river, the

islands on which as many as 63,000 Canada geese once rested, well-protected from predators by the swift water flowing on either side, are now easily reached from the shore, making the geese easy prey for wild animals, domestic dogs and people. Annual student counts of the geese using the sanctuary between 1985 and 1991 dropped from 7,500 to 3,300.[18]

Charles Colville purchased a farm beside the Isle Pierre ferry landing in 1960 and operated the ferry there from 1975 until the service was discontinued in 1982, when the lower water flows made it impossible for the loading ramps to reach far enough into the river to permit vehicles to board the ferry. "By then the water was pretty skimpy," he said during a 1993 interview in Prince George.

> There was a rock near the shore that we used to hang up on when the water was low. By the time we pulled the ferry out of the water, that rock was standing right out of the water. As the water got lower we lengthened the ramps and, in the end they weren't long enough.
>
> There was lots of water when we first went there. In the spring we had to really watch the kids because the current was very strong close to the shore. I tell people there was enough water then so whenever we went fishing we could drive up the left side of the river in a boat. Now there's hardly enough water at any time to do that.

Too much water, not too little water, has caused different environmental problems at the western end of the project. This is where all the water which once flowed eastward into the Nechako River has been turned around and is now flowing westward through the Kemano powerplant tailrace and into the Kemano River. In the 22 years between 1956 and 1978, the amount of

---

"In layman's language what he's saying is, the weeds are there and getting worse and the lower water levels of Kemano Completion haven't started yet." *Nechako Valley resident Bob Mumford, BCUCH 4.504-05.*

"There are now only a few remaining people who knew the Nechako as a free-running, unfettered stream, connecting the stable flow of water from the snows of the Coast Range to the Fraser River system. Now it is merely a creek in comparison to is original condition." *Vanderhoof pioneer Dr. Al. Mooney, BCUCH 3.380.*

water flowing in the Kemano River more than doubled.[19] These higher water flows resulted in a straightening of the river's main channel and increased the river's width by 60%. The higher waters caused flooding of adjacent lands and increased the length of the river's side channels by 250%.[20]

The river contains five species of Pacific salmon and a large population of eulachon, the fish that were the basis of the rich culture of generations First Nations people living in that area: They used this oily fish for food and rendered them into rich oil which they traded with other First Nations people living further away from the ocean. After the initial impact of the increased water flows, the concurrent increase in the length of the river's side channels appears to have improved the spawning and rearing environment for pink and chum salmon. As a result, the number of spawning pink salmon returning to the river since 1960 has increased 184% to an average of 106,000 fish, and the number of spawning chum salmon has increased 100% to an average of 40,000 fish.[21] The eulachons, coho and chinook have not fared so well since the riverbed has been changed, becoming a deeper, wider, straighter course that has eliminated the salmon spawning grounds. Native leaders report the catches of eulachons have significantly declined since Alcan began releasing more water into the Kemano River.

These recreational, fishery and irrigation issues were not taken into consideration when Alcan received its water licence in 1950 and began construction of Kemano I.

Unpleasant Diversions

[In] 1979 Alcan ran headlong into a generation that viewed both the past and the future differently than a generation that had applauded newsreels of the Kitimat Kemano project taking shape. This was a major clash in understanding.[1]

When Alcan announced its original plans to divert the Nechako River in the 1950s, few Canadians understood the long-term cost of the lost recreation and fishery potential such an industrial development would entail. Canada had entered an era when Big Industry was King. Northern-Interior BC residents were no different from other BC residents in their inability to envision the time, 30 years later, when environmentally-concerned citizens would battle industrialists over who had the right to control the last of the province's seemingly inexhaustible forest and water resources.

Prior to 1950 there was so little concern about the province's natural resources that only short-term and incomplete records are available for the amount of water then flowing in the Nechako River or, indeed, for the amount flowing in most BC rivers. These incomplete records make it difficult to determine, in anything resembling a precise way, the consequences the Kenney Dam had

---

"Alcan is a multi-national company, in the business to make money, it is the governments, federal [and] provincial and to some extent municipal, who have gotten us into this bind. It is the voting public that let this happen." *Vanderhoof resident Audrey L'Heureux, BCUCH 3.327.*

on the water flows in the Nechako.

It *is* known, however, that when the Kenney Dam was completed in October, 1952, the riverbed between it and the Nautley River virtually dried up. Ninety-eight per cent of the river's estimated mean annual flow of 7,407 cubic feet per second below the Cheslatta Falls was diverted into the reservoir until it was full. Only then was more water released into the river.[2]

That meant 627 million cubic feet of water were missing from the river every day.

No matter how you portray it, 627 million cubic feet of water per day is a lot of water. And the amount of water missing from the river becomes even more staggering when you multiply the daily loss of 627 million cubic feet by 365 to arrive at a figure of more than 228.9 billion cubic feet as the amount of water no longer flowing through the canyon on the upper Nechako during 1952.

The project had been reviewed by the federal Department of Fisheries and Oceans (DFO) and the International Pacific Salmon Fisheries Commission prior to the construction of the dam. They recommended changes in the original design of the Kemano I Project to ensure there would be adequate water flows in the section of the river between the dam and the Nautley River, and that the water temperatures be kept low enough to protect the spawning chinook. Their recommendations were ignored. Between 1952 and 1957, when all the water was being diverted to fill the reservoir, the only water being released into the upper Nechako came from the dam on Murray Lake. Water levels were so low many chinook spawning redds were left high and dry and the salmon using that section of the river as their spawning ground virtually disappeared.[3] In fact, the amount of water required to protect both the migrating salmon and the fish living in the river year round were not mentioned in the water licence issued to Alcan in the 1950s.

"This project would not be allowed to happen if it was in the backyards of the residents of the Lower Mainland, and I want you to think about that, and think about damming up the Fraser and know how you would feel if this was happening in your home." *Vanderhoof resident Glenda Olson, BCUCH 4.522.*

120

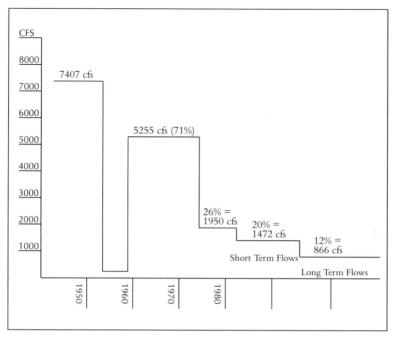

Average flows at Cheslatta Falls, showing the decline in water flows in the upper Nechako since 1950. Chart reproduced with permission from *Water Exports: Should Canada's Water Be for Sale?*

Better records are available for the changes in the river's water flow since 1957, when 71% of the water was again flowing into the river below Cheslatta Falls.[4] By 1980, the amount flowing into the river at that point was 26% of its pre-dam flows. The flow was reduced to 20% of its pre-dam flows in 1987, and by then plans were being developed to reduce the amount flowing in the upper Nechako to 12%—or 866 cubic feet per second—of the amount flowing there before the dam was built.

What puzzles today's more environmentally-aware residents of the Nechako River Valley is how few people, during the 1950s to mid-70s, expressed any concern about what was happening to the flow in the river that was so vitally important to the geography and ecology of the area. To understand their environmental nonchalance one needs to know about the recurrent boom-and-bust cycles that shaped the twentieth-century economic history of the

121

region.

The first industrial boom in the Nechako River Valley followed the signing of an agreement in July, 1903, between the Grand Trunk Pacific Railway Company and the federal government, opening the door for the construction of a railway from Winnipeg through the Nechako River Valley to the port of Prince Rupert. It was an age of rapid railroad expansion throughout Canada, and there were rumours circulating that as many as 19 railways would criss-cross the valley at the junction of the Nechako and Fraser Rivers. The population of non-natives living in the valley soared. Among the new arrivals were speculators looking for cheap land, farmers drawn to the area by promises it would become the second Garden of Eden, men looking for work on the railway and people who were just naturally drawn to new settlements.

The outbreak of World War One brought an end to this first construction boom in the Nechako River Valley. Gone were the fast-talking developers who claimed Prince George would rival Winnipeg and Chicago as a transportation hub serving a territory one-third the size of Europe. People who had sunk all their savings into land along the railway either left, or hung on, hoping for better times. Pioneer Prince George resident, Charles Olds Sr., described the deserted scene on Prince George's previously bustling main street after the construction workers and most of the city's male population had left to join the army:

> I remember sitting on the sidewalk in Prince George with my brother-in-law who had a drugstore at that time. That's all he had, just a drugstore and no customers. None. We sat on the sidewalk eating chocolates out of his store. There was absolutely no sign of life, not a man or a chicken or anything on the whole street which is now Third Avenue.[5]

Following the Armistice in 1918, the people who remained in the valley endured a major economic depression and 35 years of hardship, eking out a living by working on the railway, in the boom-and-bust forest industry, on small farms or as workers, or owners of small businesses. The depression that preceded World War Two was particularly hard on the region's already fragile economy. Sawmills closed, forcing hundreds of men into relief camps. At the height of the depression, Prince George's city council was reported to be spending $900 to $1,000 a week providing relief to people who received 40¢ a day for food and 25¢ a day for a place to sleep.[6]

The stagnant economy persisted in the valley until the demand for lumber increased with the outbreak of the Second World War, when sawmilling was declared an essential industry. When the war ended, the headsaws continued to spin in the thousands of small mills located throughout the Nechako River Valley, turning out the lumber required for rebuilding Europe's bomb-ravaged cities and for constructing new homes for the returning Canadian and American servicemen.

It was during these years that Prince George and the surrounding region earned the well-deserved reputation of being a hard-working, hard-drinking town. The booming lumber industry had drawn large numbers of husky, young loggers into the area who quickly found jobs in the hundreds of small sawmills that dotted the evergreen forests surrounding the city. When their week's work was done, they crowded into town where they filled the beer parlours and blew away much of their hard-earned money on beer, hard liquor and any other form of entertainment they could find. A Saturday night in downtown Prince George in those days was usually a pretty wild time, featuring frequent drunken brawls. Then the loggers went back out into the bush to begin another week's work. Ample testimony of the tough working conditions in those early bush mills can be found in the newspaper reports of yet another logger's death due to being crushed by lumber falling off trucks, "widow makers" crashing down on them in the woods or trucks going out of control on icy bush roads. Few of those old-time loggers escaped without losing at least one finger, and sometimes a foot or a hand, to the unprotected headsaws used in those mills.

Historian Bruce Hutchison gives an account of a visit to Prince George during the late 1940s:

[I]t still retains, in its broad streets of the land boom, its false store fronts, its insatiable ambition, a reckless, pioneer character of its people, the look and the feeling of the frontier, not to be found anywhere else in B.C. This, after all, is the gateway of the north and the north is the only frontier left in America.7

During the 1950s and early '60s the Nechako River Valley certainly was a pioneer area and, as such, attracted young people seeking to make their fortune. The result was that by 1961, 70% of the residents of the region were under the age of 35, compared with the 57% in that age group provincially.[8] Even in the best of times, the lumber industry suffers from boom-and-bust cycles. During the 1950s, when the industry was in the hands of small operators and the union's influence was limited, the cyclical nature of the industry resulted in continued uncertainty for the economies of the communities along the Nechako River. When the region's sawmills were closed, either by a downturn in the market or a strike, business died and everyone suffered.

The promise of economic security finally arrived in the valley with the industrial boom which began with Alcan's mega-project in the 1950s, and continued with the construction of three pulp mills in Prince George during the '60s. It also brought another flood of new residents to the area: In the 10 years following 1951, the population of Prince George increased by 195% and the population of Vanderhoof increased by 127%.[9]

When these newcomers looked at the Nechako River, they were unaware that a large amount of water had already been diverted from the river. In time, most of the long-time residents remaining in the valley also became accustomed to the river's reduced flow. They forgot that Alcan's licence enabled the company to remove even more of the water from the river and from the upper reaches of the Skeena system, another major BC salmon-bearing river system.

The confusion among local residents was heightened by Alcan's referring to the river's altered, post-dam flows as the "natural," "historic" or "existing" flows—a misleading terminology that continues to this day. Thus, whenever the company says the completion of the Kemano project will reduce existing flows in the Nechako by 29% in Vanderhoof and by 57% in the upper part of the river, these percentages apply to the current flows in the Nechako and disregard the water that had been diverted since the early 1950s.

This distortion has not gone unnoticed. In his critique of Alcan's baseline environmental studies, biologist Grant Hazelwood states:

The use of the word "natural" in Volume 2 (Appendices 2.1) to describe the state of the Nechako River from 1954 on, after the Kemano I alterations, is indeed straining the readers' credulity. The river prior to work in 1948 was natural. After that date, it was controlled and no longer reacted directly to environmental changes within its upper basin.[10]

Alcan uses a curious curve of logic to defend its position: The company says their 1987 proposals will change what is there today "but it will have no effect on what hasn't been there for more than 40 years." Alcan's BC vice-president Bill Rich says that

> Kemano I has been in operation since the early 1950s. Northern communities have prospered as a result of Alcan's presence in Kitimat. There has been continued growth in population, agriculture and other industrial and economic activities through the Nechako Valley. Salmon stocks have been maintained and, in fact are increasing, and none of this has been impeded by the Nechako River as it exists today.[11]

But people who were familiar with the river prior to the construction of the dam are troubled by their memories of the deeper, stronger currents that once flowed there. When asked, they can point to where those flows had left high-water marks on the piers of the older bridges crossing the river and on the remnants of the higher banks that once marked the river's edge during peak flows.

In retrospect, although Vanderhoof residents continued to use their portion of the river for swimming, boating, fishing and other recreational activities, the residents of the booming city of Prince George appeared to turn their back on the Nechako and Fraser Rivers. Access to the Nechako was blocked by the numerous small sawmills and planermills built along the river's southern shore during the 1940s and '50s. Over each mill towered a conical beehive wood-waste burner belching out a steady stream of smoke and fly ash over the city. No one complained when the city built a water-pumping station in the small clearing near the cutbanks where young people had traditionally gathered to swim in the Nechako,

---

"We are now paying a heavy environmental price for the fact that our ancestors viewed unmodified nature as chaos, something to be 'tamed'...."
John Gray, *Lost in North America*, 132.

and by the 1950s, the Nechako and Fraser Rivers were no longer considered safe places to swim. To ensure the safety of swimmers, the city built its first swimming pool soon after the dam was constructed. So, the next generation of young people gathered on the grassy slopes near the new outdoor pool, thus forgetting about the natural beauty of the two rivers that were such a major feature of the city.

For decades after the Kenney Dam's completion, the First Nations people were the only Nechako Valley residents who knew something drastic was happening to the millions of sockeye swimming up the Fraser into the Nechako on their way to their spawning grounds along the Nechako, Stuart and Nautley Rivers. The Carrier Nation had always relied on the river both as a transportation system and as the provider of a major food source, so they realized sooner than others that there were fewer big chinook coming into the upper Nechako to spawn. The dam and the sudden surges of water from behind the Skins Lake Spillway had detrimental effects on their lives right from the start. But although they were the first to speak up during the 1970s and '80s about the environmental damage already inflicted on the region, few natives spoke out about what happened to them during the two decades immediately following the construction of the dam.

Why?

To answer that question one has only to look at their history. The Cheslatta People were not the only First Nations people affected by Alcan's activities in the region. Like First Nations across Canada, the Carrier Nations living in the Nechako River Valley had been confined to small reserves a fraction of the size of their traditional territories. Their numbers were soon decimated by European diseases—such as measles, smallpox and influenza—against which they had developed no immunity. With their population dwindling and their leaders having died or having lost their way, the First Nations people found it difficult to adapt to this new lifestyle—brought on by the onslaught of European culture,

"To develop a frontier land like this, you have to rearrange the landscape. Development inevitably changes the landscape." *Bill Rich, National Geographic (July, 1986), 63.*

religion, industry and diseases—that had replaced their once strong and self-sufficient way of life. These intrusions into their territory curtailed their traditional methods of hunting and gathering their food from the land as they had done for generations upon generations in the past. Their traditional close family and communal life was destroyed when their children were taken away to be educated in non-native ways—and concurrently mistreated and abused—in church-run schools. The effect of the residential schools upon the already shattered communities was rampant social problems—alcoholism, abuse, suicide—resulting in the neutralization or death of most of their young leaders who would have been those to speak out when Alcan began removing water from the Nechako River, flooding the valleys in the river's upper reaches and sending the water rushing into the Kemano River to the east.

And again, no one spoke out in the 1960s when the company began veering from its originally stated purpose of generating cheap hydroelectric power to smelt aluminum at Kitimat and, instead, began selling hydroelectricity to the province's publicly-owned power corporation, BC Hydro. The company's move into the lucrative hydro business began when BC Hydro constructed a powerline to deliver Alcan's excess power from Kitimat to the growing community of Terrace.[12] By 1966 Alcan had a contract with Hydro requiring that the company deliver an uninterrupted supply of electricity into the region's power grid to be sold to residential, commercial and industrial users. Within two years the Crown corporation had constructed powerlines to deliver electricity from Alcan's Kitimat plant through Terrace to Prince Rupert, and another line from Terrace up the Nass River Valley to deliver power to Kitsault, where a mining company was setting up a molybdenum mine.[13] The province was pleased with the power-purchase arrangement with Alcan because it allowed BC Hydro to delay for 10 years the need to spend more than $100 million to improve its power transmission system between Prince George and Smithers, and to extend the system from Smithers to Terrace.[14]

Alcan's involvement in the power generating business took a big leap forward in 1978, when BC Hydro extended the provincial powerlines into Terrace, so that power generated at Alcan's Kemano plant began flowing into BC's power grid, which is also linked into the North American power grid. By 1980, the company was racking up power sales to Hydro worth approximately $1 million a month.[15] Valley residents started to pay attention when, in 1979, in order to generate the additional power it was now selling to Hydro, Alcan began diverting more water into its reservoir. In November, 1979, the amount of water being released through the Skins Lake Spillway dropped to 399 cubic feet per second. Even more water was diverted during 1980.[16] This increased diversion of water coincided with two years in which the amount of water flowing into the reservoir was lower than usual. Alcan was obviously taking its new role as a privately-owned power utility very seriously.

During an emotional, four-hour protest meeting held in the community on February 14, 1980, the residents of Vanderhoof vented their outrage against Alcan's plans to increase its hydro-electric generating capacity by diverting more water from the Nechako. That evening, more than 600 people crowded into the auditorium of Nechako Secondary School where they lambasted their MLA, Socred Jack Kempf, and his attempts to convince them of the economic benefits of the company's plans.[17] Over the crowd's shouts of outrage, Kempf refused to agree with their demands that he oppose the project because, he said, the province needed the development to create jobs. To pacify the crowd, he assured them a full public inquiry into the project would be held with "a complete opportunity for public input"[18] as required by government policy. The demands and cries of disbelief heard from opponents of the project during that heated, rancorous 1980 meeting were repeated frequently over the next 13 years before any such hearing was ever held on the project.

Among the most vocal opponents were First Nations' people from the nearby Stoney Creek Band, one of whom described the damage already done to the river valley to be "Like devastation only equalled by the dropping of an atomic bomb."[19] Another band member wanted the company to go away and leave them and their

---

"Question: When is a river not a river?
Answer: When it runs backward like the damned Nechako." *National Geographic* (July, 1986), 62.

land alone. "So much has been done in the past to the Indian people there is little left to take—but it looks like they are coming for the last of our valuables," said Stoney Creek elder Sophie Thomas. "You call it progress but Alcan—you can take your millions and billions and destroy someone else's valleys and rivers."

A warning letter, from respected pioneer physician and Vanderhoof civic leader Dr. A.W. "Al" Mooney, was read at the meeting, urging Alcan and BC Hydro to listen to what the people were saying if they wished to "avoid violence that is bound to occur" otherwise. Dave Merz, a spokesman for the Nechako Valley Regional Cattlemen's Association predicted millions of dollars in agriculture output would be lost in the valley if the river dried up and the region's water table dropped.

"How can you put a value on a river?" asked conservationist, Jan Erasmus. "It is so much easier to put a value on industrial benefits." Erasmus also decried the eventual loss of the hauntingly beautiful sound of migrating geese returning to the bird sanctuary at the northern edge of the village, should the water disappear from the river. "We will have to take down our Vanderhoof Canada goose that is a symbol of the community," she said. Others spoke about their fears that their once-beautiful river would be replaced by an "ugly scar of a gravel pit."[20]

Pro-Alcan support in Vanderhoof grew after Alcan announced it was planning three new smelters in BC, the first of which would be built in Vanderhoof. Once again the prospect of a big industry moving into an area and providing hundreds of well-paid jobs lured civic leaders and other residents of Vanderhoof into supporting Alcan's development plans. Before long, the once-quiet community had been split into pro- and anti-Alcan factions.

The controversy cooled off later in 1980, when the DFO finally became concerned about the decreased water flow in the Nechako. By July, 1980, two years of lower water flows and hot, dry summers had raised the temperature of the water in the Nechako above the level the DFO considered safe for the millions

---

"[T]here's no more scouring flows with the ice that would scour the gravel bars so we'll never again have 63,000 geese here." *Vanderhoof resident Peter Rodseth, BCUCH 44.447.*

of sockeye moving into the river. Since migrating salmon stop eating when they leave the ocean, by the time the sockeye reached the Nechako—after their more than 400-mile swim up the Fraser, and before moving on to their spawning grounds on the streams flowing into Stuart, Trembleur and Takla Lakes—their energy reserves were nearly depleted. The Nechako's lowered level and higher temperature could only further exhaust the fish. When the federal government sought to force Alcan to release more water from its reservoir to protect the migrating salmon, the move set off what was to become a long-running constitutional battle over who has the right to control the water flows in the river: Alcan, the BC government or the federal government. That question has not been resolved to this day.

Until that fundamental question is answered, the BC government's January, 1995, announcement that the KCP was cancelled carries little weight, because it is unclear whether or not the federal government or the provincial government can halt the project.

On the same day he announced the project's cancellation, Premier Harcourt wrote to Prime Minister Chretien advising him that "The first step necessary to terminate the Project is for the Minister of Fisheries and Oceans Canada [Brian Tobin] to withdraw the 1987 opinion letter establishing water flows associated with the project."[21] He also stated that the province had decided, on the basis of the BCUC's findings, that the water levels set out in the 1987 Settlement Agreement were insufficient "to maintain and protect fish stocks, particularly Chinook and Sockeye Salmon."[22] Eight years earlier, however, the federal fisheries minister of the time, Tom Siddon, advised Alcan president David

---

"Then what happened is Alcan drove a wedge into the community with this carrot-on-the stick approach with the smelter. And it sort of divided the community. And finally it gets to the point when you're in these type of groups where the wife says why do you have to do all this stuff? Why do you have to go to all of these meetings?.... And I guess you come up with some archaic word like 'duty' or you keep hearing phrases in the back of your mind, clichés perhaps, but they say, all that is needed for evil to exist is for good people to remain silent. And after a while you just want to walk away from it, but you can't because it's sort of like turning your back on a rape in progress." *Vanderhoof resident Craig Hooper, BCUCH 3.363-64.*

Morton that he was satisfied that the remedial measures agreed to by the Strangway working group would ensure the fish and the eggs they deposited in the Nechako River redds could be protected, "with an acceptable level of certainty," within Alcan's proposed flows.[23]

Since the federal government has the responsibility of protecting migrating salmon, and the report prepared by the BCUC recommended that the flows in the river must be increased to protect the fish, the federal government has "the primary responsibility for compensating Alcan, should any compensation be required," Harcourt advised Chretien.

Fisheries Minister Tobin's response to Harcourt's statement was to maintain that the BC government—*not* the federal government—is responsible for compensating Alcan, as it was the *provincial* government that signed the 1950 agreements that gave the company the rights to all the water from the upper Nechako River.

These shots between the provincial and federal camps were but the latest salvo in what has been a 15-year-long dispute over whose responsibility it is to control the amount of water flowing in the Nechako. The first charge in the battle began on June 16, 1980, when Federal Fisheries Minister Romeo LeBlanc—who in 1995 was sworn in as Canada's Governor General—ordered Alcan to increase the amount of water it was releasing into the river from 500 to 1,000 cubic feet per second by July 1, 1980. The increased water flows were the amount researchers determined necessary to maintain levels deep and cool enough to ensure the survival of the salmon migrating to their spawning grounds, of their eggs and of the fry hatching from those eggs.

Alcan did not comply to the federal order, but did increase the flows released into the river to 800 cubic feet per second, in response to an order from the provincial water rights comptroller issued June 27, 1980. Eight hundred cubic feet per second, Alcan said, was the amount its researchers had determined necessary to protect the fish. Alcan's actions caused NDP Environment Critic Jim Fulton (MP Skeena) to rise in the House of Commons and level a charge that, by refusing to comply with the fisheries minister's order, Alcan was pushing the minister around and, by failing to enforce his order, the fisheries minister was indicating that Alcan could dictate the water flows in the Nechako River.[24] By this time, Alcan was selling 20% of its hydroelectric production to BC Hydro and there were fears the company planned to expand its electricity sales in the province to supplement its declining aluminum-smelting revenues.

Within days of Fulton's comments, Graham Lea (NDP MLA for Skeena) raised the question, in the BC legislature, of Alcan's contract to sell power to BC Hydro. He said he had learned that Hydro had already obtained the rights-of-way for the powerlines to transport Kemano-produced power to Burns Lake.[25]

Soon community-based environmental groups entered into the fray.

The Terrace-based Skeena Protection Coalition said it was considering legal action against Alcan, claiming that the water being released through the Skins Lake Spillway into the Nechako was insufficient to protect the salmon.[26] Louise Kaneen, president of the Vanderhoof-based Nechako Neyenkut Society sent a telegram to LeBlanc demanding he take immediate action to protect the salmon moving into the river by enforcing his order that Alcan increase the amount of water being spilled into the Nechako River to 1,000 cubic feet per second.[27]

Alcan had also indicated it intended to more than double its aluminum smelting capacity in BC from 240,000 tonnes to 582,000 tonnes per year. To obtain the large amount of hydroelectricity required for this project, however, Alcan needed to expand. The company announced that its plans—the KCP—included expanding the capacity of its Kemano hydroelectric plant, diverting the remaining water from the Nechako River and diverting the water from the upper Skeena River into its Nechako Reservoir. At the time, the company was utilizing only 50% of the water allocated to it under the water licence issued in 1950—a licence that also gave Alcan the water rights over the Nanika-Kidprice water system which flows into the Skeena River and which had not yet been developed. The company now planned to utilize the water from the upper Skeena River system by building a dam near the outlet of Nanika Lake, then diverting this water into the reservoir through a short tunnel.

The announcement of these plans sparked even more protest. It spread to Prince George, where a group called Save the Nechako had begun distributing "Stop Kemano" bumper stickers and gathering signatures on a petition opposing plans to proceed with the Kemano Completion Project.[28]

In Ottawa, former Environment Minister John Fraser, the MP for Vancouver South, told a July 22, 1980, meeting of the Common's fisheries committee about Alcan's "rape of Interior B.C.," and demanded the Trudeau government hold public hearings into the project as had been promised by the former Conservative government led by Joe Clark.[29] He also pointed to Alcan's attempts to "soften up the public" to accept its new project by conducting public relations campaigns in communities the project affected.[30]

LeBlanc responded on July 25, 1980 by ordering Alcan to increase—immediately—the amount of water it was spilling from behind the dam through the Skins Lake Spillway to 8,000 cubic feet per second and, unless the weather cooled, to maintain that flow until August 20. The company responded by increasing the flow through the spillway to 7,000 cubic feet per second.[31] After August 20, Wally Johnson, director of fisheries for BC, said that Alcan might be permitted to reduce the water releases through the spillway to 1,100 cubic feet per second by September 1, and maintain that flow until March 31, 1981. By April 10, 1981 the company would be required to increase the flow to 2,000 cubic feet per second and maintain that flow until June 30, to provide the water flows and the temperatures required to rear the young chinook in the river.[32]

Those figures are important: They are significantly more than the flows the DFO agreed—seven years later—were required to protect the salmon.

The jubilation among federal fisheries ministry officials upon Alcan's releasing 7,000 cubic feet per second into the Nechako River was short-lived. Four days after the flows were increased, Alcan turned the water tap off again. Brian Hemingway, public relations spokesman for the company, said the decision to increase the water flow had been based on earlier weather forecasts: New revised forecasts for the Vanderhoof-Prince George area indicated that the heat wave was ending and temperatures were expected to drop to below normal. On the basis of this forecast, Alcan had concluded that the larger, cooling water flows were no longer required, and thus had reduced the water flow through the spillway to 600 cubic feet per second—less than 8% of the amount Fisheries Minister LeBlanc had ordered the company to release.[33]

LeBlanc responded to Alcan's action by saying that if Alcan did not comply with his order to release 8,000 cubic feet per second into the river by the next day (July 29) he would seek an injunction forcing the company to comply with his order.

That's exactly what LeBlanc did. Mr. Justice Thomas Berger of the BC Supreme Court heard the case.

Alcan claimed that *it* was the sole judge of what the water levels should be in the river because it operated the Nechako Reservoir under a water licence obtained from the province of BC in 1950, and therefore was not subject to the orders of the federal government. The DFO claimed it was meeting its responsibility for protecting migrating and resident salmon when it issued the water release order under Section 20(10) of the federal Fisheries Act. The province of BC intervened in these legal proceedings in order to protect its constitutional authority to manage its water resources. The applications for intervener status filed on behalf of the Rivers Defence Coalition[34] and the Carrier Sekani Tribal Council,[35] however, were denied on the grounds the proceedings dealt with constitutional issues.

Alcan's lawyer, Douglas Brown, argued that the temperatures in the Nechako River had cooled since the order was issued and no longer posed a threat to the health of the fish; therefore the release of 8,000 cubic feet of water per second through the Skins Lake Spillway was no longer required. The higher flows demanded by the minister were, in fact, a waste of water, he said, and could result in a serious lowering of the reservoir, which could mean a loss of production and layoffs at Alcan's Kitimat smelter. BC's water comptroller Howard DeBeck agreed, saying a requirement that Alcan dump any more than 500 cubic feet of water per second into the Nechako River "would be cutting into the water bankroll necessary to run the generators feeding its electricity-gobbling Kitimat smelter."[36]

134

Mr. Justice Thomas Berger disagreed. In an eight-page judgement he determined the federal government had the right under the Fisheries Act to order Alcan to release the water: "Alcan has not flouted the law," the judge wrote. "It has simply said, on legal advice, that it believes the minister's order is unconstitutional. I have reached the conclusion, however, that Alcan must obey.... [T]here will be an order directing Alcan to comply with the minister's directive."[37]

Berger said that because the federal minister represents the public's interest, the power to protect the public's resources should ultimately be his. This portion of his judgement lends some credence to the BC government's 1995 statements that the federal government is responsible for compensating Alcan for any damages it is to be awarded resulting from the decision to cancel the project. Berger also advised the two parties to seek a negotiated settlement to the disagreement over the amount of water necessary to protect the salmon and their eggs. The BCUC has determined the amount of water required in the river is more than that set out in the Settlement Agreement.

This constitutional controversy revolves around the fact that water is considered *property* under the control of the provinces, and the federal government has *legislative* control over ocean-based fisheries and ocean fish that migrate inland. The debate "left federal fish squirming in provincial waters" said reporter Thomas Hopkins in the August 11, 1980, edition of *Maclean's*.

In other media, the *Prince George Citizen* editorially lauded the decision as setting a fair precedent,[38] while the editor of the *Vancouver Province* continued to worry if the Montreal-based aluminum giant had become "a law unto itself."[39]

Although the injunction was issued to protect migrating sockeye, it was later expanded to include the spawning and rearing requirements of the chinook. A technical committee was established in March, 1981, composed of representatives of the DFO, the Province of BC, Alcan, Envirocon and the International Pacific

---

"Mr Justice Berger also stated 'Alcan has not flouted the law, it has simply stated, on legal advice, that it believes the Minister's order is unconstitutional'." *Alcan's Bill Rich, BCUCH 11.1642.*

Salmon Fisheries Commission (IPSFC). The committee was supposed to improve the exchange of information about Alcan's activities on the Nechako River among the parties concerned. But, when it was disbanded in January, 1983, no agreement had been reached as to the safe amount of flows in the Nechako. A warning about the damage that would be caused to the rich Fraser River salmon fishery by any further reduction in Nechako water flows was issued during 1983 by the IPSFC.[40]

While the technical committee attempted to agree on the amount of water required to protect the fish, the flows outlined in the injunction were renewed annually until July 1985, when Alcan served notice it would not continue to provide the "injunction flows." Rather, it intended to return to the Supreme Court, seeking a permanent resolution to the jurisdictional and technical issues involved in determining who had the right to control the flows in the river. The trial date was set for March, 1987, and the DFO began preparing a countersuit supporting its power to force Alcan to release fish protection flows into the Nechako.

In January 1984, four years after promising to build a smelter and other industrial facilities in the northern part of the province—a promise that was either a public relations ploy aimed at gaining Nechako River Valley residents' support for their plans to remove more water from the river, or a business decision that was overtaken by a downturn in the world aluminum market—Alcan finally unveiled its plans to establish aluminum reduction plants in Northern BC. But, because of concerns about the environmental consequences of establishing three smelters in the region, the company had reduced its proposal to two smelters with a combined capacity of 370,000 tonnes per year. That same month it applied to the provincial government for an energy project certificate to enable it to begin constructing the facilities required to produce more electricity for the two new smelters it proposed to build.[41]

The first plant was to be built between Vanderhoof and Fort St. James in an area known as 12 Mile Hill, and would have a capacity of 171,000 tonnes. The second plant was to be built at another undetermined site in northwestern BC—when world demand warranted its construction. Alcan made it clear its proposal only made economic sense if both smelters were constructed.

Therefore, although its plans for the second plant were vague, the company told the government it would not proceed with its plans to expand its activities in BC by constructing the first plant in Vanderhoof unless it had received approval in principle from the government for the construction of the second plant. Alcan proposed to expand its hydroelectric generating capacity by using the remaining water available to it under the terms of the water licence given to it in 1950. That licence authorized Alcan to divert and store all the waters in the Nechako River upstream of Cheslatta Falls and all the waters of the Nanika River watershed upstream of Glacier Creek, approximately three miles below Kidprice Lake.[42] Diverting water from the Nanika-Kidprice system meant the company would be withdrawing water from the Bulkley-Skeena River system, another of BC's major salmon-spawning rivers. The 1984 KCP also included the construction of a dam at the outlet of Murray Lake to replace the Skins Lake Spillway as the facility through which water would be released back into the Nechako River.

Once again, the provincial government offered unquestioning support for Alcan's proposal.

Developing the remaining hydroelectric potential of Alcan's Kemano project had been suggested by the BC government as early as 1970. At that time the provincial government was becoming concerned about the increasing demand for electricity and instructed the BC Energy Board to develop a long-term plan for the province to meet future energy requirements. In its zeal to increase the province's hydroelectric production, the provincial government also proposed to add the water from two more systems—Dean River and Morice Lake—to increase the amount of water available for Alcan's generators at Kemano. Although the government appeared ready to expand Alcan's water licence to include this additional water, neither scheme was included in the final plans for the KCP.

The continued talk about diverting water from the upper Skeena River into Alcan's Nechako Reservoir caught the attention of the people living along the Bulkley and Skeena Rivers and led to the formation of yet another environmental group, Save the Bulkley. The group pointed out that the planned diversion of the

137

Nanika-Kidprice system into the Nechako River not only threatened the future of the rich salmon runs up the Skeena and Bulkley Rivers, it could also mean a transfer of diseases and parasites from the Skeena River into the Nechako and Kemano River systems which could seriously harm the fish in the reservoir and the two rivers. Their fears were supported by the research done by a scientist from the DFO. A discussion paper issued by the department in January, 1984, warns that combining water from the two river systems could also result in introducing unknown diseases, different strains of diseases and parasites found in the Nanika-Kidprice system into the Nechako and Kemano River systems. The discussion paper predicted there would be no easy solution to this problem, saying that: "Although Alcan have met the sampling requirement suggested by the Department to detect diseases and disease agents, it must be recognized that no amount of sampling and examination can give complete assurance of the absence of a given pathogen."[43]

The report concludes that although there is always a risk associated with transferring water from one water system to another, the risks to the fish populations in the case of the KCP are difficult to predict, and so if the project proceeds, the two systems should be monitored carefully.

In support of its proposal to withdraw the remaining water from the upper Nechako and Skeena Rivers, as outlined in the water licence they received in 1950, Alcan's consultants released a 13-volume baseline study of the project's environmental impacts in 1981.[44] This was followed, in 1984, by a 23-volume assessment[45] of how much water would be required to protect the salmon in the Nechako and Nanika-Bulkley River systems and what damage would be done to the Kemano River when the extra water was released into it after passing through Alcan's powerhouse at Kemano.

But Alcan's plans to increase its smelting capacity in BC were thwarted by world events. Aluminum prices were falling and, on October 26, 1984, the company announced it was putting its plans for expanding its aluminum operations in BC on hold. Business leaders pooh-poohed charges that the project had been cancelled. "Their decision is simply facing economic reality. The company is working to solve this problem and their efforts can be expected eventually to put KCP back on stream," said Dale McMann, of the Prince George Region Development Corp.[46]

Anti-KCP Vanderhoof alderman Louise Kaneen was pleased with the announcement. "I am glad they finally put their cards on the table," said Kaneen, who explained she had always doubted the company was serious about building the smelter. Instead, she said, they wanted to divert the water to increase their hydroelectric power production.

People were never willing to trade the river for a smelter.... I have always said they should clean up after Kemano I before they think about anything else. I still want a federal government inquiry into the present management [of the river] and I feel there is still a need for a diversion tunnel around the Kenney Dam.[47]

Skeena NDP MLA Frank Howard said the postponement gave everyone time to reconsider the project.

I have argued for a long time that Alcan, or somebody else, should move in the direction of further processing in this area using the aluminum already being produced here. Rather than added smelting facilities, we can't over emphasize the value-added aspect for our economy. I hope Alcan's decision to postpone its additional smelting capacity will allow them time to re-examine the question of manufacturing aluminum products in this area.[48]

Five days after plans for the smelter in Vanderhoof were postponed, Alcan's Bill Rich provided the reasons for the postponement to a group of businessmen in Vancouver: "The project was put on hold to give Alcan an opportunity to assess what is happening to the world-wide economy."[49] The price of aluminum on the world market had dropped to 40¢ per pound (US) from 70¢ per pound in one year.

Ten years later, there was still no sign of a smelter in Vanderhoof. But Alcan had spent half a billion dollars expanding its hydroelectric generating capacity and the people living in the valley began to suspect Louise Kaneen had been right all along: Alcan had never had a serious commitment to building a smelter there at all. The valley residents had suspicions that the company wanted to use the water from their river to generate more hydropower that it could sell back to them—or, worse yet—export to the United States.

An Issuance of Opinions

With the issuance of this opinion, it is my conviction that the objectives of your company and my department are met. On the one hand your company is provided with certainty with respect to the amount of natural inflow which it will be permitted to divert for power production purposes. This will allow your company to commit funds to the further expansion of its power works at Kemano. On the other hand, the water being provided in accordance with this opinion will ensure that there is sufficient flow in the Nechako River to provide an acceptable level of certainty for the protection of fish and ova therein.[1]

The legal tug-of-war over who has the right to control the water flows in the Nechako River that began in 1985 has continued into 1995.

The original trial date for settling the dispute over who had the right to control the amount of water flowing in the river was March, 1987. It was expected to last five weeks.

Alcan's environmental consultants, Envirocon, had already begun preparing baseline studies for the Kemano Completion Project in 1979, based on using all the water from the Nechako and Nanika-Kidprice to which it had obtained the rights under the terms of the provincial licence issued in 1950. In 1980, Alcan changed its approach and ordered Envirocon to investigate how much water would be required to protect the fish living in those watersheds.

In preparation for their appearance in court, teams of scientists—both Alcan's and the DFO's—were also seeking the answer to the question: "How much water is safe for the chinook, who spawn in the upper part of the river and live there all year, and the sockeye migrating through the river during July and August?" Predictably, the two groups of scientists came up with different answers: Alcan argued the salmon runs would not be damaged if the company diverted all but 12% of the pre-dam flows in the upper Nechako River, while the DFO thought the fish required a minimum of 30% of the pre-dam flows.

By 1984 only Alcan's environmental consultants had released their findings. When the first volumes of what was to be Envirocon's 23-volume environmental study were released,[2] the DFO set up a team of specialists to evaluate them. The discussion paper[3] based on their findings began and ended with warnings:

> This project proposal contains elements which make it of more vital concern to salmon than any other fish habitat question we are likely to encounter in the rest of this century.[4]

The paper concluded with a statement that sounded similar to the unheeded warnings issued by Fisheries biologists prior to the construction of Alcan's Kemano I project:

> [I]t is one thing to identify and describe a possible impact upon salmon habitat, but a very different matter to pre-determine its effects with accuracy. Regardless of which scenario, or variant thereof, is finally chosen, its impacts cannot be fully understood until after Kemano Completion. It is abundantly clear to the Department that, in the face of so much uncertainty and risk to the fisheries resources of Canada, the proponent [Alcan] will be expected to engage in considerable post-project assessment and monitoring.[5]

When, on March 3-4, 1984, federal fisheries representatives held a public meeting in Vanderhoof to discuss the project as outlined in their paper, they were surprised by the strong and reasoned opposition from Nechako Valley residents to plans to divert more water from their river, and by the weakness of the arguments in support of the project presented by Alcan. A representative of the DFO described the meeting:

> The opponents of Kemano Completion were more vocal and pro-

vided more plausible arguments to support their views. In contrast, the proponents of Kemano Completion tended to indicate, without supporting argument, that in their view salmon and aluminum production should both be achievable at maximum levels. It was further suggested that this happy outcome required only the removal of attitudes of confrontation, and collaboration between DFO and Alcan.[6]

Many of the more than 300 people who attended the two-day meeting were opposed to the federal government's proposal. They made it clear to the federal representatives they were not prepared to give up most of the water from their river so Alcan could generate the power it needed to smelt aluminum in a plant, costing $2-billion to $3-billion, that it proposed to build in Vanderhoof. There were many impassioned pleas made by residents on behalf of their river. "It may be progress for your people, but not for my people. My people live off the land. It is our way of life and we can't part with it," charged Sophie Thomas, an angry elder from the nearby Stoney Creek Indian Reserve.[7] Her booming voice reflected the despair her people had felt as they watched the decline in the salmon runs in the Nechako River following Kemano I.

Others objected to the benefits accruing to large businesses from the project. "This project benefits only those with incredible financial resources," said Vanderhoof resident Randy Kaneen, who was a member of the Vanderhoof-based environmental group, the Nechako Neyenkut Society, which was calling for a full federal inquiry into the proposed diversions. He was also critical of the activities of Alcan's public relations staff who were busy ingratiating themselves with community leaders in the Nechako River

---

"We don't want any more water talk, we don't want any more go to the States. We're not going to sign nothing, we don't want nobody to sign behind door being closed. We want everybody to know what goes on now, we don't want this kind of deal again like 1952, this kind of deal is not good." *First Nations elder Leah Patrick of Fort Fraser, BCUCH 2.235.*

"They want all the water. They want everything to themself, they don't care about other people, they don't care about what's going to happen to the people. It's the money they're looking after.... They don't have no pity for another person." *Nautley elder Margaret Nooski, BCUCH 2.243.*

Valley. He claimed the "advocacy advertisements" Alcan was placing in the local media, and its threats that it would abandon the project should the public find it unacceptable, had "interfered with a rational decision-making process."[8]

Kaneen's wife, Louise, who was an alderman in Vanderhoof, said it was the job of the DFO, not the people of the Nechako River Valley, to negotiate with Alcan to protect the salmon. "Alcan's water demands will ensure massive fish kills in the Nechako," she predicted.

An angry Bob Dahler, who had farmed beside the river for 20 years, told the hearing all water licence applications to irrigate farms had been put on hold until the resolution of the issue of the water flows in the Nechako. "If we lose the right to irrigate our land, then the Kemano project deserves to be thrown out completely," he said.[9]

By now it had also become apparent that Alcan's promises of a boom in local prosperity when the smelter was established in Vanderhoof, combined with a well-organized public relations campaign directed primarily at local politicians and businessmen, had deeply divided the residents of that community. On one side were the people who questioned the economic feasibility of building a smelter in Vanderhoof, doubted the river's environment could be preserved if it were built and feared that plans to remove more water from the Nechako would reduce their once beautiful river to a nearly stagnant stream. On the other side were local politicians and business leaders who wanted the jobs and prosperity a smelter promised to bring to Vanderhoof, and the Chamber of Commerce, who had suddenly become whole-hearted supporters of Alcan's project.

Opponents of the project, such as Vanderhoof resident Louise Burgener, claimed the aluminum smelter had been dangled before Vanderhoof politicians and business people like a carrot on a stick to persuade them to support the idea of trading the river for the commercial growth a smelter would bring. "Alcan's campaign to sway public opinion was wide-ranging. Donations were given to almost every conceivable project, a public relations officer was hired and given an office and a house in Vanderhoof. Local entrepreneurs began to speculate on land and machinery for the expected construction,"[10] Burgener said later.

There were also reports that community leaders were being lavishly entertained by Alcan—wined and dined in both in the Nechako River Valley and in Montreal, where they were flown to visit Alcan's headquarters and stayed at its guest house.

Supporters of the project now included politicians such as Fort St. James mayor Russell Gingrich, Vanderhoof mayor Len Fox, and business leaders, including Prince George Chamber of Commerce president Bob Tape, and Dale McMann of the Prince George Region Development Corporation.[11] Don Grantham,[12] a spokesman for the Vanderhoof Chamber of Commerce, saw the building of a smelter in that community as an opportunity to provide high-tech jobs and 15,000 man-years of work there. "That deserves a great deal of consideration," he said.[13] Jim Togyi of the Fort St. James Chamber of Commerce declared he now supported the project because "the future of the forest industry is limited and has reached its potential. Alcan's development would stabilize the economic base in the area."[14]

All the high hopes of Nechako Valley business and political leaders came crashing to the ground on October 26, 1984, when Alcan announced it was "postponing" the start of construction on the Vanderhoof smelter. The unstable world economy during the early 1980s and a precipitous drop in the world price of aluminum were the reasons given for the postponement.[15] What the company didn't admit was that the reason world aluminum prices were falling was that the six large vertically-integrated aluminum producers, including Alcan, who had been able to dominate the world market for the metal[16] were beginning to lose control of the price of aluminum. The threat to their control of aluminum prices began when a number of independent producers, who were not vertically-integrated, began selling their reduced-but-unmanufactured

---

"They made beggars out of our local elected representatives sitting by the roadside with their cups out while Alcan steals this resource from under our very noses. And why have they gone to so much trouble to steal it? Because it is very very valuable. As somebody pointed out each cubic metre per second of water that they can take out of this river and run it through the penstocks has an estimated hydro-electric value of 1.4 million dollars annually." *Vanderhoof resident Craig Hooper, BCUCH 3.369.*

aluminum through brokers on the London Metal Exchange and the Commodities Exchange in New York.[17] Many of these new producers, particularly those in Russia and Eastern Europe, were heavily subsidized by governments who were more concerned with maintaining production and employment than making profits for their shareholders.

Other valley residents applauded the delay in the project. Among them was Prince George labour leader, Ken Stahl, president of the Prince George and District Labour Council. "We are not against jobs, but a lot of people are not thinking beyond tomorrow," he said, "If it is going to damage the rivers, let's make sure it is a viable project."[18] Delaying the project gave everyone time to consider using the additional power to develop an aluminum manufacturing industry in the region, said Skeena NDP MLA Frank Howard.[19]

Although the construction of the Vanderhoof smelter had been postponed, the two sides continued preparing to go to court, seeking a settlement of their disagreement over the safety of the fish within Alcan's proposed waterflows.

And the federal government's scientists continued to warn the government about the potential dangers of the project. Their report, "Case Histories of Regulated Stream Flow and Its Effects on Salmonid Population," released in July, 1986, disputed Alcan's claim the KCP would result in no net loss of salmon in the Nechako, Nanika-Bulkley and Kemano River systems. On the contrary, the scientists predicted there would be a 90% reduction of the salmon runs in the Nechako River if the KCP went ahead as Alcan had proposed. Their conclusion was based on a study of the impact of water regulation on 81 rivers in North America, 29 of which had been subjected to diversions and water reductions similar to what Alcan was proposing for the Nechako. The study also concluded there would be a 95% reduction of the salmon runs in the Nanika-Bulkley River system and a 60% loss of salmon runs in the Kemano River.[20]

"Alcan's stock, like many resource issues, has been one of the high flyers on the stock market this year. Since early January, it has climbed from $26.16 to a high last week of $46.75." *Montreal Gazette, 22 July 1987.*

Later, Bruce Jenkins, spokesman for Alcan's new environmental consulting firm, Triton—which had been split off from Envirocon, the company responsible for Alcan's earlier environmental studies—argued that none of these studies was directly applicable to the Nechako River. The $20-million cold-water release structure to be built in the dam would enable them to improve water temperatures in the river by permitting the release of water at colder temperatures than was possible under the existing regime. Jenkins simply said the cold-water release system—combined with habitat improvements and the addition of nutrients to the river to increase the production of food for the fish—would improve the environment for the fish. When asked to cite studies proving that all this extra activity in the river would better its fisheries environment, Jenkins pointed to the Nechako River itself, indicating the way it had recovered during the 40 years since the construction of the dam. Fish are adaptable creatures, he said.[21]

Had they been more widely known, the conclusions reached by Simon Fraser University graduate student Juan Carlos Gomez Amaral in his 1986 Master's thesis would have added more evidence to support the position of the project's opponents. His study indicates that although the project's original industrial and social objectives of increasing employment opportunities and industrial development in the north had been met, the ongoing damage to the environment and the treatment of the Cheslatta people made the project unacceptable in the 1980s. Furthermore, Amaral concluded, the overbuilding of aluminum reduction capacity and the declining prices for aluminum had now rendered the project uneconomic. He also recommended that the original agreement be reviewed, to ensure the province received fair compensation for the water used, thereby avoiding charges by the United States that the province was subsidizing Alcan's low electrical production costs.[22]

Nechako Valley residents were also upset that the studies conducted by Envirocon, Triton, and the federal and provincial gov-

"None of the controversial testimony could be entered into the record. It had been rendered irrelevant by the deal that had been struck the previous evening by the Strangway Group." *Monte Olson, BCUCH 3.390.*

ernments were concerned only about the safety of the salmon using the river were less water to be released into the upper reaches of the river from behind the Kenney Dam. No consideration was given to the needs of others using the river water: farmers, freshwater fish, birds at the wild bird sanctuary, floatplane operators, and people who swam and boated in the river or used it for other forms of recreation.

At the request of the DFO, the March trial date was first postponed to May 25, then to September 1, 1987. Throughout the adjournments leading up to the scheduled opening of the trial, Carrier First Nations leaders claimed a deal was being worked out behind closed doors which would permit Alcan to reduce the flow of water in the Nechako River.[23] "Negotiating on a without-prejudice basis is part and parcel of the legal process," said lawyer Edward John, chief of the Carrier Sekani Tribal Council. "What we are saying is, if we are not going to be involved in a public process in this case, it should be decided in court, not by backroom deals."[24]

The trial finally got under way on September 1, 1987 and the two parties began introducing the evidence their scientists had collected during more than seven years spent studying the river.

A Canadian Press report of the opening days of the trial highlights the disagreement over the water flows required to ensure the safety of the fish:

> The federal government and the Aluminum Co. of Canada are at odds with nature, as well as each other in assessing the desirable waterflows in the Nechako River.
>
> The documents discussed Tuesday in the B.C. Supreme Court indicate that 35 years ago, before Alcan built dam on the river, the natural water flow at Cheslatta Falls during July and August was 10,000 cf/s.
>
> In a continuing suit before Justice Kenneth Lysyk, the federal fisheries minister seeks to set the minimum flow during the crucial sockeye migration months of summer at 8,000 cf/s.
>
> Alcan, whose water use license for the river dates back to 1952, dismisses that as excessive and says 6,000 cf/s in the summer is sufficient for the safety of the salmon.
>
> Both sides also disagree on the desirable flow rates during other

months with Alcan claiming the minister's requirement sometimes exceeds the original natural flow.

The B.C. government, as a third party in the suit, goes further than Alcan in challenging Ottawa.

Citing the Constitution Act, Victoria says the federal minister is exceeding his power in attempting to dictate the water flows in the river over which the province has jurisdiction.[25]

The court case was suddenly adjourned on September 14, 1987, when it was announced an out-of-court settlement—which later became known as the 1987 Settlement Agreement—had been reached during four days of in-camera meetings held in Vancouver August 20-23, 1987, led by University of BC president Dr. David Strangway.[26] None of the DFO scientists appointed to the task force evaluating the environmental impact of the proposed KCP attended these in-camera, Strangway-led meetings.[27] They were astonished by the water flows outlined in the agreement because they were exactly what Alcan had been demanding all along.

Upon signing the agreement, Alcan had permission to reduce the amount of water it released into the river from behind the Kenney Dam to what are called the "short-term flows" of 1,472 cubic feet per second—meaning that only 20% of the water flowing into the upper Nechako prior to the construction of the dam was left in the river. The agreement also states that after Alcan completes construction of a water-release system, drawing water from behind the dam and releasing it into the river, it could then reduce the amount of water it released to 12% of the pre-dam flows.

The KCP's opponents living in the region were outraged by the agreement. They had always believed it was their river, and to this day they believe the 1987 agreement should be changed to give them more say in how it is managed. Other Nechako Valley residents oppose the agreement because they resent the financial benefits it bestows on Alcan, at their expense, by turning over control of the upper reaches of their river to the company. They argue the 1950 agreement should be set aside because, instead of using the power to smelt aluminum as was the original intent of the project, the company is relying more and more on selling hydroelectric power to improve the figures on the bottom line of its financial statements.

Other opponents of the 1987 agreement are the federal scientists who, during the period leading up to the 1987 court case, recommended water flows much higher than those set out in the agreement. They believed these higher flows were necessary to protect the unique gene pools contained in sockeye and chinook salmon who swim hundreds of miles up the Fraser and Nechako Rivers to reach their spawning grounds deep in BC's Central Interior.

On the other side of the legal tug-of-war are Alcan and the federal and provincial representatives who, until the BC government's January 1995 announcement that it was cancelling the project, believed they had reached binding agreements during the 1950s, and again in 1987—agreements which the company claims give it the sole right to control the amount of water flowing in the Nechako River, and hence down the Fraser and into the Pacific Ocean at Vancouver.

Alcan also claims that under the terms of the water licence issued to it by the BC government in December, 1950, it has the right to divert the remaining water from the upper Nechako, plus water from the upper Skeena, into its Nechako Reservoir. In recognition of growing environmental concerns in the valley, the company claimed it generously gave up some of these rights and added more responsibilities when it signed the 1987 agreement. It was not, therefore, prepared to make any more concessions.

The federal government claims it has a constitutional responsibility to protect the salmon and the agreements with Alcan meet this responsibility by ensuring there is enough water of the right temperature to protect the migrating salmon and their eggs which they lay in the upper Nechako.

Opponents of the project argue that 12% of a river is not enough to sustain the lives of its inhabitants, or of those beings living in the forests and communities along its length.

It should be remembered that throughout this dispute Alcan has been facing a deadline of December 31, 1999, to complete its hydroelectric developments in BC: On that date, Alcan will receive a permanent licence for all hydroelectric facilities it has installed by that time.[28]

More than three years later, Mike Healey—a research scientist, director of UBC's Westwater research foundation and a DFO representative on the Strangway working group whose recommendations had led to the signing of the 1987 Settlement Agreement—admitted the Strangway group's terms of reference had included a provision that the Nechako water flows should be "equivalent to" the level sought by Alcan.[29] The terms of reference for the committee were "To develop a program of measures and plan of implementation which will provide an acceptable level of certainty for the conservation and protection of the chinook fisheries resource of the Nechako River."[30] They made no mention of the other fish using the river, but the working group was instructed to assume a cold-water release facility would be built in the Kenney Dam.

Pat Slaney, a provincial fisheries biologist who had opposed Alcan's proposed flows before the Settlement Agreement was signed, appeared to have changed his mind suddenly, once he became a member of the Strangway working group, about the amount of water required to protect the fish. In an earlier report, Slaney had stated he believed that to protect the fish, the water flows in the Nechako River would have to be 27% more than those

---

"Engineering and computer fallibilities are referred to as acceptable levels of certainty. However you name it, it's gambling nevertheless, and in this case the odds of success at KCP are very uncertain and unacceptable, a point that Alcan are very cognizant of, because if the salmon disappear or the wells dry up or anything else happens, Alcan and their friends in high places will say, ah shucks, we tried, too bad, because it's written into the agreement that no matter what happens they are held blameless." *Geoff Laundy of Prince George, spokesperson for the Two Rivers Canoe Club, BCUCH 6.927.*

"The eye-opener for me was when the 1987 Nechako River Agreement was signed behind closed doors. My vision of Canada was slightly altered, and my sense of a system that functioned in sort of a quasi-democratic way was shattered, and I deeply resented this total betrayal of the Nechako by the provincial and federal governments, and their bribing of the local municipal governments with all sorts of shallow promises." *Craig Hooper, BCUCH 3.366.*

being proposed by the DFO, and 272% more than the flows proposed by Alcan.[31] No explanation was given for Slaney's change of mind until he appeared as a witness during the BCUC's 1993-94 hearings. At the time he said he had been recalled from educational leave to join the meeting of the Strangway group after the group had already met for one day. He was not informed of the importance of the meeting: He was told only that they were to discuss "impacts on chinook salmon in the Nechako River" as part of an attempt to negotiate an out-of-court settlement.[32]

Slaney said that because he had not been working on the issues during the period leading up to the meeting, he was not familiar with the recent developments in the Kemano controversy. "I knew nothing about the removal of Nanika/Morice or KCP, or I knew nothing about the province's agreement as part of the Settlement Agreement to pay for freshwater fish mitigation in the Nechako River," he said.[33] He was instructed only to see what he could do to protect the freshwater fish in the river, based on what was being proposed for the chinook. In other words, he was to "wear a chinook hat but to think trout."[34]

He attended the last three days of the four-day meeting, which he had believed was called in order to arrive at a set of mitigation measures to conserve the existing chinook stocks within the flows Alcan was proposing. He said he was never told he would be required to sign a final document containing recommendations that would clear the way for an out-of-court settlement. He was surprised, therefore, when, the day after the meetings concluded, his director, Dr. Narver, contacted him by phone to ask why he had not signed the document prepared by the Strangway group following the meeting.[35]

I informed Dr. Narver, when he did ask me to go back and sign the document, that Alcan's flows were what were on the table and they would have major impacts on sports fish habitat, and it would still

---

"And then we had KCP. A 1987 Agreement that imposes 19th century political and economic philosophies on people struggling to prepare for the 21st century. I know of no other resource industry in B.C. that operates today with the same environmental impacts it had in 1980, let alone in 1950." *Prince George resident Arlene Galisky, BCUCH 6.1060.*

be risky for chinook because the flows were low, and exceptionally low in winter.[36]

...

I then, a bit reluctantly, signed the Strangway Group Report under the assumption that the risk to chinook salmon would be off-set by a very major mitigation program, and I don't think I would have signed it had I not been feeling comfortable that there would be a major mitigation program. Yet today I remain concerned that a cost-effectiveness clause in the Settlement Agreement could limit the scale of mitigation that is required to do the job there, especially on sedimentation control along the river and tributary watersheds and for re-engineering and complexing the habitat of the river.[37]

When asked if, had all the information now available about the effects of the KCP been accessible to him at the time he signed the committee's report in 1987, he would have signed the agreement, Slaney said: "Given those new risks that I see there, I think I would have declined."[38] He admitted, during the BCUC hearings, that he continues to believe the low winter flows provided for in the Settlement Agreement will negate any efforts to protect either the chinook or the freshwater fishery, and that the federal and provincial governments will have to revert to an off-river hatchery to protect the salmon and freshwater fish. In his view, reverting to a hatchery to maintain a gene pool would be a failure, particularly after what happened during an unsuccessful attempt to establish a salmon hatchery on the Fraser River near Quesnel, south of Prince George.[39]

He also admitted that the province has never developed any plans for offsetting the damage that would be caused by the diversion of more water from the river. "We've never been given the funds to proceed on either the planning phases or implementing some of the earlier what I call applied research or testing phases for the provincial component. Since 1987 and thereafter there was no significant funding," he said.[40]

Under the terms of the 1987 Settlement Agreement, Alcan had assumed some new responsibilities including:

• releasing water into the upper Nechako as set out in the short- and long-term flow regimes for the river, attached to the agreement;
• paying for the construction of the cold-water release facility in the

152

Kenney Dam which, at the time the agreement was signed, was estimated to be $20 million;

• paying for the construction and maintenance of all the remedial work undertaken on the Nechako to protect the salmon;

• paying for half the costs of monitoring the river to determine how well the remedial measures were working;

• sharing with the federal government in paying the costs incurred by the two-committee system established to oversee the remedial work undertaken on the river.

Alcan also gave up its rights to divert the water from the Nanika–Kidprice river system on the upper Skeena River, and abandoned its rights to store water in the Murray–Cheslatta lakes.

Federal Fisheries Minister Siddon described the agreement as "an intelligent and environmentally responsible resolution of a long-standing and counter-productive legal dispute."[41]

Nonsense, said the project's opponents.

The day following the announcement of the Settlement Agreement, Carrier-Sekani Tribal Chief Ed John held an emotional press conference in Prince George in which he said the chiefs had instructed lawyers to review the Settlement Agreement with a view to challenging it in court. "The agreement condemns the Nechako River to death," he said.[42]

> Indians don't believe Alcan and the governments when they say that will enhance the salmon stocks in the upper Nechako River. They don't believe the federal government when it says it is looking out for Indians' interests and they believe the province is prejudiced against Indians.[43]

He went on to issue a prediction that Alcan's long-term plan was to become a privately-owned hydroelectric company in a province where most of the power is produced and distributed by the publicly-owned corporation, BC Hydro:

> This agreement is by scientists for scientists and Alcan. Look at the agreement. It permits Alcan to expand and produce more hydroelectric power for industrial use. Then look at hydroelectric power in terms of privatization and decide for yourself who will be in the best position to control hydroelectric power in this province.[44]

He also pointed out that the agreement makes provincial tax-payers, not Alcan, responsible for repairing the environmental damage done to the Cheslatta-Murray Lakes system when Alcan released water from behind its reservoir through the Skins Lake Spillway. Provincial tax-payers are also responsible for the costs of enhancing and preserving the freshwater fish stocks in the Nechako River within the lower flow regimes.

BC's Socred Energy Minister Jack Davis disagreed. He described the agreement as

> a win-win situation. The province gets an expanded power generation base which will attract new industrial development, the federal government's Department of Fisheries and Oceans fulfils its mandate to protect the fisheries resource and Alcan is able to carry on its long-term development plans.[45]

He ended the press release by thanking Alcan for being "a good corporate citizen" and for making every effort to "find an equitable solution to a complex and sensitive problem." What he didn't say was the agreement also contains a section making either the federal or provincial government responsible for the cost of any liability or expense arising from the agreement.[46]

Nor did anyone point out that under the terms of the agreement the DFO relinquished its constitutional responsibility to manage the water flows in the upper Nechako River and to ensure the safety of the salmon using the river. This responsibility had been turned over to a technical committee composed of one representative each from the DFO, the BC environment ministry, Alcan and an independent expert selected by the other members of the committee. The technical committee reported to a steering com-

---

"The people who signed the 1987 Agreement do not live in my world. Their vision seems to be one of virtual reality where a game of pretend seems to take the place of actual experience." *Arlene Galisky, BCUCH 6.1061.*

"Now two years I never go out hunt, fish even though how much I want it, I cannot go out. The fish warden last year he said he heard the fish was sick so hardly anybody went fishing and I didn't fish." *Elder Leah Patrick, BCUCH 2.235.*

154

mittee composed of senior representatives of Alcan and the federal and provincial governments.

A letter from BC's Environment Minister Bruce Strachan, before the Settlement Agreement was signed, shows he clearly understood reduced water flows would cause problems to the freshwater fish living in the river for which he was responsible. In the letter he says:

> The full impact of the proposed water release regime from the Nechako Reservoir on the above fisheries (in the upper Nechako River watershed) is unknown. However our studies indicate that there may be significant impact on the resident trout and char populations particularly by the proposed winter flow regime.[47]

He also states that his ministry's strategy for maintaining the recreational fishery in the upper Nechako was based on "a no-net-loss principle" accomplished by maintaining whatever fish populations the lower flows would support, and increasing the recreational fishing opportunities on tributaries of the upper Nechako and elsewhere in the Nechako River basin.[48] He added that the damage caused to the fishery in the Murray-Cheslatta chain by the torrents of water surging through the Skins Lake Spillway offered one of the best opportunities for improving the area's freshwater fishery.[49]

By the time Tory MP Frank Oberle (Prince George-Peace River) announced the details of the Settlement Agreement in Prince George on September 14, 1987, Strachan seems to have found a way to overlook his concerns about the possible negative consequences of the water flows Alcan was proposing, which now appeared as the flow established by the Settlement Agreement. During the press conference at which the Settlement Agreement was announced, Strachan promised worried residents: "It is expected the impact on other water licence holders from Alcan's activities will be minimal. Flows in the river will not be reduced for five years, allowing ample time to take appropriate measures."[50]

Despite government representatives' faith in the terms of the agreement, serious concerns remained about the company's ability to protect the salmon using the river. Once again it seemed as if, unless some pre-project trials were carried out, no one would know whether or not the fish would survive until after the project's completion.

Strachan later denied any knowledge of a proposal put forward by the BC government during the negotiations leading up to the Settlement Agreement in which Hydro would provide Alcan with a source of power for ten years to give it time to carry out the experiments to prove that its planned mitigation measures would work.[51]

He also failed to put in place any plans to protect the freshwater fishery in the upper Nechako River. During the 1993-94 provincial hearings into the KCP, it was revealed that his environment ministry staff had prepared a mitigation plan for the Murray-Cheslatta system and the upper Nechako River, but no money was ever provided to implement them.[52] By 1994, the staff in the regional environment ministry office in Prince George consisted of an acting regional fisheries biologist with, during the summer, a permanent staff of two biologists and a staff of field technicians who, in addition to numerous other duties,[53] were responsible for managing the fish and fish habitat in 13% of the province's land mass, including much of the freshwater fishery affected by Alcan's industrial activities in the region.

At the BCUC hearings, opponents questioned if the 1987 Settlement Agreement contravened the 1950 Industrial Development Act which paved the way for the building of the dam. The 1950 Act states that the company was given the right to divert the water from the Nechako River in order to generate hydroelectric power *for use by industry* in the region—*not* to sell to BC Hydro, some opponents pointed out.[54]

At a press conference announcing the Settlement Agreement, Oberle predicted it would result in a 2% reduction in the amount of water flowing in the Fraser River at Prince George.[55]

This figure was the first in a confusing sequence of numbers thrown at Nechako Valley residents about the ramifications the project would have on their river. Eventually, it became clear that Oberle's 2% reduction was incorrect. He was following Alcan's example by referring only to the flow reduction caused by the KCP, estimated to be 10.5%. In fact, the total reduction in water flows at Prince George—caused by all of Alcan's industrial activities in the region, plus Kemano I and the KCP—will total a 40% reduction of the flows in the river before the dam was built. Information the government representatives failed to mention at the time the 1987 agreement was announced was that the long-term flow regime for the Nechako River as set out in the agreement would result in a drop in the water level at Hell's Gate in the Fraser Canyon during September and October.[56] A DFO document released in 1988 states:

> The lower water would render the fishways [at Hell's Gate] ineffective much earlier in the season, threatening the main pink salmon run and the late sockeye runs including the Adams River run. Critical fish passage problems would also occur at three other lower Fraser locations. The 1987 Agreement mentions none of these problems.[57]

The 1988 DFO document also points out that, under the agreement, the fisheries minister had surrendered his jurisdiction over the water flows in the Nechako River:

> Both flow regimes[58] will instead be managed by a bureaucracy of technicians from the company, the provincial and federal governments and from an outside source. Whatever the conditions on the river, these managers will have no power to increase the annual water allocation but will merely distribute it throughout the year. They will also attempt to design technical remedies for the salmon losses that the agreement acknowledges could occur. The Agreement does not say what will happen if all their remedies fail.
> ...
> In effect, the power granted to the Minister of Fisheries and Oceans by the Parliament of Canada has been transferred to a non-elected steering committee,[59] and if the Steering Committee cannot agree, to a single arbitrator. A decision of the Steering Committee (or of an arbitrator) regarding the sufficiency of flows for the protection of fish and ova will be final and binding. This change is more

---

"Opponents of the project like to talk about KCP reductions relative to the Nechako River as it was more than 40 years ago before the Kenney Dam was built and before many of the people here today were born. Alcan talks about reductions from existing flows...." *Bill Rich, BCUCH 11.1655.*

than a delegation of decision-making authority by the Minister (which itself is unlawful without statutory authority). It is an abdication by the Minister of his duty. In the case of delegated authority, the Minister can always withdraw that authority. In the case of this Agreement, however, the Minister has transferred his authority in perpetuity since the Agreement is binding on the parties to it, their successors and assigns.[60]

The same document indicates other legal problems associated with the Settlement Agreement, including section 2.5 of the Agreement which is described as

an attempt (somewhat disguised) to exempt Alcan from the actions of future governments and the effects of future legislation. Turned around, section 2.5 says Alcan will not be bound by any public hearings or regulatory process, or any mitigation or compensation measure under any future statutes or regulations that are inconsistent with Alcan's existing rights.[61]

When they learned of this provision of the agreement, residents of the Nechako River Valley asked themselves if Canadian law permits one government to bind all future governments in this way. To date, there has been no clear answer to that question.

The 1950 agreement, which overrides the 1987 Settlement Agreement, states Alcan is to be granted the rights over the water and land in the Nechako Valley to enable it to generate the power it requires to smelt aluminum and for industrial developments in the region. When asked, in 1987, about this provision of the 1950 agreement a company spokesman said a number of industries requiring an assured power supply were being investigated, including thermomechanical pulp mills, at least one additional aluminum smelter, a plant to produce industrial gases and a plant producing aluminum engine blocks. With the exception of a pulp mill in Vanderhoof, none of these projects has been discussed further. And there are people who question whether a pulp mill will ever be built in Vanderhoof, given the growing shortage of wood fibre in the region and the increasingly stringent environmental standards to be met before being permitted to release effluent into the—by then—much-diminished river. Alcan has agreed to provide free power to the pulp mill for three years, but Nechako Valley residents question if this will be enough to make the pulp mill financially viable and predict that Alcan, through BC Hydro, will be selling power to the mill at the end of the three years.

The most immediate benefits Alcan received from the agreement included protection from future court action and an increase in its supply of low-cost power which it can use either to smelt aluminum or to sell to BC Hydro. The 1988 DFO document also raises the probability of Alcan going into competition with BC Hydro, the Crown corporation responsible for developing and distributing electric power in the province:

> B.C. Hydro's rate for large industrial users [the "transmission" rate] has been 2.8 cents per kilowatt-hour [KWH] since 1985. In order to make an attractive offer to a large industrial user, suppose that Alcan undercuts this rate by 25%. Alcan's rate would then be 2.1 cents per KWH. The value of the 150 megawatts would be $27.6-million annually.[62]

Nechako Valley residents now firmly believe Alcan never had any intention of constructing another smelter in BC, that instead—as many of them had suspected—it was planning to become an unregulated, privately-owned power utility. This suspicion was confirmed when, in 1988, Alcan signed a 20-year agreement to sell 2,500 gigawatt-hours a year of firm power to BC Hydro, beginning in 1995.[63] Alcan and Hydro also signed a reservoir co-ordination agreement under which Hydro could draw down the Nechako Reservoir to provide more power during periods when other BC Hydro reservoirs were experiencing drought conditions.

Thus, the BC government's announcement of the KCP's "cancellation" not only places the government in the position of violating two agreements, it places Alcan in the position of being unable to comply with both the reservoir co-ordination agreement and its agreement to begin selling power to BC Hydro in 1995.

At the hearings, Alcan's BC vice-president Bill Rich placed the total value to the province of these two agreements at more than $400 million.[64]

That's not all. Under the terms of the Settlement Agreement, despite all its talk about establishing smelters and other industries in the Nechako River Valley, there is no provision in the agreement requiring Alcan to do so. Nor does the agreement require the company to pay for any mitigation or other compensation arising from future public meetings, or to provide additional water for fish protection should the short-term or long-term water allocations set out in the agreement prove inadequate.[65] The province has also been left to pick up the tab for the costs of any damage Alcan does to the Nechako's freshwater fish populations.

A 1988 DFO document warned the federal fisheries minister:

> [W]hen rivers are regulated to allow more than 70 percent of the natural flows in all months of the year, salmon number can be maintained or enhanced. When flows are reduced below 70 per cent, the productivity of the system declines until at flows below 30 per cent the population become degraded.[66]

Remember: The Settlement Agreement enabled Alcan to reduce the water flows of the upper Nechako to 12% of their pre-dam levels and they would be not more than 21% of the natural flows in any month.[67]

Worse yet, the flow reductions were not made evenly throughout the year. Instead, a larger portion of the spring flows were diverted into the reservoir to refill it after the long winter drawdown, when inflows were low. That eliminated higher natural spring flows in the river which had served a useful purpose for centuries of the natural cycle of the river's life because they scoured debris off the spawning grounds, in preparation for the thousands of chinook salmon that would spawn there later in the year.[68]

The chinook salmon were of particular concern to federal scientists: The only available figures accounting for the number of these big fish using the river prior to the building of the dam were

---

"Direct benefits to the communities of the north and industrial expansion is a deliberate, orchestrated hoax. Thus new smelters are imaginary, new pulp mills will come only if the forest industry decides to pulp valuable timber logs." *Geoff Laundy, BCUCH 6.927-28.*

"If both Alcan and the federal and provincial governments are satisfied that the terms of the 1987 Settlement Agreement provide adequate protection for fish, why do they refuse to consider a full public environmental review?" *Rob Lemmers, spokesman for the Commercial Fishing Industrial Council, BCUCH 6.879.*

incomplete, but their estimates of chinook runs prior to 1950 range from 5,000 to 10,000 spawners, with one estimate as high as 29,000. The fish were almost eliminated from the river following the construction of the dam, when little water flowed between the dam and the Nautley River and, later, when large amounts of sediment were eroded out of the Cheslatta and Murray Lakes system and deposited in the Nechako river. By 1988, the number of spawning chinook in the river was estimated to be 1,500 and by 1994 the number of spawners had dropped to 1,144. "This recent decline in Nechako chinook numbers contrasts with all other Fraser River chinook populations which have been growing during the same period." The Nechako sockeye run would also be seriously depleted by the lower water flows, the document states.[69]

The one positive note in the agreement was that Alcan had relinquished its right to divert water into the reservoir from the Nanika-Kidprice system. But even this concession was a benefit to Alcan because it meant the company would not have to spend more than $90 million to build the dam on that system and drill another tunnel to deliver the water from the Nanika-Kidprice reservoir into the existing Nechako Reservoir. Alcan often pointed to its agreement to relinquish its rights to the Nanika-Kidprice system as evidence of its new improved, environmentally-friendly strategy. "One of the biggest concessions Alcan made in redesigning KCP was giving up its rights to the Nanika," Alcan's BC vice-president said in his opening statement before the BCUC hearings in Prince George.[70]

Although it seemed Alcan had suffered a loss when it gave up its rights to store water in Murray and Cheslatta Lakes, this too was actually a benefit to the company. According to Alcan's 1984 application for an Energy Project Certificate, the Murray Lake dam and spillway were intended to re-regulate the water being released from the Skins Lake Spillway as a fish-protection measure. In 1983 it was estimated that it would have cost more than $4 million—and now

---

"[T]he Province will grant to Alcan through legislative means, if necessary, other rights equivalent to Alcan's current rights to develop the Nanika." *Letter from BC Energy Minister Jack Davis to David Morton, president of Alcan, 2 Sept.1987.*

that responsibility had been turned over to the federal and provincial governments.

A cost-benefit analysis has never been done of all the factors affecting the Nechako River Valley as a result of the 1987 Settlement Agreement. But common sense told many residents of the valley that Alcan broke even on the deal—*at least*—and, whatever the cost, they—not the company—would pay the price.

Those who wanted to see the project go ahead note that Alcan had agreed to construct a facility near the Kenney Dam to release water from the reservoir into the upper Nechako. The cost of that facility was originally set at $20 million. By 1994 the estimated cost had risen to more than $70-million as a result of design changes and inflation. Alcan had refused to consider a recommendation made by the DFO that such a facility be built when the dam was being designed. The company's reason for refusing to install a cold-water release facility in the dam was that it would be unsafe. Closer evaluation of the cost of this facility shows it would allow the company to reduce the volume of water it is required to release from its reservoir from 500 to 65 cubic feet per second, resulting in Alcan's having an additional 435 cubic feet per second of water with which to generate power. That amount of water can generate approximately 80 megawatts, which, at 2.1¢ per KWH, is worth $14.7 million annually and, when the facility had paid for itself, the company could add that money to its annual profits.

The people in the Bulkley River Valley welcomed the section of the agreement in which Alcan abandoned its control over the water flows in the Nanika-Kidprice system because it prevented the transfer of diseases and parasites between the Skeena, Fraser and Kemano River systems and protected the water flows in the rich salmon-bearing Skeena from being diverted into the reservoir.

Despite that one little victory, at the beginning of October 1987, Pat Moss of Smithers, chairperson for the Rivers Defence Coalition, repeated her call for a full public review of the agreement and charged both governments with capitulating to Alcan's wishes. "Although provincial and federal politicians say this is a win-win deal, the only ones we see will win are Alcan's shareholders," she claimed in a news report. Moss also charged the agreement gave Alcan everything it had been asking for since 1984.

This was confirmed by an Alcan spokesman, Brian Hemingway.[71] The company was also given approval to dredge the narrow channel filled with drowned trees separating the former Tahtsa and Ootsa Lakes. The dredging was necessary to allow water to flow into the tunnels under Mount DuBose on the shore of Tahtsa Lake when the reservoir was drawn down to lower levels. The committee of fisheries technicians now responsible for controlling the water levels in the river were not required by the Settlement Agreement to report their decisions to the public, yet for several years the committee did hold annual meetings in the region to explain how it was planning to protect the fish. These meetings, however, were never very satisfactory. The scientists came armed with charts, graphs and statistical information about how they proposed to protect the fish in the river, even though there was only 12% of the water left in it.

Meanwhile, the Nechako River Valley residents attending these same meetings wanted to talk about the fact that there was so little water left in the river already it was nearly stagnant at times, and they had difficulty using it for recreational purposes. Residents who lived in the commmunities along the Nechako River system complained that the agreement gave no consideration to their needs, and it also appeared that they would be faced with the cost of changing their sewage disposal system so that it conformed with the lower flow rates in the river. The scientists had no answers for the residents' worries: They were more concerned with designing complicated artificial structures to protect the fish. One such proposal included jamming old railway tracks into the banks of the river to catch debris such as twigs, roots and trees floating down the river to create artificial "beaver dams."

There were questions about whether or not the proposed cold-water release system in the Kenney Dam would work: What about the low oxygen content of water drawn from deep in the reservoir? Could the salmon tolerate the sudden changes in temperature that would occur when they encountered the colder water after swimming long distances upstream in the warmer waters of the Fraser and Nechako Rivers? Would the facility in fact be able to deliver the amount of cold water required to cool the water flowing in the river all the way to its junction with the Fraser River? And KCP opponents continued to point out that after the project was completed, the winter flows in the Nechako River would be only slightly higher than the summer flows in the Chilako and Stellako Rivers, and less than the summer flows in the Willow River.[72]

Despite these serious concerns, local politicians and many residents of Prince George and the now deeply-divided community of Vanderhoof seemed prepared to accept the fact that the day might come when there was so little water flowing in the Nechako River that at times it would be possible to drive a four-wheel-drive vehicle 60 miles along the shores of the river between the two communities.

Most of the residents of Prince George, even facing the bleak outcome should the project proceed, remained silent. They were more distracted by the recession affecting most of Canada and which had been particularly hard on resource-dependent communities such as their own. At that time, any project that promised well-paid jobs looked good to them—no matter how short-term they were, or how much long-term damage the project would inflict on the environment. Elsewhere, although the Save the Bulkley Society in Smithers, the Carrier Sekani Tribal Council, and the Vanderhoof-based Nechako Neyenkut Society attempted to warn people about what was happening, few listened.

With all its approvals and licences in hand, Alcan began its preparations to drill a second 10-mile tunnel through Mount DuBose. This time, instead of the time-consuming drill-and-blast method used to create the first tunnel in the early 1950s, the company brought in a tunnel-boring machine that had been used to create the undersea tunnel between Britain and France. The 662-ton machine had been brought to Kemano in 300 pieces and assembled before being carried on rails into the tunnel, where its 18.8-foot rotating, grinding head fitted with 42 hardened steel cutters fractured off the rock in small chips. The chips were carried back, loaded into the 298-foot trailer which was drawn along behind the boring machine, and the debris was deposited outside the tunnel. Using this modern boring monster, Alcan was able to advance an average of 91.8 feet per day through the heart of the mountain—more than twice the rate achieved when the first tunnel was built using the old drill-and-blast method.

Nor Any Drop to Drink

"This valley has suffered enough."[1]

In 1988, the Smithers-based group Save the Bulkley Society decided to challenge the terms of the 1987 Settlement Agreement in court—an action that was the first step in what would be a four-year-long legal battle over who had the right to control the amount of water flowing in the Nechako River. The society later joined the 13-member Rivers Defence Coalition who combined their efforts in opposition to the Kemano Completion Project. Pat Moss, of Smithers, was chosen to be their spokesperson.

When the federal court approved Alcan's application to become an intervener in that first court action, the coalition decided to put the court action on hold because its members feared that, based on the history of its previous actions, Alcan would use both its position as an intervener and its deep pockets to stall, delay, place legal obstacles in the path of the courts and do everything in its power to push the court costs beyond the coalition's financial ability to proceed. The coalition also realized that even if it won that case, it would not achieve its goal of forcing the federal government to conduct a full environmental review of the project. Worse yet, Pam Moss said, even if the courts struck down the validity of the agreement, the government could simply reword it and Alcan would proceed as planned.[2] So the coalition changed its legal tactics and, on October 9, 1990, filed new documents asking the federal court to require the federal government to subject the KCP to its new

Environmental Assessment Review Process, commonly referred to as EARP.

Three days after the coalition filed its court documents, the second court action was also stalled when the federal Cabinet met and approved an order exempting the KCP and the 1987 Settlement Agreement from the EARP process.[3] Federal Fisheries Minister Bernard Valcourt said the exemption had been ordered because the environmental concerns of the federal government had been answered by the studies already completed on the project by Envirocon, Alcan's environmental consultant.[4]

A provision of the federal Access to Information Act protecting cabinet documents from the public's prying eyes for 20 years makes it impossible to find out until 2010 whether the brevity of the interval between the filing of the coalition's court documents and the federal Cabinet's decision to exempt the project from its EARP requirements were related or coincidental. There are those, including former Prince George-Bulkley Valley NDP MP Brian Gardiner, who doubt whether any documents or records will ever be found from that cabinet meeting. He predicts they've probably "disappeared."

Former federal biologist, Don Alderdice, who was one of the federal fisheries scientists who opposed the project before the Settlement Agreement was signed said that, by exempting the project from its EARP process, the federal government was trying to cover up information which would add fuel to the growing opposition to Alcan's plans to increase the amount of water the company planned to divert out of the Nechako. Alderdice and other federal scientists were convinced a further reduction in the amount of water flowing in the river would pose a serious threat to the fish populations of both the Nechako and Fraser Rivers.[5]

Alderdice was particularly angry about Valcourt's assurance that the project had already been subjected to thorough studies which satisfied all the government's environmental concerns. Alderdice reminded the public Alcan's proposal had been rejected by all the federal scientists assigned to the Kemano task force, which had been evaluating Envirocon's environmental studies at the time the 1987 agreement was signed. The government also effectively silenced their own scientists' objections by excluding them from Strangway's working group which had been instructed to find ways to protect the fish within the water flows Alcan was demanding.[6] "It's a cover-up," Alderdice said. "The only people who don't have the total knowledge of what went on are the general public."[7]

Faced with the Cabinet's exemption order, the coalition changed its legal direction again, this time challenging the validity of the exemption order. By that point, the Carrier Sekani Tribal Council had launched a separate action, claiming the exemption order was beyond the authority of the Cabinet and that it was also unconstitutional, as it would adversely affect the Carrier peoples' aboriginal right to fish.[8]

KCP's opponents were jubilant when, on May 16, 1991, federal court Justice Allison Walsh ruled in their favour, declaring the federal Cabinet's decision not to order a review of the project was "a failure to undertake a legal obligation."[9] In a wide-ranging decision, Justice Walsh dismissed Alcan's procedural objections, quashed the 1987 Settlement Agreement and ordered that the project be subjected to the federal EARP process.

"This is one of the happiest days I've ever had in my life. This is a victory for the Nechako River," said a triumphant Carrier Sekani Tribal Chief, Justa Monk.[10] He had spent most of his adult life fighting to obtain justice for the Carrier people whose dependence on canned, smoked and dried salmon for winter food had been seriously undermined by the Kemano I Project. Elders were telling him the few Nechako salmon they had been able to catch in recent years were too sick, soggy and covered with sores to preserve for use during the winter. Monk joined other central interior residents and the coalition in calling on the government to heed Walsh's findings and immediately initiate a full environmental review of the project.

When federal NDP Environment Critic Jim Fulton asked Environment Minister Jean Charest to assure the House that an environmental review panel would be set up immediately, he reminded the minister that this was the first time in the history of Canada a federal court had found the Cabinet had broken the law.[11]

Walsh's ruling was hailed as a victory by groups fighting other hydroelectric projects in Canada. Bill Namagoose, executive-director of the Grand Council of the Cree of Quebec, said the decision meant Ottawa could no longer get away with conducting only a partial study of Hydro-Quebec's $12.7-billion Great Whale Project.[12] "A proper environmental review will confirm what we have said all along—that these projects should not be built," he predicted.[13] Appeals had also been launched to stop the Rafferty-Alameda Project in Saskatchewan. Alcan's opponents feared the BC government would follow the precedent established in Saskatchewan where then Premier Grant Devine continued to press on with the construction of the dam after the court ordered a federal review of the project.[14]

Although there were predictions Alcan would appeal Walsh's decision, the Rivers Defence Coalition remained hopeful this was the end to its long campaign to have the environmental consequences of the project subjected to rigorous public scrutiny. Coalition spokesperson, Pat Moss, stated:

> This has been a 12-year struggle to get what we thought was just natural justice after initially expecting that there would be full public hearings before they made any decision. So you could say there's a sense of vindication of our position after all these years. The courts have recognized that this is what should have occurred and should now occur.[15]

Her statement refers to the fact that, since 1979, Alcan's critics had been opposing all proposals to divert more water into Alcan's Nechako Reservoir. They thought they had made their point when, on May 12, 1981, then Energy Minister Robert McClelland told the BC legislature that the KCP would not proceed without full public hearings.[16]

Despite McClelland's assurances, there was no mention of an independent environmental assessment when, in 1980, Alcan announced that it planned to divert more water into the reservoir from the Nechako River and Nanika-Kidprice system to supply the power for the three new smelters the company was planning to build in BC.

Another let-down for anti-Alcan activists came during the run-up to the 1984 federal election. During his campaign, Brian Mulroney had promised a full environmental hearing into Alcan's plans for the Nechako River.[17] But when Alcan threatened to abandon the project should the federal government fulfill that election promise, Mulroney summarily forgot it.[18]

Once the Mulroney-led Conservatives were elected, Alcan established close ties with the new government by appointing three high-profile Conservative supporters to Alcan's board of directors. The best-known Conservative appointment was Allan Gotlieb, who had served as Canada's ambassador to the United States for eight years. While in Washington, DC, he used his knowledge of the inside workings of the US government to good advantage in order to help the Mulroney government ease the negotiations of the Free Trade Agreement with the United States through the complicated American political process.

Alcan representatives also worked hard to gain Canadian support for the government's efforts to settle the Free Trade Agreement with the United States. The agreement was particularly attractive to Alcan because most of the aluminum being produced in Kitimat is shipped to manufacturing plants in the US and Asia.[19] In other words, BC provides the cheap power required to extract aluminum from bauxite, but most of the manufacturing jobs required for this process have been created outside Canada.

Other newly-appointed Alcan directors were Sonja Ingrid Bata, who was an outspoken supporter of Mulroney's unsuccessful constitutional efforts at Meech Lake, and Conservative Senator Jean-Marie Poitras, who was Finance Minister Michael Wilson's former boss. During the constitutional debate he lined up with other Conservatives as a staunch supporter of the Meech Lake accord.

Alcan's strong support for free trade was rewarded when, in turn, Mulroney handed out government appointments to three Alcan executives—the most prestigious going to Alcan's chairman and chief executive officer, David Culver: When he retired from his executive position with the company, he was made a member of

---

"Pursuit of the medium-term public interest over the short-term vested interest is the path of responsible and judicious government. But government, like any institution, is subject to error." *"Introduction," Water and Free Trade: The Mulroney Government's Agenda for Canada's Most Precious Resource, ed. Wendy Holm, xi.*

the Order of Canada by Prime Minister Brian Mulroney, one year after the signing of the Settlement Agreement. During the 1988 federal election, when free trade was the hotly-debated issue between Liberal leader John Turner and Brian Mulroney, Culver, who was previously known to be a Liberal supporter, openly broke with the Liberals' opposition to free trade to become the leader of the pro-free trade organization, the Canadian Alliance for Trade and Job Opportunities. The alliance had more than $5 million to spend on its campaign, $250,000 of which was donated by Alcan. During the election campaign the Alliance is reported to have spent $2 million urging Canadians to support the Free Trade Agreement by voting Conservative.[20]

In 1988 Mulroney appointed Alcan director Laurent Beaudoin to the Canadian Senate. In 1987 Beaudoin was featured in a government-produced video as one of the prominent Quebec businessmen speaking out in support of free trade. He got his reward in January 1989, when he was made a companion to the Order of Canada.[21] Mulroney had also appointed Alcan director Ted Newall to the prime minister's advisory group on Executive Compensation to the Public Service and to the International Trade Advisory Committee.[22]

Nechako Valley residents' jubilation over Justice Walsh's decision—to quash the 1987 Settlement Agreement and to order an environmental review of the project—was squelched in 1991, when Alcan appealed it, claiming they had been prevented from presenting all their evidence.

When the federal government joined Alcan in its appeal, environmental groups expressed their disappointment with the government's continued failure to act to protect their interests. Worse yet, instead of being informed directly of the government's decision to appeal, they had first heard about it when Fisheries Minister John Crosbie revealed the information while testifying before a Commons fisheries committee.[23]

Throughout the debate over whether or not the project should go ahead, the provincial Socred government held fast to its commitment to allow Alcan to proceed. The provincial government's support for the project appeared to waver when, on December 4, 1990, BC's Environment Minister, John Reynolds, told a parliamentary committee studying the draft legislation for the federal government's new EARP requirements that there would be both a provincial environmental review of Alcan's KCP and public hearings. When Jim Fulton (NDP MP, Skeena) pressed Reynolds for the date of the hearings, Reynolds said no date had been set and simply reiterated his original statement—"[T]here will be hearings."[24] But, by the time Reynolds left the committee meetings, he had had a change of heart and would say only that there would be "meetings" instead of "hearings" on the KCP.

These seemingly contradictory statements prompted the House of Commons committee to order Reynolds to reappear before them to answer charges that he had deliberately misled the House. He was given until the end of January, 1991, to respond. Fulton said the order not only put pressure on Reynolds to explain his statements, but would also focus more attention on the fact that the federal government had chosen to exempt this one project from a mandatory law which it had no trouble applying to other controversial projects, such as the Old Man River Dam in Alberta, the Rafferty-Alameda Project in Saskatchewan and the Great Whale Project in Quebec.[25]

Within a week Reynolds had resigned as environment minister, citing his differences with Premier Bill Vander Zalm over proposals to introduce tough new controls on pulp mill pollution as his reason for stepping down. The Socreds continued to deny they had ever meant to initiate full public hearings into the project. History has shown that to be true.

At the BCUC hearings, the testimony of former Socred Environment Minister Bruce Strachan provided a number of insights into the BC government's involvement in dealings with Alcan. When asked why the province agreed to proceed with the project without an assessment of its effects on the environment,

---

"[W]e lost trust when our representatives opposed us in court." *Louise Burgener of the Nechako Neyenkut Society, BCUCH 4.541.*

"We are a peaceful people for the most part, and probably too trusting that our elected governments will look after our interests, safeguarding our heritage and natural resources for us and future generations." *Vanderhoof resident Diane Fawcett, BCUCH 4.567.*

171

Strachan said he'd been assured by his advisers that the freshwater fishery in and around the river could be sustained and actually increased within the flows proposed by Alcan.[26] Although the cost of the remedial work required to sustain the freshwater fish would be born by the province, Strachan claimed those costs would be more than offset by the increased revenue the project would bring to the province. No cost-benefit analysis was produced to prove the truth of his claim, however, and Strachan never actually implemented any plans to protect the freshwater fishery in the river. So, to date, there have been no environmental-protection costs incurred by the province as a result of the project. And it was learned that the project would probably result in less than six permanent jobs in Kemano and, possibly, as few as one.

It became very apparent that the provincial government was in fact actively involved in the negotiations prior to the signing of the 1987 Settlement Agreement: According to Pat Chamut (Director-General of the Pacific Region of the DFO), it had been applying "very, very strong political pressure on the federal government to negotiate an agreement...."[27]

Strachan defended the government's position, saying it was an effort to avoid the winner-take-all outcome that could have resulted from the court case.[28] He says the 1987 Settlement Agreement resulted in more water flowing in the Nechako River than provided for under the terms of the 1950 agreements—which had given the company the right to divert all the water from the upper Nechako River. Had that earlier provision remained in place, it would have meant there would continue to be little water flowing in the river between the dam and its confluence with the Nautley River. Strachan was also anxious to secure the benefits of the increased industrial activity and the short-term construction jobs resulting from the project. He said that the province also preferred that the federal government not become involved in issues affecting the economic development of BC.[29]

Strachan admitted he had doubts about the environmental repercussions of the 1950 agreement, but had accepted the fact it was legally binding:

...so we were stuck on the horns of a dilemma, of wanting to be part

172

of Alcan, and stand up for their rights too, and their agreement with the Province of British Columbia dating back to 1950, and yet we couldn't let them have everything that was agreed to in 1950. So we had to reach a compromise, and we had to stay out of the courts to do it. That was generally the thinking that was going on at the time, and that's the best way I can summarize it in the position of our Cabinet generally....[30]

Strachan agreed the interests non-fisheries users of the river—such as municipalities, farmers, recreational users and others—were discussed during the negotiations leading up to the signing of the 1987 agreement, but nothing was included in the agreement to protect their interests.[31] Within months of signing the agreement, the province agreed to assist municipalities facing increased costs to improve sewage treatment or water withdrawal systems as a result of the lower flows in the river, he said.[32]

At the BCUC hearing, it was revealed that the provincial Socred Cabinet's decision to sign the 1987 Settlement Agreement was based on information that placed the value of the Nechako River salmon fishery at $1 million[33] when, other evidence showed, by 1993 it was actually worth $77 million.[34] Asked if the provincial Cabinet's decision to sign would have been different had it known the value of the fish was seventy-seven times greater than it had been informed it was, Strachan responded only with: "[N]o matter what he [then Energy Minister Jack Davis, now deceased] said about the salmon fishery, [he] had absolutely no impact on it, nor could he negotiate for it. That was a DFO responsibility as we all know."[35]

Strachan maintained the province's decision to trade jobs for fish was the correct one, despite the fact that their position was based on a severely inaccurate estimate of the value of the fish, and that the project's probable employment benefits—the jobs that might emerge at the proposed pulp mill in Vanderhoof—were just that:

"In the spring of 1987, after a lot of preparation on both sides for the legal proceedings and several postponements, Alcan and DFO re-opened discussions. We did this at the explicit urging of B.C. Energy Minister Jack Davis and B.C. Minister of the Environment, Bruce Strachan." *Alcan's Bill Rich, BCUCH 11.1661.*

probable. There would be an intensive effort to protect the fish under Alcan's flow regime, he said.

Following the signing of the 1987 Settlement Agreement, the province had made no plans to protect the freshwater fish in the river and lakes affected by the water reductions. Strachan said he did not recall a provincial proposal to guarantee power to Alcan from BC Hydro's power grid for ten years to provide time for studies to be conducted to demonstrate the effectiveness of the remedial programs being proposed to protect the fish stocks in the river.[36] Nor did he recall why that proposal was dropped. One possible explanation for its being dropped is that Alcan had until 1999 to complete its power installations on the Nechako River. At that time, the company will receive permanent licences covering all facilities then in place. If they had to wait ten years until 1997 to confirm that the remedial measures being planned for the river would work, it would be too late to complete the project before the 1999 deadline.

Strachan surprised the KCP opponents when he admitted that he did not know the positions any of the parties were taking regarding the amount of water that should remain in the Nechako River prior to the negotiations leading up to the 1987 Settlement Agreement.[37]

As the controversy over the KCP continued to heat up, Alcan decided, in June, 1991, to halt all construction activity on the project and lay off more than 800 of the people working on it.[38] The reason given for the shut-down was the uncertainty about the project's future that was created by the court decision.[39] The workers were understandably upset at the loss of their well-paid jobs at a time when there was little heavy construction activity in the province. They thought they had ensured their job security when, in February, 1989, the 17 construction unions with members working on the project signed a five-year, no-strike, no-lockout agreement. Despite that concession, they claimed, they were now

---

"...I have concluded that there is only one point upon which there is total consensus: the Kemano Project, first undertaken over 40 years ago and more recently slated for expansion, is both multi-faceted and intractably complex." *Rankin and Finlay, 7.*

"innocent bystanders caught in the middle as Alcan winds down construction."[40] "The word everyone is using is devastating," said Gail Guise, manager of the Kitimat Chamber of Commerce, who predicted the shut-down would mean that businesses in that community would lose business worth $6 million.[41] The Kitimat Chamber of Commerce launched a local campaign to rally public support for the project, which put them in direct opposition to the residents living along the Nechako River who saw themselves paying a big price for Kitimat's prosperity.

Although purchase orders and contracts worth more than $20.2 million had been placed with businesses and contractors in Prince George and Vanderhoof by April, 1990, that was a far cry from Alcan's earlier promise of a smelter costing hundreds of millions of dollars and providing hundreds of permanent jobs in Vanderhoof. It was also only 5.4% of the $379.9 million in orders and contracts placed by the company to that date. Companies elsewhere in BC, mostly in the Lower Mainland, had received Alcan contracts worth more than $263.8 million, and contracts worth $96 million had been placed elsewhere in Canada. American suppliers had received orders worth $3.6 million and orders totalling $11.4 million had been placed outside North America.[42]

Meanwhile, time was running out for the KCP's opponents. They were deeply in debt and discouraged by their unsuccessful attempts to have the federal court order an environmental review of the project. Their frustrations were increased by the statements made by Tory Frank Oberle (MP Prince George-Peace River) that,

> ...if it were started today, there was no question Alcan's Kemano Completion project would be subjected to a full environmental impact study.
>
> I can say that unequivocally, as there would be in the James Bay project (in Quebec) and the Site C project on the Peace River (in northeast B.C.). But when the hydro-electric project began in 1987, the federal government's environmental impact guidelines did not have the force of law.[43]

Alcan's opponents could not accept Oberle's explanation that, because of bad timing, the KCP would be allowed to proceed without a full environmental review while other, smaller projects would be subjected to intense environmental scrutiny by the federal government.

Opponents of the KCP received another blow on May 8, 1992, when a three-person federal appeal panel set aside Justice Walsh's decision against Alcan, thus allowing the company to proceed with the project.

The Cheslatta First Nations people had no intention of letting that happen. They were becoming increasingly upset by the way all their efforts to prevent further damage to the river and their homeland had been thwarted by the courts. "As they say in the Olympics, 'Let the Games begin' because we are not accepting that order," said Mike Robertson, a spokesperson for the Cheslatta Indian Band. "Our territory is at risk out here and we will use whatever means we have to make Alcan go through a proper environmental review."[44]

Despite the fact the federal court had now cleared the way for Alcan to resume working on the project, the company kept its construction equipment in mothballs while the coalition and the tribal council decided whether or not they would appeal to the Supreme Court of Canada. On June 2, 1992, the Carrier Sekani Tribal chiefs announced their lawyers would seek leave to appeal the decision to the Supreme Court of Canada. It took the Rivers Defence Coalition until August 31 to raise enough money to enable it to announce that it, too, would appeal the lower court decision.

The Supreme Court's rejection of the application to appeal the decision left the KCP's opponents confused about the apparent contradictions between the federal court's decision and a decision made earlier that year by a federal government committee. Their confusion arose because, on March 5, 1992, they had learned the federal government's all-party, Standing Joint Committee for the Scrutiny of Regulations had ruled the Cabinet did not have the constitutional authority to exempt the KCP from the federal law requiring a review of all large projects affecting the environment. That appeared to raise a disturbing conflict between the federal court ruling that the exemption order was binding and the findings of an all-party standing committee of the House of Commons saying the Cabinet had acted illegally and unconstitutionally when it exempted the KCP from its EARP process.

"The act does not give the Minister of the Environment an express power to grant exemptions," said Francois-R. Bernier of Ottawa, the lawyer for the Standing Joint Committee for the Scrutiny of Regulations.[45] The committee would not formally file its objections in a report to the House of Commons and the Senate until the next session of the Canadian Parliament, Bernier said.

The all-party committee's report offered little hope to Alcan's opponents, for although the committee of eight Senators and eight MPs had the power to disallow orders it disagreed with, it rarely took that action, Bernier explained. "I have no indication it intends to exercise disallowance vis-a-vis KCP," he said. Normally, the report is just presented and, in the end, public opinion "achieves the end that is sought."[46]

When announcing the parliamentary committee's decision, Liberal MP Derek Lee, who co-chaired the Common's committee with Conservative Senator Normand Grimard, admitted the appeal court judges' remarks "are at variance with our view of the law of Parliament and the general law of Canada.... I say that with respect, but you've got to remember I'm speaking from Parliament which is a separate entity from the courts," he said.[47]

"Who is in charge in Canada, the courts or Parliament?" valley residents asked themselves.

They were told the scrutiny committee reviews several thousand regulations issued by the federal government each year. It operates

---

"You need not wonder why serious scientists and serious Canadians hold MPs in such contempt. An all-party committee concludes that a problem [the reduction in the world's ozone] is second only to all-out nuclear war, and nothing is done. So who is really running the agenda, you ask? Oil companies, automotive manufacturers...vested interests." *MP Jim Fulton, Canadian Forum (Nov. 1993), 11.*

"...I will leave it to others to debate whether it is the job of a parliamentary committee or the job of the courts to decide what is lawful and what is not. This humble engineer has believed throughout his life in the simple principle outlined in a Civics class many decades ago. Parliament creates the law and the courts apply it." *Bill Rich, BCUCH 11.1671.*

under a basic principle of British-based parliamentary democracy stretching back to Henry VIII which says the executive branch of government—in this case the federal Cabinet—cannot make exemptions to the law—in this case the law requiring that large projects undergo an environmental assessment review—unless parliament gives it the power to do so.[48]

When the report was finally introduced to the House of Commons more than a year later on June 7, 1993, Lee stressed the committee was not ruling on the merits or dangers of the project, only on the Cabinet's actions in granting the exemption order.[49]

MP Brian Gardiner immediately placed a notice of motion on the Commons order paper requesting a debate on the issue. His request was ignored and, when the matter was raised in the Commons, the Conservative-dominated House passed the report without dissent or debate. "Either the government didn't know what was going on or they think they can deep-six the issue," Gardiner said following the government's apparently self-condemning action endorsing a report which denounced the federal Cabinet for acting illegally and unconstitutionally.[50] Government House Leader Harvie Andre's office pleaded ignorance when asked about the government's actions.[51]

Despite endorsing the report, the government was under no obligation to do anything about it, Gardiner pointed out,[52] and, to the dismay of those who had hoped the committee's ruling would prompt the federal government to act, the government did exactly that: nothing.

On hearing these contradictory opinions, Prince George resident Arlene Galisky, of the Allied Rivers Commission, said it was atrocious that the federal court would defend a Cabinet order its own parliamentary watch-dog says is illegal: "We are spending money on lawyers and the federal government is spending money on lawyers and here its own parliamentary committee says the cabinet acted illegally."[53]

While the appeals worked their way forward, other information was coming to light that made residents of the valley uneasy.

Early in 1991,[54] Alcan announced it was delaying the start of construction of the $24-million cold-water release facility in the Kenney Dam for the second time. Construction of the facility to release colder water into the upper Nechako River had originally been scheduled to start in 1991. But in the spring of 1990 the company announced construction would not start until 1992. The first delay was necessary because it was discovered that the cold water drawn from deep in the reservoir was too cold and contained too much nitrogen and not enough oxygen for the fish to survive. The release facility, therefore, had to be redesigned so the water temperature could be regulated by combining colder water drawn from deep in the reservoir with water siphoned off from near the surface. Before being spilled into the remains of the Grand Canyon of the Nechako River, the water would be aerated by passing it through a hollow cone valve and over a baffle-block spillway to reduce the amount of nitrogen it contained. Thus, the engineers needed extra time to redesign the facility to provide this two-stage release process.

The reason given for the second delay was the downturn in the economy and the low price of aluminum. Yet the company said that despite the delay in the start of construction, the facility could still be completed by the summer of 1994, when Alcan was scheduled to begin drawing more water from the reservoir to feed the four new 110-megawatt generators being installed at Kemano.

Suspicious Nechako Valley residents asked themselves: "What will happen to our river if Alcan proceeds to withdraw more water in 1994 without constructing the cold-water release facility?"

They learned later they had another reason to be concerned about the water release facility Alcan had agreed to build in the Kenney Dam. During the 1993-94 hearings into the project, Alcan's Bill Rich admitted that, should the facility not function properly, the 1987 Settlement Agreement did not oblige the company to make sure it worked. Worse yet, if the facility should not work properly, the agreement permits the company to release even less water into the upper Nechako River.[55]

Alcan's opponents had little reason to believe the company's assurances that construction of the cold-water release facility was only being delayed, not abandoned. After all, this was the same company that had been promising them that a yet-to-be-materialized aluminum smelter would be built in Vanderhoof. Indeed, questions were being asked whether the 1987 Settlement

Agreement required the company to construct the Kenney Dam release facility *at all*.[56]

Many Vanderhoof residents had become very weary and disillusioned by both Alcan—for the string of broken promises the company had strung them—and the provincial government—for its proposed industrial developments that were supposed to bring the economic stability they needed in the face of declining forest revenues. First, Alcan had promised a smelter would be built in their community. Then, Socred Premier Bill Vander Zalm promised them a meat-packing plant to process the thousands of cattle that were being raised on the rich forage crops grown in the valley, but were being shipped outside the region for processing. Next, a consortium of companies was proposing to build a pulp mill near their community. But the pulp mill's future was dependent on Alcan's support, and so residents questioned if *it*, too, would ever be built, because of the growing shortage of pulp logs in the region.

Fears were also growing in the minds of Alcan's critics that the additional power to be generated at Kemano once the new generators were installed would be considered surplus to BC's power needs, and would therefore be permitted to flow through BC Hydro's power grid and into Alberta and the United States. This scenario seemed all the more likely since Alcan had cancelled its plans to build a smelter in Vanderhoof and had not announced plans to increase its smelting capacity at Kitimat or anywhere else in BC. And their fears seemed to be confirmed when, in May, 1991, BC Hydro announced that, when the new generators were installed at Kemano, 285-megawatts of the electricity they generated would be purchased by Hydro for export to either Alberta or the US.[57]

That announcement brought a quick response from anti-Alcan activist Richard Overstall, a director of the Save the Bulkley Society, one of the groups affiliated with the Rivers Defence Coalition who said: "They're saying, 'Well, if we don't need it, we'll export it'."[58]

Nechako Valley residents also wondered how to reconcile Alcan's plans—to remove more water from the river with which to generate hydroelectricity to be sold to BC Hydro—with the resolution approved by Hydro directors in April, 1991, which stated: "In carrying out its business B.C. Hydro will minimize adverse effects on the natural and social environment and actively pursue opportunities to manage our resources for the benefit of present and future generations."[59] The directors also adopted a resolution establishing eight principles to guide Hydro in implementing the environmentally-friendly resolution. Included in this resolution is a principle stating the Crown corporation will "Pursue opportunities to replace in kind natural or social resources affected by B.C. Hydro's actions."

Could Hydro circumvent its environmentally-friendly resolve by purchasing power from Alcan? the increasingly suspicious valley residents asked themselves. And was there any need for BC Hydro to purchase power from Alcan?

When Hydro agreed to purchase surplus power from the KCP beginning January 1, 1995, under the terms of a 20-year sales agreement signed February, 1990, they said the additional power was necessary to help offset a developing provincial power shortage. But between 1988 and 1991 there had been a shift in Hydro's policy, and it had introduced a Power Smart program to encourage more efficient use of electrical power in the province. The need to purchase more power from Alcan had also been reduced by Hydro's decision to begin purchasing power from independent producers. The two measures resulted in a decline in the demand for power.[60]

Anti-KCP lobbyists' flagging hopes rose again in mid-1991 when it appeared Premier Bill Vander Zalm's scandal-ridden Socred party was stumbling toward an election later that year. BC's polarized two-party system meant there were no Liberals sitting in the provincial legislature, so the NDP seemed the only possible successor to the tired and troubled Socreds.

During a visit to Prince George late in 1990, NDP leader Mike Harcourt had added fuel to the lobbyists' hopes when he declared that if the federal government didn't undertake an environmental assessment of the project, the province should hold its own inquiry:

> It's time to clear the air and let the public have a say. When senior fisheries biologists accuse both governments of abandoning the fisheries resource, it's clear we must re-examine deals made behind

181

closed doors. The issue in the environmental impact process is that you weigh the environmental and economic aspects equally, rather than saying, "We're going ahead, come hell or low water, and we can patch up the environmental issues later." We say, "No, you've got to have a balance sheet that measures assets and liabilities equally, both in economic terms and jobs and the environmental harm done, and try to measure the two together." It doesn't mean you're anti-growth or anti-development. It means you're just for quality development and managed growth.[61]

The NDP carried this pro-review platform into the 1991 provincial election. John Ricketts of Prince George, the NDP candidate in the newly-formed riding through which the Nechako River flows,[62] confirmed his party's stance, saying if the NDP formed the next government, and if the federal government had not begun an environmental assessment of the project, an NDP government would conduct its own review.

Former Vanderhoof mayor Len Fox was the Socreds candidate in the riding. He dismissed as "unspecific" the allegations by federal fisheries biologists that the project threatened the future of the salmon runs in the Nechako. He defended his party's anti-review stance saying residents had had plenty of time to intervene during the long process leading up to the start of construction.[63] Fox also reiterated Alcan's position that the company had already taken action to protect the environment when it gave up the rights it had obtained in the 1950 agreements with the province to remove all the water from the upper Nechako, and when it agreed to continue releasing water into the upper river through the cold-water release facility it agreed in 1987 to build in the dam. Furthermore, Alcan had relinquished all the rights to the water flows in the Nanika-Kidprice system on the upper Skeena River it had obtained in 1950.[64]

When the provincial election ballots were counted on October 17, 1991, Fox had narrowly defeated Ricketts[65] to become one of the seven Socred MLAs remaining of the 41 who had formed the previous government.[66] NDP candidates Paul Ramsey and Lois Boone won the two other ridings which included portions of Prince George.[67] Both Boone and Ramsey had supported a review of the project, and the anti-KCP activists who had supported them were hopeful they could now count on them to ensure that the new provincial government kept its pre-election promise of a review of the project.[68]

When the NDP formed the government in October, 1991, it seriously began studying the implications of holding a review of the KCP.

They didn't like what they heard.

Lawyers examining the agreements on which the project was proceeding concluded they were legally air-tight. Worse yet, the terms of the 1987 Settlement Agreement included provisions making the federal and provincial governments responsible for obligations, liabilities or expenses arising from any public hearings or regulatory processes initiated by either government.[69] Faced with the threat that it would be forced to pay all the costs of a hearing in which the federal government did not participate—and the federal Conservative government was giving no indication that it had any intention of ever reviewing the environmental impact of the huge project—the province was reluctant to proceed alone.

The Supreme Court of Canada appeared to nudge the federal government toward accepting its responsibility to review provincial projects such as the KCP when, on January 23, 1992, it ruled its environmental assessment rules were valid, and said the Canadian government had both the right and the responsibility to carry out reviews of provincial projects.[70] The judgement defined environment in broad terms, identified its protection as one of the major challenges of the 1990s and recognized environmental reviews as essential planning tools.

"It pretty clearly shows major projects like Kemano must have an environmental assessment," commented Rivers Defence Coalition chairperson, Pat Moss.[71]

Despite increasingly aggressive prodding by northern BC NDP MPs Brian Gardiner and Jim Fulton, the federal Conservative government still refused to act.

Ottawa's reluctance to review the project was continually challenged by anti-KCP groups and First Nations organizations, who were also keeping the pressure on BC's new NDP government to fulfill its pre-election promise of holding a review of the project. The NDP's new environment minister, John Cashore, got an earful when he attended a meeting organized by the Allied Rivers Commission in Prince George on February 27, 1992. More than 250 people attended the meeting but, once again, it was the Carrier Sekani elders who spoke most eloquently about their concerns for the future of their river. Soft-spoken Stoney Creek elder Mary John[72] told the minister: "That shining water that flows in the river is not just water, but the blood of our ancestors. That is why it is so sacred to us, and year after year as long as the river is threatened, we will return to fight for its life."[73]

When he did not promise an environmental review during this meeting, Cashore was given what he later described as "a verbal spanking" by members of the audience including these words of advice from a member of the Stellaquo Indian Band: "Get out of your fancy shirts, suits and ties and get off your hind ends and go and look at the river and talk to its people."[74] Louise Burgener, president of Vanderhoof's Nechako Neyenkut Society, outlined for Cashore the 12-year fight her group had waged to save the river and then observed, "The fact that we are here today expressing those same concerns shows how much success we have had."[75]

Allied Rivers Commission spokesperson Arlene Galisky was more optimistic. "Finally tonight we start a process that should have been started 12 years ago. Finally tonight we have a provincial environment minister who has come to Prince George to listen,"[76] she told those attending the meeting.

Back at Alcan's Montreal headquarters, company chairman David Morton was threatening that unless construction of the half-built megaproject was allowed to proceed without new court challenges, the company would begin legal action against the two levels of government to recover the more than $500 million the company had already spent on the half-completed project.[77] "Unless it is clearly delineated what we have and have not got, we can't possibly proceed with a further investment of five-, six-, seven- or eight-hundred-million dollars," Morton said, following the company's annual shareholders' meeting in Montreal. "We have a hole in the ground that we don't really want. We would not have had a hole in the ground if we had not had an agreement which turns out not to be an agreement."[78]

Morton also hinted he was considering abandoning construction of the project because costs had risen to an estimated $1.3 billion. Declines in the world price for aluminum had forced the company to eliminate 6,200 jobs—or 11% of its more than 50,000-member workforce—during the previous two years. The layoffs were a result of a drop of $1.1 billion in Alcan's world-wide sales during 1990. Despite the drop in sales the company reported earnings of $543 million during 1990. But, in 1991, it reported losses of $36 million.[79] This was the second time Alcan had threatened to abandon the project when it was confronted with the possibility of an environmental review: In 1984 the company had threatened to give up plans for the project when the Mulroney-led Conservative government appeared ready to carry out its election promise to subject the KCP to an environmental review.[80]

Despite the threats of lawsuits and the withdrawal of plans for the project, opponents to Alcan's plans for the Nechako River continued to pressure the provincial government to review the project.

The Socreds and the provincial Liberals were offering no support: The Socred's opposition to a review had been clearly stated during the election; and the Liberal's new, aggressive, young leader, Gordon Wilson, who led that party's resurgence from holding no seats in the legislature to forming the province's official opposition, was also clearly opposed to one, saying it would create too much uncertainty and chase potential business away from the province. He cited Alcan's KCP and the government's failure to approve a proposal for the Windy Craggy Mine as two examples of the NDP's "do nothing" approach to business.[81] The Windy Craggy Mine proposal—to build a copper mine capable of producing 300 million pounds of copper annually near BC's border with Alaska—was later shelved by the BC government in favour of establishing a remote wilderness park in the area.

There was other opposition to the NDP government's stance on mining in general and Alcan in particular. The Mining Association

"I also believe that citizens who may be directly affected by such development should be part of the decision-making process, otherwise, we are no more than serfs as in mediaeval Europe, our future dictated by absentee landlords in Victoria and Ottawa." *Arlene Galisky, BCUCH 6.1055.*

of BC was critical of the "green" BC government, which they said was forcing mining companies to look to Latin America, particularly Cuba and Chile, as areas where they would invest their money. As evidence that the provincial government did not support the mining industry, Mining Association president Gary Livingstone also pointed to the government's refusal to approve the Windy Craggy Mine near the Yukon border, its decision to subject Alcan's KCP to a review and its new provincial water levy which was blamed for Cominco's decision to halt plans for a $100 million conversion of its aging lead smelter.[82]

Opposition to the KCP was growing throughout the Nechako River Valley and, in September, 1991, the residents of Fort Fraser and Fraser Lake joined their neighbours in Vanderhoof in their struggle to stop more water from being diverted from the river. Their decision to act followed a warning from public health officials to begin boiling their drinking water because it contained unacceptable levels of bacteria found in human and animal feces. Fraser Lake draws its water from the lake after which it is named and Fort Fraser draws its drinking water from the section of the Nechako River between the dam and the Nautley River—that is, from the section of the river where water flows had already been reduced to 20% of their pre-dam flows and would be reduced to 12% of the pre-dam flow if the KCP were allowed to proceed.

If the water is already too polluted to drink, what will be like after the project is completed? Fort Fraser and Fraser Lake residents asked themselves.

More than half the residents of the two small communities crowded into a school auditorium in Fort Fraser on November 29, 1991, to discuss the problem. At the conclusion of the meeting they had formed their own group, A River Forever, to contest Alcan's right to divert more water from the river. The spokesperson for this group, English-born Jeanette Parker, said she disliked being referred to as an environmentalist: She was, she said, acting from "an inner, spiritual, absolute belief that something was going to happen that was totally wrong." A River Forever, she said, would represent the more moderate position that there should be room enough in the valley for the river, for farmers, for recreational use, for industry and the jobs industry provides. She

186

described her growing awareness that industry had taken control of the river as being "like I'd been asleep and woken up and realized something had to be done about it because we couldn't let it happen and, if a single person could make a difference, that meant me, too."[83]

Soon the activities of A River Forever took over her every waking hour and all her energy. She admits that her heavy involvement with the group and the opposition she faced from the residents of the Nechako River Valley who favoured Alcan's project were major factors contributing to the nervous breakdown she suffered in the fall of 1993. "They [Alcan's supporters] thought I was this little upstart from England getting involved in something that was none of my business," she said. Other people told her they were afraid to get involved because it would upset their friends who were in favour of the project.

> Many people were in the pockets of Alcan so I thought I couldn't quit. If I didn't keep the bit between my teeth, I was afraid it would be all over. By the summer [of 1993] I felt everything was on my shoulders, and Janet [Romain] and Pam [Sholty] couldn't help because they had farms to run. I had a fax machine in my house, but we acted as a group. But I was constantly travelling and phoning and contacting the media.

Much of the stress came from the fact she was unable to obtain any intervener funding until the day the community hearings began in Fort Fraser. "I was frustrated. Unfortunately, a lot of bureaucrats think they're the only ones with intelligence and I was given the runaround and lied to, and I took that personally," she said. Despite the impact the campaign had on her health and her personal life, she says she has no regrets and would do it all over again if she thought she could ensure there would be a river flowing through the valley forever.

When Parker's health failed, Janet Romain, a small, wiry, spirited farmer's wife from Fort Fraser, and her lively friend and neighbour, Pam Sholty, took over responsibility for the activities of the A River Forever group. Asked why two farmers' wives had become so deeply involved in a controversial battle over the river, Sholty admitted that before she became involved in the anti-Alcan fight, she had scoffed at people who would lie down on roads and

The founders of the anti-KCP group A River Forever, Jeanette Parker (left) and Pam Sholty, at a 1992 trade show in Vanderhoof. Photo courtesy of Pam Sholty.

railways during blockades. When she and Romain got involved they were "pretty naïve" at first, thinking that if they arranged to meet with Alcan's BC vice-president Bill Rich, and "just tell him we need 30% of the river so it would flow from bank to bank, he would give it to us."

Their rude awakening to the world of multinational business came when Rich told them in no uncertain terms that the 1987 Settlement Agreement was legal and binding and, moreover, if any lawyer or government tried to take it away, Alcan would sue them.

"He told us if we had lived on Mars and came back to earth in 100 years and saw this nice little river, we would think it was beautiful because we had never seen it before," Sholty said. "I told him we didn't live on Mars and we wouldn't settle for a cute little river."

Sholty also had other, more personal, reasons for becoming involved in the A River Forever committee. "One of the reasons I got involved was I had been sick with cancer and I realized at that point in time, if I fought for it, I may not be here but that river would be here forever as a legacy for my children and my grandchildren if it is looked after properly."

Romain says she first became aware of what was happening to

the river when she asked Alcan's Vanderhoof-based community representative, retired school principal Bill McLeod, to come to their farm because they were having problems with their cattle walking across the river. The lower water flows in the river meant the Romains could no longer rely on the water to act as a barrier to keep their cattle on their property and they would have to spend money to construct a fence along the river bank to keep their animals from wandering.

> That day Alcan had shut the river down to slightly more than 12% [of its pre-dam flows] and Bill said "This is going to be high water after the Kemano Completion Project is finished" and I looked out and there was 150 feet of cobble gravel, a 50-foot river channel and another 150 feet of cobble gravel on the other side and I realized that was going to be as high as the river ever got.
>
> Before that meeting,[84] there were a lot of people in the valley who, like me, thought there would always be lots of water in the river in the summer and the fish and the aquafers would be alright and Alcan would take care of us. When we told them what we had learned they started getting angry.[85]

Nechako Valley residents' concerns about what was happening to their river increased in 1992, when dead and dying salmon were discovered near Prince George—far from their spawning grounds upstream on the upper Nechako, Stuart and Nautley River systems. It had been a hot, dry summer and when the salmon moved through the Fraser into the Nechako they encountered water well above the 70°F federal fisheries biologists considered safe for their survival that far from the ocean.

It was Prince George resident Ben Meisner who reported finding the dead and dying salmon to the media. Meisner, who has built his home on the north shore of the river and has explored the length of the river in his powerful jet boat, tells a dramatic story about how the discovery of a dying chinook—or spring as he refers to it—during the hot summer of 1992 made him so angry he has dedicated most of his free time and considerable sums of money to opposing Alcan's plans for the river.

He describes the event this way:

> I was down on my dock and I saw a spring salmon coming down the river in distress, a big female and she was loaded with roe. I

189

walked out into the river up to my chest and got her and I brought her over to the edge of the bank—she was still alive—and I held her in my arms, got her uprighted. She'd been splashing coming down the river and she had no physical bites or anything—like from a seal or an otter had been after her or an eagle. But she had a couple of sores on her.

I held her in my arms, I don't know, maybe for half an hour and I thought—you have to appreciate that fish came from somewhere off the Aleutian Islands and maybe made a trip of 15,000 miles and was coming home, passing by two thousand rivers, back up here, leaving all those other fish that went into all those other rivers on the Fraser not to say anything about all those other rivers she passed along the coast, heading to her own little stream up the Nechako which might be six feet across and a foot deep to where she was born and where she would die.[86]

When that 37-pound salmon died in his arms, Meisner became a dedicated Save-the-Nechako advocate.

She probably weighed 50 pounds when she left the ocean. I thought "Where in the hell do we human beings get the right to do this to her?" I was mad. I thought of all the effort she'd gone to to get that far up the river and all the eggs she had and not one of those was ever going to reach anything. It was like me saying to you, "I'm not going to let your children have children." It hit me that way. So you can say I became more dedicated in my approach in 1992.

Whenever Meisner took his jet boat out on the Nechako River during that summer's salmon migration season, he found more dead salmon. When he advised the DFO staff of what he had seen, they at first dismissed them as spawned-out salmon. When he disputed that, saying salmon did not spawn near Prince George, the staff of the federal fisheries office reminded him the dead salmon were no longer their responsibility: The 1987 Settlement Agreement had turned that responsibility over to a non-elected committee which was now responsible for ensuring the water temperatures in the river were safe for the fish. He should be talking to the committee about the dead fish, not federal fisheries officials, they told him.

Instead of contacting the technical committee in Vancouver, Meisner phoned a Prince George television station and, when he went back up the river the next day, he took a television camera crew with him. This time they found more dead fish, including two large sturgeon. The largest number of dead fish were the hundreds of dead sockeye they found floating in the water and caught in the weeds and brush near Bednesti Creek.

Because Meisner had begun to suspect the sockeye had been killed by the high temperature of the water in the Nechako River, he checked the temperature of the water in Bednesti Creek using the equipment he had purchased to measure the temperature of the river near his home. He found the temperature to be 54°F, well within the range considered safe for salmon. But the temperature in the main stem of the Nechako was 72°F which, according to the terms of the 1987 Settlement Agreement, was one degree higher than the maximum water temperature allowed when salmon are in the river. Meisner concluded the fish had suffered temperature shock when they moved from the higher water temperatures in the river into the cooler water temperatures in the creek.

That summer Meisner says he found water temperatures as high as 74.2°F in the river near Prince George. When federal fisheries officials discounted his findings saying he wasn't taking the temperatures properly, Meisner invited them to come with him when he took his readings. Their readings were identical. In fact at one point, he used the fisheries office's thermometer to make and record their readings when their staff person was away.

Other people living along the river also noticed what happened to it that year after Alcan released large volumes of water into the river in an attempt to cool the water. Dorothea Meyer, who has lived near the Nechako River since 1958 and swam in it regularly every summer, described her 34 years of observing the river in the following letter to the *Prince George Citizen*:

Spring runoffs and flood reach their peak usually in mid-June. During the runoff the water is brownish and turbid with roiled sediment. After mid-June the water recedes quickly and settles into its gravel bed, becomes relatively free of silt and debris and runs quite clear. One can observe the difference between runoff and July water clearly when standing on one of the bridges and looking down into the river-bed. What this means is that the river has normally cleared itself by the time of the salmon runs.

This year Alcan released so much water in July that within days the river rose very quickly to almost flood level, carrying with it huge amounts of debris, dirt and silt which had washed off its banks. Big trees and branches came floating down for weeks; the water was a dark muddy brown when it normally would be clear during this time.

Into this soup the fish swim after a long, stressful run up the Fraser River.

I saw more dead fish caught floating in the grass on the flooded shoreline than in any other year since 1958, and this was only on a short stretch of 500 to 700 yards of riverbank.

So many assumed causes were cited in the press for the mysterious fish kill, but common sense tells me that fish have to breathe oxygen. Water that normally runs clear by the time the fish reach it is totally muddied up and brown with dirt during this year's salmon run. Certainly this is not helping these fish to make that last stretch to their spawning grounds.

What possessed Alcan to suddenly release such huge amounts of water from their dam just prior to the salmon runs? The fish had to overcome a wall of mud, silt and debris as well as the sudden change in water temperature. Long before the salmon losses were made public I looked at the swollen, dirty river and could only shake my head in disbelief over such folly.

I am a non-political, non-scientific person. I am not even a fisherman or a native. But I know that if Alcan and their scientific advisers have their way, this scenario will be repeated every year in the future: the Nechako River, reduced more and more in its flow during the rest of the year, will suddenly swell up during July just prior to the salmon run and carry with it all the debris, dirt and mud which accumulated on its banks and its old river-bed during the year.

And this muddy mess rushes down to meet the salmon on their way up.[87]

By then Nechako Valley residents knew the safety of the fish in the river depended on the temperature of the water flowing in the Nechako River. But the answer to the question "What temperatures are required to ensure salmon arrive on the spawning grounds in good shape?" had not been answered. Alcan's environmental consultants claimed the fish can survive "with an acceptable level of certainty"[88] in waters with temperatures as high as 71°F. Other fisheries experts said salmon such as those in the Nechako River, who had to swim hundreds of miles to reach their spawning grounds, require water temperatures no higher than 63.5°F in order to preserve their strength and ability to spawn successfully.[89]

That summer, Ben Meisner was also shocked to discover that although Alcan frequently referred to its temperature monitoring station at the mouth of the Stuart River, there was in fact no temperature-monitoring station there. The last temperature monitoring station on the Nechako is located at Finmoore, five miles upstream from the mouth of the Stuart. Since most of the Nechako River sockeye turn into the Stuart on the way to their spawning grounds, and the Stuart is usually warmer or, at best, the same temperature as the Nechako, Meisner questioned why no one appeared to know the temperature of the Nechako's waters between the mouth of the Stuart and the point where the Nechako flows into the Fraser at Prince George.

Meisner believes before the dam was built the salmon's two-day trip through the warmer waters flowing in the Stuart was less of a threat than it is today, because the temperature of the Nechako was then much lower. "The problem is now they spend five days total time in water that's too warm from the time they leave the colder water in the Fraser trying to make it to the Stuart, and they just can't make it," he claims.

He was angered by Alcan's continuing efforts, during the BCUC's 1993-94 hearings, to convince people it can divert more water from the river without harming the fish.

Now they have a new public relations firm that writes their stuff for them and when you leave a hearing where you've given testimony, they're outside with the press releases right there saying what was wrong with your testimony—some people call them the truth police because it's their job to tell people what Alcan's version of the truth is.

It's amazing. This is the only time in history where we the people of the central part of this province are arguing with a company to try to get back something that is ours, and it is supposed to be the other way around. They're the guys that are supposed to prove to us that they can have it.

Remember this, if I'd left you as the custodian of the Nechako River after the 1987 agreement and you had looked after it in the manner it has been looked after by Alcan, you would be in jail. You promised to keep 3,100 fish in the river, you promised this in an agreement, and you've lived up to nothing. Yet you're walking around saying you're doing everything correctly. I don't know how they do it because if it was the average unclad, unwashed type they couldn't get away with this.

Do you know that the amount Alcan pays the province for the water it uses is tied to the price of aluminum and the price of aluminum has now dropped so low, I don't know where it's at, but my guess is their bill for the water in 1994 will be something like $60,000 for the use of the Nechako River. It's so low as to be absolutely pathetic.

Other serious questions were now being raised about methods the government used to obtain the agreement, including allegations federal fisheries scientists had been pressured to change the findings to conform with Alcan's demands for water.

Throughout the period when both sides were preparing for the 1987 court case, there were rumours the federal scientists had been threatened with dismissal if they failed to change their expert witness statements they had been asked to submit to support Fisheries Minister Tom Siddon's position. Proof these rumours were true became public on October 14, 1992, when MP Brian Gardiner unveiled a package of confidential letters and memos written by federal biologists documenting the internal struggle over the water flows that occurred within the DFO both prior to and after the signing of the Settlement Agreement.

In this package was a memo written July 18, 1986, by H. Mundie, of the department's fisheries research branch in Nanaimo, to Rod Bell-Irving, of the department's water use branch in Vancouver. The memo begins: "Howard Smith has asked me (June 26) to make changes to my expert witness statement of June 3 and to send a revision to you and a copy to him." Mundie goes on to say Smith criticized his statement for being too adversarial and negative. He expresses concerns about changing evidence he claims clearly indicates reducing the river flows further would reduce the salmon-production capacity of the Nechako River.

...my statement consists mainly of fact, not of opinion. Of 29 cases of regulated [river] flow, 26 resulted in reduced salmonid stocks. This outcome has a likelihood of one in 200 of occurring by chance. This hardly leaves room for subjective views.

He alleged that the department appeared to be asking him to make the argument that, since the department's proposed flows were higher than Alcan's, they were more acceptable.

The lesson of the case histories is that one cannot remove 69 per cent of the water from a river and expect to maintain salmon runs. There is, therefore, no relative merit in the DFO flows over those of Alcan; both are insufficient.[90]

Near the conclusion of the letter Mundie says Howard Smith told him those members of the department's technical staff who do not support the minister (for which read: "change their expert witness statement") "must take their game and play elsewhere."

Mundie informs Bell-Irving he sought legal advice to help him resolve his dilemma over whether he should obey orders, or tell the truth.

The answer was unequivocal; my obligation was to tell the truth under oath. I was informed that I would be in a far graver predicament if I signed an affidavit that I did not wholly believe in. I am left with no choice, therefore, but to give my first priority to the acquisition and presentation of the best possible information.

Gardiner charged, based on the information he had obtained, that it was apparently politics, not science, that motivated the federal government first to seek an out-of-court settlement, and then to exempt Alcan's project from its environmental review process.[91] Both moves, he claimed, were made because the government was afraid of the damning evidence its own fisheries biologists would give at the trial or during environmental hearings.[92]

Another man who was seriously troubled by the pressure exerted on federal fisheries biologists to change their testimony was William Schouwenburg, the senior biologist in the department's program-planning and economics branch, and the man who wrote the 380-page report of the Kemano task force which until that point had not been made public. His growing frustration about the efforts being made within the DFO to present Alcan's proposals in

195

a favourable light is apparent in his memo of October 25, 1990, which was included in the package of material obtained by Gardiner. Schouwenburg writes:

> I fully appreciate that anyone that is given the task of justifying the technical merits of the agreement under any circumstances will be stressed to the limit. As far as I'm concerned it would be like trying to keep clean while following closely behind an operating manure spreader.[93]

Gardiner had also obtained a copy of the Kemano task force report which he made available to the media. It concludes with eight recommendations about the conditions that should be maintained in the river to protect the salmon, including one stating that water temperatures should not exceed 63.5°F between the dam and the Nautley River, and 68°F below the Nautley. The Settlement Agreement requires Alcan to release enough water from behind the dam to maintain the water in the Nechako at a temperature no higher than 71°F.

In another memo written by Schouwenburg and forwarded to the members of the task force in November, 1990, together with the final version of the still-secret task force report he writes:

> I have attached copies of the exchange of correspondence I had with the Director General [Pat Chamut] which clearly demonstrates the desperate lengths to which he is prepared to go to hide the fact that the Nechako Agreement was a political and not a technical resolution to the problem. He did, however, leave me an "out" so that I could finalize the report and that I have done. Do not assume that any request from the public to see this document will be honoured. In the recent flare-up over the wonderfulness of the assessment process and the lack of public input to the final Agreement, Mr. Chamut refused to provide this document to [Dr.] Gordon Hartman [a DFO fisheries biologist]. It appears that the words "Alcan," "Nechako" and "Kemano" as well as any knowledge pertaining to those words are to [be] wiped from the minds of anyone employed in DFO other than those officially designated as spokespersons.
>
> Before I retire next March, it is my intention to write a memo to the Director General on how the suppression of technical information affects the morale of the professional staff involved as well as

raising ethical questions. Perhaps it will help us regain a clear separation between science/technology and politics that is essential for us to maintain our professional credibility.

On April 1, 1991, after he had retired, Schouwenburg returned a commendation he had received from the department for the work he did on the Kemano task force. The letter accompanying the returned commendation was also included in the package of information Gardiner released during his October, 1992, press conference. In his letter, Schouwenburg explains his return of the commendation: He thought the way in which the 1987 Settlement Agreement was being defended by the minister and federal bureaucrats tainted the professional reputations of the members of the task force who had dedicated so much of their careers to it:

> While I remained in the Department, I kept this Award posted on the wall as a reminder of how much the politicization of the public service combined with bureaucratic cynicism is responsible for the very low morale of the Department's staff. Everytime I saw such a similar award posted elsewhere, I wondered to what degree that person's reputation had been sacrificed by some self-serving politician or bureaucrat. Now that I have resigned from the public service I no longer need such painful reminders.
> ...
> Many of the terms of the Settlement Agreement run contrary to the advice given in the Kemano Task Force by the best minds the Department could muster from its ranks. Many issues are not addressed by the Agreement. This is largely because the Minister of the day and my Member of Parliament, Tom Siddon, did as he is empowered to do and made a political decision on the project.
> The terms of the Nechako [Settlement] Agreement flowed from the deliberations of the Strangway Working Group.[94] The DFO members of that working group were in essence instructed (intimidated?) by your predecessor Dr. Peter Meyboom to ensure they came up with a resolution to the problems which were consistent or compatible with Alcan's objectives. This of course meant that the positions taken by the Kemano Task Force and the team of experts involved in the preparation of our court case were to be abandoned.[95]

In October, 1990, the staff of the DFO had been advised that only their boss, Director-General Pat Chamut, was to speak publicly about the Settlement Agreement.[96] Federal scientists had also been ordered not to talk to anyone about the KCP prior to the start of the court case, in an effort to prevent information from being inadvertently released to Alcan. That ban was continued after the Settlement Agreement was signed so that nothing was known of those discussions until after fisheries biologists who had worked on the Kemano task force had either retired or left the department and were therefore free to begin talking publicly about their concerns.

The muzzling of federal fisheries biologists was just one of the obstacles facing researchers looking for the rationale behind the agreement. Non-government researchers and reporters, including myself, found that their efforts to uncover the truth—hidden by the documents, deals, deceptions, allegations and controversy that have piled up around the 1987 Settlement Agreement—were being stifled by government regulations.

Researchers likened their early attempts to uncover information about what happened prior to 1987 to peeling layers off an onion: Each time they uncovered a layer of new information, they discovered there was another layer of equally difficult-to-obtain information hidden under it. The most tireless and persistent researchers were Dana Wagg and John Hummel, who had been hired by the Cheslatta Carrier Nation to investigate the actions occurring around the signing of the 1950 and 1987 agreements. They succeeded in obtaining much of the government information that came to light later.

Many of these pre-BCUC hearing researchers, including Wagg, Hummel, and people working for Brian Gardiner, tried to use Canada's Access to Information legislation to obtain government files. In response to their applications for this information they were told the more than 80,000 pages—documents, letters, memos, minutes of meetings and other material relating to the these agreements and Alcan's activities on the Nechako River—in the federal government's files were not available because of the pending court actions launched by Alcan's opponents immediately following the signing of the 1987 Settlement Agreement.

The Cheslatta Carrier Nation's dogged determination to inform other Canadians about the damage done to their lives by the federal government and Alcan was brought to the public's attention again when, during July, 1992, the band asked BC's Attorney General Colin Gabelmann to investigate laying criminal charges against the aluminum giant under Section 182 of Canada's Criminal Code. That section of the Code states anyone who improperly interferes with or offers any indignity to a dead human body or human remains, whether buried or not, is guilty of an indictable offence and liable to imprisonment for a term not exceeding five years.[97]

This action followed Alcan's decision to release larger-than-usual volumes of water from the Kenney Dam Reservoir, which resulted in raising the level of Cheslatta Lake more than 13 feet and flooding two graveyards on the shores of the lake.[98]

Alcan said the unusually large water releases were necessary because the reservoir had been filled by the higher-than-usual amount of water draining into it from the heavy snow pack that had accumulated on the surrounding mountains during the winter.[99] Others attributed the heavy flows of silt-laden water and tree roots they saw moving through the river to the company's desperate attempts to cool the water temperature in the river before the sockeye salmon began swimming through it on their way to the spawning grounds.

By August 6, the DFO had a six-person crew at work building temporary dykes around the graveyards beside Cheslatta Lake. But the incident provided a reminder of the damage that had occurred in the area south of Vanderhoof by the rapidly fluctuating level of the Nechako River and the Murray-Cheslatta Lakes since Alcan built its first project in BC in the 1950s. "We've put up with this for 35 years and it's time someone takes responsibility for what's happening here," said Mike Robertson.

Within a month, three BC cabinet ministers[100] decided they had better get a first-hand look at the areas already affected and those that would be affected if Alcan proceeded with the KCP. The tour was co-ordinated by the A River Forever committee, and included aerial and ground inspections of the Skins Lake Spillway, Cheslatta gravesites, Cheslatta Falls, the dry Grand Canyon of the Nechako River, Kenney Dam, chinook spawning grounds, the bird sanctuary in Vanderhoof, agricultural areas, the Vanderhoof water and sewer system and a native fish camp.

At a community reception held after the tour was completed, long-time Fort Fraser resident and trapper Leo LaRoque gave his opinion about what he thought should be done with the river:

> I would be satisfied if Alcan would give us a constant flow of water in the Nechako River of no less than 2,000 cubic feet per second. Then the river could re-establish itself, we could put a canoe in and drift down it, the birds could build their nests there and nature would take over and correct the errors.[101]

LaRoque was present the day Alcan shut off the flow of water into the Grand Canyon of the river, and spoke of it at a community hearing in Fort Fraser:

> I stood on the banks of that once beautiful river and watched it go dry, a day I will never forget. The six miles of the canyon above Cheslatta Falls were left with small puddles filled with rainbow trout. They all died. Below the falls hundreds of Chinook salmon were spawning. As the water level went down the eggs were left high and dry.
>
> The beavers and muskrats had their lodges established and runways up to the water level, they too were left high and dry. And the muskrats have never recovered.
>
> Over the last four years, we have seen the Nechako River in flood conditions two and three times a year. These floods have brought down tons of silt covering most of the gravel beds. The fresh water clams are all but gone. The White Sturgeon in the Upper Nechako River is gone as well, and so are the rainbow trout and the dolly varden.[102]

The canyon is now overgrown with willow and alder thickets, he said.

Alcan's critics protested when, in 1992, federal Fisheries Minister John Crosbie appointed Alcan director, Dr. Peter Pearse, to investigate the disappearance of salmon in the Fraser River. They charged that it was inappropriate to have a director of Alcan—the very company whose activities are damaging one of the main tributaries of the Fraser River—investigating the disappearance of the fish. They believed the fish were dying as a direct result of the conditions in the river which had resulted from the 1987 Settlement Agreement.

Pearse, naturally, rejected their theory. Instead, he blamed the disappearance of the fish on overfishing—both inland and at sea—and weather disturbances—including successive El Niño[103] occurrences in the Pacific Ocean which created unusually hot, dry weather in the interior of the province, lower-than-usual water flows and higher-than-usual temperatures in the Fraser River. He also blamed the breakdown of a fishing agreement with the United States which led to American and Canadian fishers taking unusually large numbers of salmon at the mouth of the Fraser.

Most of the blame, however, he placed on the shoulders of the federal government, citing their last-minute decision to introduce native food fisheries on the Fraser River as the prime factor contributing to the salmons' disappearance. The federal government's decision was made in the wake of a Supreme Court decision, in what was referred to as "The Sparrow Case," that determined natives have a right to fish. Near riots broke out on the lower Fraser when commercial fishers objected to the decision which, although it was legally correct, threatened their ability to continue earning their living by fishing.

Alcan's opponents also criticized Pearse's report, saying Ottawa's failure to monitor the water temperatures in the 70 kilometres of the Nechako River, through which all the sockeye migrate from the Fraser on their way to the Stuart River, meant the effect of higher temperatures in that river were not considered by the study. That information was found in a less-widely distributed accompanying technical report on the Nechako River prepared by Dr. Peter Larkin, in which he states that water temperatures higher than 17.5°C (63.5°F) can cause health problems in sockeye who have swum long distances inland.[104]

This warning seemed to apply to the Stuart-run sockeye. By the time they reach the Nechako River they are nearing exhaustion after swimming more than 400 miles upstream from the mouth of the Fraser, near Vancouver, to the confluence of the Fraser and Nechako Rivers. From there, some of these sockeye must swim up to 200 miles further to reach their spawning grounds near the northern end of Takla Lake.

Water temperature readings provided by Alcan show that, on all but two days during the period from July 10 to August 20, 1992,

Cheslatta River in 1923 before the Kenney Dam was built. BC Archives & Records Service, Province of BC photo no. i-32008.

when the sockeye were in the river, the temperature of the water in the Nechako upstream from the Stuart exceeded 17.5°C. No temperatures were available for the water in the Stuart River, up which most of the sockeye swim after leaving the Nechako River on their way to their spawning grounds in Stuart, Trembleur and Takla Lakes. It is known, however, that because the Stuart River is shallow, it only draws off the warmer water from the top of Stuart Lake; thus the water in the Stuart River is usually warmer than that in the Nechako.[105]

Later that year, the RCMP began investigating the allegations that a federal fisheries scientist had been instructed to change the expert witness testimony he was preparing for the 1987 trial. When Brian Gardiner questioned Federal Fisheries Minister John Crosbie about the investigation in the House of Commons, Crosbie confirmed there had been "some kind of an investigation into this matter going on now for a year or two, but we have never been put in possession of any information as to just exactly what the investigation is about or what results have occurred."[106]

BC RCMP Inspector McAuley confirmed they had been investigating the allegations, but doubted there would be any prosecution because of lack of evidence.[107] When Gardiner questioned him about the investigation, he explained that a prosecution would be

Slumping of the banks of the Cheslatta River below Skins Lake Spillway that occurred during large water releases in 1992 in an attempt to cool the Nechako during the sockeye migration. Photo courtesy of Pam Sholty.

difficult because so much time had elapsed and many of the required documents were not available.[108] Apparently the RCMP were experiencing the same problems in obtaining the DFO documents as other researchers had in investigating the KCP. Native leaders worried that Nechako Valley residents would settle for a provincial review of the project.

That would not be enough, they said: They wanted a wide-ranging federal judicial inquiry and environmental review into Alcan's industrial developments in the region since 1950, so southern BC residents would finally learn the truth about the company's activities in northwestern BC.[109] "If the Nechako River dies, my people die," Carrier Sekani Tribal Chief Justa Monk said during a press conference in Prince George.[110] He feared the province would go ahead with the review without federal government participation.

His fears were justified.

On January 19, 1993, BC Premier Mike Harcourt travelled to Prince George to make an announcement about the project. With him were Energy Minister Anne Edwards, Environment Minister John Cashore and University of Victoria law professor Murray Rankin, who had been appointed by the government in July, 1992, to investigate the KCP and advise the government on what action it should take. When his report and recommendations were released during the press conference, they were greeted by a mixture of applause and boos.

The boos came when the government announced it would not order construction of the project halted because, as Rankin said in his report, the economic benefits were so great they outweighed even the worst-case estimates of its negative effects. "Short of

---

"While there is no doubt that the Legislative Assembly could choose to resolve the issue of compensation by means of legislation that explicitly denied compensation to Alcan, the impact of such a step on investor confidence in the province could be considerable." *Rankin and Finlay, 39.*

"I don't think that any of the nonsense that circulates about KCP has made me as angry as the suggestion that we would be so unethical or again so stupid as to do anything that could be construed as criminal." *Bill Rich, BCUCH 11.1673.*

January, 1993 (left to right): Dr. Murray Rankin, BC Premier Mike Harcourt, BC Minister of Environment John Cashore, and BC Energy Minister Ann Edwards in Prince George, making the announcement that the BCUC will hold hearings into the Kemano Completion Project. Photo courtesy of the *Prince George Citizen*.

expropriating the project, it can't be removed," Harcourt told the crowded press conference in Prince George.[111]

"Why not expropriate it?" asked some members of the audience. Others said BC and Canada should follow Norway's example: Faced with a situation much like the one developing in BC, Norway purchased Alcan's shares in Norwegian-based aluminum-producing facilities in 1979.[112]

Harcourt also announced the BC government was acting on Rankin's recommendation that there be a review of the project because, although the benefits of the KCP will be felt throughout BC, the residents of the Nechako River Valley will pay all the short- and long-term costs through the loss of most of their river. "The Harcourt Government took the only logical option it had this week when it ordered a public review of Alcan's partly-constructed Kemano completion project," commented the editor of the *Prince George Citizen*.[113] Since 1987, Prince George's only daily paper had actively reported the concerns of Nechako Valley residents and their drive to have the impact of the project assessed. At this time few other BC dailies were aware of the major environmental battle developing in central BC.

Lorna Barr, deputy chair of the BCUC, was assigned the task of heading the Commission. Two commissioners were initially appointed to work with her: Prince George geographer Alistair McVey, the chair of the College of New Caledonia's university-transfer science division, and UBC Professor Emeritus Dr. Peter Larkin, who toured the area before the dam was built and prepared a critical report on it that was presented to the half-day hearings held in Wistaria and Victoria in October, 1949. Larkin had also been responsible for the report on the Nechako River appended to Dr. Peter Pearse's 1992 report on the disappearance of hundreds of thousands of sockeye salmon on their way to the spawning grounds.

Native leader Alfred Scow was appointed to the commission later. He withdrew in May "for personal reasons" when it became apparent the area's Carrier Indians did not support the provincial review process.

Native leaders and environmental groups immediately condemned the provincial government's report for not doing enough.[114] They rejected Rankin's conclusion that the 1987 Settlement Agreement is legally binding and were shocked by the government's decision to allow the project to proceed. Justa Monk, Tribal Chief of the Carrier Sekani Tribal Council, laid down the terms under which his people would participate in the review. They included the participation of both the federal government and Alcan, and the inclusion in the commission's terms of reference the damage caused by the 1950 agreements and the project's environmental consequences along the full extent of the Fraser River.

Monk used Rankin's report to draw to the attention of First Nations people living in southern BC the potential damage the project would inflict on the Fraser's rich salmon runs. Early in February, 1993 the more than 200 chiefs and delegates attending a

---

"Rankin says 'The damage is regional while the benefits are provincial'. When you destroy the largest tributary to the Fraser, how can that be classified as regional?... We have all read Mr. Rankin's document and found many interesting statements such as: 'Alcan's strong environmental commitment'.... I am enclosing the latest Polluter's List from the Department of the Environment which shows Alcan has made the list again for the seventh time. Maybe Mr. Rankin didn't have access to that." *Glenda Olson, BCUCH 4.522-23.*

First Nations Summit in Vancouver threw their weight behind the Carrier Sekani Tribal Council's fight to halt Alcan's plans to divert more water from the Nechako, and began laying plans for a province-wide fight to save the river.

Squamish Nation Chief Joe Mathias told the delegates that the project threatened some of the world's richest natural salmon runs as well as freshwater fish—whitefish, trout and white sturgeon—on which native people living along BC's largest river depended for their food.

The delegates also supported the Carrier-Sekani chiefs' efforts to have the area to be affected by Alcan's project given interim protection. "Interim protection measures" is a process included in the BC Treaty Commission Agreement signed in September, 1992,[115] which ensures that land being subjected to environmental damage can be protected while the three parties negotiate the first treaties with most of BC's First Nations people.

That protection was never provided.

Although the Rivers Defence Coalition welcomed the news that there would finally be a review of the project, spokesperson Pat Moss said that was the only part of the report with which she agreed.[116] "The rest of his analysis we find very faulty and we are disappointed in the kind of job Mr. Rankin has done here," she said. "Essentially we don't agree with any of his analysis."[117]

The coalition particularly objected to Rankin's conclusion that most of the damage had already been done to the river by the lower flows resulting from the agreement signed in the 1950s, and the damage resulting from the 1987 Settlement Agreement was only incremental. "In fact the really serious damage is likely to occur now," she said.[118]

Premier Harcourt said he was not surprised by their reaction to Rankin's "sobering conclusions." Unfortunately, he added, most of the discussions with Alcan were completed behind closed doors. "The consequences of trying to undo that agreement are very expensive. As a lawyer, I respect legislatures and the rule of law, and whether you like the decisions made by past governments, you are bound by them," he said.[119]

Alcan's only response was to say that it would neither participate in the hearings nor resume construction until the review was completed.[120] The company was in a difficult position: By May, 1993, it had reported losses in eight previous quarters;[121] and faced with a glut of aluminum on world markets, Alcan was being urged to reduce costs by cutting back on its production.[122]

Although both the federal and provincial governments refused to take part in the hearings, on March 2, 1993, the Prince George City Council announced it would join opponents of Alcan's proposal to divert more water from the river by presenting a brief to the commissioners.

There was another piece of good news in March, 1993, when the Cheslatta People finally reached an out-of-court settlement[123] with the federal government in the action they had brought in charging the Department of Indian Affairs with, among other things, fraud, forgery and breach of fiduciary responsibility in the events surrounding the sale of their lands to Alcan in the early 1950s. Alcan had also promised to return the seriously damaged lands around the lake to the band when the KCP was completed.

By May, 1993, the federal government had agreed to "co-operate" with the BCUC's hearings. That meant it would not participate directly, but would release some of the more than 80,000 pages of documents related to the project. Most of those documents, however, could not be released without Alcan's consent. Ottawa also reserved the right to "object to the authority of the commission to obtain disclosure of information or to subpoena past or present federal government employees in order to elicit information." In other words, the gag-order remained in place and DFO employees were not allowed to take part in the hearings.

In July, 1993, Alcan announced it had changed its mind and said it would participate in the hearings after all, to ensure that its side was properly explained and that the project went ahead as planned. "We feel compelled to participate because of the likelihood that, without our participation, the review would be incomplete and therefore could lead to recommendations not consistent with the present project design," said Alcan's Bill Rich.[124]

By this time there were allegations Alcan was again secretly trying to renegotiate its 1988 agreement to supply BC Hydro with electrical power, worth a total $600 million over a number of years[125]—allegations that brought instant denials from BC Premier Mike Harcourt and launched a semantic battle over what was and was not considered government assistance. In a prepared statement Harcourt said:

> With respect to Alcan vice-president Bill Rich's statement that he hopes the BC government will help preserve the economic attractiveness [of the KCP], I can confirm that, at Alcan's request, government officials have engaged in discussions with Alcan.
>
> Alcan put forward a formal proposal to existing arrangements for the supply of power to B.C. Hydro that would have resulted in hundreds of millions of dollars in additional costs to BC Hydro and BC tax-payers.[126]

He told the legislature the meetings were arranged after Alcan threatened to take legal action against the province, charging it with breaching the 1987 agreement, and were intended as an attempt to try to settle their dispute out of court. It was during the meetings that the province became aware Alcan wanted to renegotiate its contracts with BC Hydro, he said.

On July 15, 1993, Harcourt rose in the BC legislature to confirm that the company was trying to "wring an extra $350 million from Hydro for electricity from the Kemano Completion Project."[127] The company's proposals were based on the fact the project had become uneconomic because, since construction began, the cost of completing the project had risen from $500 million to more than $1.3 billion. The increased price Alcan wanted for the power it sold to Hydro would cost BC tax-payers an additional $350 million, and Alcan's proposal was rejected, Harcourt said.[128]

Harcourt assured the legislature the government would consider a long-term agreement to purchase the excess power from Alcan's plant at Kemano at the old rates under the terms of BC's new energy policy opening the door to long-term electricity exports by BC Hydro and independent producers.[129] He gave the company 30 days to clarify its terms.

Bill Rich did so on August 11 in a letter to Moe Sihota, the BC minister responsible for BC Hydro, in which he advised him Alcan would not resume construction of the project unless it could renegotiate the amount and the price of the electricity it was committed to sell to Hydro.[130] If the company could not renegotiate a new agreement with Hydro, it would look to other markets for additional power to be generated at Kemano, said Alcan spokesman Les Holroyd.[131]

Rich denied that the company was seeking a subsidy to bail out the troubled project on which it had already spent more than $500 million. Despite the economic difficulties, he also denied Alcan had plans to abandon the project.[132] "Absolutely, categorically, there's no question in all this of Alcan abandoning or cancelling the project," he told a Prince George reporter.[133]

This exchange between the provincial government and Alcan left many of the residents of the Nechako Valley scratching their heads. Why was it Alcan thought it could renegotiate the 1987 Settlement Agreement when it no longer suited their purpose, yet refused to renegotiate it when the residents of the valley found fault with it? they asked themselves. It also added more fuel to Nechako Valley residents' suspicions that Alcan was really not as interested in smelting aluminum as it was in selling power. There were also concerns Alcan would begin exporting water after the NAFTA agreement appeared to make that possible. It would not be impossible for Alcan to capture the water exiting the powerhouse at Kemano, then carry it by pipeline or canal to be loaded on tankers docked near the mouth of the Kemano River.

The company's economic troubles came to the forefront when Alcan's CEO, David Morton, stepped down effective November 1, 1993, and was replaced by Jacques Bougie, who had been president and chief operating officer.[134] The move followed a two-year study of Alcan's world-wide operations.[135]

The company had been sailing through stormy financial waters for more than three years. It had reported a net loss of $209 million (US) during the previous 10 quarters,[136] including $122 million in 1992, and $20 million in the first quarter of 1993, compared with a combined profit of more than $3 billion between 1986 and 1990.[137] The losses were blamed on Russia's cash-strapped government's decision to begin selling large amounts of aluminum on the world market at cut-rate prices, thereby ending the ability of large aluminum producers like Alcan to control world prices of the metal.[138]

Aluminum analyst Stewart Spector of New York is reported to have responded to the shakeup at Alcan's Montreal headquarters by saying it was time for Alcan to recognize that the aluminum industry had changed forever, and the only solution to the company's problems was to reduce production.[139]

In December, 1993, Alcan's new CEO, Jacques Bougie, announced that by cutting costs he aimed to make Alcan the producer of the lowest-cost aluminum in the world.[140] Bougie had already worked with Morton to implement a two-year program to cut more than $400 million (US) from its cost base during 1991 and 1992.[141] Described as a "workaholic" and a "technocrat" when he assumed the number-two job in the company in 1992, Bougie said at that time he saw the company's future role in supplying materials for the structural parts, engines and castings of mass-produced cars. He predicted the amount of aluminum used in the manufacture of a car would double to 300 pounds between 1992 and 1997.[142]

Following the signing of the 1987 Settlement Agreement, an aluminum engine block factory had been one of the industries proposed for using Alcan's excess hydroelectric power. Like so many of the proposed benefits offered as reasons for supporting the KCP, that plan was never acted upon.

By 1994 the company was still trying to rationalize its business operations by selling some of its smaller, inefficient components, cutting back production by 156,000 tonnes (171,600 tons) including a 30,000-tonne-cut in aluminum production in Kitimat[143]—all of which was accomplished without laying off any permanent employees, Rich said.[144]

Alcan was also working to gain control of the hearings into the KCP, charged the spokesman for a Prince George-based environmental group. Everything changed after the company agreed to participate in the hearings in BC, said Dr. Peter Carter of the Nechako Environmental Coalition (NEC).[145] "They [the commissioners] said most definitely before that, consultants will be available to all stakeholders," Carter told a reporter at the *Vancouver*

Sun.[146] He was reacting to the commission's decision that its consultants would no longer produce a summary for public discussion. Instead, Alcan would provide "an information base and summary document" unless panel members decided otherwise. "Alcan is completely running the show. It's not hard to see we have an uneven playing field," he said.[147]

Although Alcan was now participating in the hearings, Carrier Sekani Tribal Chief Justa Monk still refused to attend citing, as before, the federal government's failure to participate as one reason First Nations people refused to participate. "To me it's a junior hearing. Our input into the terms of reference for the hearings has been totally ignored."[148]

He added another reason for the Carrier Nations' refusal to participate: They would not take part unless Premier Mike Harcourt guaranteed that their participation would not be used against them in the future.[149] This statement seemed to indicate that the Carrier Sekani First Nations were either worried that their participation in the hearings would jeopardize their treaty and land claims negotiations, or they were planning further legal action on the issues surrounding Kemano I and the KCP, and didn't want statements they might make during the hearings to be used against them in that action.

MP Brian Gardiner, supported the First Nations' demands that the federal Conservatives be forced to take part in the hearings, charging that government with being "the biggest culprits in this whole issue."[150]

Anti-KCP activists were becoming increasingly frustrated.

The Rivers Defence Coalition was unhappy with the way the commission was acquiring its consultants. Commission chairperson Lorna Barr had invited intervener groups to recommend the experts who should be hired to assist the commission, but, Alcan's opponents charged, the commission had gone ahead and hired its own consultants without consulting the interveners. That procedure brought charges from Allied Rivers Commission[151] spokesperson Arlene Galisky that the commission was barrelling ahead with its own agenda and ignoring public input into the process.[152] She was also unhappy because intervener groups were not consulted on the consultants' terms of reference.

The Rivers Defence Coalition had been demanding that the commission's terms of reference be broadened to look at the province-wide consequences of the KCP, particularly its effect on the Fraser River.

Intervener groups were also upset by the provincial government's decision to make only $250,000 available to assist them with hiring researchers to prepare reports and lawyers to represent them at the hearings. And they were perturbed by the way these funds were being distributed. For instance, although the commission had announced it would hold a series of community meetings in BC's central interior in September, interveners, including the Rivers Defence Coalition and the A River Forever group had received no money, and thus were unable to hire lawyers to represent them.

When a federal election was called for October 25, 1993, valley residents trying to stop the project polled the candidates in the Bulkley-Nechako riding about their position on federal participation in the hearings.

The Tory candidate, former Prince George alderman Colin Kinsley, told an audience in Houston, BC, that impediments should not be put in front of Alcan and warned the provincial government it could end up in court over the way it was handling the inquiry into the KCP.[153] Everyone knew where Brian Gardiner stood: He had been carrying on the stop-KCP fight federally for years. But that didn't stop Kinsley from claiming that Gardiner was using the Kemano issue to get re-elected.

Jean Chretien had given Pat Moss of the Rivers Defence Coalition a firm commitment that the federal government would participate in the hearings,[154] and the local Liberal candidate, David Wilbur, reaffirmed Jean Chretien's promise during the election campaign, when he said that, should the Liberals form the next federal government, all the government documents related to the project still being withheld from public view would be released,

---

"[I]f I may say respectfully, that this hearing is a convenient way of having a public tantrum but without the unpleasantness of Clayoquot Sound. We're having a democratic, sanitized process." *Geoff Laundy, BCUCH 6.931.*

and the gag-order on the federal fisheries scientists' participation would be lifted.

Reform Party candidate, Dick Harris, also supported federal participation in an inquiry. But his party's environmental platform was the briefest of all the major parties, consisting of a one-page, broadly worded document which began with the statement, "The Reform party supports ensuring that all Canadians and their descendants dwell in a clean and healthy environment."[155] When Harris was elected to represent the Prince George-Bulkley Valley Riding, interveners took a closer look at his party's policies and found only that it promised to give preserving the environment a high priority while carrying out its plans to cut $19 billion from the federal deficit within three years.

Despite the criticisms and complaints, the commissioners continued to prepare for the first community meeting and, after several delays, it was finally held on November 9, 1993, in Kitimat. It opened under a cloud of uncertainty because, after years of battling each other in the courts, Alcan and its opponents were there, but the First Nations people and the federal government were absent.

On December 20, 1993, the commission took steps to ensure that three important witnesses would provide evidence at the hearings when they issued subpoenas to Pat Chamut, director-general of the DFO for the BC Region, and to two members of his staff: Dennis Deans, chief of habitat management, and John Payne, chief of habitat conservation. The fourth person they summoned to testify before them was Duncan Hay, a private consultant and head of the technical committee directing the fisheries conservation program on the river.

The announcement that some key witnesses had been issued subpoenas ordering them to appear at the BCUC hearings came amid growing discontent with the terms of reference established for the hearings. Interveners continued to ask questions: Why was the review limited only to the *effects* of the project and not the *process* that led to the 1987 Settlement Agreement? Why were the consequences of the 1950 agreement not included? And why did it not look to the effects the KCP would have on the full length of the Fraser River?

Hearing Things

The hands of time cannot be turned back. Those who wish to find their solution by returning to 1950 or returning to 1987 are not a constructive part of the process.[1]

When Lorna Barr finally called the BCUC's first community hearing to order on November 9, 1993, she faced a room full of concerned Kitimat residents. Most of the people attending the meeting made it clear they wanted construction to resume on the Kemano Completion Project by wearing buttons proclaiming "I Support KCP."

That was to be expected.

These were the people who had benefitted most directly from Alcan's industrial activities in BC. They lived in a community planned by Alcan, whose smelter was the community's largest employer. Wages in Kitimat are higher than both the Canadian and BC averages. Although considered isolated by people living in other parts of the province, Kitimat is located in a picturesque mountain valley in BC's Central Coast Range where the residents have easy access to the ocean, mountain wilderness, hot springs, lakes and one of the world's best unregulated salmon-fishing rivers nearby, the Skeena.

The only threat to the wild salmon using the Skeena River had been Alcan's plans to divert water from its upper reaches into its

---

"We want to see this project completed." *Terrace mayor Jack Talstra, BCUCH 1.80.*

215

Nechako Reservoir. But that danger had disappeared when the company signed the 1987 Settlement Agreement which removed Alcan's right to divert the flows of the Nanika-Kidprice system into Alcan's reservoir.

When asked, few of the people attending the meeting that day saw any connection between Alcan's plans to divert up to 88% of the flows from a salmon-bearing river like the Nechako, to what might happen to the Skeena should the company succeed in maintaining the chinook salmon stocks in the upper Nechako with the planned 12% flows remaining in the river. This planned "maintenance" on the Nechako could be precedent-setting: Proposals could be put forward to divert the upper reaches of every BC salmon-bearing river—using the maintenance on the Nechako as the basis for believing it could work elsewhere.

It is also true that the residents and businesses of Kitimat and nearby Terrace had suffered severe economic set-backs when Alcan decided to halt construction of the KCP. Until that point, the residents of Kemano, Kitimat and Terrace believed their fears for the economic future of their communities had not been heard amid the growing clamour for environmental hearings into the KCP. By deciding to open the community hearings in Kitimat, the commissioners gave the residents of these communities an opportunity to make their views on the project known first.

In her opening statement, Barr established a friendly but authoritative tone by emphasizing that the commissioners wanted to keep the community hearings as informal as possible. Her soft, Scottish-accented voice, no-nonsense but patient manner and her habit of scanning the room with her dark eyes to see if anything was amiss, gave onlookers the impression she was both welcoming and in charge of what was about to transpire. No cross-examination

---

"It makes economic and environmental sense to allow the continuation of KCP, which will use existing waters to supply an increase in power rather than building another dam elsewhere in the province and flooding more land." *Kitimat resident Luella Froess, BCUCH 1.94.*

"Of 134 businesses contacted there was a combined loss of $7,340,000 due to the suspension of the project." *Sharon Taylor, President of the Terrace Chamber of Commerce, BCUCH 1.27.*

Indian village of Kitimaat with graveyard (centre right) and church (centre left), circa 1950. BC Archives & Records Service, Province of BC photo no. d-01309.

Johnson Street Camp at Kitimat during construction of the first Kemano project, circa 1950. BC Archives & Records Service, Province of BC photo no. bag1513.

would be allowed during the community hearings, she explained, but the commissioners might ask presenters questions for clarification at the conclusion of each presentation. To her left during each of the hearings sat Dr. Peter Larkin. A short man whose slightly flushed, wrinkle-free, bespectacled face and balding head gave him an angelic look that belied his decades of experience studying BC's salmon-bearing rivers and imparting his knowledge to students at UBC. This is the same man who had travelled over the Great Circle Water Route before the Kenney Dam was built to assess the dam's impact on the lakes that now lie beneath the reservoir.

To Barr's right throughout the hearings sat Alistair McVey. His dark hair, lean, heavily bearded face and inscrutable demeanour contrasted sharply with the more opened-faced appearance of the two other members of the commission. There were times during the hearings when onlookers could be forgiven for believing McVey was not listening. Then, he would surprise everyone by suddenly leaning forward and asking a penetrating question about something a presenter had just said.

Before the hearings started, Barr made it clear that the commission's terms of reference specified it was to deal only with the damages which might be caused by the 1987 Settlement Agreement, and did not include the damages caused by the agreement made in the 1950s.

When the hearings started, no one could know that before they were finished nine months later, the commission would hear 87 days of statements and testimony. Included in this deluge of talk were impassioned calls for the commission's terms of reference to be broadened; emotional statements of the concerns of Kitimat and Nechako Valley residents; long explanations of Alcan's plans for facilities and for managing the river so the chinook runs could be protected; conflicting expert testimony about hydrology and the requirements the salmon, freshwater fish and other inhabitants of the river required for survival; thoughtful comments about what

---

"We have had enough studies and reviews. Let's stop spending money and start making some. Let's get on with it. Let's give the north a chance." *Kitimat businesswoman Marjorie Fowle, BCUCH 1.100.*

(From left): Commissioners Allistair McVey, Lorna Barr (Chairperson) and Dr. Peter Larkin at the BCUC hearings in Vanderhoof. Photo courtesy of the *Vanderhoof Omineca Express-Bugle/Courier*.

the commission should recommend; and, during the technical hearings that followed these opening community hearings, careful cross-examinations by lawyers and private citizens of the different panels put forward by both proponents and opponents of the KCP.

The first official statement in the hearings was presented by Richard Wozney of the District of Kitimat, who outlined Alcan's impact on that community:

> The interruption in construction has had direct and significant impacts on the B.C. economy, particularly the economy of northern British Columbia. The effects were felt very acutely in Kitimat as many people in our area lost their jobs, much purchasing related to Kemano Completion ceased, and citizens' confidence in the local economy was shaken.[2]

Like most of the people at the meeting that day, Wozney believed the resumption of construction of the project would restore economic stability to Kitimat and Terrace. As the hearings progressed, however, it became clear that although completing the project meant the return of short-term construction jobs, residents could not count on Alcan's smelter providing employment forever.

Eventually it was learned that the completed project would create fewer than 10 permanent jobs at the generating plant in the Alcan-owned town of Kemano, and that there were no long-term guarantees that Alcan would keep its aging smelter at Kitimat operating at full capacity in the future.

There was also concern about the company's contract to deliver 285 megawatts of power to BC Hydro starting on January 1, 1995. Alcan's June, 1991, decision to halt construction of the KCP meant that that deadline would now be difficult to meet and questions were being asked about where the company would obtain the power to fulfil its commitments. Later, Alcan's BC vice-president Bill Rich admitted one option the company had was to close down one or more of its potlines in Kitimat to make that power available for sale.[3] Other options were: to combine the existing 140 megawatt power surplus already being sold to BC Hydro under short-term contracts, or to buy the additional power necessary to meet the contract deadline from Alberta or elsewhere.[4]

Many of the Kitimat residents who spoke that first day recommended that a block of the power resulting from the completion of the project be committed for use by industry established in their area. This recommendation harkened back to the 1950 agreement which cleared the way for the construction of the dam, and which stated that the company was being given the right to construct the project in order to generate electricity for use in the smelter it was constructing in Kitimat and for other industries in the region. As the hearings progressed it became clear different interpretations were given to the term "region." Some thought it meant the Kitimat-Terrace region, others thought it meant the Nechako River Valley, and still others thought it meant the entire province of BC or even Western North America.

Ray Brady, chairperson of the Kitimat-Stikine Regional District, noted on the opening day of the hearings that "in the foreseeable future if the Aluminium Company of Canada decided that the market conditions were correct and they wish to increase

---

"Economically, it is difficult to believe that the province could say no to what is likely to be among the cheapest sources of power in the world." *Richard Wozney, BCUCH 1.19.*

further smelter capacity, that they could do it anywhere in British Columbia or anywhere on the coast, and that would not be to the advantage of the Pacific Northwest."[5] He, too, urged the commissioners to ensure that future benefits from the power generated by the project be assigned to the Kitimat-Stikine area.

The presentations by business leaders from Kitimat and nearby Terrace concentrated on demonstrating the short-term benefits reaped by the region as a result of the money Alcan had already spent and would spend completing the project, and on describing the devastating effect Alcan's decision to stop construction had had on businesses in Kitimat and Terrace.

Six million dollars worth of business and 2,000 jobs were lost in the two communities when Alcan stopped construction of the project, Sharon Reeves, president of the Kitimat Chamber of Commerce, told the commissioners.[6] More than $535 million had already been spent on the project—including 1,900 contracts valued at more than $25 million placed in the Terrace-Kitimat area during 1991 alone. Contracts worth $710 million were already in place when construction stopped, more than half of which were committed to BC companies, said Sharon Taylor, president of the Terrace and District Chamber of Commerce.[7]

The two Chamber of Commerce presidents offered, as another compelling reason why the project should be completed, a statement attributed to Larry Bell, then chairman of BC Hydro: He was quoted as saying that the power Alcan had agreed to sell to the public utility upon completion of the KCP would save the Crown corporation from committing $500 million to develop other power sources.[8] At the conclusion of their joint presentation, commissioner McVey asked the two Chamber of Commerce presidents if any plans had been prepared for dealing with the economic

---

"It is my opinion...that no support exists at the informed level to use the subterfuge of a hearing process to restrict or in any way alter the flow regime arrived at by mutual consent and contractually agreed upon by the best minds and the best information available by all who entered into the KCP 1987 agreement.... What are we conducting here, an economic review? an environmental review? a police action? a fishing expedition? Does the Commission really know what it is here for?" *David Serry, BCUCH 1.65, 67.*

repercussions their communities would experience when the short-term construction phase of the project ended. They admitted there had not.

These early speakers made it clear they did not agree with the Province's decision to hold the hearings. They believed those calling for the hearings were attempting to "turn the clock back to either 1950 or 1987."[9] Nor did they blame Alcan for demanding compensation for the delays caused by the hearings because the company entered into the 1987 agreement in good faith and, therefore, had a right to expect that agreement to be honoured. "If the agreement is not honoured then Alcan has a legitimate right to expect fair compensation," Wozney declared.[10]

Wozney also claimed that trying to mitigate the damages that resulted from the 1987 Settlement Agreement was pointless, because "the major damage to the Nechako River System, to the Nechako Reservoir and to the Kemano River took place over 40 years ago. KCP will, at worst, cause only incremental damage."[11]

Other speakers pointed to Premier Harcourt's recent announcement that Alcan was seeking to increase the price it received for the power it was selling to BC Hydro as one way the province could compensate the company for the costs it has incurred as a result of the delays and the cost of attending the hearings.

It wasn't until half-way through the meeting that the commissioners heard from anyone who disagreed with Alcan's plans to remove more water from the Nechako and increase discharges into the nearby Kemano River. The dissenting voice was that of Arnold Nagy,[12] who rose to speak on behalf of the more than 2,200 people employed in the fishing industry along BC's northern coast from Bella Coola to Prince Rupert and Haida Gwaii.[13] He pointed out that there would be fewer than 10 short-term jobs created by the KCP, yet it threatened the long-term future security of the jobs of the more than 20,000 BC residents who make their livelihood in the province's fishing industry—an industry that contributes

---

"[T]urning a river system that is owned by the people and future generations of Canada over to a private company is not in the best interest of all Canadians.... It's a lot broader issue than just jobs, jobs, jobs." *Arnold Nagy, BCUCH 1.56, 58.*

"close to one billion dollars annually to the BC economy....We in the fishing industry do not believe that the KCP will be of any benefit to anyone except Alcan and its profit margin and to B.C. Hydro who will export the power generated to the United States,"[14] said Nagy, whose union, the UFAWU, is affiliated with the Rivers Defence Coalition.

The Nechako River contributes 20% to BC's total salmon production. The Kemano task force report prepared by DFO scientists before the 1987 Settlement Agreement stated that these stocks will be seriously damaged if more water is removed from the Nechako River. Other damage will occur to the runs using the Kemano River when more water is diverted from the reservoir into that river, Nagy explained.[15] The commission, therefore, should consider the project's effect on the whole of the Fraser-Nechako River system, he concluded.

Kitimat businessmen countered Nagy's arguments by saying that Alcan's previous environmental consultants, Envirocon,[16] had spent more than $22 million studying the river before it recommended the flows included in the 1987 Settlement Agreement. That should be good enough, he said. Whether or not the environmental assessment prepared by Envirocon for Alcan should be relied upon was argued about throughout the hearings.

Kitimat businessman David Serry admitted he was unable to understand why people objected to the KCP:

I have never been able to correlate the justification for the strong pockets of hostility, distrust, or conflict engendered against the proponent's corporate activity within the region, given the cost benefit accruing to the region by the proponent's corporate activities. That the original project in 1954 created dislocations and unfavourable impacts is not denied using the standards of today. This, however, is not the source of the hostility in my opinion. Perhaps the proponents' handling of ongoing and arising objections may feed hostility.[17]

Terrace mayor, Jack Talstra, described the project as "a second jump start"[18] for that community because it made more power available and attracted more people into BC's northwest region. "Right now, without the Kemano Completion Project, Alcan spends about $3.1 million a year in Terrace for goods and services,"[19]—an amount that would grow to approximately $15 million annually if construction resumed on the project, he added. "For the Lower Mainland, those are perhaps nickels and dimes, but for us in Terrace those are big dollars that we depend on in making our local economy a sound one."[20] He pointed to a proposal to build a paper mill halfway between Kitimat and Terrace as an example of an industry that would be drawn into the area by the additional power generated at Kemano upon the project's completion.[21]

Cliff Madsen, a spokesman for the Canadian Association of Smelter and Allied Workers (CASAW), the union representing workers at Kitimat and Kemano, described how it felt to be caught in the debate over jobs versus the environment: "[W]e see two extremes in this whole process. On the one side you have the NIMBYs[22] and, more recently, called the NOPEs, Not On Planet Earth. And, on the other side, I think equally extreme if they're honest, is the "'Don't ask any questions, let's just develop it, any cost any way',"[23] he said. CASAW recognizes that the old attitude "What's good for General Motors is good for the U.S.A." has been replaced by the realization that responsible corporate development must include public and community participation in the decision-making process, Madsen added.[24] In summarizing the union's position, he said it was giving "conditional" support to Alcan's plans to complete the project, provided the region benefitted "in a meaningful way"—which could be achieved by tying energy permits to provisions ensuring sustained employment was created in the region.[25]

The 1950 agreement for the sale of electrical energy generated at Kemano is limited to promoting and developing the district and does not appear to authorize the production of electricity for consumption outside the region, he pointed out.[26] Nor did the union think the original plan, put forward by Alcan in 1984, to use the additional electricity to smelt aluminum in new smelters in central BC "should be allowed to vaporize without some sort of justification or reasonable explanation."

Alcan's statement that they may eventually use the additional power generated for smelter purposes "...if and when the aluminum market warrants," well, as I said earlier on, this debate has been going on for more than a decade and the market has risen and fallen a couple of times since then. It peaked, for instance, in 1988 at $1.20 a pound, yet we still didn't hear any indication for a company during those good days about when they were making record profits, whether there was any commitment forthcoming to the additional smelter capacity. So our question is: When would such conditions warrant a statement, a commitment: Okay? We're puzzled at that.[27]

He agreed aluminum prices were not so promising in 1993, but the outlook was positive, and smelting more aluminum could still give the region the economic shot-in-the-arm it needed when the demand increased. Other options were the construction of an aluminum recycling plant and establishing a plant in the region to manufacture aluminum automobile components. He concluded his statement with this description of what happens in a community when its largest industry begins laying off people and there are further threats it may reduce production:

[I]t doesn't require a $10,000 study to get a glimpse of where we're at today with economic development at Kitimat. There's been a population decline from 14,000 to 12,000. Job reductions at the smelter continue at a steady pace. Our sons and daughters are graduating from school and then moving down south to find work. This community needs an injection of positive influence and the resumption of KCP would be, in our opinion, a lost opportunity if we didn't see beyond the construction phase. Now is a time to secure commitments for investing in the region's future.[28]

Another speaker, Marjorie Fowle, a former researcher-broadcaster for CBC, was critical of the sensational stories written and broadcast by the media which, she said, misrepresented the KCP story to audiences outside the Kitimat-Terrace region:

When I was with the media and covering a story, there were often times after reading and listening to the reports that I thought many of my colleagues hadn't attended the same meeting. Unfortunately emotion makes a better story than fact. Facts are very dry. If a reporter can file a more emotional story, it has a better chance of

---

"If all we're doing in five years from now is monitoring a generating plant that's shipping power down south, then we've missed the boat in our submission." *Cliff Madsen, CASAW, BCUCH 1.91-92.*

being picked up and even receive provincial or national exposure. That exposure is often that reporter's ticket to a larger centre or better position. It often appeared to me that the journalism schools must be stressing creative writing skills, rather than investigative journalism. Unfortunately the public erroneously believes this news coverage and these stories and emotional turmoil begins.[29]

Kitimat businessman Gerry Bloomer provided the commissioners with another description of the impact of Alcan's activity—or lack of it—on the people and economy of Kitimat. He had moved to Kitimat from Vancouver just in time to watch "convoluted legal challenges" force Alcan to wind down its construction activities at Kemano.

All of us, whether intimately or indirectly, are inextricably linked to the well-being of our three main players in this town and at tidewater. When the predominant one, Alcan, falters through some very harsh fiscal quarters with a prolific undertaking in limbo, we can all feel the loss of esteem and morale; witness the psychological and monetary wounds tearing the fabric of our small businesses and labour pools of skilled trades people asunder. Each of us senses the reverberations of abject pain with shop fronts, government services and families vanishing from this municipality.[30]

Kitimat residents were not looking for handouts, he assured them: "We've mainly been stand alone types, not relying on assistance.... We only ask to be granted the freedom to continue in this vein, unencumbered by bureaucrats and incessant lobbying of special interest groups."[31]

As they would do during each of the community hearings, the Alcan representatives attending the meetings remained silent, but listened intently to what the citizens of Kitimat and, later, the residents of the Nechako Valley were saying.

Fish Don't Swim Single File

The Nechako Valley and its immediate surrounding area is a land of great beauty. The creeks, the lakes, the mountains, the farm lands and the forests. This is our home. It is our right and privilege to live here. It is our responsibility to apply all manner of knowledge to all resources, the air, the earth, the water, to ensure prosperous and wholesome life in perpetuity.[1]

To be honest, I am really sick of listening to a group of people who don't even live in this part of the country tell us that draining a river system will not impact on the environment much beyond the banks.[2]

The steady throb of skin drums could be heard inside the meeting hall when Commissioners Barr, Larkin and McVey reconvened the community hearings nine days later on November 18, at Fort Fraser, 270 miles to the east of Kitimat. The drums were a symbolic protest by Carrier Nations people who, because they continued to refuse to take part in the hearings, chose this method of reminding the commissioners and those going into the meetings that their lives had also been damaged by Alcan's activities in the Nechako River Valley.

Many of the submissions made that day at Fort Fraser were deeply introspective and spiritual as the residents spoke of their profoundly held belief that humans cannot destroy or damage the environment without injuring themselves and their families. This more subjective, emotional manner was in sharp contrast to the hard-headed, business-like, technology-driven approach the com-

227

First Nations drummers outside the BCUC hearings in Fort Fraser. Photo courtesy of the *Vanderhoof Omineca Express-Bugle/Courier*.

missioners had heard from the residents of the region around Kitimat.

One person who spoke at Fort Fraser was Jacqueline Anne Green. She said, "I am speaking to you straight from my heart as I am not any kind of expert with a degree behind my name. I would like to speak on behalf of life itself, for the future generations of both man and all other living things that live on the Nechako River and its basin."[3]

Another young woman, Maya Sullivan, said, "The earth asks us to use her abundance wisely and gently, taking only what we need and to harvest in a manner that we may return again and again, whenever we need that particular thing. The earth asks us to help her grow, to be clean, to be in balance, to love and appreciate, to be kind, to use the medicines the earth creates naturally to heal ourselves."[4]

Most of the people who spoke at Fort Fraser made no attempt to hide their hostility toward Alcan's failure to meet its promises to them, and toward its determination to reduce the flows of the Nechako River to 12% of its pre-dam flows with no firm commitments to giving anything back to the area.

Protesters at the BC Utility Commission hearings in Fort Fraser. Photo courtesy of the *Vanderhoof Omineca Express-Bugle/Courier.*

Robert Green, a man who described himself as "an old peace-loving hippy" provided one of the best summaries of why the ordinary people living near the Nechako River were "so full of hate" when they thought of the KCP and Alcan. In a word, it was lies, he said, the lies the company had told them over the years:

> I remember a book by Mordecai Reisler [sic], "Lies My Father Told Me." Well, I've got some lies here that have been told to me over the last 14 years, some in that building that was here before this building was erected. The book should now be called lies that a trans-national told us. Here are some excerpts from the book. (*BCUCH* 2.175)
>
> "Alcan is in the aluminium business not the hydro-electric business."... "The company will not appeal a decision by the Supreme Court of British Columbia." (*BCUCH* 2.176)
>
> "While I believe the aluminium industry can grow in British Columbia and that it's especially suited to the north, it's clear we must share the water resource that's involved with the people who depend on it." (*BCUCH* 2.176-77)
>
> "I recognize that the Kemano Completion will produce jobs and taxes, but it also will be carried out in a way that the people in the north can support." (*BCUCH* 2.177)
>
> Alcan is committed to the use of the watersheds as a shared resource.... We are committed to developing a proposal for this project in concert with northern residents.... I am optimistic that some economically sound version of our project can ultimately be constructed and put into service without permanent disturbance to our regional environment. (*BCUCH* 178)
>
> By working together I believe that we can develop a project that could become a model for future development of renewable energy resources.... There must be sufficient water in the Nechako River to protect existing runs of Chinook salmon to the upper reaches of the river. (*BCUCH* 2.179)
>
> As far as the agriculture prospects are concerned these people haven't got anything to worry about. I don't know what they're all up in the air about, these farmers that are worried about water. (*BCUCH* 2.179-80)
>
> Water flows required for irrigation are much smaller than those required for other needs and irrigation can easily be provided for. (*BCUCH* 2.180)

Later in the hearings Alcan's BC vice-president, Bill Rich brought out his own list of the inaccurate information he said was being passed around by the opponents of the project.

Protesters at the BCUC commission hearings in Fort Fraser. Photo courtesy of the *Vanderhoof Omineca Express-Bugle/Courier.*

I've heard Alcan referred to during these hearings as an American company. Not so. Alcan is a publicly held Canadian company whose shares are traded on most of the world's major stock exchanges. It is Canadian controlled, and although Canadian share ownership has been known to dip below 50 per cent, this is something that doesn't happen often or for very long. At the end of 1992, almost 70 per cent of Alcan's shares were Canadian held.[5]

He also claimed that many of the people who had appeared before the commissioners had greatly exaggerated the proposed flow reductions in the Nechako River that would be instated once the project was completed. He explained Alcan's version of the flow reductions this way:

> [I]n assessing the effects of flow reduction, we can only measure against what is there now and that is why, Madam Chair, that under KCP why we say Nechako flows at Prince George as they exist today will be reduced by 12 per cent. To put it another way, 88 per cent of the existing flows at Prince George will remain after KCP. At Vanderhoof 71 per cent of existing flows will remain. In the Upper Nechako, 47 per cent of the existing flows will remain.

In other words, Rich continued to portray the water diverted in the 1950s as irrelevant, claiming the reduction in the flows of the upper Nechako River following Kemano Completion would not be 88% of the original flows as the project's critics claimed.

Farmers with land in the Nechako Valley also spoke out during the community hearings. One of them was Janet Romain, spokesperson for A River Forever, who told the commissioners that much of the river-bottom land and the fertile land on the benches above the Nechako River between Fraser Lake and the Stuart River has been developed into farms. The area's low rainfall means many of these farmers rely on irrigation to improve the production of their land. With the benefit of irrigation, the farmland in the Nechako River Valley can produce two or three crops of alfalfa hay annually. Without irrigation, it produces only one small crop, she said.

"I'll tell you one thing, Alcan has come a long way. In the 1950s and the late '40s and '50s they discriminated very heavily against the native people in the price they paid for their land when they took it away from them. They're not doing that any more. They're treating us all the same. They're treating you like fools. They're treating us all like fools." *Long-time Nechako Valley resident Robert Green, BCUCH 2.183.*

"The Kemano projects are being held by the proponents as shining examples of ... shared resource management. Hydro-electricity gets 88 per cent. The salmon get 12 per cent. And irrigation gets a tiny dollop. And that's the end of the sharing." *Janet Romain, BCUCH 2.149.*

She blamed the terms of the 1987 Settlement Agreement for the fact there is no more water available for irrigation in the upper reaches of the river, since the DFO ordered the province to issue no more water licences to farmers in that region because all the water in the river was needed for the fish.

They say that all the water left from Cheslatta Falls to the confluence of the Stuart and Nechako is required for fish. Alcan tells us that there is plenty of water for both agriculture and fish. Again, who do we believe?
...
At every public meeting we have attended the same thing was called for, more water in the river. Please do not misread the frustration that we are feeling about the highhanded way the governments have decided to allocate a resource that we feel belongs to us, the people who live in this valley.... No amount of money can buy the Nechako. The only mitigation I am interested in is more water left in the river bed.[6]

Community and business leaders in the smaller communities of Fort Fraser, Vanderhoof and Fraser Lake had other concerns. They faced a major problem in coming up with the money they would need to improve the communities' deep-drilled wells in order to provide safe drinking water, and to improve their sewage disposal systems so they could continue to discharge water back into the river when the flows are reduced. The BC government had already committed $2.2 million of tax-payers money to assist communities to improve their water and sewage systems, but that wasn't the only problem they faced, said Henry Van Andel, spokesperson for Fort Fraser and the Regional District of Bulkley-Nechako.[7] Residents were also concerned about the loss of the river's recreation and tourism value.

People living beside other water systems in the Nechako Valley, such as the Francois Lake-Stellako River system which drains into the Nechako through Fraser Lake, have not yet been affected by Alcan's activities. But they said they feared water could be drawn from those sources if the region experienced a dry period and the company needed more water to meet its sales contracts with BC Hydro.

"A dramatic drop in the reservoir's water level would cause trouble for Alcan if they were locked into an agreement to provide power, Fraser Lake could be in trouble, and Vanderhoof might as well put wheels on their canoes. We trust Francois Lake will not be looked at as a source of water," said Jill Kopy, president of the East Francois Lake Commuter Association.[8]

Low water levels will also produce problems for trappers[9] and people who have built wharves along the river, the commissioners were told.

Young people came forward at Fort Fraser to give the commissioners their views that the decisions of past governments to permit Alcan to reduce the flows in the river was affecting their lives and the lives of future generations.

"I spend a lot of time rafting down the Nechako River. I sure hope Alcan doesn't take any more water out of the river. I think they've already taken more than their share," 10-year-old Cody McNolty told the commissioners. He went on to explain that he wanted future generations of children to be able to enjoy riverrafting the way he had. "I sure hope you can help us save what is left of the Nechako River."[10]

Fifteen-year-old Mathew Green questioned why the next generation had to live with the mistakes of previous governments. In the statement he had prepared, and which was read to the commissioners by his father, Robert, he said:

> We and our children can never hope to witness the great beauty of the once mighty Nechako except within the confines of old photographs. Never can we witness the awing number of spawning sockeye which one native elder described as "...a huge mass of red which was so large it would stop the flow of the Nautley."[11]

Toward the end of the one-day community hearing in Fort Fraser there was a question about the validity of the studies on the basis of which the project was proceeding.[12] "We do not feel that a proper study has been done by independent biologists and environmentalists. We cannot depend on studies prepared by Alcan or the federal or provincial governments, as these bodies stand to gain by KCP," said John Stafford, deputy mayor of nearby Fraser Lake.[13]

The last speaker that day was the slender English-born woman who, until her health broke under the strain, had spearheaded the efforts of the A River Forever group. When Jeanette Parker strode to the intervener's table to be sworn in, few people realized she had been heavily sedated to control back spasms which had confined her to bed. Despite her pain, her voice was strong and purposeful when she described the immensity of the David-and-Goliath struggle in which her group found themselves.

In the seven months since the hearings had been announced she had repeatedly called for an honest and fair hearing in which groups such as A River Forever had adequate funding and time enough to prepare to defend the river from the onslaught of the batteries of Alcan-hired legal and environmental experts.

> We also stated there will be no public confidence in the process if the Commission, on its own accord, select [sic] the experts. Here we are seven months down the road and no further ahead. Do we have funding in place? No. Do we have experts? No. Do we have documentation and adequate time to prepare? No. So what does this tell us, Commissioners, that this is a fair and a proper hearing? No way. The experts that the Commission has hired are the Commission's experts and not our experts. Alcan has its team of experts. The Commission has its team, and we have the usual, which is absolutely nothing.
>
> We ask ourselves why. Is history repeating itself? Are we following the same trend as yesteryear's? We are growing angrier by the minute and our patience is diminishing. This is our review. We and our children have to live here, and yet our hands have been tied.[14]

In fact, her group had received their intervener funding that day, leaving them only three weeks to find a lawyer to represent them at the Phase One technical hearings which were scheduled to start December 6. She demanded the technical hearings be delayed for

---

"As students, teenagers and future inheritors of the earth, we feel that a government that gives control of a natural multi-use resource to a private corporation in perpetuity, without fully understanding future implications, is not being responsible." *High school student Lance Burgener of the Nechako Environmental Youth Alliance, BCUCH 4.432.*

"We feel ignored and betrayed by both of the senior levels of government and are very frustrated." *John Stafford, deputy mayor of the Village of Fraser Lake, BCUCH 2.196.*

four months to give them time to prepare, or, if that was not possible, some of the more contentious issues should be removed from the earlier technical hearings to give intervener groups more time to research and prepare themselves properly.[15]

After hearing repeated calls for a delay in the start of the more formal technical hearings, the commissioners agreed to delay their start until January 17, and answered the concerns of Parker and other interveners by reassigning some of the more technical water-related issues until the hydrology hearings.

When the community hearings reconvened the next day, November 19, in Vanderhoof, the commissioners finally heard from the people of the community that had been torn apart by Alcan's promises—by their hopes that a smelter would be built there, and their fears that if it was finally built, they would lose the river that is an important landmark and resource in their community.

Business and political leaders were united in their appeal to the commissioners to help them ensure that Vanderhoof continues to have a viable future. The key word repeated throughout their presentations was "sustainability." They were prepared to support the KCP if the sustainability of Vanderhoof's society, economy and environment were safeguarded, Vanderhoof Chamber of Commerce representative Henry Klassen told the commissioners.[16]

For too long the community had watched as productive forest lands were drowned in the Nechako Reservoir, the water from the river was diverted to benefit the rest of BC and more of the remaining forest resources were hauled to the larger mills in Prince George and Prince Rupert without any benefits returning to Vanderhoof.

During the long drive to force the calling of an environmental review of the project, the community had been divided into pro-Alcan and anti-Alcan camps. Mistrust of the governments and big business was intensified by the series of broken promises made to the residents of Vanderhoof including Alcan's promise of a smelter, and the provincial government's promise of a meat-packing plant. More recently, the promise of a pulp mill had been dangled before Vanderhoof residents in an effort to entice them to accept having less water in the Nechako River as it flows through their community. Henry Klassen stated:

> Many people believe the pulp mill can be a reality, while others believe that all these economic development proposals are yet another diversion game being played in order to stop resistance to diverting the rest of the river. The mistrust of others in this community has magnified. Many people are afraid to participate in the hearings because they think it might put the planned pulp mill or other economic initiatives at risk. Others have given up the fight to acquire what they feel is adequate water because they think it is a lost cause. It is an atmosphere of tension that we have lived with for years.
>
> ...
>
> The original promise that was made was that the construction of the Kemano I and KCP would benefit the northern sections of the province. As suggested in this brief, the opposite is true. The vast majority of economic benefits flow out of the north, relatively little stays or returns.[17]

Vanderhoof mayor Frank Read echoed Klassen's words when he told the commissioners that, ten years previously, the Council of the District of Vanderhoof had approved a motion supporting the project. The motion still stands. But, Read reminded them, there were conditions attached to the motion calling for guarantees that the project would not damage the environment or the community's social and economic development. Before they could agree to a further reduction in the flows in the river, Vanderhoof councillors wanted assurances that the reduced flows would not harm their community and Alcan's firm commitment to build a smelter there.[18]

Throughout the Vanderhoof hearings there were repeated calls

"Finding an appropriate and sustainable way ahead is essential because otherwise our local economy, as it exists today, does not face a very encouraging future." *Vanderhoof resident Henry Klassen, BCUCH 3.276.*

"[S]ustainability, for those who don't know what it means is this: We inherit something from the previous generation and we pass it on to our successors in at least as good a shape as we received it." *Geoff Laundy, spokesman for the Two Rivers Canoe Club, BCUCH 6.929.*

for the residents of the Nechako Valley to have more say in how the river was managed, and for the establishment of a local benefits fund to be used to assist industry to locate in the region. Mayor Read pointed to two projects—a cogeneration plant and the proposal to build a pulp and paper mill near Vanderhoof—as examples of the sort of effort that could help to stabilize the economy of the community.[19]

Vanderhoof's dependence on the future of the forest industry was highlighted by the fact that 83% of the community's wages come from that industry, said Vanderhoof sawmill operator Lloyd Larsen.[20] But two decisions made by governments over the previous 40 years had significantly reduced the ability of the area's timber supply to sustain the local forest industry: the drowning of the forests when the Nechako Reservoir was filled,[21] and the Vanderhoof land settlement program in the 1970s, in which settlers were given incentives to clear large tracts of forested Crown land for agricultural use.[22] Now, Larsen said, the mills were faced with a government drive to make significant reductions in annual allowable cuts, which would further undermine Vanderhoof's economic viability.

When Commissioner Larkin questioned Larsen about his company's[23] attempts to harvest the timber that had been under the water of the reservoir for almost 50 years, Larsen said "It doesn't look very good, it doesn't smell very good, but it might be alright once it's dried and dressed and bundled up."[24]

Denis Wood of Quesnel, who holds the title to the first deeded property on the Nechako River downstream from the Kenney Dam, pointed out that "just over 600" spawning chinook made their way to the upper Nechako River in 1993, compared with the Settlement Agreement's goal of an annual average of 3,100 return-

---

"Long-term considerations should be borne in mind, not merely the urgency of immediate problems. That mistake was made in 1949 and again in '87. You, the Commission and the government of the day, should not let this happen in '93…. There's no technical or scientific person alive who can tell me what nature is going to do to us on a year to year basis, so I think it needs to be regulated to comply with nature." *Vanderhoof guide-outfitter and mayor, Frank Read, BCUCH 3.291, 293.*

ing chinook spawners. He believes the low chinook escapement that year was directly related to the fish mortalities that occurred in 1979 and 1980, when Alcan diverted large amounts of water to produce more power to sell to BC Hydro.[25] "One wonders how the fish managed to survive for thousands of years waiting for Alcan to come along and sort things out,"[26] he commented.

Bob Mumford described why he believes the increased weed growth in the Nechako and its tributaries is responsible for killing fish: Canadian Pond Weed is invading the waters and threatens to choke off their lives when the rivers and lakes freeze over. As oxygen and light levels decline under the ice, the bulky leaves of the weeds die and begin to soak up all the oxygen from the water as they decompose. The weeds already occupy 30% of the lowered Nechako and the nearby Stuart, he said.[27]

> Weeds are like a snow fence. I think everyone here is familiar with a snow fence or wind fence. They slow the water down, it drops whatever silt or dirt it's carrying and this in turn helps the weeds to grow more, this in turn slows the water down more and a vicious circle of growth begins, referred to as positive feedback. Weeds create weeds and where they grow the area is no longer usable.[28]

The weeds also provide ideal hiding places for predator fish, such as squaw fish, that eat young salmon and form a barrier for migrating salmon.

"Fish don't swim single-file," he said.[29]

There was also a strong protest against the reduction in the Nechako's flows from the recreational users of the river. Doug Goodwin painted a gloomy picture of the future of continuing to canoe safely on the Nechako Reservoir and river should the KCP proceed.[30] He claimed that the increased fluctuations of the reservoir's water level will increase hazards to canoeists there:

> The extended foreshore, the further accumulation of drift logs, and the exposure of greater numbers of tree tops and stumps which will result from exaggerated and frequent drawdowns, will further reduce the safety factor for canoeists. Safe and quick access to the shore is mandatory for safety as well as convenience. The present conditions make this impossible for much of the reservoir. The Kemano Project can only make this condition worse.[31]

On the river itself,

[t]he unsightly vegetation encroachment on the foreshore and sand-bars, the extensive mud flats, the prolific weed growth and the subsequent smell of rotting materials will detract considerably from the paddling experience. The reduced availability of Chinook salmon will also reduce the number of sightings of eagles and bears along the waterway.[32]

Dangers like more exposed rocks and log jams will increase the likelihood of overturning or swamping, particularly, he said, by inexperienced canoeists, "many of whom have found the Nechako River to be quite a forgiving river in the past. The slow and gentle flow of the river throughout much of its length lures even novice paddlers out leaving them quite vulnerable in those places in the river where higher skills are needed. Anything which increases the dangers in these areas unnecessarily is, for us, a concern."[33]

Goodwin said that increased weed growth will also reduce the number of back eddies which provide canoeists with safe places to enter and exit the river,[34] and the thick growth at the edges of the river is not only unsightly, it will force more paddlers into the swifter, more dangerous main stem of the river. "Although it may seem backward to the non-paddler, lower water levels in general actually increase hazard. Canoes and kayaks are well-designed craft for water. Contact of any kind with land, however, even a river bed makes them unstable and potentially dangerous."[35]

"Nothing can compensate paddlers for the lack of water," he concluded.[36]

Later that day Vanderhoof resident Louise Burgener described her experiences with the increased weed growth in the river.

In the early 1980s I used to take my children, who were two and three years old at the time, swimming at a place in town called Sandy Beach. At that time there were some weeds toward the edges of the river beach, but it was still very pleasant to spend an afternoon there. Within only a few years, and that is with the injunction flows imposed by the court, I had to stop swimming there because the weed growth was so extensive that it was no longer pleasant. We had to move upriver to a spot just under the bridge for swimming and recreational purposes, and that was not very satisfactory with the cars whizzing by and all the other interruptions.

Again, referring to weed growth, I canoe frequently on the Nechako but had not been down to the confluence of the Stuart and Nechako for about five or six years. I was shocked to find that when I paddled down the Stuart and around the point to go up the Nechako, the Nechako was full of weeds. We had to paddle almost out to the centre of the river to avoid the weeds. This was uncomfortable, not only because the current is faster near the centre and so it's harder work, but also because the smell of the decaying weeds was very bad. This was in September of last year.[37]

The next presenter was pioneer Vanderhoof-based family physician, Dr. Al Mooney. A short, ruddy-faced man whose grey hair stands stiffly at attention in a bristly crew cut, he has been an outspoken opponent of Alcan's activities in Central-Interior BC since 1950. He argued against British Columbia's reimbursing the company if the project is stopped or revised to make it more acceptable to the people of the Nechako River Valley:

Alcan was given the vast area of the reservoir without charge. Huge areas of timber resources and farm lands were drowned. No salvage of timber was required as compared to the Wild Horse Dam in Idaho and the Ram Dam in Alberta where the flooded areas had been totally cleared and reservoir margins left tidy.

The commissioners also received a lesson on the long history of floatplane activity in the Nechako Valley and the dangers posed when this type of aircraft attempts to take off from the river after the flows are reduced upon completion of Alcan's project.

Dr. Paul Collard[38] reminded the commissioners that the flying careers of the founders of two of Canada's major airlines had begun in the valley:

In 1937 Ginger Coote Airways, later to become United Air Transport Ltd. under the ownership of Grant McConachie of Canadian Airlines fame, opened a base at Fort St. James. Russ Baker, who later formed Central B.C. Airlines and Pacific Western Airlines, was the base pilot, flying Fox Moth aircraft on floats.[39]

At that time freight and passengers destined for Fort St. James and further north usually arrived in Vanderhoof by rail and were taken to the floatplane facilities on the Nechako River where a plane would deliver them to Fort St. James. In 1939 Yukon Southern Air Transport[40] began floatplane service to mines, prospectors, trappers and other residents of Fort Ware, Pinchi Lake, Manson Creek, Germanson Landing, Takla Landing and McConnell, by using a variety of aircraft including Junkers, Norseman, Fokker Universal and Fairchild.[41]

Thirteen privately owned and two commercial floatplanes now use the club's base in Vanderhoof. Numerous itinerant aircraft also use the facility and an air base at Fraser Lake provides maintenance and other services to 130 floatplane customers from BC's central interior, the Yukon and Alaska, he said.[42]

How much water do these planes require to land on the Nechako River safely?

That depends on the type of float and its load, Collard said: "An Edo 3430 float, commonly used on a Cessna 185, for example, will settle about 18 inches in the water at full gross, and similarly, an Edo 4930 float, used on a Beaver, will settle to about 20 inches at full gross."[43]

When a floatplane is taxiing or taking off it requires deeper water as the float, especially the hind portion of it, settles deeper in the water, he explained. The Edo Corporation, the largest manufacturer of floats for aircraft, recommends a minimum depth of 29 to 33 inches for the two floats mentioned.[44]

But Transport Canada regulations require a minimum of six feet of water in the take-off and landing areas. The depth of the channel is defined as the minimum depth of water at low levels throughout the entire channel.[45] The existing average minimum water depths in the vicinity of the Vanderhoof Club's take-off and landing area during September and October is 36 inches, based on a river flow of 55.9 cubic metres per second. When Alcan's project is completed, the depth of the river is expected to be 4.3 to 12 inches lower, he said.[46]

The club's existing facilities do not meet Transport Canada's recommmended depths, but do meet Edo's minimum requirements for the two commonly used floats. If the KCP were to be completed, the facilities would meet only Edo's recommended depth for the Cessna floats and, in low flow years such as October, 1979, when the river's depth was recorded at 26 inches, no floatplanes could use the facilities. Dredging the channel would not help because the resulting siltation would threaten nearby salmon-spawning grounds and the channels would probably fill in. Building weirs to maintain deeper water in the vicinity of the floatplane base was a viable but expensive solution, he said.[47]

At the community hearings in Fort Fraser and Vanderhoof, few people spoke out in defence of Alcan. One person who did was farmer Gordon McFee, who, for 20 years, had been chairman of the Regional District of Bulkley-Nechako:

> It would appear that most appellants do not wish to compromise, my way or no way. We've already chased considerable industry from our province. Let's use some common sense. Alcan pays approximately $10 million into the water license annually and another $10 million in taxes to this province. We need them, and personally I have found Alcan to be a good corporate citizen that contributes to our 4-H, to our arena construction, our annual Rotary Auction.[48]

He recognized the problems resulting from the reduction in the flows in the Nechako River and suggested these be rectified by the province's reactivating plans to divert the Nanika-Kidprice system into the Nechako Reservoir. But, this time, instead of turning the water over to Alcan to generate electricity, it would be used to supply more water for the Nechako River.

The most startling statement during the community hearings in Vanderhoof was made by Vanderhoof businessman, Heinz Dube, who was an employee of Alcan between 1964 and 1975. He said that while he worked for the company, he was ordered to dump toxic materials into an area near Kitimat that is exposed to the action of tides and salt water. He described the toxic waste as "skims that came out of the holding furnaces in the smelter containing cyanide, chlorine and other toxic substances."[49]

Alcan later did an extensive search of an area in which toxic substances were reported to have been buried, finding no proof of the allegations. Residents remain suspicious, believing that the evidence of the dumping has been erased by the action of tides and salt water over the intervening 19 to 30 years.

Dube also reminded people of the experiences of the early workers at Kitimat who, when the vegetation and trees began dying downwind of the smelter, were told the damage was caused by beetles—"but the other side of the mountain was pretty good, there was no problem, they didn't make it over the top."[50]

During the second day of hearings in Vanderhoof, Nechako Valley residents finally got a chance to hear from the group of companies proposing to build a pulp mill in Vanderhoof.

George Killy, son of pioneer Prince George lumberman Ivor Killy, told the commissioners that when Alcan invited four locally-owned forest products companies[51] to develop plans for Vanderhoof Pulp and Paper in 1989, it was an attempt by Alcan to fulfill its promise, made in 1983, to bring industrial development to the community in return for its support for the KCP. The invitation came after earlier attempts to develop a smelter and a newsprint plant in the area fell through.[52]

The consortium of four companies is proposing to invest $300 million to construct a chlorine-free mill with a capacity of 210,000 tons of pulp annually on the Stuart River upstream from its junction with the Nechako. The proposed pulp mill would create 175 permanent jobs in a community which, by its own admission, was anxious about its economic future.

Although water is an important component in the production of pulp, the mechanical pulp production process to be employed in the proposed Vanderhoof plant would use 25% of the water required by the chemical process employed in older pulp mills, he said.[53] Ninety-six per cent of the water will be returned to the river where the average dilution factor will be 250 to one.

Alcan's commitment to the project was to provide free power for the first three years of the mills' operation.[54]

The consortium of companies had already spent $3 million developing plans for the project, Killy said.[55] But Alcan's decision to halt construction of the project, and the consortium's unsuccessful efforts to negotiate a power-bridging agreement with BC Hydro, had become serious obstacles to their plans for the pulp

"[I]f KCP proceeds, if the pulp mill is built here with infrastructure help, if the forest land base is preserved and if the local benefits fund as alluded to in the Rankin Report become a reality, we believe that some important building blocks towards economic and social sustainability for our communities can be achieved...." Lumberman Norm Avison, BCUCH 3.302.

mill. Timing the start of production is critical to the success of the project, he said. Pulp prices are cyclical and the consortium wants to bring the new mill into production when prices are on their way up, not after they have started to decline again.

The BCUC hearings, Killy told the commissioners, were another serious threat to the construction of a pulp mill in Vanderhoof: "If you can't see your way clear to endorsing, if you will, the settlement agreement at least such that it maintains the financial integrity of Alcan's project, then we don't have a project. It's that simple."[56]

Toward the end of the final day of the community hearings in Vanderhoof, Glenda Olson apologized to the commissioners for all the hostility that had been directed at them during the meetings— "but you must understand the frustration of the people. Interveners were promised assistance, Most opponents of the project have not received the help in time to properly prepare. It doesn't make for an even playing field."[57]

Residents of the area were also angry because the commission had not fulfilled its promise to have its hired technical consultants prepare a draft analysis and then give opponents an opportunity to question them on it, she said. Worse yet, they had recently been advised the consultants would not be producing a document and would not appear as expert witnesses: Instead, Alcan would provide the information base and summary document. The commissioners assured her the accuracy of the information contained in Alcan's summary documents would be subjected to rigorous cross-examination later in the hearings.

Olson added that the region had witnessed two *positive* developments as a result of the bitter controversy over Alcan's plans to divert more water from the river.

> One, thanks to the misinformation we have received, a number of us have become a very learned group of people. We have become amateur lawyers, biologists and economists. I have never caught a fish in my life, but I can tell you how many cubic feet per second we need in our river to keep the eggs from freezing in the winter. For that education I thank Alcan. Number two, this project has brought the aboriginal and non-aboriginal people together. We are all together in this fight to save our future. We stand together with

our native neighbours and friends shoulder to shoulder, and this bond is getting stronger every day.[58]

The lack of definitive information about the potentially detrimental effects of the KCP was to become a theme of the hearings. Using documents prepared by Alcan's environmental consultants, Louise Burgener of the Nechako Neyenkut Society was the first person to raise the question of how the commissioners could consider compensation for damages when, in many instances, little was known about the consequences of the project on the creatures living in and around the river. From Envirocon's Environmental Impact Assessment prepared in 1984 she quoted:

> The cumulative impact on Nechako River beaver cannot be stated in quantitative terms.... The potential impacts on moose cannot be stated in quantitative terms.[59]
>
> ...
>
> The impact magnitude [on peregrine falcons] cannot be stated with any certainty.... The impact on trumpeter swans, a protected species, in ice-free reaches, is unknown.[60]

Nor did Envirocon's study reveal how much money the project would cost the trappers and guide-outfitters who relied on the river to maintain their businesses, she said.[61]

Later in the hearings it would become apparent that neither Envirocon nor the provincial government knew much about the number of white sturgeon living in the river, or about what they required to survive.[62] The environment ministry disagreed with Envirocon's conclusion that there were not many sports fish such as rainbow trout in the upper Nechako River,[63] and indicated that Envirocon had also completely ignored the large population of resident whitefish in the river.[64]

Environment ministry officials later admitted they were unaware of any studies that had been done of the cutthroat and steelhead populations in the Kemano River.[65] They were unaware of any study into the potential trauma that might be suffered by the river's

---

"Those who say there never was a healthy trout population in the Upper Nechako don't know what they're talking about. I know. I caught lots of trout until Alcan started fooling around with the flows." *Denis Wood, BCUCH 3.317.*

freshwater fish population when the amount of water pouring out of Alcan's hydroelectric plant at Kemano is increased.[66] And no one seemed to know much about the potential effects of the mercury accumulating in the Nechako Reservoir as it is released from the decaying forest buried under the waters, or where this mercury might become a health hazard when the water from the reservoir is released into the Nechako and Kemano Rivers. As well, the province has never provided any funding to study the loss of freshwater fish habitat that will occur in the Nechako River if Alcan completes its proposed project.[67]

Burgener also stated that although the province had agreed to pay for the upgrading of Vanderhoof's sewage system, this agreement meant, in fact, that she would be among those paying for it. "Why would I want to compensate myself for damage that I did not cause and in fact struggled to prevent?" asked the woman who had openly opposed the project since the early 1980s.[68]

Alcan, not the provincial government, should be paying for the damages its projects cause in the river and surrounding environment, she claimed. "If not, they are being subsidized. We wonder if that might lead to problems similar to the problems experienced by B.C. softwood industries when trying to export to the United States when we're considering free trade agreements."[69]

Late in the day, another speaker, Pam Sholty, said the most important question the commissioners had to answer was one posed by Murray Rankin, who "pointed out in his recommendations regarding a KCP review, that such a review should include the question of whether the release of additional flows to the Nechako River would be in the public interest notwithstanding the cost."[70]

Sholty admonished the commissioners for not acknowledging the A River Forever group's invitation to tour the Nechako River Valley. The commission had accepted Alcan's invitation to tour its hydroelectric and smelting facilities: Why did it not want to see the end of the project which was paying the price for those facilities? she asked.[71]

What we request of the Commissioners is to ask Alcan to simulate the proposed winter flows from the spillway for several days, so that the Commissioners and staff may view the area first hand and see for themselves the pitiful challenge facing the once majestic Nechako River.[72]

The commission and its staff did tour the Nechako Valley as guests of the people of Vanderhoof and Fort Fraser in August, 1994. But, at that time, the flows in the river were high because of the additional water being released to cool the temperature in order to protect the sockeye migration. They also toured a portion of the areas in the spring of 1994 as guests of the committee which controls the river levels.

Glenda Olson says she does not believe the commissioners ever saw what the river looks like in the autumn, when wide sand bars appear on each shore after the flows are reduced to a minimum, allowing Alcan to fill up its reservoir in preparation for the long winter when inflows will be very low.

Pam Sholty predicted that in addition to the area's already large cattle production, the future would see potatoes, turnips, carrots, broccoli, cauliflower, beets, peas and raspberries grown there and shipped south, if water were available for irrigation. In response to a question from Commissioner Larkin, Vanderhoof farmer Guy Bambauer said: It's been done before—it can be done again. If the world warming trend continues and California's vegetable growing areas run out of the water they can use on their crops, places like Vanderhoof could be called upon once again to grow vegetable crops.[73] But, as Sholty noted, if the flows in the Nechako were to be further reduced, the agricultural potential of the Nechako Valley would be choked off forever.

Drumming on Deaf Ears

The Carrier Sekani nations speak with the wisdom of many generations. Fish, and the water they depend upon, is the central essence of our existence.[1]

Teach your children what we have taught our children, that the earth is our mother. You must teach your children that the ground beneath their feet is the ashes of our grandfathers. Whatever befalls the earth, befalls the sons and daughters of the earth.[2]

Despite the strong interest in the outcome of the hearings into the Kemano Completion Project among the First Nations people living in the Nechako River Valley, it wasn't until the community hearings began in Prince George on November 25, 1993, that the commissioners received any public explanation for the natives' decision to boycott the hearings.

The Cheslatta band had released fragmented statements to the press, but no one had yet appeared at the hearings to explain why the native people were refusing to participate. This action—or apparent non-action—was puzzling to many because, when the 1987 Settlement Agreement was announced, native people had been among the first to speak out against it and had often demanded a full public review of the project.

It was not First Nations representatives who walked to the front of the hearing room to explain the absence of Carrier-Sekani representatives to the commissioners, but rather the non-aboriginals who had worked with them for years. And, as each speaker began his presentation, he made it clear he was speaking on his own behalf, not on behalf of the First Nations or the Cheslatta people. But these speakers were closely identified with the band. They were Richard Byl, a Prince George lawyer who had been acting on their behalf, Mike Robertson, the band's chief researcher, and Dana Wagg, a writer and researcher employed by the band.

While they were speaking inside the meeting room, members of the Cheslatta Band stood outside the Prince George Holiday Inn in -20° weather, beating drums and handing out information pamphlets to those going into the meeting.

Byl said he believed the band's decision to stand out in the cold instead of coming in to the meeting to explain their position was due to the provincial government's failure to consult with them about the terms of reference for the hearings that could determine the future of their traditional territory.

A pamphlet prepared by the Carrier Sekani Tribal Council which was handed out during the hearings listed ten reasons for their failure to appear, the most important of which was number three, which stated:

> The Commission's process does not recognize that aboriginal people have special land and resource rights which have never been respected. These must be dealt with on a government-to-government, nation-to-nation basis. The Province cannot meet its constitutional obligations by using the Commission as a front for one-sided consultation.

In the pamphlet they urged people to ignore the review because it sought to shift the cost of the environmental damage away from Alcan and onto the backs of BC tax-payers. The commission is asking the wrong question, they claimed: Instead of asking how to lessen the damages and compensate the region for unavoidable destruction caused by the project, the question should be "Is this project worth it?"

"I am concerned that all these words may come to naught, that the Indian drumming may have fallen on deaf ears, that emotions without concrete substance may be listened to but not remembered, and that in the end it will all be politics and a decision will be made on who has the power." *Vanderhoof resident Diane Fawcett, BCUCH 4.568.*

This same question was being asked when the BC government cancelled the project in January, 1995. An evaluation of the costs of the project and the long-term projected income showed Alcan would lose a minimum of $195 million over the next 20 years, confirming what Alcan had said in 1993, when it asked the government to renegotiate its power-sales contract, to provide the company with an additional $350 million.

The tribal council's demand for government-to-government talks to deal with their concerns stems from the BC Supreme Court decision in a court action commonly referred to as "Delgamuukw" which ruled that if a government is making a decision affecting the lives of BC's First Nations people, it must first consult meaningfully with them. During the period leading up to the calling of the BCUC hearings, the tribal council released its own terms of reference which insisted on their full participation on equal terms with the federal and provincial governments, meaning that they would be involved in the setting of the terms of reference and the selection of the commissioners.[3]

No consultation was held before the hearings were announced and, when the terms of reference were announced, the Carrier Sekani Tribal Council immediately denounced them as too narrow because they included neither the consequences of the KCP on the Fraser River, nor the effects Kemano I had had on the lives of the people living in the region. Tribal chief Justa Monk, during a speech at the Lht'a Koh/Fraser River Watershed Summit Conference, in October, 1993, said:

> We are deeply concerned about the problems the salmon face in their upstream journey starting with the difficult passage at the Bridge River Rapids and Hell's Gate fishways. I respectfully draw your attention to recent remarks by biologists that the die-off of fish failing to get past these structures is much greater than previously thought. Decreased Fraser River flows, as a result of Kemano Completion, only increase this danger.[4]

At that time Monk also noted that the return of chinook to the Nechako River in 1993 was among the lowest in years, at a time when chinook runs on other upper Fraser tributaries were increasing.

Natives are also concerned about the probable loss of freshwater fish, particularly the white sturgeon which, Monk predicts, is doomed to extinction if the project proceeds.[5] At the same summit conference, he told the delegates:

> It can never be forgotten that the bountiful harvest of salmon that you all enjoy downstream, the harvest which makes the Fraser River one of the most important salmon-producing rivers in North America originates in this area. The Carrier-Sekani people are proud to speak on behalf of the fish. We are, after all, very good at it. Our forefathers have been doing it for centuries.[6]

The tribal chiefs objected to the federal government's failure to participate from the beginning of the hearings, and they claimed it was wrong to permit Alcan and BC Hydro to act as participants, "even though they are really proponents who stand to profit from the present project design. The Commission has even allowed Alcan to provide the information base for these hearings!"[7]

The Cheslatta Carrier Nation and the interveners were also annoyed that the terms of reference for the hearings had changed at least four times. The last change was made within ten days of the start of the hearings. "[I]t was at that point the chief and council of Cheslatta Carrier Nation threw up his [sic] hands and said, 'We've had enough. We cannot deal with this kind of a shifting ball park'," Byl said during the first day of hearings in Prince George. In any legal proceedings, when the terms of reference or filed documents change, there is a delay in the start of the hearings, he pointed out.

> And now we're looking at technical hearings a few months from now, or a few weeks from now, rather, that are very complicated, that are very difficult, with terms of reference that have changed at the last minute. This is simply not fair play. This is not right and the leadership and the people of Cheslatta are not prepared to participate in a forum where these kinds of things take place.[8]

The Cheslatta people had also been frustrated in their efforts to obtain all the documents related to the KCP, particularly the provincial documents describing the legal relationship between Alcan and BC Hydro. Those particular documents—which were required to determine if Alcan is an aluminum-manufacturing company, or a power utilities company masquerading as an aluminum-manufacturing company—can be found only among the complete file of KCP documents, Byl told the commissioners.[9]

If, in fact, Alcan is now a power utility company, it is required to conduct itself according to BC's laws regulating power utilities, most of which are set out in the BC Utilities Act. The act calls for any utility company that is creating or expanding its generating capacity to apply for permits before it proceeds.[10] Alcan has not done that, Byl indicated.

> I think that if I as an individual wanted to build a small hydro-electric dam on a little creek someplace, I would probably have to make more filings, hire more lawyers and do more things than Alcan has to do for this, and that is another reason why Cheslatta is disposed in the manner that it is.[11]

Alcan has always claimed it was given permission to remove more water from the Nechako River in the 1950 agreement. But the company's opponents say the agreement specified that water was to be used to generate electricity to smelt aluminum at Kitimat or for other industries in the region, *not* to sell power to BC Hydro. If it is becoming a power utility company, Alcan should be subject to specific BCUC regulations governing its activities, including a requirement that it obtain an energy permit.[12]

It is impossible for anyone to understand the Kemano project until they can study all the federal evidence and interview all their witnesses, Byl said. But because of the amount of material related to the hearings that had been released after the hearings began, that was impossible. For all of these reasons, plus the absence of the federal government in the hearings process, the Cheslatta people believed the hearings were not credible, Byl said.[13]

Within a week of the start of the hearings, the band was still indicating it was going to participate, but at that point the lack of money prevented them from obtaining the many expert witnesses they wanted to bring before the commissioners.[14] Therefore, Byl stated, the Cheslatta people believed they could make their point more effectively "by standing in 20 below beating a drum. To stand

---

"First they came and took our trees, now they want our water too."
Statement attributed to an unnamed BC Klahoose First Nations Elder by Klahoose Chief Kathy Francis, Transcripts of the Canadian Water Resources Association's conference in Vancouver May, 1992.

here is to stand here totally handcuffed and, Madam Chairman, that isn't right."[15]

Byl was latest in a long line of people who complained to the commissioners about both the amount of money BC was providing to intervening groups and the way the money was being distributed. The process for obtaining these grants to pay for their expenses had become very controversial and was further complicated by the fact that it was the provincial government, not the commission, who controlled the pursestrings on the $250,000 being provided to meet intervenors' expenses. On July 23, 1993, when the deadline for grant applications had passed, 12 applications for these funds had been received and, at that time, grants totalling $340,000 were distributed. One hundred thousand dollars was allocated jointly to the Carrier Sekani Tribal Council and the Cheslatta Band, which is a member of the tribal council. Another $100,000 was also allocated jointly to the A River Forever and the Rivers Defence Coalition. The government had delayed payment of the $100,000 to the two groups until they submitted an explanation as to how they would share the money.

Other grants given to interveners were: $35,000 to the Haisla Fisheries Commission;[16] $10,000 to the Kitimat Chamber of Commerce; $2,500 to the Nechako Regional Cattleman's Association; $2,500 to the Omineca Regional Wildlife Association. Fifty per cent of the funding allocated to these four interveners were distributed immediately, with the remainder to be forwarded when the hearings began.

Applications for intervener funding were refused to the District of Vanderhoof (because it was felt Vanderhoof had access to the money it needed through local taxes); the Nooksack Indian Tribe of the United States (because it was only indirectly involved); and a private application (because grants were not being given to individuals). An application for a grant submitted by Prince George-based Nechako Environmental Coalition had been withdrawn prior to the announcement of the distribution.

Three weeks before the community hearings were scheduled to begin the government, reacting to the complaints it was receiving from some groups who said they had not received enough money, threw an additional $80,000 into the pot. The Haisla Fishery

Commission also announced it would not be participating in the review, and thus would not need its $35,000 grant. This money was returned to the fund and the grant allocations realigned to provide an additional $15,000 to the Kitimat Chamber of Commerce and $7,500 to the Omineca Wildlife Association. The Vanderhoof District Chamber of Commerce had been added to the list of recipients and would receive $45,000; the A River Forever Group was to receive $50,000; and the Rivers Defence Coalition $100,000. When the hearings began, discussions continued with the tribal council and the Cheslatta Band about the $100,000 it had been allocated, but no decision had been reached.[17] When the hearings dragged on into August, 1994, many interveners began running out of money.

There was also growing anger at the prospect that the provincial government might end up paying Alcan's expenses as well as the interveners'. Before the hearings began, Alcan claimed that, according to the terms of the 1987 Settlement Agreement, the province might also be responsible for all of its expenses during the hearings, including the expenses incurred by the decision to delay construction of the project. Interveners privately stated that Alcan voluntarily agreed to participate in the hearings and no one ordered the company to stop construction, so it should not be eligible for compensation. Alcan's response was to say that if it had not taken part in the hearings, the commissioners would not have received all the information required to make a balanced decision.[18]

No doubt the issue of who pays Alcan—for both its legal expenses and the compensation package to be paid now that the project has been cancelled—will either be negotiated or decided by a judge. Interveners fear it may become part of a deal in which BC Hydro compensates Alcan by increasing the price that Crown corporation pays the company for the power it purchases from it.

The interveners' financial situation worsened throughout the nine months the hearings continued. The BC government did add more money to the fund, bringing the total to more than $500,000. Still, by the end of the hearings in August, 1994, the A River Forever group[19] was openly referring to the fact it could no longer pay its lawyer, David Austin of Vancouver. A tireless worker, he kept plugging on, determined that the people of the Nechako

Valley should be well represented at the hearings. His expenses were paid when he was working for the groups. But, when he was in Vanderhoof, he stayed with Vanderhoof residents and, to save on expenses, his return trip to Vancouver was sometimes as a passenger in a truck carrying a load to the Lower Mainland. When asked why he worked so hard without pay, Austin responded:

> When I first met with this group I had never seen a group of people who were being so badly screwed in my life by the unfairness of the allocation of the resource.
>
> Now I stay on because of the people. These are hard working, smart, common sense people who have ripped these farms out of the land. They are a pioneering generation who have lived close to the land and know nature humbles us and we will never be able to dominate it.
>
> These are not environmentalists. This is affecting part of their lives, not affecting someone else's life, like the environmentalists involved at Clayoquot. They don't look at the environment in the narrow sense but as a biological system that is part of everything. They also have a broader sense of community and the river and the land and how it means something to their children and future generations. They're independent pioneering people and don't like someone else having their hand on the tap. They live close to nature and they've watched the river going up and down irrationally in a way they know is not consistent with the seasons.
>
> They believe they've been lied to and now say they're not opposed to the project but you have to prove to us the project won't deal a death blow to the river and you had better be honest.

Throughout the hearings the money-starved interveners counted their pennies, volunteered countless hours, sold raffle tickets and sweat shirts to raise money and reduced their costs by sleeping three or four to a room when attending the out-of-town hearings.

"So the people you see in front of you at these meetings we're not the kind of people who chain themselves to trees or lie down in the middle of roads, we're people who understand certain aspects of this river, that love certain aspects of this river, and we want to prevent a huge injustice from being perpetrated. That's why we're here." *Vanderhoof resident Craig Hooper, BCUCH 3.367.*

Despite all their efforts, each day when they walked into the hearing room with their one lawyer they were reminded of how their resources were outflanked by those of the federal government and Alcan. On one side of the hearing room sat batteries of government and Alcan lawyers, and their assistants, and the representative of a public relations firm who—each day—issued a press release containing Alcan's version of the evidence presented that day. As the hearings progressed, these daily press releases and lists of corrections to reporters' stories of the previous day, were dubbed by reporters as the workings of "The Truth Police."

"I'd like to see how much Alcan bills to the province," Glenda Olson said at the end of the hearings. She believes that when the accounts are tallied up, the interveners should receive the same amount as Alcan.

Not everyone was polite and respectful when they spoke to the commissioners about the position of the First Nations and Byl's polite but critical comments were followed by a hostile statement by Mike Robertson in which he described the hearings as a sham lacking credibility and designed solely to restore the government's image in the eyes of the world investment community. He pleaded with the commissioners to do something to restore confidence in the proceedings.

> If I were a lawyer and my client, the Nechako River, had been sentenced to death, is it not right for me to do everything under my power to protect my client from certain death. In the case of the BCUC, the evidence that would set my client free and prove his innocence is being withheld by prosecution. The judge has already signed the death warrant and no one on the jury understands common English. My client, the Nechako River, is going to die.[20]

Robertson's speech had been fiery and he hurled many angry allegations at the commissioners and against Alcan.

His anger stemmed partially from the commissioners' actions when, after touring Alcan's facilities, they turned down an invitation to tour the Nechako River with native and community groups, saying it would be inappropriate to tour the region with the groups opposing the project. Residents of the Nechako Valley continued to urge them to tour their valley to see firsthand what was happening there. Finally near the end of the hearings they agreed, and everyone involved, including the commissioners, went on a rigorous three-day tour of the reservoir, a canoe ride down the Nechako River from Cheslatta Falls and a tour of the communities that will be affected by Alcan's project.

The anger of valley residents was also fanned by Alcan's refusal to answer questions about how much money it would make from the KCP and its refusal to restore Cheslatta Lake.

By this time, the commissioners had listened to days of criticisms of the terms of reference, which they had not set; the intervener-funding process, which they did not establish and over which they had little control; and Alcan's corporate activities and image, which were also outside their sphere of influence.

Robertson's highly critical comments were too much for Commissioner McVey. Before he responded he was careful to say he too was speaking on his own behalf.

...I'll personally tell you why I accepted the opportunity to become a Commissioner and to take the oath required of someone in my position, and that is that I, as a citizen of this country and as a resident of the northern part of this province for the last 25 years, I felt that something had to be done. I agree that there are difficulties. I'll put it that way, obvious difficulties with the entire project and its predecessor, I felt that at least by being a member of this particular Commission I could at least give people in the affected regions, and I include more than just the north of B.C. in that, the opportunity to speak openly and freely at this particular hearing, I believe does so. The process is perhaps flawed, but at least we're airing our particular views. I don't believe that we had the opportunity to air our views in quite the same way in the past.[21]

It was a tense moment and one that would be repeated at other

---

"These hearings are nothing more than a forum or a stage established by the B.C. government.... The script has been carefully written and choreographed by the government and the audience is the international investment and business community.... The non-native people are finally getting a taste of what the native peoples have endured for generations. For the first time they are being ignored and insulted by governments." *Mike Robertson, BCUCH 5.702-03, 706.*

hearings when McVey believed he and the other commissioners were being subjected to unfair criticism.

Toward the end of the hearings it was revealed that the Carrier Sekani Tribal Council had been negotiating behind the scenes on what a federal government representative called "a government-to-government basis."[22] This angered representatives of the Cheslatta band, who had not been advised of the behind-the-scenes talks about an issue that had deeply affected their lives and is one of the reasons given for Monk's failure to be re-elected tribal chief in 1994. Instead, the chiefs chose a young woman, Lynda Prince, as their new chief.

During the hearings John Watson, regional director for BC for the federal DIA revealed that the department had provided $100,000 to the Carrier Sekani Tribal Council to complete a review of all the federal documents related to the KCP that had been submitted to the BCUC by then. This was in addition to the $30,000 provided by the DFO, he said. He, too, was careful to inform the commissioners that the appearance of department officials should not be construed to be formal participation by First Nations people in the hearings. Copies of the findings of the review prepared by the tribal council, including an analysis of the consequences of Alcan's activities on First Nations' people in the region, were to be given to the commissioners prior to the completion of their review, he claimed.[23]

Native leaders did not agree with Watson's explanation of their plans for the $130,000.

"The Department of Indian Affairs and Watson were trying to discredit us by mentioning the $100,000 during the hearings," Richard Krehbiel, a lawyer employed by the tribal council, said after the hearings ended.[24] He says Watson didn't tell the commissioners his department had given the band the money after more than 100,000 pages[25] of related government documents had been

---

"[F]rom a population estimated to be 70,000 in the late 1700s, the B.C. First Nations population was reduced by epidemics to a low of 22,000 in 1929. Improved health and socio-economic conditions have resulted in a steady increase since that time to approximately 92,000 Status Indians in British Columbia in 1991." *Dr. David Martin, BCUCH 85.16040-041.*

delivered to the band. These documents were made public so late in the hearing process that it was impossible for First Nations' researchers—or anyone else, for that matter—to assess all this material properly in time to submit the evidence at the hearings. In fact, when some of the material was found to contain important new evidence, it was already too late to introduce it as evidence in the hearings.

By mid-September, 1994, a month after the hearings had ended, unopened boxes of documents remained stacked up in a room in the tribal council offices in Prince George. The money was being held until they could find someone to go through the papers and develop a position paper on the background of the project[26] and its implications for the Carrier people, said Krehbiel. "But there's no way we are giving it [the report] to the B.C. Utilities Commission," he said.

When they do complete it, the document they prepare may be used in presenting their case when they apply to the BC Treaty Commission to protect their territory, under the interim measures provisions of the process established to settle the comprehensive claims being negotiated for the territory affected by Alcan's BC activities.[27] These interim measures are intended to protect territory where it can be proven that the land, water and resources are under threat until land claims negotiations are completed.

In BC, unlike the rest of Canada, few treaties were ever signed with First Nations people. Non-natives who arrived in what is now BC began dividing up and using the land and have never dealt with Aboriginal title through either treaties or legislation.[28]

The BC Treaty Commission was established in 1991 to deal with the process of negotiating these treaties and, by August, 1994, had accepted 41 statements of intent from BC First Nations wishing to negotiate them. The Wet'suet'en claim includes the eastern

---

"I've walked the rivers, the forests and the mountains. I've seen the fluorescent ribbons hanging everywhere. I know that every bit of the earth has already been explored for its economic worth. Every bit has been squared off and valuated as a source of income. Others just don't understand that life comes from where we live, from the plants, the animals and our connections to the earth." *Sonny Greyeyes, BCUCH. 7.1079.*

end of the tunnel, through which Alcan draws off water from the eastern end of the Nechako Reservoir, and the land around the Skins Lake Spillway. The Kenney Dam is in territory claimed by the Carrier Sekani, and the Haisla land claim includes Kemano and the territory over which the transmission line from Kemano to Kitimat has been erected.[29]

The DIA's definition of its goal in settling comprehensive land claims provides some insight into what will undoubtedly become an important First Nations' influence on the final decision on the KCP. As described by Watson during the commission hearings, the goal is to:

> ensure lasting certainty of ownership of lands and resources, in other words to provide clarity as to the nature of ownership and title on lands; to stimulate economic development; to encourage Aboriginal people to participate in activities of government; to ensure the effective and meaningful involvement of Aboriginal groups in renewable resource management and environmental protection; and ensure that Aboriginal groups share in the benefits of that development.[30]

In light of that statement, it would seem that the First Nations people living in the Nechako and Kemano River Valleys may well hold a trump card in the dispute over Alcan's entire Kemano project, and the outcome of this dispute will depend on how they choose to play that card during the comprehensive land claims negotiations.

Krehbiel doesn't deny the First Nations people expect to have a strong say in how much water remains in the river.

No one is talking about the loss of the river. The thing is now to

---

"According to archaeological and anthropological studies as explained by Rich Blacklaws, U.B.C. Department of Archaeology, people of the Dene Nation first began inhabiting these sites 7,000 years ago approximately as glaciers receded creating the Fraser and Nechako Rivers." *BCUCH 6.985.*

"The riverbanks are lined with literally thousands of prehistoric food cache pits. The countryside is interlaced with ancient trails. Artifacts of a great variety can easily be located on most cultivated fields. With few exceptions, the major occupation sites occur along the rivers and near the junctions of rivers." *BCUCH 6.986.*

stop Kemano Completion Project in its present form. The position is they won't give up their lands and sell what belongs to them or trade off their rights to that land or water and now the issue is the negotiations over how it is used and that does not mean two governments deciding without full aboriginal participation.[31]

The federal government has also been negotiating settlements of specific claims including those launched by the Cheslatta and Kitimat bands related to damages they suffered during Alcan's industrial activities in the region in the 1950s.[32] The specific claims result from incidents in which First Nations claim the federal government failed to meet its fiduciary responsibility to protect their interests with respect to the reserve lands or other assets the government holds in trust for them, or its failure to live up to its responsibilities under the Indian Act.[33] Negotiations have been finalized on four specific claims related to Alcan's activities, totalling more than $7.9 million, filed by the Cheslatta and Kitimat bands, Watson said.[34]

Watson admitted the federal government did not consider First Nations' concerns when it signed the 1987 Settlement Agreement, telling the commissioners "it does not appear that Department of Indian Affairs played a direct role or a significant role in the activities leading up to this agreement."[35] Watson said that the most important concern the First Nations' people had expressed to him about the KCP was their fear the fish on which they rely for food and ceremonial purposes may disappear if the water flows were further reduced. The Haisla People are concerned about increased erosion to both reserve lands and traditional lands when flows increase in the Kemano River. Other concerns BC's First Nations expressed included potential damage to grave sites around what was the village of Kitimaat; degradation of the water quality in the Nechako River when pulp mills and municipal sewage treatment plants dump effluents into the reduced flows in the river; and the adverse effects of the reduced flows on ground and surface waters and on the related wildlife habitat on which First Nations' traditional hunting and trapping activities are based. He concluded by saying that the federal government will look at the commission's report before deciding if it will contribute more money to pay for the costs of monitoring and lessening the impacts of the KCP.[36]

Both presentations ignored some important questions raised by Victoria lawyer Murray Rankin in the report he prepared for the BC government in 1992, in which he called for the provincial review. In his report, Rankin also stated that it did not appear as if, prior to the start of the construction of the KCP, the province had had any meaningful consultation with or made any alternative arrangements for the First Nations people whose lives would be affected by the project. Rankin and BC's First Nations people were aware recent court decisions had made consultations mandatory in this instance.[37] A provincial hearing into KCP was the only way to avoid a finding of breach of provincial fiduciary responsibility and would help clarify the extent of its repercussions on their lives, he said.[38]

Without stepping too far into the tangled legal web of evolving federal and provincial responsibilities to First Nations peoples surrounding this issue,[39] it does appear that, since the affected First Nations' people refused to participate in the hearings and, instead, continued to negotiate with the federal and provincial governments on a "government-to-government" basis, they will have to be consulted now that the commission has prepared its report. Because the provincial government has decided that the project will not be completed, the consultations with BC's First Nations' representatives will, presumably, be brief, because this is what they have been demanding since the 1987 Settlement Agreement was announced. First Nations' leaders may now demand a place at the bargaining table if the company and the province attempt to negotiate a settlement. I predict the non-native representatives will also be demanding to be involved in any negotiated settlements with the company. Like the First Nations people, they learned a bitter lesson in 1987 when the provincial and federal governments went behind closed doors to negotiate a settlement. It is a lesson they will not soon forget.

The commissioners heard a sad outline of the health problems faced by First Nations people living in the region, some of which could be attributed to the effects of industrial developments, such as Alcan's huge project. Dr. David Martin[40] submitted this information:

...study shows that the age-standardized mortality rate for Status Indians in B.C. is twice the provincial rate overall, twice the provincial rate for diabetes, infectious and parasitic diseases, three times the provincial rate for external causes, motor vehicle accidents and suicide, and four times the provincial rate for digestive system diseases.[41]

Not all these illnesses were directly related to Alcan's projects, he admitted, but there are two health issues he believed should definitely be addressed were the KCP allowed to proceed.

First: Anything that increases the level of poverty experienced by the Status Indians living in the region will be a detriment to their health. "Canada-wide surveys have shown clearly that there is a positive and strong correlation between high levels of income and better health. Low individual and family incomes among Status Indians in British Columbia, especially those on reserve, restrict the capacity of families and communities to obtain adequate housing, good nutrition, and appropriate cultural and recreational pastimes," Martin said.[42] He noted that other evidence from across Canada indicates the health of First Nations people is adversely affected when there is a disruption in their lifestyle.[43]

The second health concern he brought forward is the growing fear about the amount of mercury contained in the fish caught in the Nechako Reservoir. The First Nations people living in that region and using the reservoir water have good reason to be concerned about the water they drink and the fish they eat. Heavy metals such as mercury and lead concentrate in human flesh, as they do in the flesh of the fish caught in the reservoir. In humans, high levels of mercury result in retardation, behavioural problems, neurological damage and serious illnesses including blindness, disturbances of the digestive system, kidney ailments and, in extreme cases, death.[44] The symptoms caused by mercury poisoning are now known as Minamata Disease, named after the condition first

---

"The infant mortality rate on B.C. Indian reserves was 41.2 per thousand births in 1977. Although the rate had dropped to an average of 13.89 per thousand births over the period from 1987 to 1992, this was approximately double the provincial rate of 7.36 infant deaths per thousand live births."
Dr. David Martin, BCUCH 85.16041.

observed in people who lived near Minamata Bay, Japan.

Martin noted that a study done in 1992 did not provide evidence of unacceptable levels of the heavy element in the hair and blood samples taken from Cheslatta residents.[45] The soil in that region is known to contain background levels of mercury and, at one time, the concentration of the metal was high enough for a mercury mine to be established at Pinchi Lake near Fort St. James. Vegetation and trees growing in soils containing mercury take up the heavy metal. When the trees and vegetation surrounding the Nechako Reservoir were drowned and began decaying, they released that mercury into the waters of the reservoir. Alcan says a survey of mercury levels in the Nechako Reservoir done by its environmental consultants in 1991, shows that the levels of mercury found there pose no threat to human health. Another survey of mercury levels in the reservoir was done in 1994 for New Canamin Resources Ltd., a company planning to establish a copper mine which would discharge its waste into Tahtsa Reach. That study states "Mercury concentrations were in the high parts per billion range in all species, and exceptionally high mercury concentrations...were found in one individual rainbow trout."[46]

Due to the uncertainty about what will happen to mercury levels in the lake should the KCP proceed, Dr. Martin recommended a mercury-monitoring program be put in place to determine if the amount of mercury in the tissues of the fish increased after the project's completion.[47]

He also pointed to another potentially dangerous situation for which no scientific proof had been found: the Kitimaat First Nation's worries about the hazards posed to them by exposure to the low-level electromagnetic fields emitted by Alcan's power transmission lines located in their village. "While at present much of the scientific community states that there is no evidence of a cause and effect relationship between EMF [electromagnetic fields] and cancer, the concerns of the Haisla people in this regard should not be ignored and should be taken in Alcan's siting decisions," Martin concluded.

Early on in the hearings, the commissioners heard about a more subtle—but equally damaging—consequence the project will have on First Nations' lives when Julie Johnston spoke. Johnston is coordinator for Rediscovery, Prince George, a fledgling group planning to use the river as a way to help native youth understand and become reconnected to both their culture and the environment, to enable them to develop a sense of their own worth. The organization had picked two possible sites for a program they were planning to establish in the region, both of which were on the banks of the Nechako River.[48] The proposed program would be based on the spiritual insights of the First Nations' Medicine Wheel and the Sacred Sweat Lodge ceremony, she explained.

She described the Medicine Wheel as a "teaching tool or a process of education and development that helps native people, especially children, come to understand their integration with the natural world."

> The Sweat Lodge Ceremony could be considered the experiential form of the Medicine Wheel. It is perhaps the most important, since here in Prince George alone, sweat lodges are held on a regular basis, at least once a week almost every week of the year. They are situated on the banks of the Nechako and on an island in the Nechako for a reason. How can a ceremonial sweat lodge purify the heart and the spirit without the cleansing properties of a flowing unpolluted river nearby? How can a young person take part in a solo vision quest, that traditional custom which best defines the rite of passage from childhood into adulthood, without the healing properties of a clean flowing river?[49]

In the second, more personal part of her submission she told a story illustrating how First Nations people draw healing and strength from nature.

> My grandfather died last winter across the country. I remembered these words attributed to Chief Seattle: "The shining water that moves in the streams and rivers is not just water, but the blood of our ancestors. Each ghostly reflection in the clear water of the lakes tells of events and memories in the life of my people. The water's murmur is the voice of my father's father."
>
> So to honour my father's father and to celebrate his life, I chose a ceremony on the snow-crusted banks of the Nechako River. Until you have let the swift flow of a river hold your love and sadness and sweep your grief away you will not know how important this river is to me.

An Acceptable Level of Certainty

To Alcan these hearings are about a project. To the people of the River's Defence Coalition and their constituent members these hearings are about the river, and consequently they're about their lives.[1]

The technical hearings into the Kemano Completion Project finally began January 17, 1994, one year after they were announced. Only then did the residents of the Nechako River Valley finally begin to receive answers to their questions about Alcan's plans to divert more water from the Nechako River.

The atmosphere of these hearings was different from that of the more open, personal and passionate community meetings at which the people living in the Nechako River Valley had had their say. Now the commissioners were led through long legal and technical arguments by lawyers and experts who slowly and methodically picked their way through the volumes of evidence presented by those arguing for and against the completion of the project.

Before they could wade into the complicated maze of information surrounding the debate over who would control the future of the Nechako River Valley, the commissioners had to make decisions on three hotly contested issues:

• *A delay in the hearings:* Interveners were pressing them to delay the start of the technical hearings, saying they needed more time because their intervener grants from the provincial government had arrived so late their lawyers had not had time to prepare for the hearings;
• *Open availability of documents:* They had to decide if the full text of

267

the agreements between BC Hydro and Alcan, which had previously been made available only to them,[2] should also be made available to the interveners;

• *Increased flows in the Nechako:* Could they recommend an increase in the amount of water flowing in the Nechako River if they determined that this was the only way to lessen the damages caused by the project?

The commissioners answered "Yes" to the two last issues and also met interveners' requests for more preparation time by moving consideration of some of the more complex technical issues, originally scheduled for the first phase of the hearings, into a later phase.

The technical hearings were divided into four phases, beginning with an examination of the design and construction plans for the facilities required to complete the project, followed by the hydrology phase, in which the water flows in the Nechako and Kemano Rivers would be considered; the fishery phase, in which they would be considering the safety of the fish using those rivers under the flows established by the 1987 Settlement Agreement; and, finally, the task of quantifying the environmental, social, economic and other consequences for people of the region.

Unlike the participants in the community hearings, those appearing during the seven months it took to complete the technical hearings were often subjected to rigorous cross-examination by lawyers and private interveners. Many of the KCP's opponents sat and listened as both sides presented their at times convoluted arguments, and watched as lawyers struggled, with varying degrees of success, to extract information from reluctant scientists and politicians.

When the hearings ended, the residents of the valley agreed they knew a lot more about the project than they had when they began—but many of their questions remained unanswered. And, after opposing scientists who appeared at the hearings had exposed what they saw as the flaws and gaps in the research on which Alcan's plans were based, residents were more convinced than ever that the company's plans to lessen the KCP's damage to the Nechako would not work.

There is one important question that remains unanswered to this day: How much government interference had there been in the period leading up to the signing of the 1987 Settlement Agreement? Despite numerous attempts by politicians, including former Fisheries Minister Tom Siddon, to reassure Alcan's opponents that the process leading to the agreement had not been tainted by political interference, Nechako Valley residents remained unconvinced. Their anxiety over this issue increased when, during the hearings, it became apparent that there was still no consensus among Alcan and federal government scientists about the fate of the salmon after flow reductions in the river are implemented, despite reassurances from politicians that the project could proceed without seriously damaging the fish. Therefore, in its final argument, the Rivers Defence Coalition held to the position that "the 1987 Settlement Agreement flows present unacceptable risk to the fish resources of the Nechako River. The only way to reduce this risk is to increase the flows released from the Kenney Dam."[3]

By the end of the hearings it had also become apparent to the interveners that, like all human sciences, the science of fisheries biology encompasses innumerable uncertainties and variables that must be assessed before all the answers are known. UBC fisheries and zoology professor Dr. Carl Walters, appearing on behalf of the Rivers Defence Coalition, described how fisheries scientists have dealt with the complexity of their field of study: "We have by and large taken a passive approach of pretending that we can measure everything under the sun and wave our arms and create a story from those measurements and an explanation."[4]

Alcan responded to the concerns about its ability to protect the salmon by pointing to the millions of dollars it had already spent conducting studies on the rivers; the terms of the 1987 Settlement Agreement which make the company responsible for most of the costs of protecting the salmon in the river; the information in the summary report of the Nechako River Working Group which shows what has already been done; and, of course, the fisheries

---

"The Minister [Tom Siddon] was entitled to the final say concerning the KCP, but not to mask his conclusions as scientific advice from his science adviser." *Nechako Environmental Coalition's final written argument, 24.*

experts appearing on its behalf at the hearings—all as proof of its commitment to protecting the salmon, regardless of the costs.

The commissioners appointed by the BCUC to hold public hearings on the KCP responded to the uncertainty of determining the environmental repercussions of such large projects when it said:

> All ecosystems are nestled within larger ones up to global levels so that the impacts of the changes in aquatic ecosystems to the adjacent land areas, and of those to the boreal forest and so on to considerations of global ecology and biodiversity may all be argued as relevant to the KCP. On the other hand, the higher levels of aggregation pose increasingly more complex if not virtually impossible challenges for prediction. Thus, while they have a valid basis in the philosophies of resource management, they do not provide a useful framework for making decisions at a detailed level for individual projects. In any event, it is apparent that the science of modelling of aquatic ecosystems to the level of predicting changes in abundance of various species in changing physical conditions fall far short of what is needed to evaluate the effects of KCP on the community of fishes in the Nechako River.[5]

Throughout the long technical arguments presented by both sides about whether or not the KCP would seriously harm the environment, valley residents were angered by the way the onus to prove the project's potential to damage the environment was put on *them*. Instead, they felt the onus should have been on Alcan to prove that there was no reasonable doubt as to the effectiveness of its plans to protect the salmon by releasing more water into the upper Nechako.

They were also upset when John Payne,[6] who appeared on behalf of the Nechako Fishery Conservation Program, admitted

---

"And what seems to be happening is every time things get tough it's the environment that has to pay the price and, consequently, it's the people of Canada that end up paying that price as those resources are lost and damaged beyond repair." *UFAWU spokesman Arnold Nagy, BCUCH 1.14.*

"KCP would effectively put the Nechako so close to the edge of collapse that it would require heroic measures just to keep life going in the river. We're talking intensive care, advanced life support, not just for a year, but forever." *Geoff Laundy, BCUCH 6.930.*

that cost had been the main determining factor in the decision to use the "adaptive management approach" for alleviating damages to the Nechako River salmon fishery. "Adaptive management" means the implementation of measures to reduce the effects of the lower water flows *after* the problems have been identified. Other management strategies in which all the variables affecting the fish are considered *before* the lower flows are instituted were considered too costly and time consuming, he said.[7]

Commissioner Larkin was not impressed with that plan. "It seems to me the approach you are describing is essentially empirical. You see what happens, you stick a band-aid on it. If that doesn't work, take that band-aid off and try another one," was how he described plans for protecting the salmon in the Nechako.[8]

This type of river management would lead from one crisis to the next, said valley residents. And if, in the end, the fish disappear, who could prove whether it was Alcan's fault, or due to some other unrelated factors such as overfishing at the mouth of the Fraser River?[9] That is exactly what happened in 1992 and 1994 when the numbers of chinook returning to the spawning beds on the upper Nechako River were well below the average return of 3,100 spawners to that portion of the river established by the terms of the 1987 Settlement Agreement. Alcan and DFO representatives blamed the disappearance of the fish on everything from flaws in the counting system, to over-fishing at sea, to First Nations' poaching along the river.

When the hearings ended, valley residents remained convinced the project should not be completed as Alcan was proposing. The minimum outcome presented at the hearings that they found acceptable was that Alcan be ordered to redesign the project to permit half the water remaining in the river after the dam was completed to continue to flow through the valley. In addition to these basic flows, the project's critics believe, there should be an annual week-long period of flushing flows of 17,600 to 24,700 cubic feet per second. These higher flows are required to remove sediment from the salmon spawning beds and scour off the weedbeds and other vegetation encroaching onto the riverbed in shallower areas, particularly downstream from Vanderhoof. If there are no flushing flows, they predict that they will be left with a weed-choked river with little flow, few fish and a hatchery built far away from the Nechako River where the gene pool of the Nechako chinook would be preserved.

The weeds are already increasing in the river, particularly in the slower-moving sections, as anyone swimming, boating or fishing in the river today can attest. A witness appearing for the Rivers Defence Coalition, Dr. Tom Brown, described the present condition of the river this way: "Like for example, when you get down by Vanderhoof there is a lot of macrophytes [weeds] growing along the edges of the river so you can't fish there, and also there's an awful lot of algae, so that when you throw your lure out in the water you have to haul it in and you have to clean the slime off."[10]

The increased growth of the weeds and slime was blamed, in part, on the material being released into the already reduced river flows from the Vanderhoof sewer treatment facility. By the fall of 1994, when water flows were higher than what they would be upon the project's completion, the river was already beginning to look exactly as Alcan's opponents had predicted it would once the KCP was finished. The slower water flows and weed encroachment evident in the slower-moving sections downstream from Vanderhoof led to this area being described as looking "more like a lake than a river...[with] the potential to turn into a continuous slough."[11] KCP opponents are convinced that further reductions in water flows will accelerate weed growth. "The river is now in its short-term fall flows. There is no velocity. It is moving so slowly it looks like a lake and the rocks on the bottom are kind of scummy. There's so little movement even the goose shit doesn't get moved," said lawyer David Austin,[12] after canoeing downstream from Vanderhoof in October, 1994.

Alcan criticized valley residents' demands for the flushing flows of 17,600 to 24,700 cubic feet per second, saying they will result in flooding land along the river's bank made available for agricultural, domestic and commercial use when the water flows in the

"[A]nd this is one that really sticks in the craw of our environmental group—is that they were going to maintain [the] Nechako stock gene pool at some other hatchery." *Nechako Environmental Coalition spokesperson Cecil Kelly, BCUCH 10.1545.*

river were lowered after the dam was built in the 1950s.[13] Residents answered Alcan's concerns by recommending that a system of dikes be built to prevent the flushing flows from flooding populated areas, and that the release of higher flows be sensibly timed, in order to avoid damaging farmers' fields.[14] A week-long flood would destroy newly planted fields or mature crops ready for harvest, but would do little damage to fields early in spring or following harvest. They rightly stated that much of the rich soil in the fields along the river was deposited there by floods that occurred before the dam was built, and further brief, carefully timed floods, will continue that long cycle of deposits of new silts on top of old.

When they released their final report to the BC government, the BCUC's commissioners supported valley residents' call for higher flushing flows, stating that "With KCP flows the weed problem will get worse along the length of the Nechako river from Fort Fraser to Prince George."[15] The commissioners also pointed out that the first stage of the remedial measures set out in the 1987 Settlement Agreement includes measures to improve the all-important conditions at the edge of the river and adjacent streams known as the riparian zone which, to a large extent, determine the survival of the fish. They therefore recommended that spring flushing flows of 6,000 cubic feet per second for two days every three years should be added to the river's flow regime[16]—a quantity that was well below the annual flushing flows of 17,600 to 24,700 cubic feet per second recommended by Alcan's critics.

Although the project has now been cancelled, valley residents continue to pressure the provincial government to act on the commissioners' recommendation that the release facility Alcan had planned to install in the Kenney Dam still be built. They are also demanding that both a larger water-release facility and a larger canal be built to carry the released water through the millions of tons of debris accidentally dumped into the riverbed below Cheslatta Falls since the dam was built.[17] Alcan had proposed building a cold-water release facility capable of discharging a maximum of only 6,000 cubic feet per second into the river—well below the amount of water valley residents believe is necessary to scour sediments off the river bottom and restore and enhance riparian zones and water tables along the river. If these changes are not made, the higher water flows would have to be released through the Skins Lake Spillway into the Murray-Cheslatta Lake chain and, hence, over Cheslatta Falls into the river. Such action would threaten the success of any attempts made by the province to meet its obligations to restore the freshwater fishery in the upper portion of the river and the Murray-Cheslatta Lake system. It would also mean that, despite the cancellation of the project, should Alcan carry out its pledge to return their traditional territory around the Murray and Cheslatta Lakes to the Cheslatta Band upon the project's completion, it would be returning territory that continues to be damaged by its activities.

Those who criticize the provincial government's plans to cancel the project should be aware that BC's energy production picture has changed significantly since the KCP was first proposed in the early 1980s. As a result, both Alcan's take-or-pay contract with BC Hydro—to sell 285 megawatts of hydropower to the Crown corporation beginning January 1, 1995[18]—and their reservoir coordination agreement—through which Hydro expects to receive an additional 270 megawatts from Alcan through the co-ordination of Alcan's and Hydro's reservoir releases—are no longer as critical to the province's energy self-sufficiency as they were when the agreement was signed. For one thing, Hydro's power-saving program, Power Smart, has resulted in a total energy saving of more than 1,400 gigawatt-hours annually. That's enough power to serve the annual needs of 140,600 homes and more electricity than that used by all the homes in Vancouver.[19] Other power has also been added to BC's total energy supply by the provincial program to encourage small independent power producers to generate electricity and sell it to Hydro. Less than a month before the BC Government cancelled the project, BC Hydro announced it was initiating four projects in southern BC that will increase the province's electrical production by 987.5 megawatts[20] annually by the year 2000. That is considerably more than the total of 555 megawatts Hydro would have received from its power purchase agreement and the reservoir co-ordination agreement with Alcan.

More new power will be added to the provincial power grid from Hydro's plan to install a fifth unit at the Revelstoke Generating Station which, by October, 1999, will increase that station's capacity by 460 megawatts. Other recent Hydro announcements include increasing the generating capacity of the Stave Falls generating station, 65 km east of Vancouver, by a total of 127.5 megawatts by replacing the station's five aging generators and by installing a fourth unit at the Seven Mile Generating Station on the Pend d'Oreille River near Trail, thus increasing the installed generating capacity there by approximately 200 megawatts. Hydro also announced that it is seeking proposals from independent power producers for a minimum aggregate supply of 200 megawatts to be available by October 1, 1998, and that it had begun studies to determine the feasibility of installing other generating units at Revelstoke and Mica Generating Stations, 130 km upstream from Revelstoke.

These were all early signals to Alcan's critics that the BC government no longer considered the power received from Alcan as critical to the province's energy supply.

During the hearings, the nature of Alcan's arguments about the KCP's benefits also disturbed valley residents. They had listened in amazement as Alcan's representatives told the commissioners that the construction of the dam and their plans to build a water-release facility in the dam were *benefits*. Residents thought it bizarre that Alcan could describe both the dam installed more than 40 years ago and the facility it was planning to build to correct the damage done by that same dam as the *benefits* of a second project—a project that could inflict further destruction on the river at that.

"In return for more water from the Nechako River, Alcan will mitigate some of the impacts of Kemano I. This is analogous to the owners of a pulp mill claiming they will not install new pollution control equipment unless they receive a guarantee that their timber harvesting rights will never be reduced," the residents of the valley stated in their final written argument.

Interveners found it nearly impossible to counter these statements because the hearings' limited terms of reference did not

---

"If this project is allowed to proceed, Alcan will become the largest independent power producer in the province." *Will Koop of Project North, associated with an ecumenical church organization supporting First Nations people in their fight for justice, BCUCH 6.948.*

include the consequences of Kemano I. Interveners constantly sought to include information about the 1950s agreement and the impact of the KCP in their statements, only to be told by commission chairperson, Lorna Barr, that they were outside the hearings' terms of reference—information confusing to the interveners, because the hearings' terms of reference *do* seem to include Alcan's 1950 activities in the region. The wording of the terms of reference includes the following statement:

> The British Columbia Utilities Commission (the Commission) shall conduct a public review of the Project in accordance with the following Terms of Reference. 1. In the context of the Industrial Development Act, the Conditional Water License, the 1950 Agreement, Order in Council 2883/50, the Settlement Agreement and the Amendment Agreement, the Commission shall review and assess the nature and extent of the effects of the Project on the physical, biological, social and economic environments in the Kemano and Nechako river watersheds and the Nechako Reservoir.[21]

Throughout the hearings Alcan countered its critics' complaints about the lack of public consultation prior to the signing of the 1987 Settlement Agreement by saying the DFO had informed the public of plans for the project at a series of public meetings.[22] In making this statement, the company ignored the fact that this was the period when many groups who voiced their opposition against the project at the BCUC hearings first became active in the Bulkley[23] and Nechako River Valleys. It was also the period during which the federal government itself did not agree with Alcan's plans to remove all the water from the upper Nechako. At that time, DFO scientists were working on a report that did not support the water flows established by the 1987 agreement,[24] and the department was preparing to go to court to defend its demand for the "injunction flows" put in place in 1980 by Mr. Justice Thomas Berger.

During the hearings it became apparent that there had been no public discussion prior to the signing of the agreement because Alcan was adamantly opposed to the proposal to begin any form of public consultations at that time.[25] "I think that the concern that was expressed, to my recollection, was that if there was a very open process that it would make it extremely difficult to conclude a negotiated settlement," said Pat Chamut, DFO director general for the Pacific Region.[26]

When asked about this matter later in the hearings, Fisheries Minister Tom Siddon confirmed that, although he had asked for more public consultation, Alcan had been reluctant to inform the public about the closed-door negotiations going on at that time:

> ...I felt it very important that while we were negotiating an out-of-court settlement to a matter before the courts, that in some way the interested parties be informed of the strategy and approach being taken...that I did feel there needed to be some public discussion and presentation of our approach at that time.[27]

Questions are still being asked about why Siddon changed his mind on May 22, 1987, and agreed to continue negotiating without any open public discussions.

A possible answer to that question came to light during testimony given at the BCUC hearings when it was revealed that on the morning of May 22, 1987, the federal Department of Justice received a call from Alcan's lawyer threatening to subpoena Siddon to testify in the pending court action. Forty minutes later, notes made by Siddon's adviser, Les Dominy, reveal that the minister changed his mind and was "now committed to a deal in which there will be no public process."[28]

When, at the hearings, Siddon was presented with this theory for his sudden change of mind, he denied that the subpoena threat was what had caused his about-face. But his answers to follow-up questions, aimed at clarifying his answer, were at best evasive and, without fail, unrevealing and uncooperative. What is more, as shown by the following exchange between Siddon and lawyer Richard Clark, who represented the Rivers Defence Coalition, his "answers" reflected his unwillingness to deal with the questions:

> SIDDON: And their approach and the whole objective at that time was to get this thing resolved before the trial date.
> CLARK: But that had not been your approach.
> SIDDON: That was the objective of my officials and those of the province and those of the Alcan to resolve this matter before the trial date. Now if I say that was my approach, that was my approach.
> CLARK: All right.

SIDDON: And then the approach was changed because I was not satisfied, and I can absolutely assure this Commission that that was the way in which my mind was suddenly set on the impossibility of completing before trial a negotiated settlement.

CLARK: Well, surely you recognized that long before May 22nd, didn't you?

SIDDON: Well, I'm sorry, Madam Chair, as I said much earlier, there's a lot of things going on in a Minister's life and I couldn't accept the suggestion of Mr. Clark.

CLARK: So what you want your evidence to be is that the reference to your changing an approach on May 22nd is a reference from achieving a final settlement before trial as opposed to an agreement to negotiate for three months.

SIDDON: It's not Madam Chair, what I want my evidence to be, that is my evidence.[29]

There is also confusion about what Siddon meant by his statement in a letter he sent to Alcan on September 14, 1987, after being informed of the findings of the Strangway working group: "There exist alternative ways to those flows to providing an acceptable level of certainty for the protection of the fish."[30]

Valley residents had been asking what new information had arisen during the four-day-long deliberations of the Strangway working group. Something must have come to light during that period to satisfy what the department had previously rejected of the company's water-flow proposals, and to counter, successfully, the evidence, produced by the department's own best scientists, showing that those flows—the flows now ensconced in the Settlement Agreement—would have serious effects on the fish.

That question of what new evidence had caused the federal government to capitulate suddenly to Alcan's proposed water flows was never answered during the hearings. It will probably be thrashed out as part of the looming battle over who pays Alcan

---

"QUESTION: Mr. Siddon, are you convinced that the Kemano Completion Project will have no detrimental effect to the salmon?
ANSWER: That's what I'm told and if I ever get any information opposite to that, then we'll certainly make it public, and if anything occurs that we think is endangering the resource, that will be made known...." *Westcoast Fisherman* (Mar. 1993).

whatever is determined it is due as a result of the KCP's cancellation.

Nor were there answers to Nechako Valley residents' questions about the meaning of the phrase "an acceptable level of certainty," which appeared first in the terms of reference given to the Strangway working group, and later in Siddon's letter confirming that an agreement on how to protect the chinook living in the Nechako within Alcan's proposed flows had been reached by the Strangway Working Group. Alcan's environmental consultant admitted during the hearings that he had no idea what "acceptable level of certainty" meant.[31] When asked the same question, another scientist associated with the issue said only that Siddon had the final responsibility for determining the acceptability of the flows' risk to the fish.[32]

Two UBC commerce professors defined the term this way:

An "acceptable" level of risk is essentially a normative proposition determined by some type of political process. Scientists cannot measure whether something is safe. Nor can they determine if a particular level of risk is "acceptable."[33]

Bruce Strachan, who became BC's environment minister six months before the 1987 Settlement Agreement was signed, was not much more forthcoming when he appeared before the commissioners. He said, in the months prior to the signing of the agreement, the province was pushing for "Anything that would keep us out of court and anything that would not involve us having to stick to the 1950 Agreement, because as I said earlier, that would be devastating."[34]

It was also revealed during the hearings that the decision to sign the 1987 Settlement Agreement was based on information provided to the BC Cabinet by then Energy Minister Jack Davis, who had previously been the federal fisheries minister. He advised Premier Vander Zalm and the other members of the BC Cabinet that the fishery on the Nechako River was worth only $1 million

---

"[T]he passage of time cannot become an excuse or an apology for the decisions of previous governments." *The Rivers Defence Coalition's final written arguments, 4.*

and, therefore, it would be advantageous to the province to allow Alcan to proceed with the KCP, as it would result in an industry worth $300- to $400-million annually being developed in BC.[35] The value Davis assigned to the Nechako River salmon fishery is way off the mark, said the Rivers Defence Coalition. It should be at least 75 times that amount because in 1993, which was a high-catch year, the commercial landed value of the four million sockeye attributed to the Nautley and Stuart River systems was $76.9 million. That figure would double or triple once the value of the jobs created by processing, transporting and reselling the fish was added to the price paid to the fishers.

In his testimony at the hearings, Strachan admitted that, prior to the signing of the 1987 Settlement Agreement, he was not aware of what flows were being proposed for the Nechako River by either Alcan or the DFO or what water flows the representatives of his Ministry said were required to protect the freshwater fish.[36] He also admitted the 1987 agreement contains no provision for water for agricultural irrigation, or for the water needs of future residential and industrial expansion along the river—which residents of the valley assumed, incorrectly, the provincial government would ensure were provided for in the agreement.[37] Worse yet, Strachan's ministry agreed to bear the cost of restoring the Murray-Cheslatta Lake chain and the upper Nechako River when the project was completed.[38]

If the KCP had proceeded, the potential costs to the province—for restoring the damaged upper reaches of the river alone—are conservatively estimated to be $10 million. The potential cost to provincial tax-payers becomes even more staggering when the enormous cost of restoring the severely damaged areas around Cheslatta and Murray Lakes is added to the other provincially-born costs of the project, which include upgrading the water and

---

"Our problem with this is, we are humans and not God and we make mistakes." *Vanderhoof councillor Ethel Cresswell, BCUCH 4.450.*

"We are a peaceful people for the most part, and probably too trusting that our elected governments will look after our interests, safeguarding our heritage and natural resources for us and future generations." *Diane Fawcett, BCUCH 4.567.*

sewage-treatment plants along the river so they can function properly under the greatly-reduced flow regime; the business, recreational and tourist opportunities lost because of the reduction in Nechako River water flows; and the compensation that may be demanded by First Nations peoples for their lost fishing opportunities and the damage to wildlife.

Questions about the amount of money required to lessen the damages the KCP would have caused to the Kemano and Nechako Rivers were answered in the commissioners' report. They recommended that a $15- to $20-million local benefits fund be established with money provided by Alcan, BC Hydro and the federal and provincial goverments. It would have been used to pay the cost of conducting baseline research of conditions in the river before the project's completion, to monitor and evaluate what happens after completion and to initiate any remedial measures needed, particularly on the Kemano River. The fund was to have been administered separately in the Kemano and the Nechako watersheds.

All these costs of correcting the damages caused by the KCP would be incurred so Alcan could make a profit and pay dividends to its shareholders. Consequently, now that the project has been cancelled, those costs should be taken into consideration in the pending battle over whether or not compensation must be paid to Alcan.

During the hearings the DFO biologists who had opposed the 1987 Settlement Agreement finally had their say about the events leading up to the approval of the KCP.

"I am here because I resent having my integrity and professional reputation tainted because politicians and bureaucrats preferred not to properly inform the public of all the details leading up to the Nechako Settlement Agreement,"[39] Dr. William Schouwenburg

---

"I believe DFO's failure to pursue the court case to its logical conclusion has had the same effect as defeat in the court. The provincial government Water Licensing Agency has no incentive to ensure that fish needs are incorporated into considerations when they issue a water license and I don't know if it's come up before, but the way the Water Act reads is fish aren't legitimate users of water." *Dr. William Schouwenburg, BCUCH. 51.9079-080.*

told the commissioners. He was responsible for editing the final edition of the federal task force report on the KCP which was then shelved by the government.

Schouwenburg and other federal fisheries biologists were subjected to personal attacks by Siddon in January, 1994, when, during an appearance on CBC radio, the former fisheries minister questioned the scientists' professional reputations and their motives for criticizing the agreement.

Schouwenburg said he and other federal scientists who had opposed the Settlement Agreement agreed to appear at the hearings on behalf of the project's opponents to inform the commission as to what knowledge was available when the agreement was reached. At that time, he said, all their evidence indicated the river and the salmon using it would suffer under the new water-flow regime.[40]

Alcan's fisheries experts disagreed. Their studies, and the work done by the Strangway working group, indicated to them the Nechako salmon fishery could be maintained within the water flows proposed by the company.

One of the most contentious issues was Triton's decision to use a computer program called the In-Stream Flow Incremental Methodology (IFIM) and the related Physical Habitat Simulation System (PHABSIM) to develop a flow regime designed to maintain temperatures when the salmon were in the river. Opposing scientists criticized Triton's decision to use these methods, particularly the IFIM method. When asked what he thought of using computer models as predictive tools in adaptive management programs, Dr. Carl. Walters, a professor of zoology and fisheries at UBC said:

> I suspect I probably have more experience than any other ecologist in the world at trying to develop predictive computer models for systems ranging from Kemano to the Florida Everglades to other places in the world, and I'll tell you flatly they don't work. They are not trustworthy at all. The basic problem comes from two things. One of them is that there are always physical and biological processes that no one has worked on much because they take place at scales and place[s] and time[s] where our measurement systems don't work. They're too costly to get at. These create great gaps and holes

in our models. And, secondly, even when we can identify some of those gaps, we make errors of omission in the modelling. We leave out processes. We just don't recognize them. It's not a matter of the accuracy with which we specify the parameters for those things we put in the models that causes troubles, it's the thing[s] we leave out entirely.[41]

Alcan brought forward other scientists who defended IFIM.[42] It was the best method available for determining the relationship between the water flows in the river and the habitat available for salmon, as required by the DFO's Habitat Protection Policy, Triton president Bruce Jenkins told the commissioners.

[I]n Aprïll of 1982, we judged that the IFIM methodology, which includes the modelling of habitat availability with flow but is not restricted to it, we judged that it was the most rigorous and systematic technique that was available. That there was no other technique as advanced and that it was the best methodology for us to adopt for deriving fish protection flows in the Nechako system and for fulfilling our mandate at that time.[43]

Another fisheries expert, Dr. Don Chapman of the United States, was less certain about IFIM's predictions. He admitted that a weakness of the IFIM method was it relied on an individual's professional judgement of the conditions in the river and the different flows in the river at the time measurements are taken.

It's the best around and I can quickly tell you that there are flaws in it. It's not a perfect method, and you've got to use it with caution, you've got to use it looking at macrohabitat, you've got to use it with the application of judgment, but it's the best method around and I'll defend it against Mathur or anybody else because I think it's been shown to be useful enough times, the way fish behave, that I feel the faith is justified, let's put it that way.[44]

"[T]echnologies create the ways in which people perceive reality." *Neil Postman, Technopoly: The Surrender of Culture to Technology.*

"Alcan's million dollar document here states that the mitigation procedures that are going to ensure the survival of the river is based on computer modelling and a little applied engineering, commonly known to us as damage control, in other words to fix up what they're screwing up." *Geoff Laundy, BCUCH 6.926.*

This courtroom style of pairing off opposing expert witnesses left observers wondering who was right. In the short-term, the commissioners had to decide whether or not they were convinced the salmon using the Nechako River would be adequately protected under the water-flow regime set out in the 1987 Settlement Agreement. If the project had not been cancelled, the final proof of who won the scientific debates heard during the commission's proceedings would not be evident until after the project's completion, when the final counts would come in indicating how many fish had survived this latest tinkering with the Nechako water flows.

The commissioners' report appears to agree with the questionable nature of the dependability of the predictions of the risks to the salmons' safety based on these models. They quoted the following summary assessment, in an IFIM primer, of this computer model's dependability: "Because our models and judgements are by their nature incomplete and imperfect, our predictions are likewise incomplete and imperfect. Post-project monitoring and evaluation, with the intent of evolving into adaptive management, should be considered when appropriate."[45]

Because of the gaps in knowledge about the species of fish living in the river now, and the way they use it for feeding, spawning and rearing activities, it may have been difficult, if not impossible, for anyone to determine the final outcome of the company's planned efforts to protect the fish. Disagreements emerged during the hearings over the salmon and freshwater fish production potential of the Nechako River. There appeared to be no agreement as to the requirements for rearing salmon in a hatchery so far from the ocean, or on the number of juvenile salmon lost to predator fish, or on the number of Nechako River salmon being caught in the ocean or at the mouth of the Fraser River when they are just beginning their long journey back to the spawning grounds.[46] Schouwenburg told the commissioners: "Now we have a black box in the ocean where there's a harvest taking place. We have a black box in the river where there are other harvests taking place

---

"Conflict is the name of the game when it comes to instream flow technology." *US fisheries expert Dr. Don Chapman, BCUCH 28.4794.*

and we have a whole bunch of uncertainties about such things as predation and so on. We don't really have a—we need some way of measuring production from the Nechako."[47]

Obtaining an accurate count of the number of salmon raised in the huge Nechako River system would involve a massive fish-tagging program—which has never been attempted on a river of that size. But it is apparent to both the residents of the valley and BC's fishers that only when it is known exactly how many fish the river produces will scientists be able to assess accurately how well the company has been able to meet its obligation to protect the river, and whether or not Alcan can continue to blame other factors—including ocean conditions, poaching and water conditions in the Fraser River—for the fact it has been unable to achieve the goal set out in the Settlement Agreement for an average return of 3,100 chinook to the spawning redds in the upper Nechako River.

The commissioners agreed with the critics. In their report they say: "The Commission is not convinced that the proposed stage A and stage B program on instream remedial measures will ensure achievement of the conservation goal, nor if they did, whether it could be demonstrated that they were indeed responsible.... Many years of study of a stable situation would be necessary to implement the sort of strategic framework envisaged by the NFCP."[48]

By the end of the hearings residents had a clearer understanding of Alcan's commitments under the terms of the 1987 agreement to the on-going costs of protecting and conserving the chinook and sockeye resources using the Nechako. But Alcan accepted no responsibility for the fish using the Kemano River where, DFO official Dennis Deans admitted, there will be salmon losses when more water is released into the river from the generating plant.[49]

Valley residents also point out that, had the project proceeded as planned, it would be the BC tax-payers—not Alcan—who would have been responsible for the millions of dollars annually it would have cost to protect and conserve all the fish in the Kemano and the freshwater fishery in the upper Nechako, the Nechako Reservoir and the Murray-Cheslatta Lakes. The costs would have continued for many years, if not forever, were the province truly committed to restoring and maintaining the river to its pre-project condition.

They were also surprised to learn that in the seven years since the agreement was signed, the provincial government had developed no systematic management plan for the Nechako River as promised by BC Environment Minister Strachan in a letter attached to the 1987 agreement.[50] Worse yet, when, at the request of a deputy minister, provincial fishery ministry employees prepared a request for $510,000 for the 1991–92 budget year to begin meeting the province's 1987 commitments to freshwater fisheries protection, the request was not approved. By 1993, the Omineca region's staff had been reduced to a full-time staff of two people with a discretionary budget of $32,000 to cover all fuel for the vehicles and all other expenditures except salaries. "Even if I were to direct my whole budget for 1994-95, my whole discretionary budget, it wouldn't equal the estimated amount to undertake the first year of this five-year sturgeon plan," fisheries biologist Don Cadden told the commissioners.[51]

The commissioners chastised the province for their lack of action in protecting the river's freshwater fishery. Competition for money to meet the demands for service, both federally and provincially, was blamed for the lack of funds for fish-protection programs. They recommended that, in the future, funds be earmarked for applied research and monitoring projects to ensure these fisheries are protected.[52]

In its evidence, Triton, Alcan's environmental consultants, downplayed the importance of the freshwater fishery by saying there was only a small number of freshwater fish in the Nechako River. Pat Slaney, a senior fisheries biologist with the fisheries branch of BC's environment ministry, disputed Triton's findings, noting that there is an abundant population of whitefish in the river and that Triton underestimated the population of rainbow trout living in the river.[53]

A report, prepared for the provincial government in 1983 by Dennis Ableson, was introduced at the hearings estimating the total desirable sport fish productivity of the Omineca region to be 7.32 million fish.[54] Of that amount, the report concludes, the Takla-Nechako region was responsible for the highest production of freshwater fish in the entire region. The Rivers Defence Coalition, which led the long fight to force the government to call for the hearings, cited these findings as further evidence supporting their belief that the 1987 Settlement Agreement was politically, not scientifically based and that, "even with the proposed remedial measures in place, [KCP] poses unacceptable risks to the fish resources and the environment, as well as hardship for local communities and people...."[55]

Alcan has always vigorously rejected these assertions saying "there is not one piece of evidence to support this theory."[56] Throughout the hearings and in its final arguments, the company reiterated its long-held position that the 1987 Settlement Agreement was based on sound scientific evidence and is unassailable because of the legal rights the company obtained in the 1950 agreement.

The company continued to make those statements after the project was cancelled. But Nechako Valley residents, who know the issues surrounding this controversy better than other BC residents, continue to question Alcan's motives for claiming the accuracy of their predictions of the project's risks, especially after the commissioners had identified numerous concerns about the Nechako Fisheries Conservation Program's assessment of the problems and plans to correct them.

Nechako Valley cattlemen and dairymen, represented by agricultural economist Bob Holtby, were the only valley residents who joined Alcan in its belief the hearings had proven that the river and the salmon would be protected by Alcan's proposed program of measures, and were satisfied that no further review of the project was required. "[T]he process of the B.C.U.C. hearings has been more comprehensive that [sic] anyone expected. One cannot think of any issue which could be raised at a later review that has not already been raised," Holtby said in the association's final written argument to the commission.[57]

That statement put this group of farmers on the opposite side of the fence from other Nechako Valley residents who were upset by Holtby's apparent support for Alcan.

The goal of the farmers Holtby represented was simple: They wanted to secure water equivalent to 353 cubic feet per second, or 60 cubic feet per second on an annual basis,[58] to irrigate their fields for two months in the summer, and the immediate approval of all the irrigation licences placed on hold by the provincial government. When the hearings ended, Holtby was confident they'd achieved their goal. Alcan confirmed that that amount of water could be withdrawn from the river during the irrigation season without a significant impact on fish habitat.[59] But the company rejected Holtby's recommendation that a reserve be placed on this water,[60] thus giving no guarantee that it would be available during periods of unusually low rainfall, or if global warming resulted in drier weather over the river basin. The company also said it would support Holtby's call for an irrigation board to be established in the Nechako watershed only if the Nechako Fisheries Conservation Program[61] was unchanged and the irrigation board had no power to allocate water licences, because that power belongs to the water management branch of the province of BC. This statement left other valley residents asking themselves what power this board would have, since it could not regulate the water being released from behind the Kenney Dam, or allocate irrigation licences, and had no guarantee there would be any water available for either of these purposes.[62]

The commissioners recommended that the 60 cubic feet per second—enough water to irrigate an estimated 44,500 acres[63]—be set aside.

Not all Nechako Valley cattlemen and dairymen agreed with the position taken by Holtby. Guy Bambauer, a director of the regional cattlemen's association, testified on behalf of the valley residents opposing the project. In his testimony he said the project would reduce the value of his family's property along the river and would result in long-term costs for improving irrigation and fencing to keep cattle from crossing the lowered river.

Other Nechako Valley residents who had become involved in the hearings had goals that were broader and more complex than those of the group of farmers represented by Holtby. They didn't

---

"[I]f there's some unforeseen consequences in the future that our weather pattern changes or something like that, well Alcan is not required to release any more water than is stated in these settlement agreements. So, when that water is used up for that year it's tough beans...." *Vanderhoof resident Peter Rodseth, BCUCH 4.444.*

disagree with Holtby's assertion there should be more water for irrigation, but they were not convinced that water would be there when farmers needed it for their fields, especially if global warming trends reduced the valley's rainfall. They also wanted assurances the environment and future economic sustainability of the river valley would be protected. Nothing they heard during the hearings provided that assurance. "We are not going to take Alcan's word as the Bible any more. We want to get it in writing that the water will always be there for irrigation," Fort Fraser resident Pam Sholty said after the hearings ended.[64]

BC fishers were also left with serious concerns about the commissioners' ability to protect the environment. Before the hearings ended, the United Fishermen and Allied Workers Union (UFAWU) began their own action to stop the project. First, they withdrew from the BCUC inquiry,[65] claiming it had failed to consider the effects of Alcan's projects on BC's coastal salmon-fishing industry.[66] "Salmon runs off the U.S. coast have been decimated because of dams and the same thing will happen here if we allow this massive hydroelectric project on the Nechako River," said UFAWU spokesperson Mae Burrows.

> We have been told by the Commission that their hands are tied, that impacts on the coastal fishing community cannot be addressed because of their restricted mandate. Morally we have to withdraw from the hearing process in order to expose the government's lie about a full public airing of all issues during this inquiry. We must have zero tolerance for any further species extinction, which is a real threat for Nechako chinook salmon if the Kemano project goes ahead.[67]

Two days later, UFAWU launched a lawsuit against Alcan and the Province of BC, claiming the project had been started without the energy certificate the Utilities Commission Act requires for power companies adding more than 20 megawatts of power to a facility.[68] Alcan applied for an energy certificate in 1984 when it announced its original proposal, which included two new aluminum smelters, one of which was to be built in Vanderhoof. That application was withdrawn in 1985 when plans for the smelters were put on hold and no new application had been made for an energy certificate when the revised project, which did not include any smelters, was announced in August, 1988. Nor has the province ever exempted the project from the need to apply for the certificate, the UFAWU claimed. The union introduced evidence from the BCUC hearings[69] to support its argument that Kemano I and the proposed KCP were separate projects, and that the preparations for the final design of the KCP began after the act was passed in 1980 requiring public hearings for all energy projects producing more than 20 megawatts of power.

"We think they broke the law," said Greg McDade, the executive director of the Sierra Legal Defence Fund and the UFAWU's legal counsel for the action. "The energy project approval process gives the provincial government an important right—the right to turn down Alcan's project. By not putting Alcan through the same process as other power producers, the province is ducking its decision-making responsibilities."[70]

The UFAWU reminded BC residents of Energy Minister Robert McClelland's statement of May 12, 1981:

> I can guarantee to this House that there will be no Kemano completion without an application from the Aluminium Company of Canada to the British Columbia Utilities Commission. At the time that application comes forward, there will be full public hearings in which everyone who has an interest in this matter will have the opportunity to fully debate the need for fisheries protection, environmental protection, levels-of-water protection, and all the concerns being voiced among the public today. The Aluminium Company of Canada knows that: the Aluminium Company of Canada has accepted it. It's a fact that it will not happen without the full public hearings, and that requirement of the Utilities Commission to make recommendations to the government. Then the political decision would be made by the government, as the member for Skeena seems to want to have done in advance. But at the present time this government has no request from Alcan for a project. I don't know whether we ever will have one, but if we do I can guarantee that it will be subject to full and complete public hearings held in the communities involved and offering full participation by the communities involved.[71]

That promise was forgotten in 1987 when the project was allowed to proceed without a review.

The Lower Mainland aboriginal fishing authority of the Sto:lo

Nation set aside its fight with commercial fishers, over First Nations' right to an aboriginal fishery on the Lower Fraser River, to lend its support to the fishers' union in its court battle with Alcan. "Since Kemano Completion is designed to sell power to B.C. Hydro, we agree with the Union there is no good reason Alcan should be treated any differently than any other business trying to develop a power generation project," said Ernie Cray, the executive director of the Sto:lo Fishing Authority.[72]

Alcan tried, unsuccessfully, to block the lawsuit, claiming the action was "frivolous and vexatious" and stating that the BCUC's hearings constituted a full review of the project as required. David Lane[73] countered Alcan's argument by pointing out that the BCUC hearings were not a full review of the project because the commissioners could only advise the government and, if it wished, the government could ignore the advice. In addition, he said, the Utilities Commission Act provides no means through which the energy minister of the BC Cabinet can require Alcan to implement the commission's recommendations.[74]

The hearings concluded without UFAWU participation.

By that time all the wrangling at the hearings, the court fights and the battle of the press releases had caused the residents of the Nechako River Valley to lose any trust and respect they may have had for Alcan and Triton.

What particularly stuck in the collective craw of the people living in the Vanderhoof region was the way Alcan had not openly disclosed to them that the province was going to give it the water, flowing in another unnamed river, to replace the flows in the Nanika-Kidprice system it had relinquished in the 1987 Settlement Agreement. Indeed, even in his opening statement to the commissioners, Alcan's BC vice-president Bill Rich continued to use the company's decision to give up its rights to the river as evidence of its commitment to protecting the environment. It wasn't until the technical hearings began that Nechako Valley residents learned there had been ongoing negotiations between the

---

"We have been betrayed. Through almost 14 years of negotiations and deals, we have lost trust in our government and faith in the democratic process." *Louise Burgener, BCUCH 4.539.*

provincial government and Alcan about the amount of compensation the company would receive for relinquishing its rights to the rivers in the upper Skeena River system.

When asked how that information made him feel, Jim Oryschuk, who had met with Alcan representatives many times during the 13 years he served as a member of the Vanderhoof District Council, said: "I guess this is one example that has caused myself and undoubtedly from the feedback that we get from discussing it with people in the community, that we lost faith, trust and a sense of being able to leave a meeting with Alcan's representative feeling ... confident—or all the information has been shared with us. That it's total and complete and upfront."[75]

The opponents of the project are convinced the company would never have proceeded with the project without the economic benefits stemming from the province's commitment either to compensate Alcan for, or replace the water flows it had relinquished from the Nanika-Kidprice system, and the financial benefits accruing to Alcan from its reservoir co-ordination agreement with BC Hydro. None of this information would have been made public had the hearings not been held.

These less-than-full-disclosure statements by Alcan betrayed the pioneering sense of honesty of people living in a region where binding verbal deals are made all the time, and everyone understands that if they fail to keep their word, they face dishonour in the eyes of the community.

"Ranchers are used to making business deals verbally. A handshake isn't often required, and this is done all the time with ranchers that deal with each other and they know if they reneg [sic] on a deal their reputation is shot,"[76] said Vanderhoof rancher Guy Bambauer who, although a director of the regional cattlemen's association, broke with that organization's official position by opposing the project. Bambauer made it clear that Alcan had destroyed its credibility with him. He said that if the project proceeded, there should be a written agreement outlining the terms under which landowners will be compensated and how disputes over the compensation package will be resolved.

"We have no assurances...the compensation will meet our needs. The compensation should be on-going. The losses are going to be on-going, the compensation should be on-going. If the project goes ahead, the profits will be on-going," he said.[77] He cited the on-going costs of the additional fencing to keep cattle from crossing the lowered river, the lowered value of the land if its productivity declines because of the lower water table and ranchers' inability to withdraw water from the river or its tributaries for irrigation. He charged the provincial government with abandoning local landowners to negotiate with Alcan on their own for compensation for losses they will suffer if the project proceeds. He said that when it signed the 1987 Settlement Agreement the government agreed to the deal, so it should be responsible for negotiating with Alcan for the short- and long-term costs of the project to area landowners.[78]

Residents point out Alcan's promise to compensate them for damages caused by the project was "not in writing, not enforceable, vague, controlled and, administered by Alcan, arbitrary, limited in time" and designed to place the interests of the company over their own.[79] Their suspicions were confirmed when, in his opening statement to the commissioners, Bill Rich said:

> The population of the Nechako Valley had grown since the 1950's and agriculture in particular had expanded considerably. Alcan might have argued that people who opted to locate along the river after 1950 should have informed themselves of the company's right to divert additional water. Strictly speaking, expansion in water use along the Nechako River could be interpreted as an infringement on our water rights. Alcan was only doing what it intended to do.[80]

Alcan was also unwilling to reveal to the commissioners the amount of tax it will pay the Regional District of Bulkley Nechako for the land occupied by the company's reservoir, power tunnels, cold-water release facility and other installations related to its power production facilities.[81] The fact is that under the terms of the

---

"One need only briefly review the history of the Kemano project to understand the lack of public confidence in the decision-making process." *The Rivers Defence Coalition's final written arguments, 4.*

"If Alcan takes this river, I know that anger from the injustice will brew and fester within this community." *Nechako Valley resident Cindy Serhan, BCUCH 4.585.*

1950 agreements, Alcan pays no taxes for its power—production facilities including the dam, the tunnel, the Skins Lake Spillway, the generating plant inside Mount DuBose and all its developments at Kemano. It does pay taxes of approximately $5,000 a year on the undeveloped land within its holdings and taxes on its smelter in Kitimat. It should be remembered, however, that the province pays to provide services such as roads and hospitals to Kitimat, and Alcan's provincial tax responsibilities for these services were reduced when two other industries, Eurocan Pulp Mill and Methanex, located there.

There were other examples of Alcan's representatives' inability to tell residents what they describe as "the simple truth."

When Ben Meisner tried to get Bill Rich to admit that he and Alcan president at the time, David Morton, had discussed the company's water flow proposals with Fisheries Minister Tom Siddon during the critical period leading up to the signing of the Settlement Agreement in 1987, Rich said there had been no such discussions or, if there were, he knew nothing about them.[82]

A letter introduced later indicated otherwise. It was dated August 17, 1987, and forwarded to Morton from the office of then Fisheries Minister Tom Siddon with a copy forwarded to Rich. In the letter Siddon says a meeting of scientific staff should be convened "without delay" to identify and resolve outstanding disputes over the water flows. Siddon also says "I would like to express my pleasure at the opportunity to meet with you last Wednesday,"[83] proving Nechako Valley residents' suspicions that the company had been negotiating directly with the government over the water flows.

There also appears to be evidence Rich had been directly involved in waterflow discussions with DFO deputy minister, Dr. Peter Meyboom, and Dr. Michael Healey, director of the

"The RDC has viewed these Hearings as involving two distinct but overlapping parts: process and science. One part is the political process and history that led to the various agreements which underlie these Hearings. The other part is the science and technical issues which were largely ignored in the political process. The two are intertwined because the process can place at risk the integrity of the science." *The Rivers Defence Coalition's final written arguments, 2-3.*

Westwater Research Centre at UBC[84] which led to the establishment of the Strangway working group.

Until the hearings were held, Alcan's opponents were unable to determine if the cold-water release facility would be able to deliver enough cold water into the upper reaches of the river to ensure the survival of the salmon and the freshwater fish. They now believe that in order for the facility to be successful, its deep-water intake should be placed deeper in the reservoir.

This information emerged when experts presented evidence about the secret, internal life of large reservoirs and lakes. The experts' research showed that beneath the surface of these large, deep bodies of water lie layers of water of differing temperatures and density which, depending on the velocity and direction of the winds and the underwater geography of the basin in which the water lies, are subject to the influence of underwater waves which are often many metres high. UBC Professor Dr. Gregory Lawrence and Dr. Paul Hamblin, of Environment Canada's National Water Research Institute, told the commissioners how, when the wind blows steadily from one direction over a large body of water, water piles up against the down-wind shore and the warmer surface water pushes the underlying level of colder water downwards and backwards. Since the prevailing winds over the Nechako Reservoir are toward the dam, where the facility will be built to release cold water into the upper Nechako, Dr. Lawrence said the studies done by Alcan's environmental consultants have not convinced him there will be enough cold water available at that end of the lake to release into the river and cool it down to the 21.7°C criterion established for the mouth of the Stuart River.

When the winds stop blowing, the warm water piled up against the down-wind shore levels itself, setting off internal waves in the layers separating warmer from colder and denser layers of water. Lawrence and Hamblin said that in addition to the problems inherent in the reservoir's internal waves and the warmer water piling up at its eastern end, will be the possibility that warmer surface water will be drawn down into the colder layer when large amounts of water are sucked from the colder levels by Alcan's planned cold-water release facility.[85]

"[I]f we have a severe situation where we have water from the upper layer, the warm water adjacent to the release facility, and rather than withdrawing 10 degrees C. water maybe withdrawing 15 degrees C. water..." Dr. Lawrence said.[86] The result would be that 21.7°C water could not be delivered at the confluence of the Stuart and Nechako, he said. Even if enough cold water were available from tributaries to cool off the river, these large volumes of water could result in floods downstream from the dam.[87] Alcan would experience more severe difficulty delivering water of the proper temperature to ensure the safety of migrating sockeye, should the water temperature required at the Nechako's confluence with the Stuart River be lowered to 20°C, as some scientists believe it should be.[88]

Despite criticism of their methodological and related studies, Alcan stood by the evidence produced by its hydrothermal expert's computer models, telling the commission the facility can deliver enough cold water to maintain water temperatures safe for the migrating salmon. The company's witness, Dr. J.E. Edinger of Pennsylvania, claimed Dr. Lawrence's concerns about internal waves are "over pessimistic"[89] and "[i]t is extremely unlikely that internal waves could limit the availability of cooling water to KDRF, thus the results provide further confirmation that downstream temperature criteria will be met."[90]

The commissioners concluded that the facility would probably work and, if it didn't, it could be modified to improve its performance. They also determined many of the issues raised about the supply of cold water near the facility could not be resolved until after the facility had been used for some time, and "even then

---

"I would like the validity and effectiveness of the cold water release facility planned by Alcan investigated by unbiased biological computer modelling experts.... I would also suggest that since the cold water relief is a part of the 1987 agreement, and if it proves unsatisfactory the entire agreement should be classed null and void." *Monte Olson, BCUCH 3.392.*

"Now again I have to reiterate that you cannot and I will not blame Alcan for being the principal contributor to fish population demise or mortalities in the system, but I will say that the temperature of the Nechako River is a factor in that process." *DFO scientist Dr. Ian Williams, BCUCH 42.7304.*

might only describe the probabilities that certain events might occur."[91]

To the residents of the valley, this sounded like another long-term experiment being conducted on their river.

Concern about the complex nature of the problems surrounding plans to protect the fish in the unstable environment of the Nechako River was reflected in the commissioners' report:

> The Commission is not convinced that the proposed...program of instream remedial measures will ensure achievement of the conservation goal, nor if it did, whether it could be demonstrated that they were indeed responsible. The difficulties of assigning effect to causes and of doing well designed applied research are not readily reconciled with the life-span of chinook. Many years of study of a stable situation would be necessary to implement the sort of strategic framework envisaged by the NFCP.

The commissioners went on to recommend that if the project is completed, the NFCP committee's membership should be expanded to include more interested local representatives, and it should also be required to consult with valley residents before making any major decision. With the project's cancellation, valley residents say they will continue their fight to ensure they are represented on whatever body is established to take the place of the NFCP.

Adding to Nechako Valley residents' anxiety about the project's effect on the environment in their valley was the information, provided during the hearings, that although parts of the technology used in the cold-water release facility have been used separately at other locations, all of this technology has never been applied at one location on a salmon-bearing river.[92] This information contributed to the belief shared by many of Alcan's critics that the KCP would have been a gigantic experiment to see if the Alcan's environmental consultants were correct. If the experiment had proven success-

---

"The facility as such, as you can see all the components put together there is no such facility that we know of around the world that would incorporate this and do what we intend it to do, but these are components, individual components of the facility that are widely known around the world."
Petr Holcak, Manager of Engineering for the KCP, BCUCH 11.1759.

ful, it would have been used as a precedent for diverting or withdrawing waters from upper reaches of every salmon-bearing river in North America. If it had failed, the Nechako River fish stocks would have been decimated before the Kenney Dam release facility could have been modified to ensure it performed satisfactorily. Therefore, Alcan's opponents argued throughout the hearings, the only way to avoid inflicting serious damage on the river was either to cancel the project, or to test thoroughly all the proposed fish-protection measures before the second diversion tunnel was completed.[93]

They now know a proposal to test all the fish-protection measures was put forward by the DFO during the negotiations leading up to the signing of the Settlement Agreement in September, 1987. The proposal was ignored. Other proposals ignored during 1987 included one suggesting that a more flexible flow regime, based on a percentage of the water flowing into the reservoir each year, be established. Tied to this proposal was another suggesting that a five-year period between the introduction of the short- and long-term flows be implemented, during which time studies of the mitigation measures required in the Nechako River to protect the resident and migrating salmon would be conducted.[94] These proposals too, were ignored.

No explanation has been given for why these proposals were not accepted.

Yet another disturbing feature of the 1987 Settlement Agreement, Alcan revealed during the hearings, was that although it *is* obligated to achieve the temperature criteria set out in the agreement,[95] it is not financially responsible should Nechako

---

"In this case there are those of the opinion that water of sufficient volume is required to maintain the populations of chinook salmon and there are those that think that such population can [be] maintained artificially with much lesser flows. In this case I believe the correct approach will only be evident in 30 or 40 years." *Dr. William Schouwenburg, BCUCH 51.9080-081.*

"[I]f there's no danger to the Fraser's fishery resource, why does the 1987 agreement limit Alcan's liability in the event of disaster." *Rob Lemmers of the Commercial Fishing Industrial Council, BCUCH 6.879.*

salmon runs be severely damaged as a result of the failure of its new facilities to deliver enough cold water into the river to keep the water temperatures within the range set out in the agreement. Instead, if the runs are nearing extinction, the company is obligated to take eggs and sperm from the remnants of the runs and raise them in a hatchery elsewhere.

The temperature of the water flowing in the Nechako and Fraser Rivers is a key factor in the sockeye's spawning success or failure. During the hearings valley residents learned the temperature of the water to be released from behind the dam into the upper Nechako River would be 10°C. Water that cold will inhibit the growth of the food on which the fish feed, thereby reducing the growth rate of the juvenile salmon and other fish in that area. To correct that problem, fisheries experts are experimenting with artificially fertilizing the river. Although fisheries experts reassured valley residents the fertilizer would be absorbed quickly by organisms in the river, people living downstream from the proposed fertilization sites who rely on the river for their drinking water didn't like the sound of that proposal. Why weren't we told about this? they asked.

Another question that remains unanswered today, despite the lengthy hearings is: Who in the DFO made the decision to ignore the recommendations of the department's fisheries experts and capitulate to Alcan's inflexible position on temperatures and flows? To this day there are DFO scientists who do not agree with the provision in the 1987 Settlement Agreement that 21.7°C is the upper limit for the protection of salmon.

"It's my opinion that the NFCP temperature criteria are too high and the NFCP[96] temperature protocol lacks flexibility," Dr. Ian Williams told the commissioners. He recommended a mean daily water temperature that is 2° cooler than that given in the Settlement Agreement, and no higher than 20°C. Because the fish have been moving through the river later, and their movement

---

"[I]f the program of measures don't work, they will...'maintain the Nechako stock gene pool at some other hatchery'. In other words, once the natural runs are dead, they'll go fish farming with the survivors, assuming there are some." *Geoff Laundy, BCUCH 6.923.*

along the river can now be tracked more accurately, the times the cooling flows are released should coincide with the times the different runs of salmon are actually in the river, instead of the period from July 20 to August 20—the only period present agreements claim the cooling flows are required.

"Ecosystems are not static. We are dealing with shifting environmental factors, we're dealing with shifting population timings, we're dealing with possible climate changes, and from my perspective, Madam Chair and distinguished Commissioners, it would be most welcome if this would be rewritten to take into account—tuning it to fish rather than to physical parameters," Williams told the commissioners.[97]

His concern about the effect of high water temperatures on salmon is based on evidence showing that when the temperature of a river rises above 18°C a bacterium which can be deadly to salmon becomes very active.[98] The bacteria are carried by suckers—a fish common to the Nechako—whose number was expected to increase with the further reductions of flows planned upon the KCP's completion.[99]

Concerns about salmon's ability to survive migrating long distances up the warmer waters in the Fraser and Nechako appeared to be justified when, during September, 1994, more than 1.3 million sockeye carrying an estimated one billion eggs disappeared somewhere in the rivers.[100] "When temperatures in the Fraser River soared this summer, migrating salmon started to behave in a bizarre fashion. Some started to swim downstream—away from the spawning beds they were so desperately trying to reach," Mark Hume reported in *The Vancouver Sun*.[101] The reaction among Nechako Valley residents was: "Ahah! See—I told you the fish would die when they tried to migrate through rivers that were too warm."

"So I hope I have made a case to indicate that what we're dealing with is an extremely complex system, that we cannot rely on some simple mathematical relationships to indicate problems, that the problems can be subtle and insidious, and that we, in my opinion, need to fall back on the fundamental physiology of the sockeye in order to protect those stocks." *Dr. Ian Williams, BCUCH 42.7301.*

Many reasons were put forward for the disappearance of the salmon. Commercial fishers blamed uncontrolled fishing by First Nations people living along the rivers. The Sto:lo Fisheries Authority, which represents the largest group of First Nations fishers living along the river, blamed DFO's mismanagement of the resource and the Canadian commercial fishers' aggressive fishing of the salmon making their way toward the mouth of the Fraser—a strategy employed to prevent US fishers from taking too many of the fish. Others repeated the excuses that the DFO fish-counting system was faulty, which was the same reason given when salmon disappeared in the rivers following the warm summer of 1992. Others blamed the laws protecting harbour seals that consume large numbers of salmon, or the DFO's inability to enforce the regulations governing salmon fishers.

Scott Hinch, a professor of aquatic biology with UBC's Westwater Research Centre, presented evidence supporting the Nechako Valley residents' contention that the salmon died because water in the Fraser and Nechako Rivers was too warm for them to survive during their long swim upstream. Hinch revealed that he had found evidence that most of the early Stuart sockeye run had died on their way to their spawning grounds up the Nechako after the temperature of the river rose quickly to more than 21°C, the highest temperatures he had ever recorded in the system. The higher temperatures increased the fishes' metabolic rate which—coupled with the facts that migrating salmon stop eating when they leave the ocean and that the warmer water causes them to move more slowly through the river—resulted in their dying of starvation.[102]

The commissioners agreed and recommended that the target water temperature at the confluence of the Nechako and Stuart Rivers should be dropped one degree from 19.4°C degrees to 18.4°C degrees, and that the period during which that tempera-

---

"We were waiting there for them. We know the river, how they travel and when they should have arrived. They just didn't show up." *UBC fisheries scientist Scott Hinch, describing how he watched and waited near their spawning beds for the more then 183,000 Stuart River sockeye in 1994, most of whom failed to appear, Vancouver Sun, 17 Sept. 1994, A3.*

ture was to be maintained each summer be changed from "July 15 to August 15," to "as required" to protect salmon runs arriving earlier or later than those dates.[103] This adjustment would provide more protection for both the chinook travelling up the Nechako beyond the Stuart River and for those salmon, mostly sockeye, entering the warmer waters of the Stuart River.

Freshwater fish are also affected by high water temperatures in the Nechako River. For example, during the summer of 1994, white sturgeon were found dead along the shores of the Fraser and Nechako Rivers. The breeding, migration and eating habits of these ancient fish are so poorly understood that Don Cadden, acting regional fisheries biologist for the fish and wildlife branch of the BC environment ministry, said it was risky and misleading for Alcan to suggest that the lower flows in the Nechako River will be adequate to protect the sturgeon.[104] Rainbow trout are also stressed by high water temperatures, the commissioners were told.

Evidence was produced during the hearings indicating there could be more occasions when water temperatures became too high for salmon to migrate safely into the upper reaches of the Nechako and Fraser Rivers. This evidence showed that Alcan's water-flow predictions are based on a period of higher-than-average precipitation in the Nechako Valley watershed. If global warming predictions are true, or if there is a long period of lower-than-average precipitation in the valley, Alcan will be faced with the difficult decision of whether to use water for power production, or to release it into the Nechako River to protect the salmon.[105]

When the hearings ended, Nechako Valley residents were still asking themselves: Since Alcan claims that the KCP is such a good project, why does it continue to fight against holding a full, public environmental review of its proposals?

One Day All This Will Be Ours

Stated in the most dramatic terms, the accusation can be made that the uncontrolled growth of technology destroys the vital sources of our humanity. It creates a culture without moral foundation. It undermines certain mental processes and social relations that make human life worth living. Technology, in sum, is both friend and enemy.[1]

The questions and controversy swirling around the Kemano Completion Project have focused on the safety of the fish living in the river and the power that can be produced by the diverted river water. What has been overlooked throughout this debate—in the research, in the terms of reference for the BCUC hearings, in the out-of-court negotiations and the in-court legal wrangling—is that at the end of the day, this is a battle over who will control the water flowing in the Nechako River.

The fight to protect the river is a striking example of how difficult it is for ordinary, law-abiding citizens, especially those living very close to their land, to force their governments to respond to their demands. The residents of the Nechako River Valley are not philosophical environmentalists. They are people whose livelihood, way of life and future are threatened by a major industrial development which, they believe, will force them to adjust to environmental changes over which they have no control. The controversy began as a regional dispute over who controls the river in which Alcan has always contended it held the trump card in the form of the agreements and licences it had obtained from the provincial government in 1950.

The government's control over the issues and the ramifications this corporate power and control had over the lives of the residents of the Nechako Valley were not revealed until the controversy received province-wide attention as the BCUC began examining the environmental effects of the agreements and licenses issued to Alcan by the federal and provincial governments. Only then were the valley residents able to state publicly their belief that they, not Alcan, should control the flows in their river. If that control does not rest in their hands, Nechako Valley residents remain convinced they will be unable to protect their lifestyle and ensure the future prosperity of the region.

Their recommendation that they be empowered to assert that control over the river, either through a regional water management board or as an integral component of the Fraser Basin Management Board's larger mandate to protect the Fraser River, was endorsed in the commissioners' report.

Valley residents also now know that before they can regain control of the historic river that has carved out the contours of their valley, the federal and provincial governments must first regain their rights to control the water flowing through the valley.

Both governments continue to claim they have that right. But evidence introduced during the BCUC hearings raises troubling questions about whether or not the federal government can order an increase in the flows in the upper Nechako River to protect migrating salmon, especially when the order is opposed by Alcan. Everyone who understands the controversy surrounding the KCP knows that Alcan demonstrated just how hard it is prepared to fight to maintain the water flows it wants in the river since 1980—the year the federal government obtained an injunction ordering the company to release more water into the river to protect the salmon. That long-simmering dispute led to Alcan's 1985 decision to ask the court to uphold its right, under the terms of its provincial water licence, to decide how much water should be in the river. That court action was set aside by the signing of the 1987 agreement and, therefore, there has never been a clear legal ruling on the question of who controls the water flows in the Nechako River.[2]

The BCUC found, as opponents of the KCP predicted they

would, that there are too many uncertainties tangled up in the complex biological question of whether or not salmon can be protected within the flows established by the 1987 agreement for them to endorse the proposed flow regime. They recommended flow-increases ranging from 189.6 to 338 cubic feet per second.[3]

If the flows are not increased, the commissioners concluded there would be three serious potential threats to the present and future production of salmon on the river: an increase in the number of young salmon killed in the river by a rising population of coarse fish hiding in the weedbeds spreading along the length of river; higher water temperatures posing a threat to migrating salmon; and an increase in the number and severity of the obstacles the already tired fish must overcome on their way to their spawning grounds.

Valley residents believe these problems already exist in the river, and say that the federal fisheries ministry should immediately exercise the authority it claims it has and order Alcan to release more water into the river from the reservoir.

Alcan argued throughout the hearings that the only conditions under which any federal fisheries minister can order the release of more water into the river is if the company breaches the conditions of the 1987 agreement. If such is the case, the opponents of the project say that it confirms their fears that the federal fisheries minister has unlawfully delegated his fiduciary responsibility to protect the fish to the two committees established by the 1987 Settlement Agreement.

Based on the history of Alcan's operations both in BC and elsewhere in the world, Nechako Valley residents are convinced that whenever the company's authority is challenged, it will begin the

---

"It is the policy of Alcan Aluminium Limited to achieve compatibility between the environment and the processes and the products of its operations. Alcan and its subsidiaries will take those practical steps necessary to prevent or abate adverse impacts on the environment which may result from their operations and products. They will respect the local legal standards and quickly implement such changes as are appropriate to achieve compliance. They will minimize waste and seek to achieve the most efficient use of energy and other raw resources." *Alcan's Environmental Policy Statement from its 1991 annual report.*

same style of protracted legal stalling tactics it began to use in 1980. Since that time, Alcan has applied heavy pressure on political leaders, spent time and money seeking to gain the support of local politicians and opinion leaders, threatened to make tax-payers responsible for its lost profits, sought to escalate the cost of court actions so high its opponents could not afford to continue and has conducted a questionable public relations blitz aimed at convincing local leaders and residents its project could proceed without harming one fish. In short, Alcan has done everything in its power to protect its interests regardless of what may happen to valley residents' lives and the environment.[4] And so, when the BC government announced it was cancelling the project, it came as no surprise that Alcan immediately threatened to sue for damages.

Meanwhile, as the three parties to this dispute continue to argue, the damage continues in the Nechako River Valley.

Since the signing of the 1987 Settlement Agreement, a four-member technical committee has been overseeing the day-to-day management of the river. Their objective is to protect the fish by monitoring the flows and conducting applied research on the river. At the time of the hearings, the committee was made up of John Payne of the DFO, Clyde Mitchell of Triton Environmental Consultants (Alcan's consultants during the latter part of this controversy), Al Martin, who represents the province of BC, and Duncan Hay, the independent chair of the committee selected by the other three members. Their testimony during the hearings revealed that there is a remarkable degree of unanimity among the committee members on issues which have generated so much public controversy.

Final approval of the technical committee's plans rests with the steering committee, whose members are senior representatives of Alcan—usually Bill Rich—and representatives appointed by the federal and provincial governments of the day. Under the terms of the 1987 Settlement Agreement, this two-tiered committee system responsible for managing the river has also assumed the federal fisheries minister's responsibility for ordering increased releases of water from the reservoir when that is considered necessary to protect the fish. If the committee members cannot agree on a proposed water flow, the dispute is referred to an arbitrator, not the federal fisheries minister.

Neither committee was required to report their activities to the people living in the valley and no independent body reviewed their work. Worse yet, as former DFO employee, William Schouwenberg, told the commissioners:

> The way in which this technical committee has been established and is being run, Alcan's consultants (Triton), are in effect evaluating their own predictive performance. This is not a healthy situation and it should not have been allowed to occur. The technical committee should have been made up entirely of individuals who had no direct involvement in the Settlement Agreement and thus no vested interest in the outcome of the resulting investigations. As it stands the neutrality test cannot be met by all members of the technical committee. Secondly, I suggest that any member of the technical committee should not be in a position to profit from the decisions made by that committee. That test is also not met by the present situation.[5]

Schouwenberg's allegations of conflict of interest result from studies commissioned by the technical committee which were contracted to members of that same committee.[6]

As far back as 1985, the federal government was warned about Alcan's poor record of co-operating with any attempted fish protection measures in a discussion paper prepared for the federal fisheries department's habitat management branch in Vancouver:

> At some point in the discussion paper the past record of ALCAN in cooperating with fisheries agencies should be reviewed. It is not a good record. The failure to do more than token cleaning of the reservoir is a public disgrace. The recalcitrance in discharging water for fisheries purposes both when the reservoir was filling and in recent years, should be put on the public record so that there will be an appropriate scepticism about ALCAN promises for the future. I simply do not believe one word of the current ALCAN conservation propaganda. It is similar to what was said 30 years ago and, judging by the record, is likely to be as insincere. To read the discussion paper, one wouldn't guess that ALCAN had a reputation as a poor performer.[7]

No one listened to the warning then. And today Nechako Valley residents wonder how many people are still ignoring it in their pursuit of the project's completion—regardless of the environmental costs.

The 1987 Settlement Agreement also appears to have seriously restricted the province's ability to issue water licences on the upper Nechako River. During the hearings, Dennis Roberts of Prince George, the regional water manager for the BC Ministry of Lands and Parks, admitted that in 1990 he was ordered by the federal DFO to issue no more licences allowing water withdrawal from the Nechako upstream from the Nautley River.[8] The ban was needed, he was told, to ensure there is enough water available to cool the river water when the salmon are migrating, once the KCP has further reduced the river's flows. Since 1990, he said, he had turned down five applications for water licenses for that reach of the river.[9]

The only other source of water for the upper reaches of the river is the natural inflow into the Cheslatta River system. That water is also no longer available to area residents because, within days of the signing of the 1987 Settlement Agreement, an Order in Council was issued reserving the unrecorded waters of the Cheslatta River and its tributaries draining into the Nechako for the exclusive use of the DFO to protect fish.[10] The reserve remains in place to this day.

A "temporary" cap of 53 cubic feet per second has also been placed on the amount of water that can be withdrawn from the river between the Nautley and downstream to the Stuart River. The cap represents the amount of water flowing into that section of the Nechako River from the Nautley River.[11] Anyone applying for a licence to withdraw water from this section of the river which would result in increasing the total amount withdrawn to more than the cap of 1.5 cubic metres per second, must prove their water withdrawals will not be detrimental to the fish. This "temporary" cap on water withdrawal is to remain in place until the long-term flows set out in the 1987 Settlement Agreement have been established and "the river and the fish populations have successfully adapted to the reduced flows."[12] Judging by the reductions in the numbers of chinook and sockeye spawners returning to the river in recent years under the short-term flows imposed on the river by the Settlement Agreement, the reserve on these flows may be in effect for a long time, if not forever, should the long-term flows go into effect.

The people living in the valley know the restrictions placed on their use of the water from their river is already hindering their agricultural, industrial, recreational and residential development. These restraints would have become worse had the KCP proceeded as planned. Alcan controls the pursestrings for much of the work being done to offset the damage caused by the reduced flows, so cost has been the major factor in determining which projects would proceed. Valley residents predicted the outcome of Alcan's cost-based decision-making process would be the incremental degradation of the river's delicate inter-related biological systems.

Throughout the BCUC hearings, Nechako Valley residents asked themselves why the company continued to fight so hard to retain control of the water when, in July, 1993, Alcan's Bill Rich admitted that falling aluminum prices and the increased cost of carrying out the KCP threatened to make the project uneconomic. Rich revealed that the company was asking the provincial government to review

> the economic terms of the half-built project. I am hopeful that Alcan and the government, working together, can agree on the best course for the future of Kemano Completion for both Alcan and British Columbia. The resulting two-year delay has changed the economics of the project. Being able to complete the job on time, meet contracts and establish sales revenue to support the financing is as much a part of the project as the construction work itself.[13]

No independent cost-benefit analysis of the this project has ever been done. When lawyer David Austin attempted to elicit information about the economics of the project, Alcan refused to divulge the company's financial information. To this day, Austin and the people he represents in the Nechako River Valley believe the project makes no economic sense. Why then, they ask, is the company fighting so hard retain control of this water?

Some information about the economic difficulties Alcan faced

"Today's Kemano Completion will yield less power and cost more money than was ever envisioned by Alcan, but still we want to build the project."
Alcan's Bill Rich, BCUCH 11.1688.

in its efforts to complete this project was released when Premier Mike Harcourt announced the project would be cancelled. It indicated that if the existing 20-year power sales contract between Alcan and BC Hydro were extended for 50 years at the current price of 2.837¢ a kilowatt hour, Alcan would lose $195 million over that term.[14] For Alcan to break even over the next 50 years, maintaining the flows set out in the 1987 Settlement Agreement, BC Hydro would have to increase the price it pays Alcan by 193% to 8.31¢ per kilowatt hour, for 30 years after the current 20-year contract expires.[15]

Every additional cubic foot of water released from behind the Kenney Dam to flow along the Nechako's historic route to the Fraser River makes Alcan's already money-losing KCP even less economically viable. Therefore, the commissioners' three scenarios in which the long-term flows in the Nechako River would be increased by 189.6, 264, or 338 cubic feet per second[16] would make the KCP progressively less economic for the company. During the hearings it was revealed that each cubic metre of water—or each 35.314 cubic feet of water—can be used to produce power worth $1.6 to $1.8 million annually.[17] That means the commissioners' proposed flow increases would remove $8.6, $11.9 or $15.3 million from Alcan's annual income. Harcourt acknowledged this fact in his cancellation speech when he pointed out that in order for the project to become economic within 50 years under the three increased flow regimes proposed by the commissioners, BC Hydro would have to pay Alcan 11.54¢, 12.65¢ or up to 13.72¢ per kilowatt hour for the power purchased from the company for 30 years after the present 20-year power purchase agreement expires.

How did Alcan get itself into this predicament? The answer lies, as Rich stated in 1993, in the rising costs of completing the project. When Alcan announced the project in August, 1988, it predicted it would cost $500 million to complete.[18] In September, 1990, the price had risen to $800 million.[19] And by October, 1993,

---

"My guess is Alcan makes no profit on its smelter operations in today's market. The hydro-electric facility is its license to print money." *Denis Wood, who owns property on the upper Nechako River, BCUCH 3.315.*

in the project outline Alcan provided to the BCUC, the company said it had already spent $535 million on the project and estimated it would cost another $818 million to complete, making the total cost of the project $1.353 billion. That's a 126% increase in costs over five years. The cost of completing the project has undoubtedly increased since 1993. Some of those costs are attributable to the interest on money borrowed for the work done on the half-finished project. It should be remembered that it was Alcan who decided to halt work on the KCP in June, 1991. At that time the company said it had made the decision because of uncertainties created by the court actions it was facing and falling aluminum prices.

Why, then, is Alcan fighting so hard to retain control of the project despite sky-rocketing costs and what appears to be its lack of any obvious pay-backs?

A look back into history provides some clues to the answer to that question. When BC's coalition government invited Alcan to come to BC almost 50 years ago, the company was looking for a site where it could generate cheap hydroelectric power for smelting aluminum. At that time valley residents were not generally aware a provision in the 1950 agreement gave Alcan up to 50 years to determine whether or not the political climate, aluminum prices and other business opportunities—such as power sales to BC Hydro—would make a future expansion of the facilities economically viable.

The first 50 years of Alcan's history in BC is almost over and Alcan is probably looking 50 years into the future. What does the company see there now?

There are two theories. One suggests that despite the losses it will suffer from power sales in 1995, the company may be able to profit from the sale of more of the power it is able to produce cheaply at Kemano in the future. By 1994, Alcan was selling electrical power worth more than $34 million annually to BC Hydro. In January, 1995, the price to Hydro increased from 1.2¢ to 2.837¢ a kilowatt hour, thus more than doubling Alcan's income from the sale of power. The value of that power is expected to increase in the future, particularly at a time when shortages are developing in western North America and demand is expected to increase in the

US where there is growing concern about the safety of nuclear power generators.

At present, the only obstacle to Alcan's selling power directly to the United States is Hydro's monopoly over the power flowing through the provincial power grid. Hydro purchases all the power available from independent producers, including Alcan, transports it throughout the province and, when there is more power available than is used in the province, Hydro sells it outside the province, often to the US.

Hydro's monopoly over power distribution in BC, however, could soon be broken by the complex interplay of domestic and international trade agreements being signed by Canada. The cumulative effect of these agreements could force Hydro to give all power producers in North America equal access to its grid, with the possible outcome that when—or even before—Alcan's contracts with Hydro end, Alcan could send all its excess electrical power directly from Kemano into the US where it could demand a higher price. And, since Alcan did not fulfill its plans to build more smelters that would have used the power from the proposed KCP, all the power produced by the Nechako River could be sold into the American market. During the BCUC hearings, fears were expressed that, should the price of electrical power continue to increase, Alcan may decide to shut down more of the potlines in its aging smelter at Kitimat and sell that freed-up power into the US, too. As its contribution to reducing the world's supply of the metal, the company has already shut down one potline at Kitimat—thus freeing the 60 megawatts of power once used to power those reduction cells, making it available for sale. It is possible that, in the future, it could shut down other potlines in the increasingly inefficient plant and, using its new-found equal access to Hydro's power grid, direct that power south of the border, where it can already command prices as high as 4¢ per kilowatt hour.

"Some say that Canada has been exporting water for years in the form of electricity; once we dam a valley for hydro-electric power, what is the difference if some of that water is piped to California to keep lawns green in Beverly Hills?" *Jerry Thompson, "Diverting Interests," 81.*

Remember that it is BC's unique geography that enables Alcan to produce this power for .5¢ per kilowatt hour, and that while until January, 1995, Alcan had paid the water rental fees on the water it used, now that cost has been assumed by BC Hydro. This is viewed by Nechako Valley residents as yet another tax benefit bestowed upon Alcan by the BC government.

The power Hydro now buys from Alcan for 2.837¢ a kilowatt hour, it turns around and sells for an average of 4.7¢. In addition, Hydro pays the province approximately .5¢ for the water rental used to manufacture this energy. Prior to 1995, the arrangement was more profitable for the province because Hydro paid Alcan 1.7¢ to 1.9¢ per kilowatt hour, and out of this, Alcan, not Hydro, paid the province the approximately .5¢ water-use fee.[20]

The fear that Alcan may be considering selling power directly into the US was heightened by BC Supreme Court Judge Robert Hutchison's decision in the UFAWU's action against Alcan. Rather than order that the project must obtain an energy project certificate, Hutchison determined that BC's 1949 Industrial Development Act, which was enacted to pave the way for Alcan to establish itself in Northwestern BC, had such sweeping powers that, unless it is repealed or amended, all subsequent energy project legislation does not apply to any additions to Alcan's projects in BC.

It would appear, then, that one avenue available for the BC government to enforce its decision to cancel the project would be to repeal or amend the 1949 Industrial Development Act. Nechako Valley residents have always believed the provincial government erred when it agreed to give Alcan a perpetual water licence covering all facilities installed by the end of 1999. Even the much-reviled Columbia River Treaty contained a provision that the treaty was to be renegotiated after 30 years. But there is no such provision in the 1987 Settlement Agreement. Why, they ask, must Nechako Valley residents be forced to live with an agreement, signed 45 years ago, that restricts their opportunities for economic growth and offends current concerns about the project's potential to cause further environmental damage to the river? There are other precedents for setting terms for reviews and reapplications for water licences. When BC Electric—the predecessor of BC

Hydro—began the Bridge River Project in the late 1950s, it was given a water licence that expires in 2019, and Ontario's water licences have fixed terms with performance reviews half-way through the term of the licence. The least the government can do, valley residents believe, is replace Alcan's water licence with a 30- to 40-year licence with a performance review after 15 to 20 years.

Hutchison also pointed out that the 1950 agreement between Alcan and BC empowered the company only to develop power for smelting aluminum or other industrial developments in the region. Alcan's critics are still asking if this means Alcan cannot sell power elsewhere in BC or to the US. That question must be answered before the matter of the KCP is settled.

When the UFAWU decision was announced, Canada was already entangled in a growing web of trading blocks which appear to threaten the Canadian provinces' ability to manage and control the use of their natural resources, including water and power. Behind the scenes, there was mounting concern about the likelihood of Canada signing the Energy Charter Treaty which, as of mid-November, 1994, had been signed by 36 countries, including the members of the European Union. The treaty was proposed during the rush of Western investors into some of the republics that had formerly been part of the Soviet Union to help rebuild their faltering economies, and to prevent them from sliding into anarchy or back into Communism. Canada originally sought to become a signatory to the treaty in order to protect the interests of Canadians investing in the former Soviet republics by ensuring they would be granted treatment equal to that being offered to investors from other countries, including Europe and the United States. When it became apparent the treaty was evolving into a binding trade and investment treaty, attention turned to the effect it could have on expanding the scope of Canada's commitments under existing treaties, including NAFTA. As of January, 1995, Canada still had not signed the treaty. On the other hand, no one has announced that Canada will not be signing the treaty and, as Nechako Valley residents now know, there is no reason to believe that the signing of this treaty is not being considered behind the scenes.

In the short-term, the European Union views the treaty as providing more secure access to the former Soviet Union's oil supplies, thereby decreasing their dependence on oil supplies from the Middle East and undermining the OPEC producers' ability to control the world price of oil. The long-term goal of the treaty is that it constitute the first step in an agreement linking all European countries' energy supplies into the treaty. For Canadians wishing to control their resources, at least one clause in the treaty could become a problem: It specifies that all countries signing the treaty must provide each other with access to their energy transmission systems equal to that provided nationally. Although the US and Canada obtained an exemption to the effect that the treaty does not apply to transmission between just two countries, there is concern that the treaty may extend to Crown corporations such as BC Hydro. If this were to transpire, the treaty would constitute one more step toward eliminating Hydro's ability to prevent Alcan from selling power directly to the company's customers in the US and, through energy swaps, to Mexico.

So, 50 years in the future, Alcan's sale of hydroelectric power will have taken on much larger dimensions, including the business value of direct electricity sales to the US.

The second theory about what Alcan could accomplish with its BC operations in the next 50 years is the export of the millions of gallons of water flowing into the Nechako Reservoir each year. There are those who believe this water could be exported to the US and on into Mexico under the terms of the NAFTA. By mid-December, 1994, it was announced that Chile is expected to be the next of many countries in South and Central America to join the continental bloc.

Since the agreements were first made public, complex arguments have been put forward for and against claims the FTA and the NAFTA have opened the doors for Americans to demand equal access to Canadian fresh water.

Sceptics—who include politicians who claim large-scale water exports to the US will never be permitted—scoff at the notion that once Canada begins exporting water, it will be difficult, if not impossible, to stop that flow. They sound much like the people who, in the 1950s, could not see the future value of the trees drowned when Alcan flooded the valleys occupied by the Great

Circle Water Route. Even if water exports are not being contemplated *now*, powerful lobbies coupled with a lucrative market create a persuasive engine that could easily change politicians' minds.[21]

The investors' rights provisions, an entirely new feature of international agreements included in the NAFTA, introduced a threat to Canada's freshwater resources potentially even more serious than the sale of Canada's water to North American markets. For the first time, these rights enable private investors living in another signatory country to sue Canada for damages caused to their investments by any Canadian regulatory decisions which allegedly reduce the value of their investments.[22] This would mean, for instance, that an American or Mexican investing in a Canadian water export project that might have its right to export water withdrawn or altered, could sue the Canadian government for damages. Until the NAFTA, these suits could only be laid by one signatory state against another. One would hope that the prospect of American and Mexican investors suing Canada for losses incurred now and in the future would prompt the federal government to get its act together to protect Canada's water interests by preventing the granting of any right to export water. Otherwise, once a company has the right to export water, Canada's regulatory ability is trumped by international private property rights.

Canada's international trading obligations already caused this country a direct sovereignty set-back when, in May, 1994, in an effort to reduce advertisers' ability to seduce more young people into smoking, the federal health minister introduced regulations requiring that cigarettes be sold in plain packages. This action caused Ambassador Julius L. Katz to appear before the House of

---

"The sequence of key staples that have been central to Canada's economic viability is well known: fish, furs, wheat, timber, metal, minerals, pulp and paper, oil and natural gas. That fresh water is next on the list as the ultimate Canadian export is powerfully suggested by historical experience nearly four centuries old." *Canadian political scientist James Laxer in Holm, 129.*

"It took me some time to realize just how powerful the wealthy corporate elite is in Canada." *Jim Fulton, Canadian Forum (Nov. 1993): 11.*

Commons Standing Committee on Health to argue that the regulations violated the investors' protection provisions of three trade agreements signed by Canada: the NAFTA, the Paris Convention for the Protection of Industrial Property, and the Uruguay Round Agreement on Trade-Related Aspects of Intellectual Property Rights. His claim was based on a legal opinion signed by former US trade representative Carla Hills, who was the US trade representative and chief United States negotiator during the NAFTA negotiations with Canada and Mexico. Hills, working on behalf of the tobacco industry, stated that in her opinion the Canadian proposal was "an expropriation of property rights requiring the payment of...compensation...[which could amount] to hundreds of millions of dollars."[23] Katz concluded his argument by saying that if Canada decides to adopt a plain packaging requirement, it would face severe economic consequences, including American sanctions on Canadian exports—such as softwood lumber, wheat and pork—that have already been hit hard.[24]

The water export debate also raises this question: Once Canada begins exporting water south to the US and Mexico, will it be possible to stop the flow? The complexity of the issues involved in this debate were confirmed when delegates at a 1992 international water export conference were unable to agree on whether or not the export of water was an acceptable option for Canadians. Delegates supporting free trade in water argued it was a commodity no different from oil, gas, minerals and lumber and should be traded accordingly. Opposing speakers argued that water is *not* like other commodities because it—unlike oil, gas, minerals and lumber—is essential to life and its export should therefore be prohibited.[25]

In anticipation that international trading obligations may force Canada to begin exporting water in the future, the delegates concluded that there are steps Canada should take now to preserve its economy and its environmental health, to ensure that the export of water is economically viable and that the control of Canada's water

---

"If we want our children to have choices, then we must consider the long-term consequences of a natural resource management decision." *Arlene Galisky, BCUCH 6.1060.*

remains in the hands of Canadians. They recommended that Canada must either take action to ban water exports, or else develop clear criteria and policies for meeting what some delegates see as the inevitability of increased demands that this country share its fresh water with its southern neighbours.[26]

One conference speaker, Ehor Boyanowsky, predicted that attempts to export water from Canada could result in violence or even war between the two countries. The Simon Fraser University criminologist told the delegates that

> [o]nce any country, especially one as powerful as the USA, views another as a source of a primary resource, inspiring industries, cities, farms to spring up in the desert that would be dependent upon that resource for survival, that country, in this case Canada, would become a holding tank. Water would become a national security issue and the US Marines the final arbiters. We would cease to exist as an independent nation in any way at all.[27]

This is one extreme view of the growing importance of water export issues in this country, and elsewhere in the world.

Another more moderate warning about future struggles to control North American water supplies were heard by those attending the BCUC's hearings in Vancouver on May 27, 1994, when former federal fisheries scientist Dr. Harold Mundie stated:

> Conflicts over water are going to increase, and they will very likely be the main feature of the first half of the next century. I do not know how the problems will be solved, but if they are to be solved they will require the very best and honest efforts of our ablest people. If our senior politicians, senior bureaucrats, captains of industry and managers behave as they have behaved in the Kemano Completion Project, there is no hope, not only for the protection and preservation of fisheries as a public resource, but for any of us.[28]

Other people say that fights over water will never materialize because the Free Trade Agreement, the North American Free Trade Agreement and the growing roster of intercontinental trade agreements on which Canada's name appears has already placed the hands of the US and Mexico firmly on Canada's water taps.

Among those who believe American access rights to Canada's water resources are firmly entrenched in the agreements is Toronto trade lawyer Barry Appleton—a constitutional and international lawyer who has been called to the bars of Ontario and New York, where he serves on the US Court of International Trade. In 1994, he stated: "Clearly, the GATT tariff item contemplates that unprocessed goods, such as snow and ice will be included in this category (water). On this basis, one must conclude that natural water will be treated as a good under the NAFTA, even when it is in its natural state. Accordingly, the NAFTA will apply to ground and surface fresh water in its natural state."[29]

Canadians can be excused for being confused on this issue. In December, 1993, in an effort to assuage Canadians' fears that these agreements will force Canada to begin exporting large volumes of water, the federal government released a document it said represented an agreement between the governments of Canada, the US and Mexico proclaiming:

> The NAFTA creates no rights to the natural water resources of any Party to the Agreement.
>
> Unless water, in any form, has entered into commerce and become a good or product, it is not covered by the provisions of any trade agreement, including the NAFTA. And nothing in the NAFTA would oblige any NAFTA Party to either exploit its water for commercial use, or to begin exporting water in any form. Water in its natural state in lakes, rivers, reservoirs, aquifers, waterbasins and the like is not a good or product, is not traded, and therefore is not and never has been subject to the terms of any trade agreement.
>
> International rights and obligations respecting water in its natural state are contained in separate treaties and agreements negotiated for that purpose.[30]

Sceptics note that there is no evidence indicating the paper was signed by the US or Mexico. More worrying is the fact that the statement is not a part of the NAFTA itself, and is thus unlikely to carry any weight when water disputes inevitably appear before a NAFTA international trade dispute panel. Such panels will deal with each dispute in terms of the agreement itself, not in terms of any explanatory statements issued by any or all governments. Moreover, the wording of the statement itself suggests that whatever state the water might be in—whether in a pipeline, reservoir, river, lake or even in an underground aquifer—once it has been bought and sold, all provisions of the trade agreements apply.

In response to a letter from US environmentalists in late 1993, US Trade Representative Michael Kantor set the record straight about how that country interprets this particular point: "[W]hen water is traded as a good, all provisions of the agreements governing trade in goods apply, including the national treatment provisions."[31]

This was the first official American interpretation of the water export issue under the terms of the NAFTA.

Some Americans were also becoming concerned about the NAFTA provisions permitting exports from one country to another. While Canadians were asking themselves in 1993 if the NAFTA meant they would be forced to export water to California, Felix Smith of Carmichael, California, wrote a letter to Vic Fazio, then vice-chair of the Democratic Caucus of the United States Congress, expressing the worries of Californians that the agreement might force them to export water to Canada or Mexico. In response to Smith's letter, Fazio said: "Nothing in NAFTA gives Mexico or Canada the right to purchase California water. Nothing in NAFTA requires the state to sell water to Canada or Mexico. In short, NAFTA does not confer on other parties a right to exploit our water resources."[32]

This statement brought the following response from BC Minister of Employment and Investment, Glen Clark:

> The analysis asserts that NAFTA poses risks to national, provincial and state control over water. It argues that NAFTA "encourages...the development of a continental market" in fresh water property rights and that it could "provide an effective means of stimulating" a continental commodity market in fresh water itself— the very lifeblood of our ecosystem.[33]

Clark pointed out that there were numerous misleading or inaccurate statements in Fazio's letter: His assertion that the NAFTA does not pose a threat to the sovereignty of the US or any of its states, and his belief the final decisions of the arbitration panels, which will decide any disputes arising from the NAFTA, are not binding before United States domestic law.[34]

Despite government reassurances that large-scale water exports from Canada "will never happen," there is no federal legislation in place to prevent it from happening, and proposals to rearrange

Canada's water flow, diverting much of it south into the US or even to Mexico, continue to pop up like mushrooms after a rain. The BC government is expected to introduce legislation banning inter-basin transfers of water during 1995.

The two most massive proposals to transfer water across the border into the US are the Great Recycling and Northern Development (GRAND) Canal project and the North American Water and Power Alliance (NAWAPA). The $100-billion GRAND project was publicly promoted prior to the FTA negotiations by Simon Reisman, Canada's chief negotiator. Reisman proposed that Canada should exchange its water for access for Canadian-manufactured goods to US markets. The GRAND proposal calls for a dam to be built across the outlet of James Bay, closing it off from Hudson's Bay and then turning it into a freshwater basin by trapping all the fresh water flowing into it from 20 rivers. The trapped water would be diverted south through the Great Lakes into the US Midwest and as far west into the Canadian Prairies as Lake Diefenbaker.

There are those who believe the controversial Rafferty-Alameda Dam complex in southern Saskatchewan is an early component of the proposed GRAND Canal project because it will be used to transport water south from Saskatchewan's Lake Diefenbaker into North Dakota.

The GRAND proposal has slipped into the background, as has another huge diversion project based in Quebec—the Great Whale Project, which has been strongly opposed by the Cree First Nations people who live in the area that would be flooded. Putting these massive water diversion projects on the shelf is probably an attempt to ensure that they do not become a decisive factor in the Quebec sovereignty referendum, expected to be held in 1995. But there are no guarantees they won't resurface later.

The second major water diversion project, NAWAPA, is of the most concern to BC residents. The sweeping concept of this proposal calls for the building of a series of dams to divert the flow of BC, Yukon and Alaskan rivers into a deep mountain valley, known as the Rocky Mountain Trench, running the length of British Columbia. This feature of BC's geography is the world's second-largest potential natural reservoir, surpassed only by the Great Rift

Valley in Africa. The upper reaches of both the Fraser and the Columbia Rivers lie in the Rocky Mountain Trench, so their flows would, therefore, be diverted by the proposed reservoir.[35] If it is ever completed, the NAWAPA reservoir will be more than ten times larger than Alcan's Nechako Reservoir which, when it was built, stored 35 million acre feet of water. No one knows exactly how much water is stored there now because, as is the case with most of the world's reservoirs, it has been slowly filling up with silt. This fact has led some people to the intriguing prediction of a future when dam spillways will become artificial waterfalls—when nature will have done what it always strives to do: restore itself. Behind the dams there would be a flat landscape slowly filling with trees and plants, inhabited by birds and bugs, and through which the water would flow, as it did in the past, but at a higher elevation.

What would happen to all the water the NAWAPA project proposes to store in the Rocky Mountain Trench?

It could be diverted eastward and southward. The east-flowing water would provide irrigation to water-starved regions in Alberta and Saskatchewan, and would then flow on to the Great Lakes, raising the level in all the lakes including Lake Michigan, which is wholly in the United States. From there the water could be diverted into the Illinois and Mississippi Rivers. The resulting rise in these rivers would enable ocean freighters to reach St. Louis and provide a safer water supply to US communities whose existing water supplies are polluted.

"Larger than California and Oregon and Washington stitched together, flooded by up to two hundred inches of rain annually, bisected by big rivers whose names few people know, British Columbia is to water what Russia is to land. Within its boundaries are, in whole or in part, the third-, fourth-, the seventh-, and eighth-, and the nineteenth largest rivers in North America...The Fraser River alone gathers nearly twice the runoff of California; the Skeena's flow approaches the runoff of Texas; both run to sea all but unused." *Reisner, 487.*

"One of the most serious challenges facing the United States regarding water is what to do with dams that are full of silt. Many smaller dams in the east have become virtually useless: indeed they are something of a menace in times of flooding." Conservationist Andy Russell, "What About Tomorrow," in Holm, 118.

The south-flowing water would also be siphoned off to be poured onto the increasingly dry deserts of 33 American states including Arizona, California, Idaho, Texas, Montana and, possibly, Northern Mexico, where much of it would be used to water what are often referred to as "farmers' fields," but are actually the fields controlled by agribusiness—conglomerates that control every stage of food production from the fields, through the manufacturing process and onto supermarket shelves. We also know some of it would be used to fill desert-dwellers' swimming pools, hot tubs and jacuzzis and provide water for their bathtubs, washing machines, dishwashers and lawn sprinklers.

There is an insidious side-effect experienced by the soils in hot, dry climates that are subjected to long-term application of large volumes of irrigation water. Much of the irrigation water evaporates, and what remains percolates down through the soil, picking up fertilizer salts and dissolved mineral salts. When it eventually flows back into the irrigation canals or rivers, its salt content is elevated. Most of the river water in the Western US is used to irrigate a large number of such fields as it makes its way to the Pacific Ocean.[36] As the water picks up dissolved mineral salts from the soil, it accumulates heavy concentrations of salt. The worst salinity problem can be found in California's San Joaquin Valley, one of the most productive farming areas in the world. Unfortunately, an impermeable layer of clay underlying the valley prevents the irrigation water from draining off, so it collects on top of the clay, waterlogging the land and drowning the plants. As the surface water evaporates in the valley's 90° to 110°F temperatures, salt crystals form on the surface of the fields. This problem is compounded by the fact that, despite the huge diversion projects to carry water onto these fields, 40% of the irrigation water used in the valley is drawn from underground sources. As those aquifers are depleted, they become contaminated with saltwater drawn in from the Pacific Ocean.[37]

According to one version of it, the NAWAPA proposal would

"This is a plan that will not roll over and die. It may be fifty years or it may be a hundred years, but something like it will be built." *Diehard NAWAPA booster Governor Tom McCall of Oregon, in Reisner, 490.*

give Canada the capacity to generate up to 38 million kilowatts of hydroelectricity in addition to providing water to irrigate crops in Canada's grain-growing areas. BC would then pay the price of further endangering its valuable salmon stocks; flooding tens of millions of acres; and dislocating hundreds of thousands of people. The city of Prince George, for example, with a current population of 75,000 and a trading population of more than double that, would partially or completely disappear under NAWAPA's proposed reservoir,[38] as would the cities of Whitehorse in the Yukon Territories,[39] and Fort Steele, Canal Falls, Fairmont and Invermere further south.[40]

Some say this extreme re-organization of the flow of Canadian rivers to satisfy the United States' insatiable thirst for water will never happen. But anyone studying a modern map of BC will discover that portions of this project are already in place. The Bennett Dam in northern BC forms Williston Lake, which has already flooded the Finlay and Parsnip Rivers that once flowed through the northern Rocky Mountain Trench. Further south lies a reservoir created by the Libby Dam, built on the south-flowing Kootenay River, behind which forms Lake Koocanusa in the southern part of the Rocky Mountain Trench.

Grand schemes such as NAWAPA may be postponed for a while and politicians may deny they will ever come to pass, but they have a habit of being resurrected. Following World War Two, a plan similar to NAWAPA was proposed by European industrialist Axel Wenner-Gren. The surveys he conducted in the Rocky Mountain

---

"Although many (U.S.) Southwesterners concede that it is no longer feasible for the desert to sustain so many humans, no one seems to know how, in a free society, to stop the growth." *Thompson, 67.*

"If the United States should ever ask Canada to ship water to an American region, Canadians should understand that the so-called "need" is artificial and political, not biological or economic." *Richard Bocking, in Holm, 101.*

"The human race has an abundance of water. It is simply in the wrong place." *Francis Date, US President Richard Nixon's ambassador to the United Nations, at the 1992 Vancouver conference on continental water issues.*

Trench northeast of Prince George were used by the BC government as the basis for the building of the Bennett Dam which created Williston Lake (really a reservoir) and, like Alcan's Kenney Dam, drowned millions of trees.

Author Jerry Thompson warns that Canadians cannot afford to become complacent about water diversion projects simply because environmentalists forced the proponents of the grand water diversion schemes of the 1960s and '70s to abandon their proposals. Canada, he says, continues to divert its rivers "at a feverish pace."[41]

> In fact, geographers J.C. Day of Simon Fraser University, in Burnaby, British Columbia, and Frank Quinn of Environment Canada have discovered that the volume of water diversion in Canada is considerably greater than the next two leading countries, the United States and the former Soviet Union, combined.[42]

The geographers' study shows that "If all this flow were concentrated into a mythical new river, it would be Canada's third largest, behind only the St. Lawrence and Mackenzie rivers."[43]

The money to be made by exporting water continues to attract the attention of big and small business entrepreneurs. In 1991 there were three applications for licences to export small amounts of water from the Kemano and Kitimat River Valleys alone.[44] They were not approved, but can be reactivated quickly whenever there is an indication the provincial government is willing to approve them.

One large inter-basin, water-transfer proposal is still being actively pursued. In January, 1994, the Texas-based Pipeline Digest Newsletter[45] contained a report about a proposal by Multinational Resources Inc.[46] of Vancouver, BC to build dual, 315-mile long, 10-foot wide water pipelines to divert one million acre feet of water annually from the upper reaches of another tributary of the

---

"To keep the U.S. Southwest blooming, visionary engineers are proposing to replumb the waterways of Canada, again." *Thompson, "Diverting Interests."*

"If this scenario is followed, B.C.'s great rivers will be only a memory, and the salmon will be an epicurean delicacy of the past, a miracle of nature living only in legend." *Bocking, "Canada's Water: For Sale?" 130.*

Fraser River, the North Thompson River, into the Columbia River in the United States. The project's main proponent is Bill Clancey of Vancouver, who was closely associated with BC's previous Socred government and is a founding member of the Bank of British Columbia. Clancey's American partner is Gerald Shupe of KVA Resources, an engineering and dam-building company in Bellevue, Washington. The company characterizes the proposed water withdrawal as representing only 1% of the water flowing in the Fraser River. But First Nations Chief Nathan Matthew, of the Simpcw people, indicated that it is also 25% to 30% of the upper reaches of the North Thompson River at the point near Valemount, BC, where the water will be withdrawn.[47]

A private environmental assessment on this project is being conducted by Triton Environmental Consultants, the same firm that did the environmental assessment work for Alcan's KCP.

To assess the size of Multinational Resources Inc.'s proposed diversion, one should know that one acre-foot of water is equivalent to 271,322 Imperial gallons. This project would draw off 27 billion gallons of water annually from the upper reaches of the North Thompson River. A research document prepared for the project provides clues about how such projects will be sold to residents of BC and Canada. Under the cover page headline, "Wealth of the Future is Water," and subtitle, "$500 million net every year to BC," the report praises the project as visionary, practical and realistic. It goes on to say that:

> British Columbia has 2 per cent of all the water in the world. Every day, 487 billion gallons of B.C. water, dump into the ocean. A fraction of that water could make British Columbia debt free and wealthy.

In its all-out effort to portray the North Thompson diversion project as beneficial to BC, Multinational Resources Inc.'s report links what it sees as British Columbians' wasteful dumping of billions of gallons of water into the ocean with the spectre of future famine:

> California's population continues to mushroom; it is expected to leap from 30 million in 1990 to 49 million in 2020. To sustain its population growth, California will be forced to take water from its agriculture industries. California provides the U.S. and Canada with

one half—50%—of its fresh fruit and vegetables. It irrigates 9.2 million acres to meet this demand; it takes 3.5 million acre feet to irrigate a million acres of land. It takes 22 gallons to produce one orange, 51 for one cantaloupe. The correlation is obvious. Farm land will revert to desert and food production will decline. Over the past several years, farmlands have decreased by a half-million acres. The next decade will see a similar trend.

I am reminded of a time when BC was more self-sufficient in the production of its own vegetables and fruits which grew in the irrigated fields of the dry, hot interior of southern BC—the northern part of the same desert on which vegetables and fruits grow further south in the US. More and more of these crops are now being imported from the US and Mexico where, ironically, they now say they need Canadian water to grow the vegetables we see in our supermarkets.

Similar dislocations in the production of farm crops occurred in the US when millions of tax-payers' dollars were spent to divert water onto their drier desert areas to enable agribusinessmen to prosper there. By 1993, economists found the cost of delivering water to the Westlands Water District in Southern California was $97 per acre foot, but farmers were being charged $7.50 to $11.80 per acre foot—resulting in an estimated subsidy of $500,000 per year to the average-sized farm in that region. The subsidy amounts to $217 per acre per year on land producing an average annual revenue of $290.[48] "This means that 70 percent of the profit on what is supposed to be some of the richest farmland in the world comes solely through tax-payer subsidization—not crop production," says author Marc Reisner. Worse yet, much of the land irrigated in the Westlands Water District is used to grow cotton and, by the 1980s, there was a surplus of US-grown cotton—which may explain the flood of cotton clothing coming into Canada from the US. Reisner continues:

"Water planning is often the embodiment of the North American faith that resources are almost limitless in quantity; whether it be land or trees or minerals or water. To many Americans, and some Canadians too, it is a logical progression of this idea that would carry the American search for more water north into Canada." *Bocking, "Canada's Water: For Sale?" 118.*

So the same subsidies that were helping to enrich some of the wealthiest farmers in the nation were at the same time depressing crops' prices elsewhere and undoubtedly driving unsubsidized cotton farmers in Texas and Louisiana and Mississippi out of business.[49]

The same could be said of the fate of farmers in BC's southern interior.

There is a moratorium on the consideration of applications for bulk exports of water by tanker from BC's rainy coastline. There are currently four active licences which were obtained before the moratorium was placed on approval of further licences. Three of the four are for relatively small amounts of water: 200 acre feet per year. The fourth is for 5,387 acre-feet—potentially a commercially viable amount—from BC's northwest coast. This licence was originally held by a company called Kermodi H2O. The company went bankrupt in July, 1994, but was reconstituted by some of the company's investors under the name White Bear Water Limited. BC's environment ministry approved the transfer of the old Kermodi license to the new company, along with the standard condition that works be constructed, the licence be exercised and export commence by a specified date, in this case before the end of 1994. As of mid-January, 1995, the licence had not been renewed—but that doesn't mean it is dead. In the past, governments have found ways to renew licences retroactively and could well do so again in this case.

During the summer of 1994, White Bear Water Limited advertised for investors in a major Mexican financial newspaper. If investors are found and if the company satisfies the conditions of its licence after obtaining an extension from the environment ministry, it may be in a prime position to use NAFTA's investment provision to thwart the provincial government's announced intention to prevent bulk water exports. BC residents may well ask whether this is not reason enough not to renew the company's licence now, before their province is led into a water export battle should the company seek to increase the amount of water it can send into the United States or Mexico.

Is there a shortage of water in the United States?

No, says author Richard C. Bocking. There is a shortage of

cheap water in the United States and, particularly in California, there is considerable room for water conservation projects to reduce the wasteful misuse of the large amounts of water already pouring into the state through federal government subsidized water projects.[50] But, he warns, there *will* be a US water shortage if that country continues to provide irrigation water to farmers for a price significantly less than the cost of delivering it to them, and if the present level of wasting and degrading water supplies continues as Americans continue to ignore newer, more efficient water technologies: "if the future is viewed as a simple projection of trends in the face of which North Americans are helpless and incapable of exercising choice or control."[51]

There is another troubling matter concerning Alcan's operations in BC: No one seems to be asking what effect Quebec's possible separation from Canada might have on Alcan's industrial activities in BC.

Alcan's headquarters are in Montreal and it has three aluminum smelters in Quebec, including a new smelter which it opened in 1991. As of July 9, 1993 all but three of its directors lived in Quebec: one director lives in BC—regional vice-president Bill Rich, in West Vancouver; one lives in the US state of Georgia; and the third lives in Jamaica. During 1990 and 1991, the company spent more than $200 million to construct aluminum manufacturing plants in Oswego, New York and Terre Haute, Indiana. A third plant in Russellville, Kentucky was scheduled for completion early in 1993. Alcan also totally or partially owns facilities related to aluminum production in Kingston, Ontario; Warren, Ohio; Detroit, Michigan; Roseburg, Oregon; Jamaica; Germany; the United Kingdom; France; Italy; Switzerland; Ireland; South America; Brazil; Argentina; Uruguay; Australia; Japan; India and Guinea in

---

"How was the Kemano hydro-electric power sales implicated with NAFTA?" *Vanderhoof resident Peter Rodseth, BCUCH 4.443.*

"To a degree that is impossible for most people to fathom, water projects are the grease gun that lubricates the nation's legislative machinery. Congress without water projects would be like an engine without oil; it would simple seize up." *Reisner, 308.*

Africa.[52] Yet it has not built a single processing or manufacturing plant in British Columbia.

Without being aware of it, Alcan and federal and provincial politicians have taught the once complacent, politically naïve residents of the Nechako Valley that they should not rely on either the federal or provincial governments to protect their interests. And if those governments don't act quickly to make certain the KCP is *legally* dead and to correct the injustices and environmental damage already inflicted on the region, the politicians responsible to those residents may come to regret their lack of action.

A major task assigned to the BCUC was to determine how to mitigate the damages the KCP would have caused to the Nechako River Valley. By the end of the hearings it was apparent that unless the project is cancelled and control of the river's flows is returned to those who live in the valley, residents are unlikely to accept any settlement of this dispute, no matter how much money they are offered to compensate them for the reduction in the flows. In fact, valley residents repeatedly told the commissioners that there is no way they could be compensated for the loss of the river.

In November, 1994, the BCUC ordered BC Hydro, as part of its next integrated review process, to review its agreements with Alcan, weighing "whatever costs are associated with implementing the contract, including social costs, against the costs of not implementing the contract."[53] In other words, the commission asked Hydro to consider not only the social and environmental costs of completing the project, but also the costs of not completing the project.

"I don't believe these three Commissioners can stop Alcan. Mayor Frank Read (of Vanderhoof) can't stop Alcan. Premier Harcourt can't stop Alcan. Prime Minister Chretien can't stop Alcan. I do believe that the people of the valley can stop KCP." *Vanderhoof resident Bruce Hill, BCUCH 3.99.*

"...I realize that nationalization is a smutty word these days, having as it does the overtones of socialism, but the government can reinforce its courage by taking a page from the life of that great socialist pioneer, the great builder of dams himself, W.A.C. Bennett, who in 1958 nationalized the British Columbia Electric Company and formed B.C. Hydro and Power Authority from the remains." *Geoff Laundy, BCUCH 6.932.*

If this review is completed, it will be the first cost-benefit analysis of the KCP. Throughout all the controversy around this project there has been no independent assessment of the economic impact of the project on the province or of its environmental impact on the Fraser River. Critics claim that without those studies the province has continued to move forward blindly into a project which may have serious implications for all of BC.

Opponents of the project believe that when the cost of the damages to the environment and the long-term social costs to the valley residents and BC's salmon fishers are accounted for in the cost-benefit analysis, it will be clear it does not make economic sense for the KCP to proceed.

Nechako Valley residents who oppose the project received a big boost when the BC Liberal Opposition pushed the NDP Government to the brink of deciding to cancel the project on October 11, 1994. On that date, Liberal leader Gordon Campbell surprised the province by announcing he was opposed to the KCP. Until then, many valley residents had thought Alcan was waiting until the next provincial election when, with the help of business and industry, a more-friendly-to-business Liberal government would be installed in Victoria. Until Campbell's announcement, discussions on the river's future had consisted mainly of technical debates over whether or not the salmon could survive in the flows prescribed for the Nechako River under the terms of the 1987 Settlement Agreement. When the Liberals came out strongly in opposition to the project, they yanked the political initiative away from the NDP, forcing them to face the fact that the only way they could recoup any political benefit from the long examination of Alcan's activities on the river was to consider refusing to allow it to proceed.

Adding fuel to the fervour of those calling for the cancellation of the KCP was the year-long campaign against it conducted by colourful CKNW radio broadcaster and former Socred MLA, Rafe Mair. He was almost solely responsible for informing Lower Mainland and Vancouver Island residents about the controversy that had been brewing in the central interior of the province for many years and that could have major consequences for the Fraser River—a river many BC residents emotionally regard as the province's main artery. As Mair has expressed it: "British Columbia and the Fraser River are almost interchangeable terms. KCP will be the beginning of the end for the Fraser. Everybody admits there's a risk in this project. If you have a risk and take out the time constraints, it becomes a certainty. If Alcan is wrong, it is catastrophe for the Fraser."

By the end of 1994, Nechako Valley residents were optimistic that they were going to be victorious in the David-and-Goliath struggle.

When Harcourt announced he was cancelling the project in Vancouver on January 23, 1995, 500 miles north of Vancouver in Prince George, Nechako Valley residents were gathered in a hotel ballroom, where they heard Health Minister Paul Ramsey (NDP Prince George-North) make the same announcement. In the room were gathered the First Nations' leaders who had been the first to speak out against the project and the non-native valley residents who had participated actively throughout the hearings. It was a triumphant moment—but they realized the announcement did not mark the end of their fight.

There remains a big unanswered question: How will the province minimize the cost of extricating itself from its agreements with Alcan?

Harcourt made his first move on January 23, when he said he was asking the federal government to withdraw the letter (14 Sept. 1987) Siddon wrote to Alcan president David Morton, in which he said he believed salmon could be protected within the flows Alcan wanted "with an acceptable level of certainty." That letter led to the signing of the 1987 Settlement Agreement three days later.

On February 1, 1995, Harcourt told UFAWU members: "If this letter is not withdrawn and replaced with new water flows, Alcan can destroy fish by withholding water and mismanaging the system."[54] Later, he urged BC fishers and other interveners in the Alcan hearings to keep the pressure on Ottawa to withdraw Siddon's letter of opinion and replace it with a demand for new water flows. Reducing the amount of water available to Alcan for producing power would make the KCP more uneconomic than it already is, and would be one certain way to kill it.

When the federal government refused to withdraw the letter, interveners waited to see if Harcourt would follow through with his threat to take legislative action to halt the project permanently.[55]

They are understandably wary about the effectiveness of instigating more legislative action to cancel the project when, in the past, both the federal and provincial governments have failed to enforce the power they already have. Alcan's critics point to the way the federal government has failed to exercise its powers, within the Fisheries Act, to order more water to be released into the river. They are also aware of how the provincial government has looked the other way when BC Hydro—contrary to the the terms of the 1950 agreement limiting Alcan's ability to sell power for use only in the region—entered into a power purchase agreement with Alcan for power that will be distributed throughout the province and, eventually, into the United States.

In his January 23, 1995 letter, Harcourt reminded Prime Minister Chretien that the federal Cabinet's decision to exempt the KCP from its own Environmental Review Process violated the government's constitutional responsibility to protect ocean-going fish. By granting that exemption, the federal government by-passed a process that would have shown the project posed a serious threat to BC salmon stocks—another reason, Harcourt contends, that Ottawa, not BC, must take the lead responsibility for negotiating with Alcan to establish what, if any, compensation was due to it as a result of the project's cancellation.

Two days later, Harcourt also wrote Minister of National Revenue David Anderson, charging that Alcan had received tax deferrals totalling $900 million for its projects in Canada.[56] The $900 million is actually the amount of tax deferrals and other benefits Alcan received from its operations throughout the world: The Canadian government's share is not segregated from that total amount. Anderson has refused to provide the full details of the amount of deferred taxes, credits and other benefits the federal government had given to Alcan,[57] saying all tax information is confidential and the government would require the written permission of Alcan to reveal this information.[58]

A clue to one major tax deferral the federal government bestowed on Alcan can be found in an examination of the co-ordination and sales agreements signed by Alcan and BC Hydro in February, 1990—the same agreements which, at the start of the BCUC hearings, Alcan and Hydro had been very reluctant to release. At the beginning of the hearings, interveners were given only summaries of these agreements; after considering interveners' arguments that those documents must be made public, chairperson Lorna Barr ordered that the full text of these agreements must be made available to Alcan's critics. When interveners were able to examine the full text, they found a curious provision that at least 80% of the electricity produced from the KCP would be considered to have been used in Alcan's existing smelter in Kitimat.

Why?

Vancouver lawyer David Austin asked that question in a letter he wrote to Anderson, stating:

> This is rather odd because the electricity from the original generating facility [Kemano I] has been used to operate Alcan's aluminum smelter in Kitimat since the 1950s. Alcan has no other aluminum smelting facilities in British Columbia and no new additional aluminum smelting capability is going to be added as part of KCP or in the foreseeable future.[59]

As any good lawyer would, Austin already knew the answer to his question when he wrote the letter: The provision was included because there is a 30% federal tax deferral for the capital costs incurred for a new manufacturing project and, by structuring the agreements this way, the illusion is created that the new power from KCP is to be used for manufacturing. In 1990, the Mulroney-led federal government agreed that Alcan would have a 30% tax deferral rate instead of the 4% rate permitted on projects that do not result in new manufacturing capacity.

On Alcan's project, for which the total capital costs have now been estimated to have risen to more than $1.3-billion, a 4% tax deferral rate would yield $52 million; a 30% rate yields $390 million. Alcan's capital cost allowance on the KCP will be less if the project is not completed.

"The BC government is not consulted on federal tax rulings. There is an agreement with Ottawa they can give any ruling they want and BC won't know about it," Austin said.[60] "So a federal government that wants to aid a Montreal-based business like

Alcan—and indirectly Quebec—could do so even if the decision had an adverse effect on BC, and BC wouldn't know about it."

The federal government is not alone in its generosity to Alcan. Since the 1940s, when Premier "Boss" Johnson first urged Alcan to establish a smelter in BC, the province of BC has also been generous in its handling of Alcan's tax matters. On November 3, 1954, the BC government approved an Order In Council exempting Alcan from paying taxes on most of the land, and industrial and utilities improvements occupied by the company's projects in the region from south of Vanderhoof to the Pacific Ocean at Kemano. This exemption was accomplished by the province's decision to designate all the land occupied by most of Alcan's major installations as industrial townships. Thus, for the past 41 years, neither the province nor the two regional districts which have Alcan installations within their boundaries have been able to assess taxes on the company's dams, spillways, underground tunnels, power generating facilities, transmission lines and the townsite of Kemano. Alcan does pay taxes on its smelter in Kitimat and approximately $5,000 in taxes annually for the unimproved lands within its control. The converted assessment value of the Kitimat plant is approximately $47.6 million, so the smelter alone represents 25% of the converted assessment value of $190.1 million on the land in the eight municipalities and seven electoral areas within the Regional District of Bulkley-Nechako, in which most of these facilities are located. If all of Alcan's facilities were included in the region's tax base, it would result in a significant improvement in the region's ability to provide services there. Some of Alcan's installations are also located in the Kitimat Stikine Regional District.[61]

Because Alcan has not been paying 41 years' worth of taxes on most of its BC facilities, it has been the provincial tax-payers who have picked up the tab for the cost of provincial services—such as the highways and health services—provided for these regions, as well as the cost of constructing Hydro's power transmission lines over which Alcan may soon be able to transmit its excess power into the US where it can command higher prices.

Remember that the terms of the 1987 Settlement Agreement make BC, not Alcan, responsible for the enormous cost of restoring the fisheries in the upper Nechako River, the Cheslatta-

Murray Lakes chain and the Nechako Reservoir. The cost of restoring the Cheslatta-Murray system alone has been estimated to be more than $10 million. In addition, the province has already agreed to provide more than $2.2 million to communities along the river to upgrade sewer and water systems which would have been rendered less effective by the KCP. No estimates are available for the total cost of mitigating the damages Alcan's activities have already caused to the upper Nechako River and the Nechako Reservoir, nor is anyone willing to put a figure on the cost of the lost salmon fisheries potential of the Nechako and its related watersheds. Canadian tax-payers' dollars also paid the federal government's $7.4 million settlement paid to the Cheslatta People for damages they incurred as a result of Alcan's activities in their traditional territory.

Harcourt assured BC fishers that he was prepared to discuss the cold-water release facility in the Kenney Dam which the commissioners had recommended be built even if the KCP does not proceed. This facility is critically important both to BC's ability to improve the freshwater fishery in the upper Nechako, the Nechako Reservoir and the Murray-Cheslatta Lakes and to the Cheslatta T'ens' plans to restore the flood damage done to their traditional territory around the lakes.[62] Soon the DFO will release the results of their study aimed at finding out what happened to all the BC salmon that disappeared from the Fraser River in 1994. Saving the Nechako River sockeye salmon run, and the smaller chinook runs using the river, could be an important first step in avoiding the collapse of BC's salmon runs.

It remains to be seen if the federal government will pay all, or part, of the cost of constructing the cold-water release facility which will improve the federal government's ability to protect the salmon using the river. Given the federal government's experience in Eastern Canada where, because of the collapse of the cod fishery it is now paying Newfoundland fishers $1.9 billion to tie up their boats and stay home, its reluctance to co-operate in efforts to protect BC's equally vulnerable fishery may lead to similar payouts on Canada's West Coast.

And what will Alcan's contribution be to this project?

Numerous other issues have been raised since the announced

cancellation of the KCP: What will happen to the 20-year contract Alcan has to sell power to Hydro? How are the federal and provincial governments going to deal with decisions about the water flows in the Nechako River, now that the programs put in place by the 1987 Settlement Agreement are in jeopardy? Will Alcan carry out its threat to sue the provincial government for its decision to cancel the project? What role will BC's First Nations communities play in how these issues are resolved? Will they finally play their trump card by forcing Ottawa to deal with this issue?

Nechako Valley residents have always alleged that the 1987 Settlement Agreement was a political decision, not a scientific one—a belief supported by the commissioners' report which showed that salmon stocks are endangered by the Settlement Agreement flows.

There are those who allege that the provincial government's 1995 decision to cancel the project was also a political decision. If BC's threat of cancellation is fulfilled, it will be an important conservation decision that will go a long way to ensuring preservation of the Nechako River Valley's environment. It will be an important sign that the old-style wooing of Big Business, regardless of the cost to the environment, is becoming a thing of the past.

Many obstacles confront the government's efforts to carry out this decision. Nechako Valley residents know they cannot rest on this victory, that there is work to be done to get the federal government to accept its responsibilities to First Nations and non-native Nechako Valley residents alike. They will also have to maintain their pressure on the provincial government to ensure that it doesn't, once again, lose sight of what they believe to be its ultimate goal: the closing of the final page ending the history of a fatally flawed project.

During their long fight to protect their river, Nechako Valley residents have been taught to judge governments on what they do, not what they say they're going to do. The final chapter of the story of Alcan's Kemano Completion Project will be a stern test of how much confidence BC residents can have in the words of today's federal and provincial governments.

Notes

359 Billion Beer Glasses

1 Kitimat businessman David Serry, BCUCH 1.64.

2 Bulletin 2M-931-6608, "The Francois-Ootsa Lake District," Fort Fraser Recording Division, Bureau of Provincial Information, 1931.

3 Angela Croome, "The Kitimat Story," *Discovery* 17.4 (Apr. 1956): 362.

4 Ibid.

5 Ibid.

6 Ibid.

7 Bulletin 2M-931-6608.

8 According to the *New Encyclopædia Brittanica*, Prince Edward Island is 2,185 square miles in size. Water drains into the Nechako Reservoir from 5,500 square miles.

9 Croome.

10 Ibid.

11 Ibid.

12 Ibid.

13 Harry Jomini, "The Kenney Dam," *Engineering Journal* 37.11 (published by the Engineering Institute of Canada) Nov. 1954: 12.

14 Ibid. 17.

15 Ibid.

16 Ibid.

17 Croome.

18 Equivalent to 229,120 acres or 92,499 hectares.

19 One acre foot of water is enough water to cover an acre of land with one foot of water.

20 Jomini.

21 Ibid.

22 The members of the Wilderness Advisory Committee were Bryan Williams, Ken Farquharson, Derrick Sewell, Les Reed, Roger Stanyer, Valerie Kordyban, Peter Larkin and Saul Rothman.

23 "Wilderness Mosaic: The Report of the Wilderness Advisory Committee" presented to BC Environment Minister Austin Pelton, Mar. 1986.

24 The BC Park Act describes Class A Parks status as "intended to preserve and/or provide an opportunity to utilize outstanding natural, scenic, historic, and recreational features for the use, inspiration and enjoyment of the public of B.C. They have a high degree of protection from exploitation and alienation. Recreation areas are administered according to the principles of multiple land use, which may include recreation, logging and mining up to and including foreshore areas."

25 F.T. Matthias (assistant manager, Aluminum Company of Canada, Ltd.'s BC Project), "Kemano, Underground," *Engineering Journal* 37.11 (Nov. 1954).

26 Ibid.

27 Ibid.

28 Ibid.

29 Description provided by the author's brother, John Warner.

30 Juan Carlos Gomez Amaral, "The 1950 Kemano Aluminum Project: A Hindsight Assessment," 29.

31 Ibid. 30-31.

32 Duncan Campbell, *Global Mission: The Story of Alcan*, Vol. 2, 82-83.

33 More commonly referred to as 900 megawatts.

34 The two figures are different because there are times when one of the eight generators must be shut down for maintenance and repairs.

35 BC Hydro's Power Smart program uses 10,000 kilowatt hours as the average annual consumption of a home in BC.

36 It is also almost enough electricity to supply three cities the size of Prince George which, as of 31 December 1993, had a total of 25, 614 residences.

The Sound of a River Dying

1 Glenda Olson, BCUCH 4.521-22.

2 *Maclean's*, 15 Dec. 1951: 15.

3 "Physical and Hydrological Studies, Baseline Information," (Envirocon Ltd. for the Aluminum Company of Canada, Ltd., 1984) shows that the past operation of the reservoir reduced the flood magnitudes at Fort Fraser by 20%, at Vanderhoof 17% and Isle Pierre 11% (Vol. 2, 812).

4 According to a pamphlet entitled "Kemano: BC Power Operations" (published by the Aluminium Company of Canada Ltd., 25 Oct. 1962), water drains into its Nechako Reservoir from 5,450 square miles. Prince Edward Island's size is 2,184 square miles and Rhode Island is 1,214 square miles.

5 Campbell 73.

6 Document C0037 filed in the BCUC's Kemano hearings.

7 Murray Rankin and Arvay Finlay, "Alcan's Kemano Project: Options and Recommendations," a report prepared for the BC Cabinet (Oct. 1992) 15.

8 Campbell 74.

9 "Record of Hearings on Applications by the Aluminium Company of Canada, Ltd. for water licenses on the Nechako and Nanika Rivers," Victoria, 31 Oct. 1949.

10 Ibid.

11 Ibid.

12 Ibid.

13 Ibid.

14 Cyril Shelford, *From Snowshoes to Politics* 133.

15 Campbell 74.

16 Ibid. 75.

17 "Record of Hearings on Applications by the Aluminum Company of Canada, Ltd. for water licenses on the Nechako and Nanika Rivers."

18 Ibid.

19 Ibid.

20 Campbell 75.
21 Dr. Ian McTaggart Cowan, Report for the BC Game Commission, 1949.
22 Ibid.
23 Ibid.
24 Ibid.
25 Letter from Forester, E.G. Oldham, to C.D. Orchard, Deputy Minister Lands and Forests, 21 Sept. 1950.
26 "Record of Hearings on Applications by the Aluminium Company of Canada, Ltd. for water licenses on the Nechako and Nanika Rivers."
27 From a 1993 interview with the author.
28 Shelford 134.
29 *Victoria Daily Colonist*, 28 Oct. 1951, 1.
30 Campbell 74.
31 Rankin and Finlay 13.

Knocking on the Floodgates of Opportunity
1 Vanderhoof pioneer, Dr. A.W. Mooney, in a letter dated 2 Apr. 1993, forwarded to the BCUC.
2 B.J. McGuire, "Aluminum: The Story of Fifty Years of Growth by the Canadian Industry," *Canadian Geographic Journal* (July 1951).
3 Ibid.
4 The Aluminum Company of America (Alcoa) later changed the name of its Canadian-based operations to Aluminum Company of Canada Ltd., and then Aluminum Limited, which assumed ownership of the Aluminum Company of Canada and 33 other small Alcoa subsidiaries around the world. By the mid-1930s the separation between Alcoa and its Canadian operations was complete; Alcoa is now one of Alcan's major competitors
5 "A Case Study of Alcan Aluminum Limited," Royal Commission on Corporate Concentration" (Feb. 1977) 11.
6 Ibid. 12.
7 McGuire ix.
8 Bodsworth, Fred, "Aluminum Hits the Road Again," *Maclean's* (15 Dec. 1951): 40.
9 Ibid.
10 MP for Rosetown-Biggar, Saskatchewan.
11 Overstall, Richard, "The Sovereign State of Alcan," *Telkwa Foundation Newsletter* (Spring, 1983): 2.
12 Ibid.
13 Ibid. xi.
14 "A Case Study of Alcan Aluminum Limited" xi.
15 Campbell 1.
16 According to the US Department of Mineral Commodity Summaries, 1992, the world's production of aluminum in that year had risen to 18.5 million tonnes annually, with the United States producing 4.1 million tonnes. Canada's production was the second-largest in the world.
17 "A Case Study of Alcan Aluminium Limited" 18-19.
18 Ibid. 20.

19 Ibid.
20 Ibid. 144.
21 Campbell 55.
22 Ibid. 51-52.
23 Ibid. 55.
24 Ibid. 53.
25 Ibid. 56.
26 DuBose, McNeeley, "The Nechako-Kemano-Kitimat Development," *Engineering Journal* 37.11 (Nov. 1954): 1-2.
27 When the Liberals were defeated in the 1957 election, C.D. Howe and Fisheries Minister James Sinclair were appointed to Alcan's Board of Directors.
28 *Prince George Citizen*, 31 May 1951.
29 *BCUCH* 11.1627.
30 Campbell 58.
31 Ibid. 58-59.
32 Ibid.
33 *Hansard*, 25 June 1948.
34 Campbell 63.
35 A subsidiary of the construction company Morrison Knudsen Company Inc. of Boise, Idaho.
36 Campbell 60.
37 Ibid. 64-65. DuBose estimated the capacity of the Chilko-Taseko project at 860,000 h.p. and the northern system between 1.3 and 1.55 million h.p.
38 Ibid.
39 Ibid. 65.
40 Ibid. 65-66.
41 Rankin and Finlay 14.
42 *Burns Lake Review*, 22 Dec. 1949.
43 The Nanika River system—which runs into the Skeena River, not the Nechako River—was not dammed during the first phase of Alcan's industrial activity in BC.
44 Overstall 3.
45 Fisheries and Oceans document 19-4-1988 34A:37.
46 Ibid.
47 Campbell 65.
48 *Western Business and Industry* 25.6 (June 1951): 94.
49 Canadian Census 1986.
50 Rankin and Finlay 15.
51 Section 1(3) of the 1950 Industrial Development Act.
52 Campbell 95.
53 *Prince George Citizen*, 15 Mar. 1951, 1.
54 *Prince George Citizen*, 24 Mar. 1951, 1.
55 *BCUCH* 40.6819.

Coffins in the Lake
1 Prince George lawyer, Richard Byl, *BCUCH* 5.685.
2 W. Kaye Lamb, ed., *The Journals and Letters of Sir Alexander Mackenzie* 306.
3 W. Kaye Lamb, ed., *Simon Fraser Letters and Journals*, 1806-1808 222.
4 Ibid. 196.

5 Ibid.

6 His first fort was established at McLeod Lake, followed by Fort St. James, Fort Fraser and Fort George.

7 The rich history associated with the Nechako and Stuart Rivers led to that route being one of the 31 historical waterways and trails chosen in 1990 for further study under the Recreation Corridors Program.

8 Norman Lee, *Klondike Cattle Drive* (Heritage House Publishing).

9 Ron Piper, et al., "Proposal for the Cheslatta Development Project."

10 Harmon, Daniel Williams 242, 246.

11 *BCUCH* 5.681.

12 Cheslatta T'en submission to the BCUC meeting regarding KCP, in Prince George, on April 2, 1993.

13 The meeting took place on October 24, 1949, in Wistaria on the shore of Ootsa Lake. It was adjourned and reconvened in Victoria on October 31, 1949.

14 Cheslatta T'en submission to the BCUC meeting regarding KCP.

15 *Prince George Citizen*, 8 June 1991, 5.

16 Cheslatta T'en submission to the BCUC meeting regarding the KCP.

17 Ibid.

18 Ibid.

19 *Windspeaker*, 14 Sept. 1992, 8.

20 *Prince George Citizen*, 8 June 1991, 5.

21 Ibid.

22 Rankin and Finlay 17.

23 *BCUCH* 5.685.

24 *BCUCH* 11.1676.

25 *BCUCH* 5.686.

26 The exact length of the river is difficult to determine because its size, and that of Cheslatta Lake into which it empties, have both been altered by years of successive flooding.

27 This letter was read into the record of the BCUC hearings; see *BCUCH* 5.689.

28 *Windspeaker*, 14 Sept. 1992, 9.

29 *BCUCH* 85.16024.

30 *BCUCH* 85.16023-024.

31 *BCUCH* 85.16024.

We Are All River Gods

1 Richard Bangs, "Introduction" to *Rivergods: Exploring the World.*

2 John Appleton, "The Nechaco [sic] Valley," *Westward Ho!* 2. 6 (June 1908).

3 Bulletin No. 29, "The Nechako and Endako Valley," B.C. Bureau of Provincial Information, 1931.

4 Draft Report, "Recreation Planning Study of the Nechako and Stuart River Corridors," B.C. Ministry of Forests, June 1990.

5 Bruce Hutchison, The Fraser 258.

6 Rosemary Neering, *Continental Dash: The Russian-American Telegraph.*

7 Norman Lee, *Chilcotin Cattle Drive: The Journals of Norman Lee.*

8 George LaBrash, *BCUCH* 2.452 .

9 Morice 16.

10 Ibid.

11 "Recreation Planning Study of the Nechako and Stuart River Corridors."

12 Jessie Bond Sugden, *In the Shadow of the Cutbanks* 1-2.

13 Ibid.

14 "Recreation Planning Study of the Nechako and Stuart River Corridors."

15 The Report of the Kemano Task Force (page) 54 estimates the water flows in the Cheslatta River prior to the construction of the Kenney Dam from 177 to 317.8 cubic feet per second. After the construction of the dam they ranged from 4,591 to 15,009 cubic feet per second.

16 Margret Nooski, *BCUCH* 2.242-44.

17 Ken Ponsford, *BCUCH* 2.244.

18 Peter Rodseth, *BCUCH* 2.435 .

19 The DFO discussion paper, "Toward a Fish Habitat Management Decision on the Kemano Completion Project" (1984), reports the tailrace discharges at the Kemano powerhouse gradually increased from 1660 cubic feet per second in 1956 to about 3880 cf/s in 1978.

20 Ibid. 41.

21 Ibid. 42.

Unpleasant Diversions

1 Alcan's BC vice-president Bill Rich, *BCUCH* 11.1604.

2 William J. Schouwenburg, ed., "Report of the Kemano Task Force" 8.

3 Kenneth Jackson, ed., "Toward A Fish Habitat Decision on the Kemano Completion Project" 1.

4 Report prepared by the Rivers Defence Coalition.

5 Bev Christensen, *Prince George, Rivers, Railways and Timber* 75.

6 Ibid. 85.

7 Hutchison 257.

8 From the 1961 Canadian census, comparing the population of District 8 with the provincial totals in each age group.

9 According the Canadian census, the population of Prince George was 4,703 in 1951 and 13,877 in 1961. Part of this increase can be accounted for by the fact that, in 1954 the City of Prince George incorporated a large block of occupied land located near the city's western boundary. The population of Vanderhoof was 644 in 1951, and 1,460 in 1961.

10 "Critique of Alcan Environmental Baseline Studies," Spruce City Wildlife Association and the BC Wildlife Federation (Dec. 1981).

11 *BCUCH* 11.1656.

12 Rankin and Finlay 20.

13 Ibid.

14 Ibid.

15 Ibid. 21.
16 Information provided by the BC Environment Ministry.
17 *Prince George Citizen*, 15 Feb. 1980.
18 Ibid.
19 Attributed to Trev Thomas, *Prince George Citizen*, 15 Feb. 1980.
20 Attributed to Joyce Philpot, Ibid.
21 Letter from BC Premier Mike Harcourt to Prime Minister Jean Chretien, 23 Jan. 1995.
22 Ibid.
23 Letter from Fisheries Minister Tom Siddon to David Morton, president, Aluminum Company of Canada, 14 Sept. 1987.
24 *Prince George Citizen*, 16 July 1980.
25 Ibid.
26 Ibid.
27 *Prince George Citizen*, 18 July 1980.
28 Ibid.
29 The Conservatives formed the government following the election of May 22, 1979. Trudeau was re-elected February 18, 1980.
30 *Prince George Citizen*, 23 July 1980.
31 *Prince George Citizen*, 28 July 1980.
32 Ibid.
33 *Prince George Citizen*, 29 July 1980.
34 An anti-Alcan coalition of the BC Wildlife Federation, Canadian Association of Smelter and Allied Worker, Gulf Trollers Association, Nechako Neyenkut Society, Save the Bulkley Society, Steelhead Society, United Fishermen and Allied Workers' Union, Pacific Trollers Association, Federation of BC Naturalists and the Prince George Environmental Coalition.
35 Representing the more than 14,000 Carrier First Nations people, many of whom have lived along the Nechako River and its tributaries for thousands of years.
36 *Maclean's* (11 Aug. 1980): 19.
37 *Prince George Citizen*, 5 Aug. 1980.
38 *Prince George Citizen*, 6 Aug. 1980.
39 *Vancouver Province*, 11 Aug. 1980.
40 The commission was appointed under a convention between Canada and the United States for the protection, preservation and extension of the sockeye and pink salmon fisheries in the Fraser River system.
41 Alcan's Application for an Energy Project Certificate filed with the BC government in January, 1984.
42 Summary of Salmon Studies Conducted on Nechako, Morice and Nanika River Systems Relative to the Proposed Kemano II Power Development, Fisheries and Marine Service of the International Pacific Salmon Fisheries Commission, February, 1979.
43 Jackson 53.
44 "Kemano Completion Hydro-electric Development Baseline Environmental Studies" (Envirocon, 1981).
45 "Environmental Studies Associated with the Proposed Kemano Completion Hydro-electric Development" (Environcon, 1984). The twenty-third volume, entitled "Impact Management," was never released.
46 *Prince George Citizen*, 27 Oct. 1984.
47 Ibid.
48 Ibid.
49 *Prince George Citizen*, 31 Oct. 1984.

An Issuance of Opinions

1 Letter dated September 14, 1987 from Minister of Fisheries and Oceans Tom Siddon to Alcan. It is attached to the 1987 Settlement Agreement.
2 The twenty-third volume has not been made public.
3 Jackson.
4 Ibid., Wayne Shinners, "Preface."
5 Jackson 69.
6 Overview prepared by D. Alderdice of the public meeting held March 2 and 3, 1984 in Vanderhoof, forwarded to R. Bell-Irving, chief of Department of the DFO's water use unit in Vancouver.
7 *Prince George Citizen*, 5 Mar. 1984.
8 Ibid.
9 Ibid.
10 See Sheila Peters, "Kemano Completion—Who Wins?," *Today's Business*: 19-22.
11 *Prince George Citizen*, 5 Mar. 1984.
12 In 1993, Grantham was elected a councillor of the City of Prince George.
13 *Prince George Citizen*, 5 Mar. 1984.
14 Ibid.
15 *Prince George Citizen*, 31 Oct. 1984.
16 By being vertically integrated these companies controlled production of aluminum—straight from the mining of bauxite, through the refining of alumina and its reduction into aluminum, to the fabrication of the metal. The six firms were Alcoa, Alcan, Reynolds, Kaiser, Pechiney and Alusuisse.
17 "Social Benefits and Cost Analysis of the Kemano Completion Project," Document R0185, Vol. 73 of the public review file of the BCUC hearings.
18 *Prince George Citizen*, 14 Sept. 1987.
19 Ibid.
20 D.W. Burt and J.H. Mundie, "Case Histories of Regulated Stream Flow and its Effects on Salmonid Populations," Department of Fisheries and Oceans, July, 1986.
21 *BCUCH* 31.5290-303.
22 See Amaral,
23 *Prince George Citizen*, 2 Sept. 1987.
24 Ibid.
25 *Vancouver Sun*, 2 Sept. 1987, A15.
26 The members of the committee were Don Chapman, Dennis Deans, Mike Healey, Bruce Jenkins, Colin Levings, Clyde Mitchell, Bruce Sheperd, Pat Slaney and Glenn Stewart.
27 The members of the KCP task force were director, R. Bell-Irving, R. Hamilton, L.

Jaremovic, H. Mundie, S. Smis and W. J. Schouwenburg. D. Alderdice, J. Jensen, J.A. Servizi and C. Shirvell also conducted research for the task force.

28 Provision of the 1950 agreements between the company and the BC government.

29 *Vancouver Sun*, 20 Dec. 1990.

30 Barr, et al., "Report and Recommendations to the Lieutenant Governor in Council, Kemano Completion Project Review" 28.

31 Pat Slaney, "Expert Witness Testimony Prepared on Behalf of the B.C. Ministry of Environment, Pre-1987" 9.

32 *BCUCH* 68.12255-256.

33 *BCUCH* 58.10203.

34 *BCUCH* 58.10305.

35 *BCUCH* 58.10225. The document was prepared by Mike Healey of the DFO, with the assistance of Alcan's consultant, Bruce Jenkins.

36 Ibid. Pages 10226 and 10227 contain testimony that the winter flows under the long-term flow regime set out in the Settlement Agreement are 7% of historical mean annual flows, and could be less than that at times.

37 *BCUCH* 58.10225-226.

38 *BCUCH* 59.10456.

39 *BCUCH* 59.10454.

40 *BCUCH* 59.10455.

41 DFO news release, 12 Oct. 1990.

42 *Prince George Citizen*, 15 Sept. 1987.

43 At that time the Socred government in BC was refusing to discuss land claims with BC's First Nations, saying their rights had been extinguished when BC joined confederation.

44 *Prince George Citizen*, 15 Sept. 1987.

45 Press release issued by Davis, 14 Sept. 1987.

46 See Section 2.5 of the 1987 Settlement Agreement.

47 Letter signed by BC Environment Minister Bruce Strachan to federal Fisheries Minister Tom Siddon, 23 Aug. 1987.

48 Ibid.

49 Ibid.

50 *Prince George Citizen*, 14 Sept. 1987.

51 *BCUCH* 68.12255-256.

52 *BCUCH* 58.10203.

53 Ibid. 10305. For a complete list of the regional biologist's duties see *BCUCH* 58.10306.

54 *BCUCH* 4.542.

55 *Prince George Citizen*, 14 Sept. 1987.

56 Fisheries and Oceans document 19-4-1988 34A:43.

57 Ibid.

58 The short-term flow regime for the Nechako as set out in the agreement will be in effect until Alcan completes construction of a cold-water release facility in the Kenney Dam, and the long-term flow regime in effect in perpetuity after the facility is completed.

59 This three-person committee oversees the work of the technical committee and is made up of senior-level representatives of Alcan, the DFO and BC's Environment Ministry.

60 Fisheries and Oceans document 19-4-1988 34A:43.

61 Ibid.

62 Ibid.

63 One gigawatt is equal to one billion watts.

64 *BCUCH* 11.1686.

65 *BCUCH* 11.1687

66 Fisheries and Oceans document 19-4-1988 34A:43.

67 Rankin and Finlay 22.

68 Fisheries and Oceans document 19-4-1988 34A:43.

69 Ibid.

70 *BCUCH* 11.1647.

71 *Prince George Citizen*, 3 Oct. 1987.

72 According to information provided by the Water Survey of Canada the average high water flows in the Chilako and Willow Rivers during May was 1,950 cubic feet per second and 4,700 cf/s respectively and the average high water flows occuring during June in the Stellako River were 2,200 cf/s. The opponents of Alcan's plans to withdraw more water from the Nechako calculated that when the project was completed the winter flows in the river would average 2,558 cf/s.

Nor Any Drop to Drink

1 Trapper Leo LaRocque of Fort Fraser, *BCUCH* 2.220.

2 Stated in a telephone interview with the author, 4 Mar. 1994.

3 The Kemano Completion Project Guidelines Order SOR/90-729.

4 Government of Canada news release, 12 Oct. 1990.

5 *Vancouver Sun*, 18 Oct. 1990.

6 Ibid.

7 Ibid.

8 *Prince George Citizen*, 27 Feb. 1991.

9 *Vancouver Sun*, 17 May 1991.

10 *Prince George Citizen*, 16 May 1991.

11 Commons Debates, 16 May 1991.

12 *Globe and Mail*, 17 May 1991.

13 Montreal Gazette, 18 May 1991.

14 Ibid.

15 *Prince George Citizen*, 16 May 1991.

16 *Hansard*, 12 May 1981, 886.

17 In a letter signed by Prime Minister Brian Mulroney, sent to Pat Moss, chairperson of the Rivers Defence Coalition.

18 *Globe and Mail*, 24 Apr. 1992.

19 Amaral 52.

20 *Vancouver Sun*, 8 Jan. 1991.

21 Ibid.

22 Ibid.

23 *Prince George Citizen*, 16 May 1991.

24 Environment Policy and Law Vol 1. No.10 (Jan. 1991).

25 Ibid.

26 BCUCH 68.12170.
27 BCUCH 40.6855.
28 BCUCH 68.12168.
29 Ibid. 12234.
30 Ibid. 12235.
31 Ibid. 12240.
32 Ibid. 12242.
33 Ibid. 12248.
34 Ibid. 12249.
35 Ibid. 12251.
36 Ibid. 12254.
37 Ibid. 12258-260.
38 *Prince George Citizen*, 21 June 1991.
39 BCUCH 13.2066.
40 *Prince George Citizen*, 29 June 1991.
41 Ibid.
42 *Prince George Citizen*, 1 June 1990.
43 *Vancouver Sun*, 27 May 1991.
44 *Prince George Citizen*, 8 May 1992.
45 *Prince George Citizen*, 5 Mar. 1992.
46 Ibid.
47 *Prince George Citizen*, 25 May 1993.
48 Ibid.
49 On June 3, 1993.
50 *Montreal Gazette*, 8 June 1993.
51 Ibid.
52 *Prince George Citizen*, 25 May 1993.
53 *Prince George Citizen*, 6 Mar. 1992.
54 *Prince George Citizen*, 15 Feb. 1991.
55 BCUCH 12.1888-892.
56 BCUCH 12.1889.
57 *Interior News*, 22 May 1991.
58 Ibid.
59 *Vancouver Sun*, 10 July 1993.
60 Ibid.
61 *Prince George Citizen*, 19 Oct. 1990.
62 The Prince George-Omineca Riding—which includes a portion of Prince George and all the other major communities along the Nechako River and its tributaries including Vanderhoof, Fort Fraser, Fraser Lake and Fort St. James—was formerly the Omineca riding represented by Socred Jack Kempf. It was formed when the two ridings centering on Prince George were realigned into three ridings. Only 57% of the more than 19,000 voters in the Prince George-Omineca Riding live in Prince George. The rest live in the predominantly Conservative portion of the riding west of the city.
63 Fort St. James Caledonia Courier, 21 Nov. 1990.
64 Ibid.
65 By 6,421 to 5,799 votes.
66 In 1994 he transferred his allegance to the BC Reform Party.
67 Boone defeated the former Socred Environment Minister Bruce Strachan, who was involved in negotiating the 1987 Settlement Agreement.
68 The party standing in the new legislature was 51 NDP, 17 Liberal and 7 Socreds. The standing when the legislature was dissolved was 41 Socred,

25 NDP and 3 vacant seats.
69 Section 2.5 of the 1987 Settlement Agreement.
70 *Prince George Citizen*, 24 Jan. 1992.
71 Ibid.
72 *Stoney Creek Woman*, written by Bridget Moran, tells the remarkable story of this quiet, dignified woman's life growing up in the wilderness near Vanderhoof.
73 *Prince George Citizen*, 28 Feb. 1992.
74 *Prince George Citizen*, 28 Feb. 1992.
75 Ibid.
76 Ibid.
77 *Financial Post*, 24 Apr. 1992; *Globe and Mail*, 24 Apr. 1992.
78 *Globe and Mail*, 24 Apr. 1992.
79 *Financial Post*, 24 Apr. 1992. All earnings and losses are reported in US dollars.
80 *Globe and Mail*, 24 Apr. 1992.
81 Interior News, 26 Aug. 1992.
82 *Calgary Herald*, 9 July 1993.
83 From an interview with the author in October, 1994.
84 The public meeting held in Fort Fraser, 29 Nov. 1991.
85 From an interview the author conducted with Sholty and Romain, 12 Mar. 1994.
86 All information from Ben Meisner was provided in an interview with the author on 23 Feb. 1994.
87 "Letter To The Editor," *Prince George Citizen*, 16 Oct. 1992.
88 This phrase caught the attention of Alcan's opponents who questioned its validity after it appeared in a letter written to Alcan President David Morton by Fisheries Minister Tom Siddon on September 14, 1987, the same day the 1987 Settlement Agreement was signed.
89 Dr. Peter A. Larkin, "Analysis of Possible Causes of the Shortfall in Sockeye Spawners."
90 The reference is to a 69% reduction in the amount of water left in the river after the dam was built, not 69% of the river's original flows.
91 *Prince George Citizen*, 14 Oct. 1992.
92 Ibid.
93 Memo from W. Schouwenburg to D.L. Deans, chief of the habitat manager division, DFO, 25 Oct. 1990.
94 Neither Schouwenburg nor Mundie were part of the Strangway working group nor were any other DFO employees opposed to the proposed Settlement Agreement with Alcan.
95 Letter from W. Schouwenburg to Bruce Rawson, Deputy Minister, DFO, 1 Apr. 1991.
96 See W. Schouwenburg's letter 25 Oct. 1990, in which he refers to a telephone call from Deans "reminding me that Pat Chamut was the Department's only spokesman insofar as the Nechako Agreement was concerned."
97 *Prince George Citizen*, 24 July 1992.
98 Ibid.

99 Ibid.
100 Environment Minister John Cashore, Aboriginal Affairs Minister Andrew Petter and Agriculture, Fisheries and Food Minister Bill Barlee.
101 *Prince George Citizen*, 18 Sept. 1992.
102 *BCUCH* 2.237.
103 El Niño is a term used to describe a sequence of events in the Pacific Ocean which result in unusually warm water circulating north off the BC Coast. When this occurs it disrupts weather patterns all along the coast of North America and is thought to affect fish migrations.
104 Larkin, "Analysis of Possible Causes of the Shortfall in Sockeye Spawners."
105 *Prince George Citizen*, 12 Dec. 1992.
106 *Caledonia Courier*, 6 Dec. 1992.
107 Ibid.
108 Ibid.
109 *Prince George Citizen*, 23 Nov. 1992.
110 Ibid.
111 *Prince George Citizen*, 20 Jan. 1993.
112 Shortages of electricity for other power-consuming industries and the differing goals of the Alcan and the Norwegian government were cited as two of the main reasons for that government's decision to buy out Alcan's Norwegian operations. See Campbell Chapter 12, "Alcan in Scandinavia."
113 *Prince George Citizen*, 21 Jan. 1993.
114 *Prince George Citizen*, 20 Jan. 1993.
115 By First Nations representatives, Premier Mike Harcourt and Prime Minister Brian Mulroney.
116 *Prince George Citizen*, 20 Jan. 1993.
117 Ibid.
118 Ibid.
119 Ibid.
120 Ibid.
121 *Globe and Mail*, 10 May 1993.
122 *Montreal Gazette*, 17 Apr. 1993.
123 Reportedly for more than $6 million.
124 *Vancouver Sun*, 10 July 1993.
125 Ibid.
126 Ibid.
127 Statement by Premier Harcourt in the BC legislature, 15 July 1993.
128 Ibid.
129 Ibid.
130 *Vancouver Sun*, 13 Aug. 1993.
131 Ibid.
132 Ibid.
133 Ibid.
134 *Vancouver Sun*, 24 Sept. 1993.
135 Ibid.
136 *Montreal Gazette*, 24 Sept. 1993.
137 *Toronto Star*, 24 Sept. 1993.
138 *Vancouver Sun*, 24 Sept. 1993.
139 *Montreal Gazette*, 24 Sept. 1993.
140 *Globe and Mail*, 16 Dec. 1993.
141 *Financial Post*, 4 Mar. 1992.
142 Ibid.
143 *BCUCH* 11.1621
144 Ibid.
145 *Vancouver Sun*, 13 Oct. 1993.
146 Ibid.
147 Ibid.
148 *Prince George Citizen*, 15 July 1993.
149 Ibid.
150 Ibid.
151 One of the 13 groups affiliated with the Rivers Defence Coalition.
152 *Prince George Citizen*, 9 July 1993.
153 *Houston Today*, 30 June 1993.
154 In a letter Chretien forwarded to Moss, dated October, 1993.
155 *Vancouver Sun*, 16 Oct. 1993.

Hearing Things

1 Richard Wozney, spokesperson for the District of Kitimat, *BCUCH* 1.18.
2 *BCUCH* 1.17.
3 *BCUCH* 12.1969-970.
4 *BCUCH* 2.164-66.
5 *BCUCH* 1.27.
6 *BCUCH* 1.31-32.
7 Ibid.
8 *BCUCH* 1.27.
9 *BCUCH* 1.15
10 *BCUCH* 1.16
11 *BCUCH* 1.19
12 Spokesperson for Locals 31 and 37 of the United Fishermen and Allied Workers Union (UFAWU).
13 Haida Gwaii is the Haida name for what are also called the Queen Charlotte Islands.
14 *BCUCH* 1.53, 55.
15 *BCUCH* 1. 55.
16 Triton Environmental Consultants had replaced Envirocon as Alcan's environmental consultants in 1989 when a group of Envirocon's senior staff negotiated a management purchase of that company and formed a new environmental consulting company which they renamed "Triton." The new company retained most of the Envirocon's senior staff including Bruce Jenkins, the former president of Envirocon, who was also named president of Triton. Envirocon's findings are contained in a 22-volume report, the twenty-third volume of which has not been made public
17 *BCUCH* 1.74.
18 *BCUCH* 1.77.
19 *BCUCH* 1.79.
20 *BCUCH* 1.79-80.
21 He was referring to a proposal by Orenda Forest Products, who have obtained a timber supply in the Nishga Valley north of Terrace and were proposing to spend $500 million to build a paper mill which would create more than 140 full-time jobs.
22 The acronym for Not In My Back Yard.
23 *BCUCH* 1.85-86.

24 *BCUCH* 1.85.
25 *BCUCH* 1.87.
26 *BCUCH* 1.87-88.
27 *BCUCH* 1.88.
28 *BCUCH* 1.91.
29 *BCUCH* 1.99
30 *BCUCH* 1.101-02.
31 *BCUCH* 1.115.

Fish Don't Swim Single File
1 Vanderhoof resident Henry Klassen, *BCUCH* 3.275.
2 Nechako Valley resident Cindy Serhan, *BCUCH* 4.583.
3 *BCUCH* 2.160-61.
4 *BCUCH* 2.223
5 *BCUCH* 11.1620.
6 *BCUCH* 2.148, 149-50.
7 *BCUCH* 2.127-28.
8 *BCUCH* 2.139. Francois Lake drains into the Nechako River through the Stellaquo River.
9 *BCUCH* 2.238. Approximate 25 trappers will be affected by the KCP.
10 *BCUCH* 2.220.
11 *BCUCH* 2.172.
12 *BCUCH* 2.202.
13 *BCUCH* 2.204.
14 *BCUCH* 2.259-60.
15 Parker's recommendations that discussion of issues—such as the cooling water flows, the water-release facilty to be installed in the dam, the impact of the co-ordination agreement between Alcan and BC Hydro and the operation of the reservoir—should be delayed received wide support from other groups, including Alcan.
16 *BCUCH* 3.288.
17 *BCUCH* 3.281-82; 275-76.
18 *BCUCH* 3.289.
19 *BCUCH* 3.287.
20 *BCUCH* 3.301.
21 *BCUCH* 3.300. The speaker, Norm Avison, estimated that 46,000 hectares of prime forest land was flooded by the reservoir.
22 *BCUCH* 3.296.
23 L and M Lumber Ltd.
24 *BCUCH* 3.303.
25 *BCUCH* 3.322-23.
26 *BCUCH* 3.317.
27 *BCUCH* 3.505.
28 Ibid.
29 *BCUCH* 3.506.
30 Goodwin claimed more than 200 canoeists and their families regularly use the river and the reservoir.
31 *BCUCH* 3.337.
32 *BCUCH* 3.347.
33 *BCUCH* 3.338-39.
34 *BCUCH* 3.337.
35 *BCUCH* 3.340.
36 *BCUCH* 3.350.
37 *BCUCH* 3.545.

38 Collard was the spokesman for the Vanderhoof Flying Club.
39 *BCUCH* 3.403.
40 Yukon Southern Air Transport amalgamated with Canadian Pacific Airlines in 1942.
41 *BCUCH* 3.404.
42 *BCUCH* 3.406.
43 *BCUCH* 3.407.
44 *BCUCH* 3.408.
45 Ibid.
46 *BCUCH* 3.409.
47 *BCUCH* 3.412-13.
48 *BCUCH* 4.424.
49 *BCUCH* 4.460.
50 *BCUCH* 4.460. Research has shown there were harmful fumes being released from the smelter and the company has installed emissions controls systems to deal with them.
51 The four companies are L & M Lumber Ltd./Nechako Lumber Co. Ltd. of Vanderhoof, Apollo Forest Products Ltd. of Fort St. James, Lakeland Mills Ltd. and The Pas Lumber Company Ltd. of Prince George. Killy holds shares in both the Prince George companies. Tembec Ltd., of Quebec, is also a member of the consortium of companies planning to build a pulp mill in Vanderhoof.
52 *BCUCH* 4.465.
53 *BCUCH* 4.468, 485. The actual water requirements for the proposed pulp mill are .17 cubic metres per second or 612 cubic metres per hour.
54 The power is estimated to be worth a total of between $45- and $50-million annually.
55 *BCUCH* 4.473.
56 *BCUCH* 4.477.
57 *BCUCH* 4.523.
58 *BCUCH* 4.530.
59 Environmental Impact Assessment, Vol. 21 (Envirocon, 1984) 177.
60 Ibid. 179.
61 Ibid. 205. Burgener's quotations from Envirocon's study appear in *BCUCH* 4.546.
62 *BCUCH* 59.10568-572.
63 *BCUCH* 58.10240-241.
64 *BCUCH* 58.10250-251.
65 *BCUCH* 59.10543-550.
66 *BCUCH* 59.10551.
67 *BCUCH* 59.10560.
68 *BCUCH* 4.546-47.
69 *BCUCH* 4.547.
70 *BCUCH* 4.553.
71 *BCUCH* 4.556.
72 *BCUCH* 4.557.
73 *BCUCH* 4.573-74.

Drumming on Deaf Ears
1 Justa Monk, tribal chief Carrier Sekani Tribal Council, *Watershed*, Nov. 1993.
2 Chief Seattle, 1854.
3 *Watershed*, Nov. 1993.

4 Ibid.

5 By the fall of 1994, Monk's dire predictions appeared to be coming true when large numbers of mature sturgeon were found dead in the Lower Fraser River.

6 *Watershed*, Nov. 1993.

7 From a statement handed out by Carrier First Nations people protesting the provincial hearings into Alcan's KCP.

8 *BCUCH* 5.694-95.

9 *BCUCH* 5.696.

10 *BCUCH* 5.697.

11 *BCUCH* 5.698.

12 This issue was later debated in provincial court by the UFAWU, but the judge ruled that Alcan was not required to apply for an energy project certificate for the KCP.

13 *BCUCH* 5.702.

14 *BCUCH* 5.698-99.

15 *BCUCH* 5.699.

16 The Haisla are the First Nations people in whose traditional territory Kitimat is located.

17 *BCUCH* 1.6-14.

18 *BCUCH* 11.1690.

19 During the hearings The River Forever group, the Vanderhoof District Chamber of Commerce and the District of Vanderhoof and the Regional District of Bulkley Nechako pooled their funds and hired one lawyer.

20 *BCUCH* 5.704.

21 *BCUCH* 5.709.

22 *BCUCH* 85.16008.

23 *BCUCH* 85.16030.

24 From a private interview in Prince George, 10 Sept. 1994.

25 By mid-September, 1994, the number of pages of documents on the KCP forwarded to the tribal council numbered more than 120,000, and boxes of papers were continuing to arrive.

26 The Carrier people refer to Kemano I and the KCP as one project.

27 *BCUCH* 85.16021.

28 *BCUCH* 85.16018.

29 Rankin and Finlay, 50.

30 *BCUCH* 85.16018-019.

31 From a private interview in Prince George, 10 Sept. 1994.

32 *BCUCH* 85.16018.

33 *BCUCH* 85.16022.

34 *BCUCH* 85.16024-026. Watson explains the details of these specific claims and reveals Cheslatta people received a settlement of $6.95 million for one claim and $475,970 for a second. The Kitimat Indian Band has settled two of the specific claims arising from Kemano I activities, one for $430,000 plus $60,000 in related costs, and a second for $9,000 plus a six-acre replacement reserve.

35 *BCUCH* 85.16027.

36 *BCUCH* 85.16036.

37 Delgamuukw v. British Columbia (1991), which requires the provincial Crown to engage in "reasonable consultation so that (adversely affected) Aboriginal people will know the extent to which their use might be terminated or disturbed" and make "suitable alternative arrangements" for these communities.

38 Rankin and Finlay, 51.

39 Ibid. 40-53.

40 Program medical officer for the Pacific Region of the Medical Services Branch of Health Canada, which is responsible for providing health services to First Nations people living on reserves.

41 *BCUCH* 85.16042.

42 *BCUCH* 85.16042-043.

43 *BCUCH* 85.16043.

44 *Physicians Guide to Rare Diseases*, Jess. G. Thoene, ed.

45 *BCUCH* 85.16044-045.

46 Pre-application for a Mine Development Certificate prepared by Hallam Knight Piesold Ltd. of Vancouver for New Canamin Resources Ltd. for its proposed Huckleberry Project, Article 8.5.6.

47 *BCUCH* 85.16047.

48 *BCUCH* 6.985.

49 *BCUCH* 6.987-88.

An Acceptable Level of Certainty

1 Rivers Defence Coalition lawyer Christopher Lemon, *BCUCH* 10.1540.

2 Intervenors had been given a summary of Alcan's reservoir co-ordination agreement and hydro sales agreement with BC Hydro.

3 Final argument forwarded to the BC Utilities Commission by the Rivers Defence Coalition 29.

4 *BCUCH* 55.9706.

5 Report and Recommendations to the Lieutenant Governor in Council, Kemano Completion Project 141-42.

6 Chief of the DFO's Habitat Conservation Unit in the department's Habitat Management Section in Vancouver.

7 *BCUCH* 64.11421-424.

8 Ibid. 11421.

9 Argument and summary of evidence for the BCUC Review of the Kemano Completion Project submitted by the District of Vanderhoof, Regional District of Bulkley Nechako, The River Forever and the Vanderhoof District Chamber of Commerce 34.

10 *BCUCH* 53.9306.

11 The argument and summary of evidence for the BCUC Review of the Kemano Completion Project submitted by the District of Vanderhoof, Regional District of Bulkley Nechako, The River Forever and the Vanderhoof District Chamber of Commerce 54.

12 Austin represented residents of Vanderhoof, Fort Fraser and Fraser Lake during the hearings.

13 Alcan Smelters and Chemicals Ltd.'s reply to the final submissions of intervenors 55.

14 The argument and summary of evidence for

the BCUC Review of the Kemano Completion Project project submitted by the District of Vanderhoof, Regional District of Bulkley Nechako, The River Forever and the Vanderhoof District Chamber of Commerce 55.

15   Report and Recommendations to the Lieutenant Governor in Council, Kemano Completion Project 125.

16   Ibid. 160.

17   After the construction of the dam, higher-than-usual water releases through the Skins Lake Spillway eroded river banks or broke through saddle dams, rerouting the flows through a new channel back into the river.

18   The contract date was not met, nor was the contract renewed.

19   See the June-July 1994 issue of Service Digest published by BC Hydro.

20   See BC Hydro BC 21—three project plan announcements and one request for proposals.

21   The first of the eight Terms of Reference established by the BC government for the BCUC's investigations into the KCP.

22   Alcan Smelters and Chemicals Ltd.'s reply to the final submissions of intervenors 6.

23   Bulkley Valley residents became concerned because the water flows from two lakes on the upper Bulkley River, the Nanika and the Kidprice, were included in Alcan's original plans to increase its hydroelectric generating capacity. The Bulkley flows into the Skeena River, another major BC salmon-bearing river.

24   The Report of the Kemano task force edited by William J. Schouwenberg, that was withheld from public scrutiny until it was given to NDP MP Brian Gardiner in 1990.

25   *BCUCH* 44.7530 and *BCUCH* 30.5178-179.

26   *BCUCH* 44.7531.

27   *BCUCH* 82.15487.

28   *BCUCH* 46.7912.

29   *BCUCH* 82.15493.

30   *BCUCH* 30.5185 and Hearing Exhibit 131E.

31   *BCUCH* 30.5186.

32   *BCUCH* 44.7477.

33   *BCUCH* 45.7750-775 and Hearing Exhibit 354, 10.

34   *BCUCH* 68.12188.

35   *BCUCH* 68.12181.

36   *BCUCH* 68.12,258-260.

37   *BCUCH* 68.12261-264.

38   *BCUCH* 68.12269-270.

39   *BCUCH* 51.9072.

40   For more information on the information provided to the commissioners by federal scientists, see *BCUCH* vols. 51-54.

41   *BCUCH* 55.9670-671.

42   Alcan Smelters and Chemicals final written arguments to the BCUC hearings 62.

43   *BCUCH* 28.4772.

44   *BCUCH* 28.4797.

45   Report and Recommendations to the

Lieutenant Governor in Council, Kemano Completion Project Review 118.

46   *BCUCH* 51.9077.

47   Ibid.

48   Report and Recommendations to the Lieutenant Governor in Council 146. NFCP: Nechako Fisheries Conservation Program, which has been developing and overseeing plans to protect the salmon using the Nechako.

49   *BCUCH* 49.8639.

50   *BCUCH* 58.10192-193.

51   *BCUCH* 58.10340.

52   Report and Recommendations to the Lieutenant Governor in Council, 158.

53   Ibid. 10251.

54   The huge Omineca region is divided into three subregions: the Findlay-Omineca, the Takla-Nechako and the upper Fraser River.

55   Final written argument of the Rivers Defence Coalition 2.

56   Alcan Smelters and Chemicals Ltd.'s reply to intervenors' final submissions 7.

57   The Final Argument before the BCUC Concerning the Kemano Completion Project from the Nechako Valley Regional Cattlemen's Association and the Nechako Valley Dairymen's Association 9.

58   They were seeking up to 10 cubic metres per second in the portion of the river upstream from its confluence with the Stuart River, for irrigation purposes.

59   Alcan Smelter and Chemicals Ltd.'s reply to the final submission of the Cattlemen's and Dairymen's Associations, Tab 8, 1.

60   Ibid.

61   The NFCP includes appointed representatives of Alcan, the federal and provincial governments and an independent representative chosen by the three other parties and, according to the 1987 Settlement Agreement, has final say over the amount of water released into the river.

62   After the final arguments were submitted, the farmers represented by Holtby asked him change the final written arguments he had submitted to the commissioners by removing all criticisms of the claims of other valley residents and restricting his comments only to farmers' demands for more irrigation water.

63   Report and Recommendations to the Lieutenant Governor in Council 177.

64   From a telephone conversation with the author, 26 Oct. 1994.

65   Although it withdrew from the inquiry, the UFAWU remained a member of The Rivers Defence Coalition which continued to participate in the hearings.

66   UFAWU news release, 27 June 1994.

67   Ibid.

68   Ibid. 29 June 1994.

69   UFAWU's arguments filed with the Supreme Court of British Columbia, 3 Oct. 1994, 10.

70 UFAWU news release, 29 June 1994.

71 See *Hansard*, 12 May 1981, 886.

72 Sto:lo Fisheries Authority new release, 20 Sept. 1994.

73 Environmental organizor for the T. Buch Suzuki Enironmental Foundation, which is also a plaintive in the court action against Alcan launched by the UFAWU in June, 1994.

74 UFAWU news release, 3 Oct. 1994.

75 *BCUCH* 78.14443.

76 *BCUCH* 81.15189.

77 Ibid.

78 *BCUCH* 81.15190.

79 The arguments and summary evidence presented to the BCUC by the District of Vanderhoof, Regional District of Bulkley Nechako, The River Forever and the Vanderhoof District Chamber of Commerce 57.

80 *BCUCH* 11.1643.

81 *BCUCH* 71.13145.

82 *BCUCH* 33.5848-850.

83 Hearing exhibit 365.

84 *BCUCH* 41.7028-029.

85 For a more detailed explanation of the study of the internal dynamics of large lakes and reservoirs, see *BCUCH* 25.

86 *BCUCH* 25.4280.

87 *BCUCH* 25.4280-281.

88 For Dr. Ian Williams' explanation of the impact of water temperature on migrating salmon see *BCUCH* 42.4273.

89 Alcan Smelter and Chemicals Ltd.'s final written arguments to the BCUC 45.

90 *BCUCH* 20.3340.

91 Report and Recommendations on the Kemano Completion Project 62-63.

92 *BCUCH* 11.1759-760.

93 Nechako Environmental Coalition's final submissions to the BCUC on the Kemano Completion Project 15.

94 *BCUCH* 46.7881. At that time the DFO was seeking a short-term flow of 18% of the inflow into the reservoir and a long-term flow of 11% of the inflow into the reservoir.

95 Attachment D to the letter, dated 25 Mar. 1993, approving the Kenney Dam Release Facility.

96 Nechako Fisheries Conservation Program established by the technical committee set up by the the 1987 Settlement Agreement to monitor and control the water flows in the Nechako River.

97 *BCUCH* 42.7305.

98 The Columnaris bacteria; see *BCUCH* 42.7387.

99 Ibid.

100 *Vancouver Sun*, 17 Sept. 1994, A3.

101 Ibid.

102 Ibid.

103 Report and Recommendations to the Lieutenant Governor 156.

104 *BCUCH* 58.10334-335.

105 *BCUCH* 13.2110-113.

One Day All This Will Be Ours

1 Neil Postman, *Technopoly: The Surrender of Culture to Technology*, "Introduction."

2 In his 1985 judgement approving the federal government's application for an injunction ordering Alcan to release more water into the river, Mr. Justice Thomas Berger did determine the federal government had the right, under the Fisheries Act, to order Alcan to release more water. But that was before the signing of the 1987 Settlement Agreement which assigned that responsibility to a non-elected committee.

3 Possible Schedule of Flows for Fish Protection, Report and Recommendations Lieutenant Governor in Council, revised Table 1.

4 When valley residents complained to Canada's regulatory body about Alcan's television advertisements that claimed not one fish would be harmed by the KCP, and not one watt from the project would be exported to the United States, the ads were ordered to be discontinued.

5 Exhibit 485 filed during the BCUC hearings, 11.

6 The final written arguments of the Rivers Defence Coalition, 23.

7 Comments on the discussion paper "Toward a Fish Habitat Management Decision on the Kemano Completion Project" prepared by Dr. Peter Larkin and forwarded to Rod Bell-Irving in April, 1984.

8 *BCUCH* 22.3830-831.

9 *BCUCH* 22.3846

10 *BCUCH* 22.3830.

11 *BCUCH* 22.3846.

12 *BCUCH* 22.3843.

13 Alcan Smelters and Chemicals Ltd press release, 9 July 1993.

14 A paper entitled "Economic Viability of KCP" released by the BC government at the time of Harcourt's cancellation of the project, 23 Jan. 1995.

15 Ibid.

16 Possible Schedule of Flows for Fish Protection, Report and Recommendations Lieutenant Governor in Council, revised Table 1.

17 *BCUCH* 33.5850-851; 34.5926; 50.8867.

18 Alcan press release, 10 Aug. 1988.

19 Letter from Vancouver lawyer Chris Sanderson of Lawson, Lundell, Lawson & McIntosh to David Good, assistant to the deputy minister of fisheries, 10 Sept. 1990.

20 For a discussion of how the same water-diversion projects being proposed today were being proposed back in 1972, see Richard C. Bocking's *Canada's Water: For Sale?*, particularly Chapter 7.

21 *BCUCH* 70.12588-631.

22 Letter written by BC Minister of Employment and Investment Glen Clark, to Congressman Vic Fazio, 9 June 1994.

23 Statement of Julius L. Katz before the Standing Committee on Health, House of Commons, 10 May 1994.

24 Ibid. Katz was speaking on behalf of two US-based companies which own Canadian trademarks: Philip Morris International Inc., which has an interest in the Canadian tobacco company Rothmans, Benson & Hedges Inc.; and R.J. Reynolds Tobacco Company, which wholly owns the Canadian tobacco manufacturer, RJR Macdonald Inc.

25 For complete information on the proceedings of this conference (held in Vancouver, May 7-8, 1992) sponsored by the Canadian Water Resources Association, see Water Export: Should Canada's Water Be For Sale?, published by the conference sponsors.

26 Ibid. 293.

27 Ehor Boyanawsky, "Water Wars: Public Responses to Environmental Threat," in Water Export: Should Canada's Water Be For Sale? 273.

28 BCUCH 52.9115.

29 Barry Appleton, Navigating NAFTA: A Concise User's Guide to the North American Free Trade Agreement 201.

30 Statement by the governments of Canada, Mexico and the United States issued December, 1993.

31 Letter by US Trade Representative Michael Kantor to Northwest Environmental Advocates, 28 Oct. 1993.

32 Letter from Congressman Vic Fazio to Felix Smith of California dated 19 Nov. 1993.

33 Letter from BC Minister of Employment and Investment Glen Clark, to Congressman Vic Fazio, 9 June 1994.

34 Ibid.

35 Reisner 488.

36 Eighty per cent of California's water and 87% of Arizona's water is used for irrigation, and the amount used for irrigation in eight other American states—Colorado, New Mexico, Kansas, Nevada, Nebraska, North Dakota, South Dakota and Idaho—is as high or higher (see Reisner 9).

37 For a more complete explanation of the damage caused by over-reliance on irrigation in California, see Reisner.

38 BCUCH 22. 492

39 James Laxer, "Why Canada's Exporters Can't Help Themselves," in Holm, 135.

40 Thompson 68.

41 Ibid. 67.

42 Ibid.

43 J.C. Day and Frank Quinn, Water Diversion and Export: Learning from Canadian Experience.

44 BC government water license register report.

45 15 Jan. 1994 edition.

46 In 1993 the company was known as Multinational Water and Power Inc.

47 Thompson 77.

48 Reisner 483.

49 Ibid.

50 Richard C. Bocking. "The Real Cost of Dams, Diversions, and Water Exports," a presentation made at the Water Export: Should Canada's Water Be For Sale? conference. See 277-86 of the proceedings.

51 Ibid. 101.

52 Alcan Aluminum Limited's 1991 annual report.

53 Decision of the BCUC in the matter of the BC Hydro and Power Authority 1994/95 revenue requirements application, 24 Nov. 1994.

54 From Harcourt's speaking notes for a speech to members of UFAWU, 1 Feb. 1995.

55 News release issued by the Premier's office, 23 Jan. 1995.

56 Letter from Harcourt to David Anderson, 25 Jan. 1995.

57 Ibid.

58 Letter from Pierre Gravelle, Q.C., to lawyer David Austin, 24 May 1994.

59 Letter from David Austin to Minister of National Revenue David Anderson, 2 Apr. 1994.

60 From an interview with the author in Vancouver, 5 Feb. 1995.

61 Tax information from Exhibit 671 filed with the BCUC hearings.

62 Ibid.

Bibliography

Books

Anderson, Terry, et al. Water Export: *Should Canada's Water Be for Sale?* J.E. Windsor, ed. Cambridge, Ont.: Canadian Water Resources Association, 1992.

Appleton, Barry. *Navigating NAFTA: A Concise User's Guide to the North American Free Trade Agreement.* Scarborough, Ont.: Carswell Thomson Professional Publishing, 1994.

Bocking, Richard C. *Canada's Water: For Sale?* Toronto: James Lewis & Samuel, 1972.

Bangs, Richard. *Rivergods: Exploring the World.* San Francisco: Sierra Club Books, 1985.

Berton, Pierre. *Drifting Home.* Toronto: McClelland & Stewart, 1973.

Campbell, Duncan C. Global Mission, *The Story of Alcan.* Vol. 2 and 3. Montreal: Alcan Aluminum, 1985-90.

Christensen, Bev. Prince George, *Railways and Timber.* Burlington, Ont.: Windsor Publications, 1989.

Gray, John. *Lost in North America: The Imaginary Canadian in the American Dream.* Vancouver: Talonbooks, 1994.

Harmon, Daniel Williams. *Sixteen Years in Indian Country The Journal of Daniel Williams Harmon 1800-16.* Toronto: MacMillan, 1957.

Holm, Wendy, et al. *Water and Free Trade: The Mulroney Government's Agenda for Canada's Most Precious Resource.* Toronto: James Lorimer & Company, 1988.

Hume, Mark. *Run of the River.* Vancouver: New Star Books, 1992.

Hutchison, Bruce. *The Fraser.* Toronto: Clarke, Irwin and Co., 1950

Lamb, W. Kaye, ed. *The Journals and Letters of Sir Alexander Mackenzie.* Cambridge UP for the Hakluyt Society, 1970.

Lamb, W. Kaye, ed. *Simon Fraser Letters and Journals 1806-1808.* Toronto: MacMillan, 1960.

Lee, Norman. *Klondike Cattle Drive.* Mitchell Press, 1964.

Morice, Father A.G. *The History of the Northern Interior of British Columbia.* Fairfield. Wa.: Ye Galleon Press, 1971.

Neering, Rosemary. *Contenental Dash: The Russian-American Telegraph.* Ganges, B.C.: Horsdal and Schubart, 1989.

Reisner, Marc. Cadillac Desert: T*he American West and Its Disappearing Water.* Vancouver: Douglas & McIntyre, 1993.

Shelford, Cyril. *From Snowshoes to Politics.* Victoria: Orca Book Publishers, 1987.

Sugden, Jessie Bond. *In the Shadow of the Cutbank.* Self-published, 1985.

Articles

Appleton, John. "The Nechaco (sic) Valley," *Westward Ho!* 2.6 (June 1908).

Bodsworth, Fred. "Aluminum Hits the Road Again," *Maclean's,* 15 Dec. 1951.

Boyer, David S. "The Untamed Fraser River," *National Geographic,* July 1986.

Croome, Angela. "The Kitimat Story," *Discovery,* Apr. 1956.

Day & Quinn, "Water Diversion & Export: Learning from Canadian Experience", James Lorimer & Company.

DuBose, McNeeley. "The Nechako-Kemano Development," Engineering Journal 37.11 (Nov. 1954).

Jomini, Harry. "The Kenney Dam," *Engineering Journal* 37.11 (Nov. 1954).

Matthias, F.T. "Kemano, Underground," *Engineering Journal* 37.11 (Nov. 1954).

McGuire, B.J. "The Story of Fifty Years of Growth by the Canadian Industry," *Canadian Geographic Journal,* July 1951.

Overstall, Richard. "The Sovereign State of Alcan," *Telkwa Foundation Newsletter,* Spring 1983.

Peters, Sheila. "Kemano Completion—Who Wins?" *Consumer Newsmagazine,* published by Prince George Consumers United Services Ltd. (July 1989): 19-22.

Thompson, Jerry. "Diverting Interests," *Equinox,* Apr. 1993.

Wise, L.L. "Setting Up Shop in the Wilderness for Huge Aluminum Hydro Project," *Engineering News-Record,* 25 Sept. 1952.

Government Records and Reports

Agreement signed by Aluminum Company of Canada and His Majesty the King in right of the Province of British Columbia, December 29, 1950.

Alcan Smelter and Chemicals Ltd. final written arguments to the B.C. Utilities Commission.

Alcan Smelters and Chemicals Ltd. reply to the final submissions of intervenors.

Argument and summary of evidence for the BCUC Review of the Kemano Completion Project submitted by the District of Vanderhoof, Regional District of Bulkley Nechako, The River Forever and the Vanderhoof District Chamber of Commerce.

Alcan's Application for an Energy Project Certificate filed with the B.C. government in January, 1984.

Barr, Lorna, Peter Larkin and Alistair McVey. Report and Recommendations to the Lieutenant Governor in Council, Kemano Completion Project, December, 1994.

Bulletin 29, "The Nechako and Endako Valley," B.C. Bureau of Provincial Information, 1931.

Bulletin 2M-931-6608, "The Francois-Ootsa Lake District," Fort Fraser Recording Division, Bureau of Provincial Information, 1931.

Burt, D.W. and J.H.Mundie, "Case Histories of Regulated Stream Flow and its Effects on Salmonid Populations," Department of Fisheries and Oceans, July, 1986.

Cheslatta T'en submission to the B.C. Utilities Commission meeting regarding the Kemano Completion Project, April 2, 1993 Prince George.

Decision of the B.C. Utilities Commission in the matter of the B.C. Hydro and Power Authority 1994/95 revenue requirements application, November 24, 1994.

"Recreation Planning Study of the Nechako and Stuart River Corridors" (draft report), B.C. Ministry of Forests, June 1990.

Environmental Studies Associated with the Proposed Kemano Completion Hydro-electric Development. Environcon, 1984. Vols. 1-22.

Final written arguments forwarded to the B.C. Utilities Commission by the Rivers Defence Coalition.

The Final Argument before the B.C. Utilties Commission Concerning the Kemano Completion Project from the Nechako Valley Regional Cattlemen's Association and the Nechako Valley Dairymen's Association.

Fisheries and Oceans' document 19-4-1988 34A:37.

Fisheries and Oceans document 19-4-1988 34A:43.

Industrial Development Act, Government of B.C., 1950.

Jackson, Kenneth ed. "Toward A Fish Habitat Decision on the Kemano Completion Project, Department of Fisheries and Oceans," January, 1984.

"Kemano Completion Hydro-electric Development Baseline Environmental Studies," Envirocon, 1981.

Kemano Completion Project Guidelines Order SOR/90-729.

Larkin, Dr. Peter A. "Analysis of Possible Causes of the Shortfall in Sockeye Spawners in the Fraser River: A Technical Appendix to the report, Managing Salmon on the Fraser by Dr. Peter H. Pearse," 1992.

Larkin, Dr. Peter A. "Comments on the discussion paper 'Toward a Fish Habitat Decision on the Kemano Completion Project'."

Nechako Environmental Coalition's final submissions to the B.C. Utilities Commission on the Kemano Completion Project.

Permit for Nechako Reservoir issued to the Aluminum Company of Canada, December, 1950 by Government of B.C.

Pre-application for a Mine Development Certificate prepared by Hallam Knight Piesold Ltd. of Vancouver for New Canamin Resources Ltd. for its proposed Huckleberry Project.

Rankin, Murray and Arvay Finlay. "Alcan's Kemano Project: Options and Recommendations," October, 1992.

Record of Hearings on Applications by the Aluminum Company of Canada, Limited for water licenses on the Nechako and Nanika Rivers, Oct. 31, 1949.

"Recreational Planning Study of the Nechako and Stuart River Corridors, B.C. Ministry of Forests" (draft report), June, 1990.

Schouwenburg, William J. ed. Report of the Kemano Task Force, Department of Fisheries and Oceans, April, 1990.

Settlement Agreement signed September, 1987 by Alcan, Department of Fisheries and Oceans and Government of B.C.

Social Benefits and Cost Analysis of the Kemano Completion Project. Document R0185, Vol. 73 of the public review file of the B.C. Utilities Commission Hearings.

Statement of Julius L. Katz before the Standing Committee on Health, House of Commons, May 10, 1994.

Statement by the governments of Canada, Mexico and the United States issued December, 1993.

Summary of Salmon Studies Conducted on Nechako, Morice and Nanika River Systems Relative to the Proposed Kemano 11 Power Development, Fisheries and Marine Service of the International Pacific Salmon Fisheries Commission, February, 1979.

Transcripts B.C. Utility Commission Hearings into the Kemano Completion Project, 1993-1994, Vol. 1-87. All references to these transcripts appear as BCUCH, followed by volume and page number.

United Fishermen and Allied Workers' Union's arguments filed with the Supreme Court of British Columbia, October 3, 1994.

Water Licence 19847 issued to the Aluminum Company of Canada Ltd., December 29, 1950.

"Wilderness Mosaic: The Report of the Wilderness Advisory Committee," B.C. Environment Ministry, March, 1986.

Conference Proceedings

Water Exports: Should Canada's Water Be For Sale? Proceedings, Canadian Water Resources Association, College of New Caledonia, 1992.

Thesis

Amaral, Juan Carlos Gomez. "The 1950 Kemano Aluminum Project: A Hindsight Assessment." Master's Thesis. Burnaby, B.C. Simon Fraser University, 1986.

Periodicals

Maclean's, various issues.

Westcoast Fisherman, Mar. 1993.

Western Business and Industry, 25.6 (June 1951).

Studies

"A Case Study of Alcan Aluminium Limited, Royal Commission on Corporate Concentration." February, 1977.

Critique of Alcan Environmental Baseline Studies, Spruce City Wildlife Association and the B.C. Wildlife Federation. December, 1981.

"Physical and Hydrological Studies, Baseline Information," prepared by Envirocon Ltd. for the Aluminum Company of Canada. Vol. 2.

Piper, Ron, Mike Robertson and Vaughn Daily, for the Cheslatta People. "Proposal for the Cheslatta Redevelopment Project." Grassy Plains, 1991.

Pamphlets

"Kemano: B.C. Power Operations." Aluminum Company of Canada Ltd. 25 Oct. 1962.

Newspapers

Burns Lake Review, 22 Dec. 1949.

Victoria Daily Colonist, 28 Oct. 1951.

Various issues of: Caledonia Courier; Calgary Herald; Financial Post; Fort St. James Courier; Globe and Mail; Houston Today; Interior News; Montreal Gazette; Prince George Citizen; Toronto Star; Vancouver Province; Vancouver Sun; Watershed.